Counseling Adults in Transition

Jane Goodman, PhD, is Professor Emerita of counseling in the Department of Counseling, School of Education and Human Services Education, Oakland University, Rochester, MI. She received her masters and doctoral degrees in Guidance and Counseling from Wayne State University, Detroit, MI. She formerly worked as a consultant and trainer for the Continuum Center, Oakland University, Rochester, MI, and served on the Counseling faculty of Eastern Michigan University. She was the 2001–2002 President of the American Counseling Association, 2005–2006 Chair of the American Counseling Association Foundation, and 1994–1995 President of the National Career Development Association. Dr. Goodman is a Fellow of the National Career Development Association.

Dr. Goodman's awards include the Distinguished Service Award from the Michigan Counseling Association, Group Worker of the Year Award from the Michigan Association for Specialists in Group Work, and Champion of Career Development from the Michigan Career Development Association.

Nancy K. Schlossberg, EdD, is Professor Emerita at the University of Maryland, College Park, in the Department of Counseling and Personnel Services, College of Education, and Director of the Center of Human Services Development. She received her doctorate in education degree in counseling from Teachers College, Columbia University. She served on the faculties of Wayne State University, Howard University, and Pratt Institute and was the first woman executive at the American Council on Education (ACE), where she established the Office of Women in Higher Education. Dr. Schlossberg served as a Senior Fellow at ACE's Center on Adult Learning.

Dr. Schlossberg's awards include: Fellow of three divisions of the American Psychological Association (APA), Fellow of the Gerontological Association, the 1983 APA G. Stanley Hall Lecturer on Adult Development, and Distinguished Scholar at the University of Maryland (1983). She was named as one of the Eminent Women in Psychology by the American Psychological Association and was listed in *Who's Who of American Women* in 1993. In addition, Dr. Schlossberg has received highest honors and awards from the following national organizations: the National Career Development Association, the American College Personnel Association, the National Association for Women in Education, and the American Society for Training and Development.

Mary L. Anderson, PhD, is an assistant professor in the Department of Counselor Education at Radford University and former Visiting Assistant Professor in the Counseling Department at Oakland University in Rochester, MI, where she earned her doctorate. Her research interests include spirituality and transitions, group work, and counselor supervision. Dr. Anderson is active in professional organizations, both at the state and national levels. She has served in leadership positions, including co-president of the Michigan Association of Counselor Education and Supervision.

Counseling Adults in Transition

Linking Practice with Theory

3rd Edition

Jane Goodman, PhD

Nancy K. Schlossberg, EdD

Mary L. Anderson, PhD

SPRINGER PUBLISHING COMPANY

NEW YORK

Springer Publishing Company, Inc.
11 West 42nd Street
New York, NY 10036

Acquisitions Editor: Sheri W. Sussman
Managing Editor: Mary Ann McLaughlin
Production Editor: Anne Williams
Cover design by Joanne Honigman
Typeset by Graphic World Inc.

09 10 / 5 4 3

Library of Congress Cataloging-in-Publication Data

Goodman, Jane, 1942-
    Counseling adults in transition: linking practice with theory.—3rd ed. / Jane Goodman, Nancy K. Schlossberg, Mary L. Anderson.
        p. cm.
    Rev. ed. of: Counseling adults in transition / Nancy K. Schlossberg, Elinor B. Waters, Jane Goodman.
    Includes bibliographical references (p. 295) and index.
    ISBN 0-8261-3784-9 (alk. paper)
    1. Counseling. 2. Adulthood. 3. Middle age—Psychological aspects. 4. Middle-aged persons—Counseling of. I. Schlossberg, Nancy K., 1929- II. Anderson, Mary L. III. Schlossberg, Nancy K., 1929- Counseling adults in transition. IV. Title.

BF637.C6S325 2006
158'.3—dc22
                                                    2006042379

Printed in the United States of America by King Printing

We have all, in the past few years, experienced the transition of becoming grandparents. To the generations who preceded us, leaving us their legacies, and to those who enrich our lives with new meaning and joy; to our parents, our children, and our grandchildren, we dedicate this book.

J.G., N.K.S., M.L.A.

Contents

PART II WHAT ARE WE LIKELY TO HEAR?

PART III WHAT CAN WE DO WITH WHAT WE KNOW AND HEAR?

List of Figures and Tables

Preface

In the decade since the second edition of this book, the world has become more complex. The pace of change continues to accelerate, and adults experience ever more intrapersonal, relationship, and work transitions. The ability to communicate instantaneously makes everyone part of a global community. We not only experience our own transitions but also vicariously experience the transitions of those far away. We have watched on television as people faced the devastation of a tsunami in Southeast Asia, hurricanes and floods in the southeast United States, and terrorist attacks in New York, Washington, D.C., Madrid, Bali, and around the world. Technology continues to change our lives, individually and collectively. E-mail communication is now commonplace, and cell phones provide access to areas too remote for telephone wires.

Adults need coping strategies to face the challenges of this complicated world. There is an increasing need for counselors and other helping professionals to understand cultural diversity, and we as a profession are increasing our focus on the role of spirituality in the lives of today's adults. We are also, as a profession, taking more responsibility for advocating on behalf of our clients, as well as teaching them advocacy skills.

This third edition expands on those areas—all of which have gained increased attention in recent years. In addition, we are including a special appendix on non-events, the things that you expected to happen that do not. It was written by Nancy Schlossberg and encompasses practical suggestions and exercises for helping adults navigate the disappointments that accompany not having life follow your intended script.

Nancy Schlossberg presented her transition theory in the first edition of this book, placing it in the context of other theoretical work on adult development. The second edition, with Elinor Waters and Jane Goodman,

added more focus on what counselors hear and included practical suggestions for what to do with what they hear. This third edition, with Jane
Goodman, Nancy Schlossberg, and Mary L. Anderson, affirms our belief
that the model is still an excellent basis for conceptualizing what we do to
help adults cope with transitions because it brings both the theoretical
underpinnings and the applications into the 21st century.

Jane Goodman

Nancy K. Schlossberg

Mary L. Anderson

Acknowledgments

We thank the graduate students who helped us with research and with their questions and life stories. We also thank Sheri W. Sussman, our editor at Springer, for encouraging us to write this third edition.

PART I

What Do We Need to Know?

INTRODUCTION

To set the stage for what counselors need to know, the reader is introduced to an overview of adult development theories. These illustrate the different ways adult behavior can be explained. Some believe adults can change at will; others believe that they can change only if the environment changes. Some theorists assume that changes are inevitable and part of the developmental process, whereas still others theorize that the transitions one initiates and weathers make the difference in adult behavior.

Once the larger landscape showing these different perspectives is in place, the reader is introduced to the transition perspective in great detail. This includes examining the transition process itself and the factors that make a difference as clients go through this process.

This first part provides the cognitive framework for practitioners so that they can understand adults in a more comprehensive manner. The knowledge about adult development and transitions provides counselors and other helpers with the necessary background so they can enable clients to manage transitions more creatively.

CHAPTER 1

Adult Development Theories

Adults face times that are increasingly challenging. A central theme in our current social context is *change*, reflecting the dynamic impact of forces across demographic, social, cultural, technological, political, and historical domains. Discontinuities are created by a number of factors that include shifting and globalization of business environments, the increasing multiculturalism of many nations, and other geographical and political events. As escalating and sweeping changes have become the norm, life can feel increasingly complex and unsettling. It is predicted that the changes in the 21st century will continue to accelerate and intensify, forcing people to cope with the impact of these changes on their lives (Buhler, 2000). The assumptions about adulthood that have been accepted throughout history are increasingly challenged by a landscape in constant flux. Indeed, today continuity is the exception, and adjusting to discontinuity has become the norm of our era. Whether people accept the changes around them or not, they may find that their old strategies no longer work in today's social context. Those who do not master adaptation are likely to find themselves trapped into obsolescence as the world continues to change around them (Bateson, 1989).

As counselors, our goal is to help adults explore, understand, and cope with what is happening in their lives. We help them increase, or at least maintain, their capacity for love, work, and play—goals often conceptualized in terms of increased competency, maturity, mental health, or a similar catch-all phrase. Theorists, whose work we will discuss later in this chapter, often talk about adults' capacity to continually invest in life, that is, the ability to respond, cope, and adapt to the challenges of life. Indeed, Smelser and Erikson (1980) organized a book around the themes of work and love in adulthood, based on Freud's (1961) definition of maturity as the "capacity to love and work." How can we, as counselors, most effectively assist adults as they strive to cope with the transitions—or meaning of the transitions—that they encounter in their lives? How can we find the best way to support them in handling the stresses that accompany the changes confronting them?

One of the best ways of achieving these goals is to connect a knowledge of adult developmental perspectives to our already acquired helping skills. The more we as practitioners know about adult development, the more effective we can make our responses and programs. Connecting a theoretical knowledge base to our practical counseling skills helps us to be more creative and more connected to the adults we try to help.

Before we focus on a framework for using adult development knowledge (see Chapters 2 and 3), we present an overview of four major theoretical perspectives: developmental, contextual, lifespan, and transition. Although these conceptual perspectives are discussed separately here, in actuality they overlap, interact, and build upon one another. This chapter serves as the foundation upon which the transition framework is based.

THEORETICAL APPROACHES TO
UNDERSTANDING ADULTHOOD

All of us are theorists. We are continually making assumptions about whether or not we can change ourselves, our partners, our children, our parents, or our friends. The assumptions we make reflect our theories about adult behavior. In this chapter, we will compare the way different theorists explain adult behavior. Although we believe that transition theories offer the most useful framework for understanding adults coping with change, it is important to recognize the value of established theories along with newer, evolving theories.

A theory is a set of abstract principles that can be used to predict facts and to organize them within a particular body of knowledge. A theory of adult development would thus suggest how cognition, personality, and other characteristics might evolve over an adult's life course. Ideally, theory should go beyond predicting the different aspects of adult development by offering new ideas that relate to things already understood. A current challenge for counselors is meeting the needs of increasingly diverse clients, conceptualizing their issues, and strategizing treatment plans that are culturally sensitive, which requires an intentional approach that is theoretically grounded. This type of approach often necessitates a thoughtful integration of both existing and emerging theoretical orientations.

The study of adulthood, however, has not yet produced such rigorous or ideal theories; current theories offer interesting but essentially untested predictions about the course of adult life. In our review of theoretical approaches, we place the four "perspectives" on adult development on a continuum according to the degree to which they encompass predictability or variability in the life course.

The Developmental Perspective: Age and Stage Perspectives

The first perspective, the developmental perspective, emphasizes the sequential nature of adult development and is the one most familiar to both counselors and the lay public. Stage theories of development can be categorized into three types: *normative-crisis* models based on the resolution of specific, crucial issues; *life-span* models based on individuality and change over the course of life; and *domain-specific* theories that are related to the unfolding of ethical and moral, cognitive, ego, or various kinds of identity development. Again, it should be noted that overlap exists among these domains of development, although they are presented here separately.

Traditional *normative-crisis* models of adulthood view development as relatively universal across the lifespan, with each stage related to a specific crisis that must be resolved. These theories have been generally accepted as a comprehensive mapping of the stages of adulthood. A review of current articles, however, reveals that important questions regarding adulthood are open for further research, especially regarding how much of adulthood remains to be mapped (Raskin, 2002). Additionally, criticisms of these models have emerged in our current social context. Critics have proposed that normative-crisis models may be outmoded, especially in that they emerged at a time when men and women had fairly rigid roles with men expected to work and women expected to stay home to care for the home and raise children (Feldman, 2006).

Development Based on the Resolution of Specific, Crucial Issues

This view of adult development is based on the assumption that human beings pass through an invariable sequence of developmental stages that are not necessarily linked exactly with chronological age. Erikson (1950) postulated a well-known broad view of development, involving eight stages of progression in psychosocial development. Each of these stages is characterized by a crucial issue that must be successfully resolved before an individual can move on. Some people move through the stages faster than do others, and some people may become arrested at one stage and never successfully move on. The adult stages involve the issues of identity (vs. confusion), intimacy (vs. isolation), generativity (vs. stagnation), and ego integrity (vs. despair).

Vaillant (1977, 2002) built upon Erikson's theory and proposed a view of the changes that take place in personality during middle and later adulthood. He conducted a 50-year longitudinal study of well-educated men and women and suggested that an added period of adulthood would be between 45 and 50. He termed this stage as *keeping the meaning* versus *rigidity* and viewed adults in this stage as the guardians of their cultural traditions and values. He described this as the time of life when adults must recognize that the world is not perfect. With this realization, meaning may be developed through an acceptance of the strengths and weaknesses of oneself and others. Vaillant also addressed what he termed *career consolidation*. He found that those people who were able to achieve intimacy were then able to deal effectively with their careers, which in turn led to the achievement of generativity and integrity. Vaillant (1982) also conducted a longitudinal study of inner-city men and found the same progression through Erikson's stages, although the external circumstances and details of life looked very different.

Erikson's work has provided a context for the well-known "identity status" research (Josselson, 1987) that classified individuals into categories based on their identities. In a longitudinal study of 34 women, Josselson (1987) concluded that the different pathways women follow in their identity development tell more about women than merely examining their social roles. In other words, what is relevant is not whether a woman is a mother, a worker, or a single parent or childless, but rather the way in which the woman separates from family and anchors or commits to the adult world.

Although there is no pure type, Josselson identified four general categories (or statuses) of women:

1. Foreclosures are those women who stick with their families' expectations. These women often adopt their parents' standards and follow their career direction.
2. Identity achievers are those who have tested new waters, are forging their own identities, and keep focusing on the future. These women are more concerned with their own view of themselves than the foreclosures who are more concerned with their parents' expectation.
3. Moratoriums are those who struggle to make commitments but have not found the right niche. Although open to choice, they fear too many options. They are struggling to find their own identity.
4. Identity diffusions are those who are drifting and avoiding an identity. This group has the most difficulty forming stable relationships. They are the most troubled.

Josselson asserted that women's development is tied to *relationship connections* (p. 169) and that women's identity achievement depends on a process of differentiation within attachment—a process Josselson termed *anchoring*. Whether in work, family, or social areas, the central aspect of identity for women appears to be the self-in-relation rather than the self, standing alone.

Gender-specific identity models have been applied in a broad way to women (Downing & Roush, 1985). These conceptualizations describe women's identity development as a process, moving from passive acceptance of patriarchal, external definitions of womanhood to a more personalized, internally organized definition. These models have come under criticism because they do not capture the diversity and the complexity of women's self-concepts or address the experiences of racial/ethnic minority women. Moradi (2005) has proposed a *womanist identity* development model that aims to move beyond the focus on a specific aspect of identity (gender), to capture women's multiple personal and group identities (e.g., race/ethnicity, class, and sexual orientation) that shape their identities. According to Moradi (2005), the term *statuses* seems warranted as a replacement for *stages* to bring attention to the fact that women may exhibit multiple identity development attitudes at the same time; these attitudes could well vary across time or contexts, especially relative to the level of work–family conflicts experienced.

The issues of career choice, identity, and transition experienced by women are strongly affected by family influence along with social gender role expectations. Much of present research focuses on the work–family conflict and balance that remain salient issues for women (Hawley, Goodman, & Shaieb, 2002). For example, Sinacore and Akcali (2000) found little impact on men's job satisfaction and self-esteem due to family environment, whereas Phillips-Miller, Campbell, and Morrison (2000) found that the women in their study experienced significantly greater marital/family stress on their careers and perceived less spousal support for their careers than did their male counterparts.

Development Based on Age

Levinson (1978, 1986) focused on relatively universal, age-linked developmental periods of adulthood that unfurl in an orderly sequence. Stable (structure-building) periods alternate with transitional (structure changing) periods. In 1969 Levinson began a longitudinal study with a group of 40 men, aged 35 to 45, who represented a wide variety of occupational and social characteristics. Levinson and his associates explored in depth six distinct periods, each closely linked to age. Extended and subsequent research has refined these six stages as follows:

1. Early Adult Transition on Leaving the Family (ages 16–20)
2. Entering the Adult World (ages 21–29)
3. Settling Down (ages 30–34)
4. Becoming One's Own Person (ages 35–39)
5. Midlife Transition (ages 40–42)
6. Restabilization (ages 43–50)

Each period is characterized by its own developmental tasks. For instance, during the Settling Down period, an individual is concerned with establishing a place in society, that is, affirming one's own integrity and becoming a full-fledged adult, and with advancing toward one's goals.

Levinson's formulations, referred to as *seasons of life,* allow for individual variation, yet emphasized an underlying sequential order and similarity. His findings showed "relatively low variability in the age at which every period begins and ends," and his later research (Levinson, 1989, 1996) suggested that the hypothesized patterns operate in women's lives as well. A review of four dissertation studies investigating the applicability of Levinson's theory to women's lives (Roberts & Newton, 1987), however, indicated limited support for the theory. In these studies, women were found to progress through the same developmental periods at roughly the same ages as had men in Levinson's work. However, despite similarity in the timing of the periods and the nature of the developmental tasks, both the strategies for addressing the tasks and the outcomes were different for the women in these samples. The authors discussed the "split dreams" reported by these women, involving a generalized image of work and family rather than a specific image of self-in-occupational-role, as lending a tentative, provisional, and conflicted quality to women's lives throughout much of early adulthood and into middle age.

The life structures of these women appeared less stable than those of their male counterparts in Levinson's studies because of the greater complexity in the dreams they attempted to integrate into their lives and the obstacles they encountered in doing so. This leads to a greater variety in the "seasons" of women's lives in which the timing of family events plays a far more critical role than age-related changes. Findings such as these reflect a pattern of moving away from age-based determinants of behavior stemming from the greater diversity of roles held by women relative to men, and the increased complexity in living out those roles.

Today, women struggle to combine multiple commitments, which are vulnerable to conflict and interruption. Also, the physical rhythms of women's reproduction create sharp discontinuities and shifts as women experience puberty, menopause, pregnancy, birth, and lactation. The ability to adapt and improvise becomes central to the reality of women's lives as they put together a mosaic of activities and deal with the conflicting demands on their time and attention (Bateson, 1989).

Another thread of research relates to how ethnic background interacts with Levinson's stages. Ross (1984), in a study of Mexican immigrants, found that subjects followed the general sequence hypothesized by Levinson, but differed dramatically in attained education (which influenced occupational choices), mentoring (with family members filling this role), occupational goals (with focus on providing security and independence), family (with strong ties to extended family), and transition (with transition to a new culture overshadowing later life transitions). In studies of Levinson's model as applied to African Americans, Ruffin (1989) and Gooden (1989) found mixed support. Ruffin's study of African American professional women found that racial identity strongly influenced the developmental phases, with the formation of intimacy especially salient during early adulthood, support for occupational goals sought in family and friendship networks rather than "mentors," and achievement aspirations related to becoming successful in a White world. As noted above, further research on multiple identities is needed to address the complexity of people's development.

In his research on professional and working class African American men, Gooden (1989) found limitations in Levinson's theory with regard to both race and socioeconomic status. The school teachers in his study, for example, fit Levinson's theory better than did the "street men." Gooden also discussed the impact of victimization in the early lives of African American men in terms of difficulties in finding mentors, developing the capacity for intimate, long-term relationships, and forming and sustaining "the dream" in a context of limited opportunity and numerous obstacles. Gooden noted that African American adult development must be viewed in a context of "how individuals encounter and respond to social opportunities and restrictions in their efforts at forming a viable life" (p. 88)—a reminder of the strong impact of race and class in the life course. It would seem that theories of racial identity should be incorporated into age-related conceptualizations such as Levinson's if we are to understand the lives of racially diverse groups of adults. In this respect contextual and stage theories clearly interact.

Domain-Specific Development

Another group of stage theorists view individuals as moving through domain-specific sequences of stages. Each domain is characterized by a qualitative difference in the way people view the world within that particular domain.

Based on extensive interviews with women, Belenky, Clinchy, Goldberger, and Tarule (1986) proposed a developmental progression by which women view the world:

1. Silence, a voiceless position in which all knowledge is subject to external authority.
2. Received knowledge, in which the individual can receive and reproduce but not create knowledge.
3. Subjective knowledge, in which knowledge is personal and private, subjectively known or intuited.
4. Procedural knowledge, in which there is investment in objective procedures for obtaining and communicating knowledge.
5. Constructed knowledge, in which knowledge is seen as contextual, objective and subjective strategies are valued, and the individual can see herself as a creator of knowledge.

Loevinger (1993) described a sequence of ego development in several stages. At the earliest self-protective stage, individuals conform, follow rules, and think in stereotypes; at a higher stage, individuals develop increasing self-awareness and the capacity to think in terms of alternatives, exception, and multiple possibilities; most mature is the autonomous stage, in which adults make commitments, tolerate ambiguities, and incorporate opposites. Because people are at different stages of development, adults facing similar transition problems will process those experiences differently—some in a simplistic way and others in a more complex, autonomous manner.

Kohlberg (1984) developed a theory of moral development that evolved out of the thinking of Piaget (1952), Dewey (1933), and Baldwin (1948). These theorists proposed that people develop philosophically and psychologically in a progressive fashion. Through his research, Kohlberg developed a sequence of six stages of moral development, which progress through three levels. The first level, termed *preconventional,* includes judgments that are based on reward and punishment (stage one) moving to judgments based on the consequences for self or loved ones (stage two). The second level, termed *conventional,* includes judgments based on whether authorities approve or disapprove (stage 3) to judgments based on obeying the laws of society (stage 4). Level three, termed *postconventional,* suggests judgments based on social contracts or collaboration (stage 5), moving to judgments based on ethical principles that apply across time and cultures (stage 6). Kohlberg's stages of moral development describe a continuum from being motivated to obeying rules by fear of punishment, to conforming to society, to being internally principled and autonomous. These stages of moral development are similar to Loevinger's ego progression.

Gilligan (1988) asserted that there are qualitative differences in the way men and women process and interpret the world and challenged Kohlberg's moral development theory on two grounds: procedural and substantive. Procedurally, Kohlberg's studies focused on men, but the results were applied to both men and women. Substantively, Gilligan (1982) argued that different issues are central to women's moral development: the issues of attachment, responsibility, caring, and interdependence. A woman's moral development proceeds from concern for survival, to concern for responsibility and not hurting others, to seeing herself as meriting care equally with others. Gilligan asserted that the view of adulthood needs remapping, to show that caring and interdependence are central to human experience.

Somewhat related to moral development are stages of spiritual faith development, one of which was proposed by Fowler (1991). Fowler's seven stages embrace the formal structural–developmental models proposed by Kohlberg and Piaget but differ in their emphasis on emotions, feelings, and imagination. Fowler's stages move from the symbolic images of childhood, to the critical reflection, personal responsibility, awareness of paradox and polarity, and selfless devotion that aware adults are capable of experiencing.

In all of these limited-domain theories, development is viewed as a progression from the simple to the complex. The movement is projected as going from an external orientation (the individual is dependent on the authority or judgment of others) to an inner orientation (an individual takes responsibility for the consequences of his or her own actions), from absolutism and dogmatism to increasing tolerance for ambiguity and uncertainty, from a tendency to perceive those outside one's own immediate group in stereotypic terms to increasing awareness of individual differences and greater empathy with others, and from a strong posture of group conformity to a mature focus on interdependence with others.

One area of limited-domain theories gaining increasing attention involves "identity development theories" referring to one's membership in a particular (often socially oppressed) group. In explicit recognition that identity is a "social psychological concept" (Deaux, 1993)—that is, largely socially determined—these models are especially important in counseling. Identity theories aid both clients and professionals in understanding, predicting, and normalizing experiences, as well as in identifying difficulties that may stem from developmental processes and tasks (Fassinger, 1991). In addition, they help members of oppressed groups identify and articulate their needs and responses vis-à-vis their own group as well as the larger culture, and they aid counselors in sorting out issues that arise in the therapeutic relationship.

One group of such theories is related to racial/ethnic identity development. Initial work in this area focused on the development of activism and racial identification of African Americans in the political upheaval of the 1960s. Later work (Helms, 1990, 1995) focused on extending this work to counseling situations. Models of the racial identity have also been applied to Asians and Hispanics (Sue & Sue, 2002; Szapocznik & Kurtines, 1993).

Helms (1995) pointed out that all of these racial identity models posit five stages and propose an on-going conflict between one's internal views of two groups—one's own and that of the dominant culture. These models also assume that the identity transformation process is set in motion by a social movement that makes it possible for minority group members to rebel against socialization experiences and seek new ways of being. Assumptions that underlie these models include the following (Helms, 1995):

1. The notion of biculturality: the idea that minority groups develop model personality patterns in response to White racism.
2. The belief that some styles of identity resolution are healthier than others.
3. The sense that these stages are distinguishable and can be assessed.
4. The assumption that affective, cognitive, and behavioral elements are involved.
5. The conviction that the cultural identification affects both intra- and inter-cultural interaction.

Most of these models begin with a lack of awareness of one's racial identity, even denigrating one's own culture and idealizing White culture. The next stages involve confrontation with the reality of oppression, subsequent immersion in one's racial group, and rejection of the dominant White group. The final stages involve the internalization of identity, increased self-esteem, and interpersonal relationships, which are not restricted by race or social group membership. As Helms pointed out, these theories are essentially cognitive theories, with identity transformation dependent on a combination of personal readiness, prior cultural socialization experiences, and educational experiences.

Models of racial identity have come under criticism for their one-dimensional approach, in that the emphasis on a singular aspect of identity ignores the reality of many people's lives as members of more than one subordinated group (Reynolds & Pope, 1991). In a study of racial development among college students, White (2002) used a thematic analysis method to look at basic themes that participants expressed regarding their identity development. The themes reflected a much more holistic, fluid, and complex process that challenged the predictability of established racial identity models. Another study looked at African American women's identity and the interaction of race and gender, and the researcher concluded that current theories of racial identity development seek to impose one-dimensional models on a multidimensional process. These participants encountered oppressive stereotypes unique to African American women, especially the stereotype of African American women as being innately incompetent in all aspects of life. They also described good relationships with other women, especially mothers and daughters, as an important part of their self-defined identities. The results suggested that the relational concept of gender identity development should be incorporated into models of African American identity development for women (Harris, 2005).

Another area that has been overlooked is the racial development among multiracial people. These individuals are often viewed as fractionated people, with their identities composed of fractions of race, culture, and ethnicity (Sue & Sue, 2002). The complexity of these individuals' social experiences and how their multiple realities affect their development has not been adequately researched or understood. These complex dimensions of individuals' experience are difficult to fit into the socially, culturally, and politically constructed definitions of "Black" or "biracial" (Rockquemore, 2004).

As stated above, multidimensional identities are difficult to fit into one-dimensional models of development. Although racial identity development models have made important contributions to the counseling field, they do not capture this complexity. Further research is needed to move beyond the focus on one aspect of a person's identity to better capture the diversity in the identities of the people who are being described. This approach could provide a better framework to enrich understanding of the complexities of individual's identities (Moradi, 2005). According to Sue and Sue (2002), enhancing multicultural understanding requires a balance and sensitivity about both the importance of race that encompasses issues of prejudice, discrimination, and systematic racial oppression and the existence of other, and often complex, group identities.

As counselors in the field became increasingly aware of a number of oppressed groups, efforts were made to extend racial identity models to other cultural identification processes. As with models of women's identity (Peck, 1986) and feminist identity (Downing & Rousch, 1985; Helms, 1995, Moradi, 2005), theorists developed models of gay identity development (McCarn & Fassinger, 1991) built on the earlier models of racial identification. There are significant differences, however. Racial minority identity development involves changing attitudes toward the meaning of an apparent identity and typically occurs within the context of potential family and community support. Other kinds of identity development involve a new awareness and articulation of a personal identity that is often not supported in one's environment.

The struggle for gay identity involves one's internal perceptions that may be in contrast to the external perceptions or assumptions about one's sexual orientation (Sue & Sue, 2002). Fassinger (1991) observed that gay identity development often involves the confrontation of both external and internalized oppression. It occurs over and over in situations in which an individual's sexual orientation is ambiguous and frequently involves a context of overt prejudice, lack of family support, and few, if any, role models. Gay persons of many racial/ethnic groups also risk potential loss of their primary racial community. Integrating the experience of people who struggle with marginality and biculturalism into our clinical work challenges us as counselors and can transform and enrich our understanding of human behavior.

In summary, developmental theories cover many domains but have in common the assumption that people's development—whether cognitive, moral, spiritual, ethnic, or psychological—progresses through predictable stages. At this time, most writing in the areas of gender, racial/ethnic, and homosexual development is theoretical, with research findings that are inconclusive or contradictory. It can be concluded, however, that development is more complex for persons marginalized from the dominant culture, in that they must confront and integrate more aspects of themselves (Phinney, 1990, 2000). Further research to capture the complexity of this process and to address multiple group identities is much needed.

The Contextual Perspective

In the second perspective we will discuss—the contextual perspective—adulthood is viewed primarily in relation to the context within which it occurs. People live, grow, and experience changes within the social context around them. Individuals experience career transitions, choices, and stability as these are all incorporated into the daily contextual issues of everyday life (Hawley, et al., 2002). For example, although old, the study of bakery workers in France (Bertaux, 1982) illustrated the importance of context. According to this study, the individual life stories of bakers and their wives were a direct result of the structure and nature of the work world in which they participated. Most bakery workers worked at least six nights a week, from 3:00 am, or earlier, until noon, totaling at least nine hours per night. This meant that whether "they were from rural or urban backgrounds, Catholic or agnostic, fat or thin, married or single, they worked at least 54 hours a week." As Bertaux stated, this fact

> Determined most of the rest of their lives . . . weekly time budget, family life . . . health (which declines after age 40 because of long hours and working in front of an oven), [and] activities outside work. . . . For bakery workers there is no reading, no participation in cultural activities, no movies; for, as they say, because of the chronic lack of sleep they tend to fall asleep "as soon as the lights are off." (p. 133)

This pattern of living, this same life story recurred over and over, "as a direct consequence of the structure of relations of production" (p.134). Bertaux's findings are relevant to those working with adults because they suggest ways to help people identify the social factors that may lie at the root of some of their personal concerns. When counselors overlook contextual factors in any type of counseling situation, the client may be left ill-equipped to integrate personal changes when returning to his or her family and community (Hawley et al., 2002).

Environment also has an impact on such transition problems as the popularly accepted *midlife crisis*. This concept emerged with Levinson's (1978) seasons of life model in which he defined the period of the early 40s to be a time of intense psychological turmoil. Although this became a general expectation about midlife, research findings do not support this idea. Adults may not experience turmoil but rather a shifting of concerns. More research is necessary to establish the specifics of these changes and whom they do and do not affect. The majority of people may find midlife to be a particularly rewarding time, with ongoing involvement with family, friends, social groups, and their careers. And those who have regrets may be motivated to change the direction of their lives, thus ending up better off psychologically (Broderick & Blewitt, 2003; Feldman, 2006; Stewart & Vandewater, 1999).

Researchers such as Rosenbaum (1979) and Kanter (1977) first challenged the popular view attributing the midlife crisis to an individual's confrontation with aging. They suggested an alternate view that focused on the impact of organizations on individuals. Rosenbaum plotted the pattern of a cohort's promotional mobility from 1962 to 1975 and studied the relation between promotion and age, controlling for sex, race, education, and level in the hierarchy. He found that promotion chances increased gradually for those without bachelor's degrees until age 35 or 40 and then gradually declined. Promotion chances for those with bachelor's degrees, however, reached a peak of <60% at about age 35 and then declined abruptly to <20% 5 to 10 years later. Thus, Rosenbaum concluded that the promotion selection system tended to withdraw active consideration from those with bachelor's degrees after age 40. Rosenbaum postulated that this precipitous decrease in people's chances for promotion after 40 was likely to be traumatic and, therefore, lead to the psychological reactions that are often attributed to midcareer or midlife crisis. Kanter (1977) corroborated Rosenbaum's position. She proposed that people's problems stem basically from organization structures rather than from intrapsychic issues. She locates "a large measure of the responsibility for the behaviors people engage in at work and their fate inside organizations in the structure of the work systems themselves" (p. 10).

Occupational environment factors affecting personality and learning capacity were also identified by Kohn (1980). Twelve dimensions significantly affect psychological functioning when all other pertinent factors are statistically controlled. The most important of these dimensions is *substantive complexity,* which may be defined as "the degree to which the work, in its very substance, requires thought and independent judgment" (p. 197). Individuals whose work is substantively complex demonstrate stronger intellectual functioning over time.

Some theorists examined the impact of context on individual lives in an even broader perspective, namely, the state. Mayer and Schoepflin (1989), for example, presented an interesting analysis of the way in which the state, through legislation, social programs, and economic regulation, provides a general framework for the individual life course. They maintained that the state set the boundaries for entry into and exit out of the educational system, marriage, occupational structure, and even illness and disability, effectively turning these personal transitions into public life events. In their view, the need for efficient administration of the legal, social, and economic order leads to more rigid age stratification, weakened social bonds, and an external rather than individually created order throughout life. They were concerned that the institutional order determining much of the social fabric of our lives may lead increasingly to the irrelevance of the person and his or her biographical contexts. This in turn may cause people to become passive rather than active in planning the course of their lives.

Another view of the impact of context came from Hagestad and Neugarten (1985). They stated that cultures have different age systems that "comprise norms which regulate status and role occupancy across the span of life. For the individual, such norms provide a scheduled set of transitions . . . they create a sense of what lies ahead" (p. 3). Nearly all cultures celebrate rites of passage for birth, puberty, marriage, death, and other predictable punctuation marks of the life course. Many of these changes in social identity lead to "new social roles, rights, and obligations" (Hagestad & Neugarten, 1985). A full understanding of these transitions in the life course requires an examination of cultural age norms and age constraints as well as consideration of three kinds of time: individual, family, and historical (Hareven, 1992). For instance, a decision to have a baby appears to be an individual couple's decision; yet the decision is dependent on the social and demographic factors operating in the couple's culture at a particular time.

As an example of the impact of historical time on adult transitions, Hiner (1985) compared the differences in Colonial and present-day responses to the death of one's child. He noted that the high infant mortality rates during the 18th century had a profound impact on the character and duration of married life, particularly for women, who literally spent all of their adulthood bearing and raising children. Marriages were more frequent and of shorter duration, and the loss of a child was an expected reality of adult life. Hiner contrasted this situation with today's ideologies, which idealize long-term partnerships and fewer children. Loss of a child today is an unexpected and particularly traumatic experience.

Neugarten and Neugarten (1987) emphasized that to understand a particular life history, one must view it in its appropriate historical context. Clearly, as historical times change, social prescriptions for age-appropriate behavior also may change. For example, people are living longer, and the postparental period has consequently lengthened considerably. At the same time, economic maturity for many young people is being delayed while a larger proportion of them attend college and go on to graduate or professional schools. In addition, there has developed what has been humorously called the "boomerang generation," that is, adult children who return home for a time, or several times, while getting situated in the world. Patterns for women have also changed radically, with most women now combining work and child-rearing. In many families child-rearing practices are changing as fathers slowly begin to share responsibility with their working wives.

These kinds of historical trends have a definite impact on the chronological and social norms for age-appropriate behavior, norms that appear to be blurring and loosening in today's society (Neugarten & Neugarten, 1987). In adulthood, there seems to be little biological necessity for such norms; the most dramatic biological change after puberty is menopause, which itself has become surrounded by many emotional myths. Research, however, suggests that responses to menopause are closely tied to other midlife events (such as children leaving home), which in turn are very much influenced by environmental, cultural, and historical contexts.

This blurring of age-defined roles and tasks, often referred to as the "fluid life cycle," represents flexibility and freedom for many. Others, however, some of whom may appear in counselors' offices, find it difficult to adjust their timetables. For example, some young men and women may feel inadequate if they have not met their achievement and family goals by the age of 35, even though they are likely to live into their 80s. When people maintain traditionally defined internal timetables that are at odds with their actual situations, they are susceptible to anxiety and conflict (Neugarten & Neugarten, 1987).

Additionally, in a pluralistic society such as ours, subgroups may have their own age-normative systems. Factors such as race, socioeconomic status, disability, sexual orientation, and geographic location may determine differences in age-defined behavior. For example, the length of the "coming out" process for gay people (Fassinger, 1991) may delay the establishment of permanent relationships and the creation of families. Similarly, occupational prejudice and discrimination may impede and delay career attainment for specific minority groups. These variations become especially obvious when we attempt to apply general normative theories to our intervention efforts.

Another source of change and challenge is *history-graded* changes. Researchers who propose a *life-course* perspective view development as an intersection of chronological age, family-related roles, and membership in a particular birth cohort experiencing historical events. This is an especially salient issue in the context of fewer or weaker social bonds combined with expanding and heightened threats and a pervasive sense of vulnerability in what has been termed an *age of anxiety* (Broderick & Blewitt, 2003). We need not look far to see many examples of profound historical events and can only imagine the impact these are having for the different age cohorts experiencing them.

It is evident then that a body of literature is now accumulating in which researchers explain behavior by analyzing the social context in which it occurs. For example, a newer theoretical approach, the *constructivist* perspective, has emerged in response to our postmodern, multicultural age. The postmodern worldview offers an alternative to modernism, which is based on an objectivist, reductionistic quest for truth and knowledge. This logical positivist worldview dominated the first half of the 20th century, with most scientific methods of study designed to explore some behavior of social patterns of current interest. A problem, however, is that because of the rapid rate of social change, the phenomena of interest are transformed before the study is complete (Gergen, 2000). Another limitation to modernism is that scientific truth is culturally dependent and value laden. Within the postmodern perspective people are actively constructing their mental realities rather than simply coping with an objective "truth." This approach emphasizes that people develop as they construct meaning and make choices within their social/cultural context. According to White (1996), "the constructivist approaches are based on the assumption that we are constructive—that we are engaged in a process of actively building our reality or world view, instead of there being an 'objective' world that can be known independent of the knower" (p. 8).

The constructivist perspective has an established usefulness for understanding how people make sense of their experience. Although the modern emphasis on the objective dimension served to give recognition to the dominant culture's voice, the constructivist approach focuses on a person's private sense (Savickas, 2003). Yet social constructions are often developed within institutional contexts. Understanding the process of constructions is fundamental, especially when one is looking at race/ethnicity, social class, sex/gender, and sexuality. Understanding these systems involves the recognition of the inequality and domination that have an impact on people's development (Orr, 2000). The constructivist approach is thus compatible with system-based theories while being relevant to the lives of women and non-Eurocentric worldviews (Brott, 2001; Brown, 1996). The preferred technique of constructive therapies is the exploration of personal narratives with the therapeutic goal of meaning-making and personal development (White, 1996).

Regardless of the focus of investigative attention, the result is to examine individuals by also accounting for the sociological and ecological factors that affect them and the meanings that are constructed out of this experience. As counselors, we must be aware of these perspectives of adult development. When appropriate, these theoretical lenses can help us to recommend interventions designed to change the environment of clients or to alter the way clients cope with their environment. We will discuss the important role of counselors as advocates in the last chapter of the book.

The Life-Span Perspective

The third perspective on our continuum—the life-span perspective—focuses on individuality and issues of continuity and change. Development is viewed as a process of adaptation taking place within multiple contexts that vary for individuals, thus leading to very different pathways through the lifespan. Some theorists see continuity among individuals over the course of life whereas others see so many individual pathways that variability becomes the cornerstone of adulthood. Kagan (1980, 1998), for example, wondered why social scientists have invested so much effort in a search for stability and continuity. He questioned the premise that information about a growing child is sufficient to explain his or her life course. In examining conclusions about a Berkeley longitudinal study in which 166 people were observed from birth through adulthood, he noted: "When the subjects were seen at age 30, 12 years after their previous interviews, the researchers were shocked by the inaccuracy of their expectations. They were wrong in two-thirds of the cases, mainly because they had overestimated the damaging effects of early troubles" (1980, p. 64). Counselors who are aware of the findings of this study can caution adults against using early problems as a rationale for being "stuck" and not taking responsibility for their actions as adults.

Neugarten (1982) also emphasized variability, which she called individual fanning out. She pointed out, for example, that 10-year-olds are more similar to each other than are 60-year olds, and stated:

> Perhaps the most consistent finding to emerge from the study of aging is that people grow old in very different ways. [There are] . . . striking variations between successive groups who reach old age . . . between ethnic . . . urban and rural, and . . . socioeconomic groups. This is to say nothing of the idiosyncratic sequences that widen the divergence among individuals. The result is that 60-year-olds or 80-year-olds are extremely heterogeneous groups. (p. 6).

Pearlin (1982), in his work on strain and coping, echoed Neugarten's emphasis on individuality and variation. He maintained that human variety is as rich as people's historic conditions and current circumstances and that even within the same cohort, the impact of conditions may differ because of variations in coping resources. Thus, in his view it was untenable to speak of either ages or life stages as though undifferentiated people were following a uniform life course. Pearlin and Lieberman (1979) found that the adult experience differs according to whether an individual is a man or woman, member of a minority or a majority group, young or old, rich or poor, or healthy or ill.

Pearlin (1982) also argued that one life phase or event should not be overly dramatized, and cited the *midlife crisis* as a case in point. It is known that crises can occur at any period and that, in fact, young adults have more strains on them than do other age groups. Yet the media and some writers continue to dramatize a crisis in midlife, the inevitability of which is not corroborated by hard data. Pearlin's caution applies to any theoretical perspective; overemphasizing any particular life event, period, or transition (such as retirement or the birth of a child) risks categorizing people as if they were all the same.

Brim and Kagan (1980) championed a life-span development approach. Their view opposed stage theories, because "stages cast development as unidirectional, hierarchical, sequenced in time, cumulative, and irreversible—ideas that are not supported by commanding evidence" (p. 13). Life-span theorists identify life events as markers, milestones, or transition points that play a pivotal role in individual development, thus giving shape and direction to the various aspects of each individual's life.

A key aspect of life-span developmental theory is the role of adaptation to the continuous influences on people's lives. Adaptation can take different forms including: growth, maintenance/resilience, and regulation of loss. *Growth* involves adding new characteristics, understandings, and skills, whereas *maintenance/resilience* involves finding ways to continue functioning when facing challenges or suffering a loss. *Regulation of loss* involves adjusting expectations and accepting a lower level of functioning. All of these adaptive processes occur throughout the life span, and it is through these adaptive processes that successful development unfolds (Broderick & Blewitt, 2003). Whitbourne (1996) addressed coping and adaptation over the lifespan and saw adaptation as the continuous evaluation of life experiences rather than reactions to discrete events. An individual's life-span construct is subject to change as the individual meets experiences that contradict it or are totally incongruent with it. For instance, the act of coping itself may result in an altered life story as individuals distort the meaning of events toward the maintenance of their self-esteem. Coping may also alter an individual's aspiration levels toward greater congruence with his or her environment when it is clear that failure to achieve aspirations does not stem from the individual's inadequacy. Thus, in this model, the adaptation process takes on different configurations, depending on whether an event is consistent or inconsistent with an individual scenario.

Effective adaptation may actually increase in midlife because of an increase in complex, integrated self-descriptions that indicate an ability to blend both strengths and weaknesses into an organized picture (Labouvie-Vief & Diehl, 2000). In fact, studies reveal that middle-aged adults who feel a sense of control over the aspects of their lives experience higher levels of psychological well-being (Bandura, 1997; Smith et al., 2000). Greater mental health and satisfaction have also been attributed to a firm commitment and involvement in reaching goals, with people involved in creative projects experiencing their lives as more satisfying (Staudinger, Fleeson, & Baltes, 1999; Nakamura & Csikszentmihalyi, 2002). Another factor that boosts psychological well-being is good relationships; research supports the idea that marriage brings about well-being to both genders, although women are more sensitive to the quality of the marital relationship (Marks & Lambert, 1998). Additionally, research supports the idea that success in handling multiple roles is associated with psychological well-being. This is particularly relevant to women, who are generally happier today than during former eras because of satisfaction derived from both family and vocational achievements (Christensen, Stephens, & Townsend, 1998).

As noted earlier, theories of individual development also need to be seen in the light of gender differences, an area of burgeoning research in the past several decades. Although further detailed discussion is beyond the scope of this chapter, differences in behavior and maturity that are ascribed to men and women are often the most striking differences among individuals. We return to Gilligan's (1988) work. Based on her findings that responsibility and care were central to her subjects' lives, she saw interdependence as a critical component of adult development. The view of the heroic individual marching up a sequence of stages and ladders is no longer adequate but must be replaced by a view of the individual rene-gotiating interdependence in ever-changing circles of attachment.

In a widely cited study on differences between women and men, Fiske and Chiriboga (1990) found that women in their sample generally had less positive self-images than did the men, felt less in control of their lives, and were less likely to plan for transitions. At the same time, their affective lives were richer and more complex, and they had a greater tolerance for ambiguity. Men anticipated placing more value on expressive and inter-personal goals as they grew older, whereas women expected to direct their interests outward and to become more concerned with contributing to society and doing good in the world. The "crisscrossing trajectories" of men and women at successive stages reflect different types of develop-mental changes, as well as different scheduling. Gutmann (1987) asserted these notions in his cross-cultural study of older men and women.

The reality of adults' lives today is characterized by variety and diversity, influenced not only by gender and culture and the roles people have, but by the timing of the stages they move through. For example, some people marry and have children at relatively young ages whereas others wait until their 40s to pursue family life. Others may never marry or live with a partner yet may choose to be a parent. These changes in the social context have challenged models that relate stages to age (Barnett & Hyde, 2001; Fraenkel, 2003). Newer models conceptualize development based on particular events in an adult's life. These models, called *life events models*, propose that the events in adults' lives, not age, determine the course of their development (Helson & Srivastava, 2001; Roberts, Helson & Klohnen, 2002). In other words, rather than looking at critical periods in adults' lives, they are looking at life events that are specific to the individual. The implication of this is that two people of very different ages may share commonalities in significant life events and thus in their personality development.

The Transition Perspective

The fourth theoretical perspective in adulthood—the transition perspective—focuses on life events entailing change. Fiske and Chiriboga (1990) conducted a longitudinal study of what they labeled as "ordinary people"—four groups of men and women in San Francisco: (a) graduating high school seniors, (b) newlyweds, (c) middle-aged parents, and (d) preretirement couples—with each group being obviously on the threshold of a major transition at the start of the study. These individuals were interviewed five times over a 12-year period. The overriding question—How do adults change over time?—was answered in a number of ways. They found that the groups differed considerably in their general outlook on life, the stresses they faced, and their attitudes toward those stresses. The researchers concluded that it is less important to know that a person is 40 years old than it is to know that a person is 40 years old, has adolescent children, is recently divorced, is about to retire, and so on. Men facing retirement, for example, encounter many of the same problems whether they retire at age 50, 60, or 70. Newly partnered individuals of any age are engaged in similar tasks of bonding, discovery, and negotiation. In short, transitions are more important than chronological age for understanding and evaluating an individual's behavior.

Schlossberg (e.g., 1981, 1991) presented a transitional model that incorporated both anticipated transitions—the scheduled, expected events that are likely to occur for the individual and that can be anticipated and rehearsed—and unanticipated transitions—the nonscheduled events that are not predictable. That model, described in detail in Chapters 2 and 3, is the cornerstone of this book.

Transitions are often experienced as frightening or traumatic. Hudson (1991) characterized life for adults as being "on a raft floating down a commanding river . . ." and the transitions as "the white waters of the river" that test every skill we have as "we slide over rocks and rapids and swirl about in unforeseen directions" (p. 51). He stated that the river metaphor captures two aspects of dealing with transitions. One is a sense of chaotic power beyond our control and the other is a sense of adventure requiring our continual readiness and vigilance.

Theorists have positioned transitions within a developmental framework, defining them as *turning points* or as a period between two periods of stability (Levinson, 1986). Moving through a transition requires letting go of aspects of the self, letting go of former roles, and learning new roles. People moving through transitions inevitably must take stock as they renegotiate these roles. Transitions often involve significant life events that require coping with what is perceived to be a crisis situation. Innate growth and potential may be realized through addressing and coping with these significant life events (Brown & Lent, 2000).

Within a developmental framework, the transitions themselves are viewed as occurring in stages, with each stage relating to the next for adaptation and successful adjustment. Within this perspective, a transition occurs over a period of time between life phases or life stages. Whether viewed as a time of crisis or as a developmental adjustment, transitions present a unique opportunity for growth and transformation (Bridges, 1980; Hudson, 1991; Schlossberg, Goodman, & Waters, 1995). A symbol that captures the essence of a transition is the Chinese word for crisis, which combines the symbols for danger and opportunity. Its literal translation is "opportunity riding a dangerous wind" (Corlett & Millner, 1993).

The cognitive appraisal model lends understanding to how people evaluate and cope with changes in their lives. This model, developed by Lazarus and Folkman (1984), emphasizes the process by which individuals adapt to events. It assumes that an individual appraises the significance of an event for its possible negative impact on his or her well-being and then determines what personal and social resources are available for dealing with the event and what the consequences are likely to be. After action has been taken, the individual then reassesses the situation. The coping strategies adopted can be instrumental (changing the environment) or palliative (minimizing individual distress).

Newer research about the role of positive emotions and coping with stress has been prompted by recent evidence regarding both negative and positive emotions that co-occur throughout the stress process (Folkman & Moskowitz, 2004). According to Folkman & Moskowitz (2004), coping is a complex, multidimensional process that is sensitive to both the environment and to personality dispositions, which influence the appraisal of stress and the resources for coping. They stated that, despite gains that have been made in understanding coping, researchers have only begun to understand the concept. They maintained that much of the problem is that coping is not a stand-alone phenomenon, as it is embedded in a process that involves the person, the environment, and the complex relationship between them.

APPLYING THE THEORETICAL PERSPECTIVES

Table 1.1 and case studies illustrate the fact that counselors' theoretical perspectives do, in fact, influence (a) their assessments of an individual's behavior and (b) their plans for intervention.

Let us take the following two cases: one, a White midlife man, and the other, a single woman giving birth to a baby.

Case of the Midlife Man

My name is Alex and I'm 48 years old. I just found out that I lost my job. I was in middle management at a manufacturing plant. One day I pulled up to work to see all these limos lined up outside. It was right

Table 1.1 The Adult Experience: Perspectives and Concepts

Developmental	Contextual	Lifespan	Transitional
Age -Invariant sequence of developmental stages -Life structure, dream, mentor *Resolution of Issues* -Unfolding of life and resolving of inner issues -Identified hierarchical stages -Differential issues for women, for different races and cultures *Domain Specific* -Hierarchical sequence in ego development, moral development, intellectual development and faith development -Different ways of knowing for men and women -Models of racial and gender identity development -New models address complex, multiple identities -Gay identity development often involves the confrontation of both external and internalized oppression	-Career mobility results from organization structure -Midlife crisis, a sociological phenomenon -Individual progress determined by opportunity structure -Intellectual capacity dependent on substantive complexity at work -Cultures provide age systems and age norms -Fluid life cycle today -Importance of historical period in setting norms and constraints -Sociological and ecological factors affect individuals -Meanings are personally constructed out of experience	-Process of adaptation -Individual variations -Fanning out -Fluid lifespan -Early trauma not predictive of later behavior -Differential distribution of strains by sex, age, different patterns of coping -Perspective, not theory -Opposed to stages related to age -Impact of events and mediating variables -Adult lives today: variety and diversity -Life events are specific to the individual	-Stage, not age -Coping with transitions: balance of resources to deficits -Sex differences -Coping, not life events, is central issue -Coping is a multidimensional process -Transitions: may be anticipated or unanticipated -Energy is used in all situations involving change -Transitions are often experienced as overwhelming or traumatic -Transitions offer unique opportunities for growth and transformation

then that I knew. Those limos were for all the guys like me who have company cars. I was told to clean out my desk, and I would be taken home. I was in that company for 24 years. I was a loyal employee all that time—never took a sick day. The people who worked under me respected my work ethic, and many of them were downsized too. It just makes me so mad. How am I supposed to pay the mortgage? My wife is so stressed out, I heard her crying herself to sleep last night. She's worried about our son's tuition for the private school he attends, and our daughter's skating lessons.

Bad as the layoff would be under any conditions, it is even worse right now. My father just came to live with us. My mother died last year, and he is getting increasingly confused. We found out that he was not eating or bathing properly, that his bills were unpaid, and that he often forgot his medications. We are afraid he has the beginnings of Alzheimer's disease. We were hoping to have help with him during the daytime so my wife could continue to take the kids to their activities, but now we just can't afford that.

I just don't know where to start looking for a new job. And who's gonna want a guy like me? I was thinking about retirement coming up, not being in a new job. I don't even have a resume worked up yet, let alone any interviews lined up. I've just got to move on, but I feel so stuck right now. I don't know if I am more angry, scared, or sad. To be honest, I feel really hopeless and don't know where to start to put things right.

Each of the four theoretical perspectives, as depicted on Table 1.1, can provide us with a lens to examine Alex and the crisis he is experiencing.

The *developmental* perspective would ascribe the crisis that Alex is facing to normal developmental unfolding. For example, according to Levinson, Alex could be conceptualized as a man at midlife who is facing the discrepancy between his goals and the realities of his life. Developmentalists may choose to normalize what Alex is experiencing. Interventions would most likely be short term, with an emphasis on the tasks of this life stage. At some point, Alex will reach the realization that he must move ahead through his own actions or begin to fall into stagnation. He will have to find the internal and external resources to gain a new perspective to facilitate his further growth and evolvement into generativity. Much of this may be dependent on his previous positive or negative resolutions of the crises and tasks of earlier pivotal points in his life.

The *contextual* focus could be on the organizational context of Alex's current crisis. The impact of the work environment would be a focus, along with changing either the context of Alex's work or changing Alex's responses and reactions to his job loss. The other context is his family situation, as Alex seems to feel overwhelmed with the financial dependence of his family members and the pressing needs of his father's declining health. The historical context might involve these expectations of him to be the sole supporter of his family and to stay in the company he had been with for so many years. The constructivist perspective would emphasize working within Alex's perspective as he shares his story. His problem-saturated story would be challenged by looking for opportunities to highlight the positive alternative stories within his story. The dominant narratives of society regarding his work and identity might be challenged to empower Alex to reconstruct his story to conclude with positive outcomes that are culturally sensitive to Alex's situation. A key to this process would be Alex uncovering and reclaiming what is meaningful to him and taking action to construct a meaningful future.

Life-span theorists might view Alex as an individual whose life experience is unique and evaluate his circumstances accordingly. Alex has encountered some challenges for which he wasn't prepared with the sudden loss of his job and his father's deteriorating health. Dealing with these situations will entail redefining and reexamining his goals and finding ways to adapt. Adaptation for Alex could take the different forms of growth, maintenance/resilience, and regulation of loss. *Growth* could involve adding new understandings and skills, whereas *maintenance/resilience* would involve finding ways to continue functioning when facing challenges of his family situation and the loss of his job. Counseling interventions could focus on both the job situation and his family environment and also address his personal feelings of helplessness. The approach would most likely be creative and not constricted by the parameters of formal theory; rather it would involve addressing Alex's unique set of issues.

Transition theorists would reexamine Alex's personal and work transitions, by assessing his resources for coping with his unanticipated job loss and family situation. Although this transition may be viewed by Alex as the most distressing and challenging of times, the unique opportunities for growth and development would be emphasized by helping him to expand his coping repertoire.

Case of the Single Expectant Mother

My name is Sandra and I am 42 years old. I am so excited and scared at the same time—I just found out that I am pregnant. I always wanted to be a mother, but thought I was beyond hoping for that to happen. My ex-husband and I went through a series of fertility tests and concluded that it was my fault that we never had a child. He got tired of all the focus on having a baby and was frustrated by my depression following the tests. We've been divorced for over a year now and I just started dating again. I met Rich at work, and although he's married, we have the most beautiful relationship. He's been so supportive of me through my recovery from my divorce, and I've been so happy with the time we can find to be together. He doesn't even know yet, and I am scared with how he might react when he finds out. He's very protective of his own children who are 7 and 9 years old and wouldn't think of getting a divorce until they are older. My closest friends don't even know about Rich. Guess I've been too embarrassed to tell them. That goes for my family and my parents too. I really want this baby, despite what anyone might say. And besides, I wouldn't even consider an abortion because it's against my religious beliefs. I worry though, about what it will be like for my child growing up with only a Mommy. And I don't want to lose Rich. I keep wondering what people might say at work. What if I lose my job? I've only been there for a few months, and Rich is my supervisor. Keeping the baby could be a mistake, but I don't see any other way to go on.

Developmental theorists would conceptualize Sandra's case from several developmental perspectives. According to Levinson, she is in the stage of Midlife Transition, yet she is in many ways in the stages of just entering the adult world of work and settling down with a baby. Levinson's stage formulations allowed for individual variations, yet he emphasized an underlying sequential order, which is a concern in Sandra's case. Her situation also exemplifies the split dreams referred to earlier in this chapter, with the complex and conflictual quality to her choices that could probably result in dissatisfaction with both her family situation and her career. She also exemplifies the varied timing that women can experience regarding age-based determinants of adult behavior. Her situation could be conceptualized developmentally regarding her identity development. A central aspect of her social, family, and work identity is her isolation and lack of social support outside her relationship with Rich. This relationship and her decision to have the baby could fit into Kohlberg's stage of moral development, with Sandra probably being in the conventional stage with fear of punishment. Using Gilligan's lens, we might conclude that Sandra's main concern is on survival and her responsibility to not hurt her baby. Each of these developmental conceptualizations provides insight into what Sandra might be experiencing. Developmental interventions would center on supportive strategies to facilitate Sandra progressing developmentally through this life stage.

The *contextualists* would view Sandra's situation in the context of her work situation and family expectations. There could be expectations for her to somehow marry the father of her baby, or her family might provide support upon learning of her situation. The historical context could have influence in that single parent households have become more acceptable and common. Sandra's social context could change, depending on her reactions to the whole situation. The constructivist approach would take into account the fact that Sandra's reality is constructed through her telling of her story. Interventions would include a collaborative and supportive exploration of her story, with an optimistic orientation. The goal would be to empower her through emphasizing her strengths, leading to an expansion of her perspectives and options. The therapist would focus on what has worked in Sandra's life and would convey confidence in her ability to come up with solutions to her problems. Any dominant expectations from the larger society would be challenged as Sandra works toward constructing her preferred story line for her future and the future of her child.

Life-span theorists would highlight the uniqueness of Sandra's situation and interventions would be tailored based on her specific situation. The focus could be on the impact on her resulting from the job situation, decisions regarding the baby, and her feelings of isolation. An individualized conceptualization and approach would be considered the most appropriate way to proceed to increase her ability to adapt to her circumstances and continue her development.

Transition theorists would assess Sandra's resources for coping, and a key focus would involve identifying her sources for support and strengthening her resources as she deals with the situation at work and becoming a mother with her family around her.

CONCLUSION

Examining our theories is important because it helps us to clarify our views and assumptions of adult development. Our aim here was to provide a quick overview of different theories and to set the stage for showing how theory affects practice. As we develop the transition perspective, we will see how all the theories described so far feed into it, making it an eclectic theory that looks at context, development, lifespan, and the construction of meaning.

CHAPTER 2

The Transition Framework

Adults are individuals—some are healthy, some are unhealthy; some are sexually alive, others are uninterested; some are happy, some are sad; some are productive, others are disintegrating; some are coping, some are collapsing. The transition framework, originally developed by Nancy K. Schlossberg (1981, 1984) and presented in this book, incorporates the notion of variability while at the same time presents a structural approach so that counselors and helpers do not need to approach each situation anew.

Adults in transition are often confused and in need of assistance. Often they can identify the issues that trouble them—they are "burned out," getting divorced, forced to change jobs, or discriminated against. These issues, in turn, often relate to their ability to love, work, and play. When they are able to explore the issue more fully, understand the underlying meaning, and develop a plan, they are more likely to be able to cope effectively and resolve the problem.

Friends, coworkers, and professional and paraprofessional helpers can learn about issues of major concern to most adults, they can listen to the adult in transition in a way that facilitates exploration, they can provide a framework for the adult to better understand his or her situation, and, finally, they can influence the adult to cope more creatively.

To help adults explore, understand, and cope, helpers need to increase their communication skills, their counseling skills, and their knowledge of adult development. In short, helpers need to be able to weave their skills and knowledge at each phase of the helping process—whether it is exploring why the individual can or cannot love, work, or play; understanding the underlying reason for the issue; or developing strategies to help adults cope more effectively with life.

OVERVIEW OF THE TRANSITION MODEL

The transition model provides a systematic framework for counselors, psychologists, social workers, and other helpers as they listen to the many stories—each one unique—of colleagues, friends, and clients. The transitions differ and the individuals differ, but the structure for understanding individuals in transition is stable. The transition model has three major parts:

Approaching Transitions: Transition Identification and Transition Process
Taking Stock of Coping Resources: The 4 S System
Taking Charge: Strengthening Resources

To summarize, Approaching Transitions identifies the nature of the transition and provides an understanding of which perspective is best for dealing with it. Transition Identification asks what change is impending— a new baby, a job change, a personal change, a relationship change? Is it anticipated, unanticipated, or a non-event? Knowing more about it and being able to describe it help get the discussion moving about what is troubling or challenging a client. Even more important than the mere identification of the change is specifying the degree to which the particular transition changes the client's life. Three people describing a similar transition, for example, job loss, are not talking about the same event. To understand its significance, the counselor needs to see how the job loss has changed each individual's roles, relationships, routines, and assumptions.

The Transition Process locates where the adult is in the transition. Did the client just learn of the impending job loss? Is the person in the first week after the job loss? Or is it a year after the loss? Reactions to any transition change over time, depending on whether one is *moving in, through,* or *out of* the transition.

Taking Stock of Coping Resources: The 4 S System provides a way to identify the potential resources someone possesses to cope with the transition. The 4 S's refer to the person's *Situation, Self, Support,* and *Strategies.* No matter where one is in the transition process, no matter what the transition is, one deals with it differently depending on these resources.

Taking Charge: Strengthening Resources demonstrates the use of new strategies. Even though some transitions are out of our control, we can control the way we manage them—we can strengthen our resources, our 4 S's. Figure 2.1 depicts the model. Part 1, Approaching Transitions: Transition Identification and Transition Process, is detailed in this Chapter. Taking Stock of Coping Resources: The 4 S System is described in Chapter 3. The rest of this book, particularly Chapters 7, 8, and 9, describes the many ways counselors can help people "take charge."

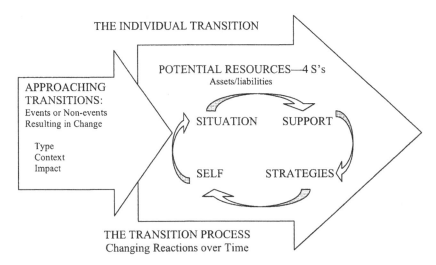

Figure 2.1 The individual in transition.

APPROACHING TRANSITIONS

A transition, broadly, is any event or non-event that results in changed relationships, routines, assumptions, and roles. Transitions often require new patterns of behavior, but we prefer not to use the term *crisis* because of its negative connotations. A transition may well be a life event that involves gains as well as losses. Moreover, crisis implies a dramatic event, and we need to be concerned with less high-profile events as well as non-events.

Transitions include not only obvious life changes (such as high school graduation, job entry, marriage, the birth of one's first child, and bereavement) but also subtle changes (such as the loss of career aspirations or the non-occurrence of anticipated events, such as an expected job promotion that never comes through). Thus, an event or a non-event can be defined as a transition if it results in change.

Parkes (1971) proposed the term, *psychosocial transition,* which he defined as a change that necessitates "the abandonment of one set of assumptions and the development of a fresh set to enable the individual to cope with the new altered life space" (p. 103). A transition is not so much a matter of change as of the individual's own perception of the change. For our definition, a transition is a transition only if it is so defined by the person experiencing it. If, for example, menopause does not have much impact on a particular woman and does not change her set of assumptions or her relationships, then, in our view, it cannot be regarded as a psychosocial transition (though, of course, it is a biological change). If, however, another woman experiences menopause as an event that marks her passage from youth to old age or from sexuality to non-sexuality, it does constitute a transition for her. For yet another woman who sees it as freedom from the necessity of using birth control, it is also a transition—a positive one.

Types of Transitions

The first step in approaching a transition is to identify the type of transition that has happened or is happening: Was it anticipated or unanticipated? Or is it a non-event?

Anticipated Transitions

These transitions comprise those normative "gains and losses or major alterations of roles that predictably occur in the course of the unfolding life cycle" (Pearlin & Lieberman, 1979, p. 220). These expected events include marriage, the birth of a first child, a child leaving home, starting a first job, and retiring. Many adults find that having an opportunity for role rehearsal, whether mental, vicarious, or real, can ease an anticipated transition. For example, many young adults find that babysitting for nieces and nephews gives them at least some idea of what parenthood will be like.

Unanticipated Transitions

These transitions comprise the "nonscheduled events" that are "not predictable." These usually "involve crises, eruptive circumstances, and other unexpected occurrences that are not the consequence of life-cycle transitions" (Pearlin, 1980, p. 179). "Events of this type in the occupational arena include being fired, laid off, or demoted; having to give up work because of illness . . . being promoted, and leaving one job for a better one. Divorce, separation . . . premature death of a spouse, . . . illness or death of a child represent such events in the parental arena" (p. 180).

Brim and Ryff (1980) made another useful distinction between events that have a high probability of occurrence in the life of the individual (getting married, starting work, having a child, or retiring) and those that are improbable and happen to comparatively few people (inheriting a fortune, being convicted of a crime, or having one's home destroyed by an earthquake or flood). The need for preparation for unexpected events has been underscored by the many natural disasters that have occurred worldwide, including earthquakes, mudslides, floods, and hurricanes.

These events are striking examples of the ramifications of unanticipated transitions. During the 2005 hurricanes in the southern regions of the United States, people all over the world watched massive evacuations on television and agonized with displaced people who had to decide what possessions they would save given only days, and sometimes hours, notice.

Bright and Pryor (2005), writing about the application of chaos theory to career counseling, reminded us that, "reality as individuals experience it . . . [is] richly complex, nonlinear, and serendipitous" (p. 302). Coping with change involves the person, the environment, and the complex relationship between them.

Non-event Transitions

These transitions are the ones an individual had *expected* but that did not occur, thereby altering his or her life—the marriage that never occurred, the promotion that never materialized, the child who was never born, or the cancer that did not metastasize. For example, a couple who had counted on having children may finally, in their mid-40s, realize that this will not occur. The realization that the expected transition did not and will never occur alters the way they see themselves and might also alter the way they behave. Generally, four types of non-events can be identified: personal, ripple, resultant, and delayed. These circumstances are discussed in detail in our Highlighted Appendix on non-events on pages 279–294.

Let us use retirement as an example to summarize the types of transitions—anticipated, unanticipated, and non-event. Planned retirement is anticipated. Retirement because the plant where you work closed is probably unanticipated. For those forced by economic necessity to continue working (and who are able to find work), retirement is a wished-for but non-occurring non-event. Thus, it is not the transition itself that determines its meaning for the individual; rather it is whether the transition is expected, unexpected, or never occurring. Clearly, one person may be thrilled at a non-event (such as being cancer free after a diagnosis of cancer), but another may be very sad with the realization that a promotion is not ever likely.

Several other points about types of transitions need to be mentioned. These points involve the concepts of relativity, context, and impact.

Relativity

An anticipated change for one person—going to college—might be unanticipated for another. For example, a school janitor who had always wanted to go to college anticipated never having that opportunity. On the day the last child graduated from the college, the family presented the father/

janitor with an application blank filled out for the state university. He completed several years of college and was, at our last interview, an emergency substitute teacher. A non-event for one person—not getting married—can be a planned decision for another and not a transition at all.

As mentioned, the same event has different meanings for different individuals. George and Siegler (1981) interviewed 100 adults older than age 50, asking them to identify the best and worst events of the past year, as well as of their whole lives. For one person retirement was "the best"; for another it was "the worst." For some it was planned and for others unexpected.

The individual's appraisal of the transition is key. Does the individual see it as positive, negative, or benign? One person might define retirement as positive, a challenge, an opportunity. Another might see it as the next step before dying, the end of a productive life. One's appraisal will clearly influence how one feels and copes with the transition or non-event.

Context

The relationship of the individual to the event or non-event resulting in change is central to our understanding of transitions. Does the primary event start with the individual (his or her illness) or with some other person (his or her boss's illness)? Is the transition personal (the individual has lost his or her job) or interpersonal (the individual has had a disagreement with his or her employer)? Or is the transition involved with the public or the community (does the individual feel disgraced by having to go on unemployment)?

Often if something is happening to an individual, resources can be mobilized. After the initial shock of losing her job, Marge began a job campaign and found another job. But if something is happening to someone else, for example, doom impending for an adult child, the individual often can only sit by, suffer, and offer support. We need to note that many feel the tragedies and excitements happening to their children as if they were happening to themselves.

What is the arena in which the transition occurs? Pearlin and Schooler (1978) wrote: "The problems of everyday life" are identified as the "persistent life strains that people encounter as they act as parents, jobholders, and breadwinners (p. 3). The researchers identified key strains in the areas of occupation, marriage, and parent roles by interviewing 100 people in an unstructured manner and then developing a structured interview with 2,300 people between the ages of 18 and 65 living in the Chicago area. Further, they showed the differential impact of life strains on different segments of the population (Pearlin & Lieberman, 1979). This useful way of viewing various arenas of life—occupation, marriage, and parenthood—in terms of unexpected "non-normative events" and expected normative and persistent problems can be extended to other arenas, such as economics, health, and education. Of course, what starts out as personal and economic—lack of income through the job loss—can also affect family relationships and precipitate other transitions. Studies confirm the negative effects of involuntary job loss on the well-being of individuals and families; unemployment has been correlated with increases in substance abuse, mental health problems, physical illnesses, and spousal abuse (Herr, Cramer, & Niles, 2004).

To summarize, the primary setting for a transition affects our reactions. The transition may involve the self, friends, family, work, health, or economics. In the George and Siegler (1981) study, individuals chose their best and worst life experiences. Most of these experiences resided in the family setting, followed by self and work. Worst life events were typically in the health setting, followed by family and self. Retirement can be a "best" experience if it makes possible a long-desired trip, or it may be a "worst" experience if it is necessitated by ill health.

Impact

For an individual undergoing a transition, it is not the event or non-event that is most important but its impact, that is, the degree to which the transition alters one's daily life. Thus, when an event, for example, a partner's business transfer involving a geographical move, creates problems for an individual, we need to look not only at the type and context but also at the impact of the event on the individual's relationships, routines, assumptions about self and the world, and roles. We may assume that the more the transition alters the individual's life, the more coping resources it requires, and the longer it will take for assimilation or adaptation. More empirical work must be done on events that happen to someone else but have impact on the individual we are trying to help. We need to distinguish those whose life patterns are changing because of others' transitions rather than their own.

One way of examining the impact of a transition is to assess the degree of difference between the pre-transition and the post-transition environments. Lieberman (1975), studying four groups of old people who made radical changes in living arrangements, concluded that the intensity of stress experienced depended not upon the individual's subjective interpretation of the change in living arrangements (whether it was welcomed or feared, whether regarded as a change for the better or the worse), but rather ". . . upon the degree to which an individual is required to make new adaptations associated with environmental change. . . . The greater the difference between the Time 1 life space and the Time 2 life space, the higher the degree of stress and consequent adaptive requirements" (p. 151). He found that the individual's success or failure in adapting to the new environment was strongly correlated with the similarity or dissimilarity of the pre-transition and post-transition environments, despite the individual's attitude toward or definition of the change.

Wapner (1981) compared pre-transition and post-transition environments ranging from nursery schools to nursing homes. Each person lives in "multiple worlds" in the family, work, and community. Thus, positive, desired changes may have as great as or even a greater impact than negative ones because individuals may find it harder to recognize the need for support in such situations.

Wapner's "psychological distance map" (1981, p. 225) provided a graphic opportunity to compare the interactions in the old and new environments. By using such maps, we can look, for example, at families who move geographically and ascertain the degree to which they maintain prior contacts as well as the number of new contacts made. Thus, we have a better idea of the impact of the transition on relationships, routines, assumptions, and roles. A person who moves or enters a nursing home who is able to maintain most of his or her former contacts will experience the transition very differently from someone who loses all contacts.

Parkes (1971), however, believed that changes in the "life space" are important only insofar as they affect the individual's "assumptive world," which includes "everything we know or think we know. It includes our interpretation of the past and our expectations of the future, our plans and our prejudices. Any or all of these may need to change as a result of changes in the life space" (p. 103). The life space is changing constantly, but not all these changes call for a major restructuring of the assumptive world.

This theory conflicts with the views of theorists such as Holmes and Rahe (1967) who originally showed the impact of multiple life events on physical health. To study this impact, they developed a Social Readjustment Rating Scale (1967) that assigns numerical values to different kinds of life events, with "death of a spouse" ranking at the top of the scale and items such as "vacation," "Christmas," and "minor violations of the law" at the bottom. The Holmes–Rahe scale ascertains the probable degree of stress connected with a given life event and its relationship to an individual's general state of mental and physical health. The cumulative numerical values of the life events that a person experiences during a given period of time, for example, one year, serve as an index of that person's general health. The person who has gone through a number of changes in a relatively short period of time is more vulnerable to illness.

But as Dohrenwend, Krasnoff, Askenazy, and Dohrenwend (1978) pointed out, the Holmes–Rahe scale must be used with reservations. In the first place, the numerical values represent empirically derived averages and are subject to individual variation. Thus, a person who has suffered the loss of a loved one around Christmas time may for many years afterwards find the holiday season more stressful than other events given a higher value on the scale.

In the second place, the stressfulness of a particular event depends not so much on the event itself as on the balance between a person's liabilities and assets at the time the event occurs. The Peri Life Events Scale (Dohrenwend et al., 1978, p. 205) expands the Holmes-Rahe scale by including 102 items covering categories such as school, legal matters, finances, social activities, and health; it also differentiates between whether the event happened to the individual directly or to a significant other. Finally, the important point is that the birth of a baby will have different meanings for the newly widowed or newly fired person than for a person in a relatively quiescent period. One man forced to take early retirement explained that it was particularly difficult because that year his wife left him and his father had moved in because of a debilitating illness.

To summarize impact: Assessment of a transition's impact on relationships, routines, assumptions, and roles is probably the most important consideration in understanding an individual's reactions. This is a key point. Sometimes a transition changes everything. Al moved from Bozeman, Montana, to San Francisco, California, to become vice president of a high-tech company. His relationships with colleagues changed; his daily routines changed—not just at work but learning his way around in the new city; and his assumptions about himself as someone with a big title changed. His roles remained the same: He was still a father, husband, son, and son-in-law. Years before, Al had worked as an accountant in Bozeman but had changed from one company to another. He clearly had made a change, but it was not nearly as extensive: He lived in the same house and still saw himself as an accountant. Of course, his relationships also changed as he acquired new colleagues.

Or let us look at divorce. Clearly with this event there are changed relationships, routines, assumptions, and roles. For many, changed assumptions about themselves and their world become paramount. Jill said, "I am no longer part of a couple. Am I deficient in some way since I cannot keep a marriage together?" She stayed in the same house with her two small children but began to think about ways to get more training so she could earn a decent salary to raise her children.

Summary

To understand the meaning a transition has for a particular individual, we need to examine the *type* of transition (anticipated, unanticipated, or non-event), the *context* of the transition (relationship of the person to the transition and setting in which the transition occurs), and the *impact* of the transition on the individual's life (on relationships, routines, assumptions, and roles). This point needs to be further underscored. Often people in the midst of one transition experience other transitions, which makes coping especially.difficult.

THE TRANSITION PROCESS

Although the onset of a transition may be linked to one identifiable event or non-event, transitions are really a process over time. Six months, 1 year, and sometimes 2 years pass before one moves fully through a major transition. For example, if you interview a person before a move, during the move, 6 months after the move, and again 2 years later, you will get entirely different responses. Reactions continually change. The only way to understand people in transition is to study them at several points in time.

Transitions take time, and people's reactions to them change—for better or worse. At first, people are consumed by their new role such as being a new graduate, a new widow, an unemployed worker, or a recent retiree. Gradually, they begin to separate from the past and move toward the new role, for a while teetering between the two. A retired teacher reported that his first month after retirement was very difficult as he was so used to his routine, his relationships, and his professional identity. But now, 6 months later, he is very comfortable with his new set of activities. He is very active in an exercise program, serves as a volunteer mediator, and is participating with the League of Women Voters.

The process of leaving one set of roles, relationships, routines, and assumptions and establishing new ones takes time. According to Bloch and Richmond (1998), transitions affect the whole person: emotional being, physical being and mental functioning. Transitions have an impact on many aspects of a person, affecting his or her life roles and self-image; thus, "to change we often have to let go of some part of ourselves, or of something we hold dear" (p. 6). Transitions may provide both opportunities for psychological growth and dangers of psychological decline. For example, some of the elderly subjects who moved to nursing homes (Lieberman, 1975) "remained intact in the face of radical environmental change" (p. 156), "whereas about half suffered marked declines behaviorally, physically (including death), socially, or psychologically" (p. 142). Interviews with men whose jobs had been eliminated (Schlossberg & Leibowitz, 1980), with couples who had recently undertaken geographical moves, with adult learners in undergraduate programs (Schlossberg,

Lynch, & Chickering, 1989), and with clerical workers (Charner & Schlossberg, 1986) confirmed that the transition process often has both positive and negative aspects for the same individual.

In the job elimination study, one man saw his job loss as a "kick in the back" but at the same time recognized it as an "opportunity to get out of both my job and my marriage." Another man reported feeling "a little shaky but at the same time hopeful." In the geographical study, one woman talked about the miserable experience of moving: "I kept thinking, if only I were back home," but at the same time she described the move as an opportunity for her and her husband to break away from their families, with whom they were "almost too close." The ambivalent nature surrounding many transitions explains the different stories a person tells a helper or friend at one point and 2 months or 1 year later.

Lipman-Blumen (1976) described the transition process as moving from "pervasiveness" (an awareness that the transition permeates all of a person's attitudes and behaviors) to "boundedness" (the change is contained and integrated into the self). Thus, in the early stages, a person is totally conscious of being a new graduate, a new widower, a new mother. In the later stages, the person is aware of having graduated, having been widowed, having become a mother, but this awareness has become only one of the dimensions of living. Knowing this result makes it easier for a counselor to help a client see a light at the end of the proverbial tunnel.

Similarly, Moos and Tsu (1976) identified two phases to the transition process: "An acute phase in which energy is directed at minimizing the impact of the stress, and a reorganization phase in which the new reality is faced and accepted. In the acute period, feelings may be denied while attention is directed to practical matters. . . . The reorganization phase involves the gradual return to normal function" (pp. 14–15). Hill (1965) believed that reaction to a crisis takes a roller-coaster form: the crisis event occurs; the individual dips down into a period of disorganization, then gradually rises up again, and levels off into a period of reorganization.

There is also a wealth of literature dealing with human adaptation to specific types of transitions that presupposes a series of phases. For example, based on her work with terminal cancer patients, Kübler-Ross (1969) identified five stages experienced by people who realize they are dying:

Denial and isolation
Anger and resentment
Bargaining
Preparatory depression over impending loss
Acceptance

Similarly, bereavement over the loss of a loved one moves from "almost global denial or 'numbness,' . . . bitter pining and frustrated searching, . . . succeeded by depression and apathy . . . with a final phase of reorganization when new plans and assumptions about the world and self are built up" (Parkes, 1971, p. 106). Lindemann (1965), who has done extensive research on grief, maintained that if the person does not do the necessary "grief work," passing through each of the stages in its turn, trouble can erupt later on.

Brammer (1991) defined transitions as both ordinary changes and extraordinary changes that occur continually throughout people's lives. He described a transition as *a journey through,* usually to something unknown, requiring the courage to take risks and the ability to cope with fear. Brammer conceptualized the levels of adaptation to transitions: *adaptation,* when one adjusts to change; *renewal,* when one sets goals; *transformation,* when one experiences rebirth; and *transcendence,* when one reaches the ultimate level for meaning-making of both the transition itself and one's whole life, as well.

Hopson (1981) wrote, "Integration not only involves renewal but also incorporates an acceptance that the transition is now complete. This means that it has become part of one's history. . . . It will have an influence over future directions, but it is not imprisoning one in the past" (p. 38). This outcome can take the form of acceptance, deterioration, or renewal. It is not possible to assess the final outcome until the person has experienced the range of phases or stages outlined. Thus, a helper interviewing a client in the self-doubt phase might consider that the person has opted for deterioration only to find 6 months later a new sense of hope.

William Bridges—Endings, Neutral Zones, Beginnings

Bridges (2004) discussed the transition process as having three phases: endings, neutral zones, and beginnings. Although we intuitively like to begin at the beginning—that is, the new job, the new baby, the new relationship— Bridges makes a convincing case that every beginning, every transition, starts with an ending. He wrote that endings are the first phase of transition. The second phase is a time of confusion before "life" returns to some sense of normalcy, and the third phase is one of renewal.

Endings

Bridges provided an example of endings when he described a woman dealing with a new baby. She was really confronting the ending of the family of two, moving into the relationship of three in a family. He wrote, "Considering that we have to deal with endings all our lives, most of us handle them very badly. This is in part because we misunderstand them. . . . We take them too seriously by confusing them with finality—that's it, all over, never more, finished" (1980, p. 90).

Endings involve disengagement, disidentification, disenchantment, and disorientation (1980, p. 92). Not everyone experiencing an ending has to go through these in any prescribed sequence, however; nor does everyone have to go through all four aspects. Still, in one way or another, people do disengage by separating from the old roles and routines. Bridges offers the example of a woman's reactions to her husband's leaving her. She says, "My self-esteem, as a woman and as a person, was all tied up with his reactions to me. I didn't just lose a husband. I lost my way of evaluating myself. He was my mirror. Now I don't know how I look any more" (p. 95). After a period of mourning for her losses she began to see that there were some possible opportunities. "Connie's life transition was a turning point in her life. . . . It had begun with an ending, and the ending had begun with a disengagement" (1980, p. 95). "Divorces, deaths, job changes, moves, illnesses, and many lesser events disengage us from the contexts which we have known ourselves. They break up the old cue-system . . . with disengagement, an inexorable process of change begins. Clarified, channeled, and supported, that change can lead toward development and renewal" (1980, pp. 95–96).

Related to disengagement is the need to disidentify with one's previous role. One man who had presided over an international agency was not reappointed. The same year he was pushed out of his job, his daughter died of cancer. This was the first time he did not have an assistant handling the mechanics of a trip abroad. He felt that he had no identity, no frame of reference. As Bridges says, "No longer being . . . wife or a salesman, no longer being the old me or a young person is a source of panic. That is when it is important to remember the significance of disidentification and the need to loosen the bonds of who we think we are so that we can go through a transition toward a new identity" (1980, p. 97). Endings can also include periods of disenchantment and disorientation-periods during which, as Bridges describes it, we may become a "person floating free in a kind of limbo between two worlds" (1980, p. 98).

Neutral zones

Disenchantment and disorientation are preludes to the next phase, neutral zones. Bridges wrote: "We need not feel defensive about this apparently unproductive time-out at turning points in our lives, for the neutral zone is meant to be a moratorium from the conventional activity of our everyday existence" (1980, p. 114). Many students take what in Europe is called a "gap year" between graduation from college and work in the field they trained for. They may work at a less demanding job, travel, or do some combination of the two. The concept of a gap year provides for social recognition of this neutral zone moratorium.

For some who can afford it, the moratorium might involve going to a spa. For others, it might be a weekend in the country; and for some it might be a leave of absence from the job. One woman, with a limited income and no chance for a weekend away, requested a day with no responsibilities each Mother's Day. Whatever it is, it is a time to be—not to think of who you were or who you might become, but just a time to experience the "here and now" and to "smell the roses."

Bridges described this as a period of emptiness, almost like being suspended in time between the old life and the new life. During this period, a person is betwixt and between, having left old roles, relationships, routines, and assumptions but not yet in a new life with new roles, relationships, routines, and assumptions. In one way it is like being in a rudderless boat.

Beginnings

Beginnings come "when the endings and the time of fallow neutrality are finished" (Bridges, 1980, p. 134). These beginnings often take the form of external career changes. We read about doctors who become artists and housewives or househusbands who take up real estate. A 25-year-old man debating between social work or medicine, chose social work because he could not make the kind of commitment to the required lifestyle and rigor required of medical students. However, he feared that at 40 he would regret his decision. The counselor pointed out that what he did for the next 15 years did not have to determine his whole life. At 40 it is not too late to make a new beginning; in fact, new beginnings are possible all through life.

Bridges's work is an example of a theory-to-practice model. He conceptualized the transition process. He showed its relevance for individuals as they deal with their own transitions (1980), and he demonstrated its applicability to the corporate world in his book, *Surviving Corporate Transition* (1988). He showed how everyone—including business firms—goes through endings, neutral zones, and beginnings. He provided many illustrations that help individuals understand transitions and even relax in the face of change. The knowledge that every beginning begins with an ending and that endings break up habits, routines, and roles helps explain why so many individuals hold on endlessly to bad relationships or stultifying jobs. Bridges specifically illustrated how managers can use this knowledge. For example, every change, whether a new boss or an introduction of technology, results in potential loss of attachments, turf, structure, future, meaning, and control (1988, p. 40). Employees must be allowed to grieve for what is lost.

A study of adult learners (Schlossberg, Lynch, & Chickering, 1989) indicated that graduation forced a reformulation of goals. As one set of goals is reached, for example, finishing a degree, there is an inevitable let-down; for once again a sense of purpose must be reconstructed. The adult learners are giving up classes, advisers, and the goal of becoming, but have not yet moved to a new set of activities and self-definition. Change involves loss as well as new possibilities. Bridges summarized the entire transition process when he wrote, "Endings and beginnings, with empti-ness and germination in between" (1988, p. 150).

Helen Rose Fuchs Ebaugh—The Process of Role Exit

Ebaugh (1988), a sociologist, concentrated on endings, the process of leaving a role. She interviewed ex-doctors, dentists, police officers, air traffic controllers, teachers, military personnel, athletes, professors, con-victs, prostitutes, transvestites, and nuns.

She found that exiting from a role is a unique process. "Role exit is a process of disengagement from a role that is central to one's self-identity and the reestablishment of an identity in a new role that takes into account one's ex-role. Role exit is a process that occurs over time" (1988, p. 23). The process begins with an individual having doubts, then looking for reactions that can be either positive or negative, and then seeking alternative roles (p. 84).

A student wrote a paper on mothers giving up custody of their chil-dren. She selected the topic after reading Ebaugh's book, mainly because she had such negative feelings about women who would voluntarily give up custody. Using the role exit framework, she looked at the process of women as they made the decision and the process of creating a new role—still mother but not with custody. She found that it was a painful process. Incidentally, her views of this group changed dramatically after the study; she gained great respect for many, did not categorize them neg-atively, and became aware of the stigma we attach to certain ex-roles.

Ebaugh's studies were mainly of those individuals voluntarily exiting from their roles. Unstudied are the many forced into leaving a role they loved—the push to make people retire early or the announcement of a spouse or partner that he or she is in love with someone else and there-fore is forcing the end of a relationship. In a pilot study of college presi-dents leaving the presidency, we found that the major difference was whether the person left voluntarily or saw the "handwriting on the wall" (McEwen, Komives, & Schlossberg, 1990). In another major difference related to gender, the men we interviewed were not as open in their responses, not as willing to talk about the pain of leaving one role and carving out a new role as the women were.

Ebaugh (1988) pointed out that many therapists "first encounter role exiters who are going through the vacuum stage of the process . . . this period is one of extreme anxiety and creates a sense of normlessness. . . . Sometimes the greatest help a therapist can give an individual 'caught' in the vacuum stage is to help [the individual] . . . begin to identify as an ex and move on to the creation of new role" (p. 209).

Self-help groups offer support to people seeking to connect with others "in the same boat" and thereby reduce loneliness and confusion. It takes time to leave a role and establish new roles, new reference groups, and new norms. The new life, though, is always built on the identity that went before. As one learns new roles, some remnants of the previous role always remain. For example, there is a tremendous difference between two elementary school teachers, one of whom had belonged to a religious order whereas the other had served as a police officer. They each have a "hang-over identity" from their previous roles.

Arnold Van Gennep and Barbara Myerhoff—The Rites of Passage

Van Gennep (1960), an anthropologist, identified a process common to all societies. "The life of an individual in any society is a series of passages from one age to another and from one occupation to another. . . . For every one of these events there are ceremonies whose essential purpose is to enable the individual to pass from one defined position to another" (pp. 2–3). Rites of passage include events that separate the individual from the group, such as graduations; incorporate the individual into a new role, such as marriage; or acknowledge an in-between status, such as pregnancy, labeled as a period of "liminality." Whether it is a rite to acknowledge separation, incorporation, or liminality, the rites have an "over-all goal to insure a change of condition or a passage from one magico-religious or secular group to another" (p. 11). Though written in 1960, these concepts apply today. In the film *Rites of Renewal,* the late anthropologist, Barbara Myerhoff, discussed the role of rituals, ceremonies, and rites of passage in helping people mark "the transition of an individual from one phase of life . . . to another" (1985). In this film, Myerhoff described the three stages of a ritual.

First, the individual is segregated. Observe any ceremony—graduation, retirement, or wedding—and note the separation made obvious by the placement or dress of the persons in question.

Second, the individual moves into a state between the old role and the new role, liminality in Van Gennep's terms and the Neutral Zone in

Bridges's. The person is still a baby and not a baby, still a worker and not a worker. As Myerhoff stated in the film, "That middle stage, the marginal one, the liminal one, is an especially interesting one because that's where the person is neither one thing or another" (1984).

The final phase of the ritual is "reincorporating the person . . . back into society as a new creature with a new identity" (Myerhoff, 1985). For example, high school graduates entering college are not sure of their identities. The final phase of the transition occurs when they develop identities other than those connected to the high school roles and relationships they previously had. Rituals thus help people make sense of the paradox inherent in many transitions—that there is no single truth, there are many truths; that individuals are part of the past, but also the future. We clearly see the importance of using rituals to help people deal with the transition process. It is just as important to develop rituals for non-events. For example, we have rituals for events such as a promotion or publishing a book, but not for the non-event of not getting promoted or not finding a publisher for your book. We suggest ways of developing rituals for these non-events in the Appendix on pages 279–293.

Frederick Hudson—Cycle of Renewal

Frederick Hudson (1991, 1999) conceptualized transitions as a normal and inevitable part of living. He defined a transition as "a natural process of disorientation and reorientation that alters the perception of self and world and demands changes in assumptions and behavior" (1991, p. 96). He stated that transitions follow predictable patterns and that adults can learn how to anticipate and move through them. Hudson highlighted the positive function of transitions and stressed that, although they can be disorientating and painful, they are most always pathways for growth and discovery.

Hudson (1999) defined a transition as "a cycle of renewal," and each phase of the cycle is described in terms of characteristics and personal skills required to navigate the transition. A transition, according to Hudson, progresses in four phases. Each phase is defined by its unique characteristics, and each phase requires its own tasks and activities. His concept of phases provides a circular map of a transition, cycling from *getting ready,* to *launching,* and *plateauing,* to *sorting things out.* He also includes the concept of the *mini-transition,* which is a repairing and updating of the same life structure when only minor changes are necessary.

Phase I, entitled *Go for It,* involves *The Heroic Self* and is the positive part of the cycle. Phase II, termed *The Doldrums,* is characterized by a protracted sense of decline. This phase is followed by Phase III,

Cocooning, which is an emotional "time out" and a time to heal, reflect and discover new directions. Hudson described this as a soulful time that gives birth to a new beginning. Phase IV, *Getting Ready,* is a time for experimenting, training, networking, and testing possible paths.

According to Hudson (1991), the healthy person is a fluid and interacting participant in the wider world. Although he acknowledged the increasing chaos of our times, he challenged people to live creatively with the chaos. He described this process as "collaging your way through time and space. . . . You arrange and rearrange your colors and shapes as you move along . . . assembling and disassembling yourself and the universe around you" (pp. 202–203). He stated that dealing with complex change is an unpredictable and informal process and yet requires life-cycle skills. These skills are those that are needed for dealing with each phase of the transition with the overall goal of generating self-renewal.

Bloch and Richmond—Hope and Spirituality

According to Bloch and Richmond (1998), energy is used in all situations involving change, and a person's assumptions are central to a positive outcome. They also stated that those who meet the challenges will hold the assumption that the universe always works for us. Furthermore, those who have hope are more apt to deal with transitions by utilizing productive strategies. These strategies require abandoning old, tightly held images, letting go of the familiar, and trusting ourselves and the world around us. This adaptation requires inner work and going deep within to find the strength to make the change. It is really about having a sense of hope: "When we have hope, our spirits are tuned in to the spirit of the universe" (p. 71).

According to Bloch (2004), living beings are in a dynamic state, moving between order and chaos. She compared these phase transitions to the movement of water among the three phases, liquid, solid, or ice, and gas or steam. She stated that phase transitions, whether sought or not, present the opportunity for creativity and the emergence of new forms. Bloch and Richmond (1998) stated that change affects the whole person: emotional being, physical being, and mental functioning. They stated that change has an impact on many aspects of a person, affecting his or her life roles and self-image: "To change, we often have to let go of some part of ourselves, or of something we hold dear" (p. 6). Change comes not just by actions, but through an inward sloughing off of old patterns. Some people emerge better, others recoup from loss and break even, and others stay the same or spiral down and despair. They described spirituality as a source of energy and stated that this energy can be utilized in times of distress. As individuals strive to become whole, they move toward self-completion, which serves to increase their adaptive capacity.

Unifying Themes—An Integrated Model

Each of the preceding theorists defined transitions as an integral aspect of human development and as a challenge to personal transformation and growth. Each conceptualized working through transitions as an active process requiring energy, strategies, and courage on the part of the person. Dealing with transitions entails both inner work and outer work. Within each theory people must first recognize and work through the loss and confusion associated with a transition. Transitions are viewed as entailing risks and associated fears, and the strategies for moving through relate to the outer world.

The goal within each of these theories is adaptation and further development through working through the phases of the transition. All agree that people will react individually in how they move through them. Successful outcomes are seen as dependent on the person's perceptions of the transition, their resources and limitations, and their overall ability to cope with the transition. Each of the theorists agrees that transitions are indeed a time of opportunity, yet have the potential to be resolved either constructively or destructively. Although transitions represent a natural and necessary aspect of adult development, they are viewed as the times that are most distressing and challenging, yet unique in the opportunities for growth and development.

Bridges presented an overview of the transition process that applies to both individuals and organizations. Ebaugh delineated exiting from a role. Hudson talked about transitions as a normal and inevitable part of living, and Bloch and Richmond focused on energy and hope. Each of these theorists focuses on transition, but each comes to the topic with a different perspective (see Figure 2.2).

To restate: In any transition, the first stage can be conceptualized as either moving in or moving out. People who move into a new situation, whether a new marriage, a new job, or an educational environment, have some common agendas and needs. They need to become familiar with the rules, regulations, norms, and expectations of the new system. Institutions need to devote a great deal of time to orientation, a process designed to help individuals know what is expected of them.

Once in a new situation, adults confront issues such as how to balance their activities with other parts of their lives and how to feel supported and challenged during their new journey. Applying this to adult learners, we see that the *moving through* period begins once learners know the ropes. Because it can be a long transition, learners may need

MOVING IN
New Roles, Relationships,
Routines, Assumptions

Learning the Ropes;
Socialization

Hang-over Identity

MOVING OUT
Separation or Endings

Role Exit

Disengagement from Roles,
Relationships, Routines,
Assumptions

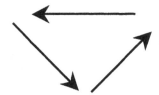

MOVING THROUGH: BETWIXT OR BETWEEN
Period of Liminality

Groping for New: Roles, Relationships, Routines, Assumptions

Neutral Zone: Period of Emptiness and Confusion

Cycle of Renewal

Hope and Spirituality

Figure 2.2   Integrative model of the transition process.

help sustaining their energy and commitment. In other areas of life, this in-between time can evoke new questions about the transition: "Did I do the right thing?" "Why am I bored?" "Can I commit to this transition?" Many jokes about the "seven-year itch" stem from this middle period when reevaluation takes place.

Moving out can be seen as ending one series of transitions and beginning to ask what comes next. Grieving can be used as a model to explain this phase in the process. People feel grief in many situations of loss other than those most commonly recognized as bereavement. When leaving familiar surroundings and people or ways of functioning and interacting to which one has become accustomed, one experiences disequilibrium. Changing jobs, moving, and returning to school, all are transitions in which adults mourn the loss of former goals, friends, and structure.

Another important point is that the larger the transition—either good or bad—the more it will pervade an individual's life. At first, one is a beginning student, new widow, or new parent. A period of disruption follows, in which old roles, relationships, assumptions, and routines change and new ones evolve. Then, finally and gradually, the sharp awareness of having graduated, living alone, or having become a parent becomes only one of the many dimensions of living—the transition has been integrated.

Retirement—An Example of the Transition Process

Incorporating retirement transitions into your life takes time. At first, people are consumed by exiting from their past role and figuring out a new life. The change is consuming, whether the person's role was a CEO of a small family business (a homemaker) whose home responsibilities have totally diminished or a newly retired CEO of a company, they gradually, begin to separate from the past and move toward a new life.

In Schlossberg's (2004) studies of retirees, she found that they follow many paths during this process: some *continue* in a modified way what they once did, others experiment and *adventure* into new activities like the researcher turned massage therapist; others *easy glide*, taking each day as it comes; others *search* for their place in the sun; some stay as *involved spectators* like the former lobbyist who is now a news junkie; and others unfortunately *retreat*. Many, of course, combine paths.

Each retiree has a psychological portfolio, which is the bridge that connects past work and future retirement. The portfolio consists of one's identity, relationships, and meaningful involvements.

Identity

This is key to the psychological portfolio. What do you put on a calling card? How do you identify yourself when you meet someone? As one man said sadly, "When people ask what do you do, I don't know how to answer. Should I say, 'Nothing?'" Miriam, a skilled dentist, could not wait to retire so that she could do carpentry. She had her workshop ready the day she retired. Yet it took her 2 years to say to herself and to others that she was a professional carpenter. Incorporating a new identity takes time.

Relationships

Relationships play a critical role in one's psychological portfolio. Cal, a retired professor, claimed that what he missed most was "schmoozing."

He was having difficulty replacing work relationships—a must to keep your psychological portfolio strong. In addition, readjusting to family relationships can be challenging. Cal amazed himself when he heard himself screaming at his wife at the check-out counter about the brand of cereal she had bought. Now that he was no longer working full time he went grocery shopping with her. Adjusting to being at home with her after 50 years of spending days apart takes time.

Meaningful Involvement

Meaningful involvement is a necessary component of one's psychological portfolio. Sociologists Moen and Fields (2002) concluded that peoples' work provides social as well as financial capital. After retirement, participation in volunteer or part-time work is an effective way to build up your social capital. Many studies point to the relationship of volunteering and mental health and even longevity. Working often leads persons to feel competent, useful, and, most of all, that they "matter." If you feel that you matter and that your life has meaning and purpose, then clearly you have the necessary assets in your psychological portfolio.

THE RESOLUTION

At some point, transitions are assimilated into one's life. For example, a woman hearing that she has been diagnosed with breast cancer will be totally absorbed in her reactions, her search for the right treatment, and her facing the many decisions to be made. The process of hearing the initial diagnosis, dealing with the treatment plan, and seeing herself and her body in a new way takes time. Eventually she is someone who had cancer. She is no longer absorbed; she has dealt with the medical and psychological treatment. She incorporated her new sense of herself, aware that this is now part of her reality, but has regained her sense of well-being.

A man who was forced to relocate will at first be totally absorbed in the logistics of moving himself and his family—selling his house and buying another. He will be focused on his wife's search for a job in the community and his children's registration in and adjustment to a new school. He will then be able to focus on his emotions about the move, positive and negative, and the learning curve to be up to speed in his new position. And all of these reactions will be mediated by his explanatory style.

SUMMARY

The transition framework is based on the following premises that:

Adults continuously experience transitions.

Adults' reactions to transitions depend on the type of transition, the context in which it occurs, and its impact on their lives.

A transition has no end point; rather, a transition is a process over time that includes phases of assimilation and continuous appraisal as people move in, through, and out of it.

These primary elements apply to non-event transitions as well as to those triggered by specific events. Those events we thought might happen that do not are often of critical importance in the lives of adults and are often underplayed or ignored. Yet they can have a profound influence on our ability to love, work, and play. Non-event transitions are elaborated on further in a special chapter, presented as an Appendix. This Appendix, written by Nancy K. Schlossberg, includes exercises for helping adults navigate non-event transitions, as well as theoretical and descriptive material.

Factors That Influence Transitions

The transition framework presented in Chapter 2 and here in Chapter 3 is designed to depict the extraordinarily complex reality that accompanies and defines the human capacity to cope with change. Four major sets of factors (see Figure 3.1) influence the ability of the individual to cope during a transition:

1. The *Situation* variable—What is happening? For example, the transition to retirement differs from the transition of having a first baby.
2. The *Self* variable—To whom is it happening? Each individual is different in terms of life issues and personality.
3. The *Support* variable—What help is available? Supports and available options vary for each individual.
4. The *Strategies* variable—How does the person cope? People navigate transitions in different ways. We call them the 4 S's.

THE 4 S SYSTEM: SOME CONSIDERATIONS

The 4 S System—Situation, Self, Support, and Strategies—describes the factors that make a difference in how one copes with change. These four sets of variables can be regarded as potential assets and/or liabilities. To understand how these assets and liabilities work, we need first to examine their interrelationship and how one goes about appraising them, but it is equally significant to examine options faced by different individuals and groups in our society.

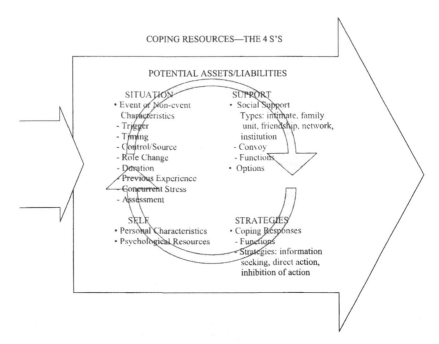

Figure 3.1 Coping resources—the 4 S's.

Balancing Assets and Liabilities

Coping effectiveness is best examined and explained by using a model that balances opposing forces. Individuals have both assets and liabilities and resources and deficits, as they experience transitions. Fiske and Chiriboga (1990) identified individuals high on both resources and deficits. Those high on one and low on the other, and those low on both. They argue that a model incorporating both resources and deficits, rather than the degree-of-impairment model, is more meaningful because people have multiple strengths and limitations.

To clarify this mix of resources and deficits, we will look at two women diagnosed with multiple sclerosis. For both, the experience is painful, incapacitating, and psychologically distressing because of the uncertainty of the condition. One of the women has ample assets to balance this deficit in her physical well-being. She has a tenured position in a university, a highly supportive family, as well as friends and colleagues who rally around her, and a coping personality. The other woman is low on assets at this particular point in her life. She has recently had a double mastectomy, thus her physical stamina and her self-esteem are low, and she has just gone through a divorce, which suggests that part of her support system has crumbled. In addition, this particular disability threatens her very economic survival by making it impossible for her to work as a carpenter, a job requiring great physical stamina. Moreover, her ability to cope has never been better than average. At this benchmark, her liabilities far outweigh her assets, making her life especially difficult.

The 4 S model then, rather than assessing a person's mental condition in terms of health or sickness, employs a ratio of assets to liabilities and allows for changes in the ratio as an individual's situation changes. This approach partially answers the question of why different individuals react differently to the same type of transition and why the same person reacts differently at different times. The difference may be that the assets–liabilities balance has changed: Assets may outweigh liabilities, making adjustment relatively easy, or liabilities may now outweigh assets, so assimilation of the transition becomes correspondingly more difficult. It is important that psychologists and others in the helping professions delay diagnosis of someone as "ill" when, in fact, all that may be needed is a temporary shift in the balance of assets to liabilities.

Appraisal of Transitions

Lazarus and Folkman (1984) defined a transition as a transaction between individuals and their environment. The individual's appraisal of the transition is key. Does the individual see it as positive, negative, or benign? An individual's appraisal will clearly influence how that individual feels and copes with the transition event or non-event.

Lazarus and Folkman wrote:

> Although certain environmental demands and pressures produce stress in substantial numbers of people, individual and group differences in the degree and kind of reaction are always evident. People . . . differ in their sensitivity and vulnerability to certain types of events, as well as in their interpretations and reactions. Under comparable conditions, for example, one person responds with anger, another with depression, yet another with anxiety or guilt, and still others feel challenged rather than threatened. Likewise, one individual uses denial to cope with terminal illness whereas another anxiously ruminates about the problem or is depressed. One individual handles an insult by ignoring it and another grows angry. (p. 50)

> . . . In order to understand variations among individuals under comparable conditions, we must take into account the cognitive processes that intervene between the encounter and the reaction, and the factors that affect the nature of this mediation. If we do not consider these processes, we will be unable to understand human variation under comparable external conditions. (pp. 22, 23)

Lazarus and Folkman suggested that individuals make two types of appraisals simultaneously. Primary appraisal refers to the perception of the transition itself—is it positive, negative, or irrelevant? If stressful, is it perceived as a challenge, a threat, or a loss? For example, 10 parents experience having their youngest child begin college. For some it may signify the end of their parenting role; to others, it may mean freedom to follow their own interests; and to still others, it may have no impact at all.

In addition, individuals engage in secondary appraisal during which they assess their resources for coping with the transition. These coping resources include the 4 S's—Situation, Self, Support, and Strategies. A woman might be facing job loss, a negative transition, but feels she has the resources to cope with it, or she might be dealing with a positive transition such as a promotion, but deems her resources for coping with it as low. One woman declined a wished-for job offer because her personal situation was negative—her son had just been diagnosed with cystic fibrosis, and her husband had left her. Her situation and supports were so low that she could not deal with any major transition—even a positive one.

The results of the secondary appraisal influence the individual's selection of coping strategies. There is a feedback loop. For example, a person might appraise early retirement as a great opportunity but then may become anxious about taking advantage of it due to the assessment of the 4 S's. This might then force a reappraisal of the desirability of early retirement and a decision not to take it. People make assessments and arrive at decisions like this all the time.

As we pointed out in Chapter 2, the transition process consists of reactions over a period of time. As reactions change, an individual's perspective can shift from feeling "this is forever" to one of "this too shall pass." It is useful for helpers to share this knowledge. As Caine (1974) pointed out in her book on widowhood, "I am convinced that if I had known the facts of grief before I had to experience them, it would not have made my grief less intense . . . [but it] would have allowed me to hope" (pp. 91–92). An individual's appraisal and reappraisal of a transition and of his or her resources for coping, can be examined in light of the 4 S's.

A Multicultural View of Options

As we have already noted, individuals constantly assess their transitions and resources for coping. These resources, according to Sussman (1972), include the individual's options, which may be actual, perceived, utilized, or created. Sussman developed "an option-maintenance model" stating that the central variable in determining whether people feel successful when coping with a transition resides in the number of options that people feel they can exercise. Sussman further contended that options are directly related to self-esteem. Chronic job loss or feeling forced to stay in a low-level job or an unsatisfactory marriage can erode an individual's confidence and self-esteem.

Sussman discussed two levels of options: structural and psychological. Structural options are related to the availability of options. When unemployment is structural, more people are affected and the individual alone can do less about it. Opening up the opportunity structure requires political action, such as legislative changes in the retirement age, thus changing the options for older people. Psychological options are related to the individual's skill in perceiving and utilizing alternatives (Sussman, 1972).

The history of oppressed groups in this country, such as African Americans, other ethnic minorities, women, and elderly persons, reflects a shift from a time when many individuals accepted that there were no options for their group to a time when the group organized to fight to change the opportunity structure. The ability to create new options is not restricted to political activists. Career development experts run workshops designed specifically to help people take control of their lives, break out of their boxes, identify what they want, and create their own jobs and options.

Thus, options can be both objective (at one time there were few professional jobs for African Americans) and subjective ("because I am African American I will not apply to medical school"). A fine line exists between actual options and the perception of actual options. Further, political action groups may assist in the creation of options for some groups, for example, women wanting to be astronauts. Thus, any discussion of options is highly complex and involves the interaction of the actual world with the individual's perceptions and actions.

At a workshop on transitions, counseling psychologist Donelda Cooke (1994) was asked to critique the 4 S model from a multicultural perspective. According to Cooke, a multicultural perspective is not one of just numbers or labels. Reporting cases or vignettes that reflect diversity of color, ethnicity, gender, or age is only a first step.

Cooke's overriding message concerned the necessity of carefully examining the assumptions and worldview of others—the ways that different people make meaning in the world. As she said

> It is important to ask how the model applies to the low-income African American mothers from an inner-city Baltimore community I interviewed for a research project, the Caucasian female client I saw in counseling who had cerebral palsy and was a victim of rape, the student who struggled with her sexual identity because her traditional Italian family would never accept that the one girl in the family was a lesbian, the 19-year-old Caucasian male student who was confined to a wheelchair three years ago and experiences insensitivities and discriminatory practices on a daily basis.

Cooke urged that sociopolitical and cultural values be the context in which others are understood

> By looking at various groups' experiences regarding domination, oppression, and co-existence, you can begin to understand the amount of control individuals have over the circumstances in their lives, or the limited choices they may have in their assets, liabilities, and resources. While the theory leaves room to explore the sense of control one has over one's transitions, unless sociopolitical constraints are boldly articulated, readers from privileged classes can too easily overlook them.

Everyone uses coping strategies, everyone has some kind of support system, everyone has a personal way of being in the world, and everyone has a unique situation. Yet there is an overriding concern. Some individuals' Situation, Self, Support, and Strategies are qualitatively so restricted that one cannot consider the 4 S's alone. As Cooke said, one's resources for coping—the 4 S's—are determined by the outside world. If people's concerns relate to feeding their families or dealing with ill children without health insurance, their resources are qualitatively different than those of middle-class professionals.

THE 4 S SYSTEM: A DETAILED VIEW

Situation

Every individual's situation varies according to the following factors:

- Trigger—What set off the transition?
- Timing—How does the transition relate to one's social dock?
- Control—What aspects of the transition can one control?
- Role change—Does the transition involve role change?
- Duration—Is the transition seen as permanent or temporary?
- Previous experience with a similar transition—How has the individual met similar transitions?
- Concurrent stress—What and how great are the stresses facing the individual now, if any?
- Assessment—Does the individual view the situation positively, negatively, or as benign?

Trigger

A transition, as we have defined it, can be anticipated or unanticipated, an event or a non-event, as long as it alters one's life. Triggers can be external, such as a decade birthday, and have internal consequences, such as an awareness that time is running out. Triggers stimulate individuals to look at themselves and their lives in a new way. For example, a change in health—a heart attack or cancer—can act as a trigger for rethinking work and relationships. Job changes, especially job losses, trigger reevaluation. For one man, the trigger was being in bed for 5 months with a slipped disk, coupled with the death from cancer of one of his closest friends: "If I can get sick, if John can die, then life is not forever." For another, being at a wedding of a friend's child can trigger the realization that one's adult children are not married and one might never be an in-law or a grandparent.

A transition can also be triggered by something that happens to someone close to the individual: A husband's retirement may trigger a fear of aging in his wife; a wife's mastectomy may trigger fears of death in her husband. Other triggers can be class reunions, movies, and books.

Aslanian and Brickell (1980) differentiated transitions from triggers: A *transition* is a "change in status . . . that makes learning necessary. The adult needs to become competent at something that he or she could not do before in order to succeed in the new status" (pp. 38–39). A *trigger*, however, is a specific life event that precipitates "the decision to learn at that point in time" (p. 39). The trigger is not necessarily directly related to the transition, as in the example of an unemployed woman, suddenly widowed, who enrolls in a medical technology course to become qualified for a job. The transition is her change of status from nonworker to worker; the triggering event is her husband's death, in itself, a major transition.

Timing

As noted, most adults have built-in social clocks that are their barometers to judge whether they are "on time" or "off time" with respect to family, career, and self issues. To be off time, whether early or late, can make individuals feel uncomfortable. Certain transitions, for example, getting married, having children, going to college, taking a job, and retiring, used to be linked in people's minds to a certain age. Today, these rigid timetables are loosening as people's lives follow irregular paths. Despite the more fluid lifespan, many still use age to define how they are doing.

Transition events or non-events are also experienced as happening at "good" or "bad" times. For example, an adolescent in senior high school will resist a family geographical move as being at a bad time. A newlywed couple may define a move away from parents and in-laws as happening at a good time. The couple's parents, who have recently become in-laws, however, may see it as a bad time. A major illness at a time of job loss would be both bad and off time. Thus, events, both anticipated and unanticipated, can occur at better or worse times, making it easier or more difficult for individuals to go through the transition process.

Control

The source of some transitions is internal, a deliberate decision on the part of the individual, whereas the source of others is completely external, and the transition is forced upon the individual by other people or by circumstances. The worker who retires because of ill health or a plant closing probably finds retirement more difficult and troubling than the worker who retires voluntarily. Similarly, couples often experience considerable negative stress in connection with residential moves when the move is forced upon them by the job requirements of one of them. The issue here is how an individual perceives control over his or her own life.

Judith Rodin (1990), the psychologist who studied the relevance of control in determining one's mental health, has paid particular attention to aging and control. She wrote "Across the life-span, every significant developmental transition provides new challenges for perceived and actual control. . . . Through middle adulthood and into old age, new demands and issues impact on one's sense of control. . . . Therefore, one's overall level of self-efficacy may remain stable, although the domains in which one feels competent are likely to change and become less numerous" (pp. 11–12).

Even if the transition is beyond the individual's control, the response to it can be within the individual's control. The two sources of control—internal and external—interact. Counselors can help adults explore the degree to which the trigger or transition is in or out of their control and the degree to which they can control their reactions to it.

Role Change

Many, but not all, transitions involve role change. We have already noted that role changes are an important aspect in determining the impact of a transition. Fiske and Chiriboga (1990) distinguished between role gains (such as getting married, becoming a parent, taking a job, or getting a job promotion) and role losses (such as getting divorced, retiring, or being widowed). Regardless of whether a transition involves a role gain or loss, some degree of stress accompanies it.

For instance, LeMasters (1957) found that the period after the birth of the first child often constitutes a mental health crisis for the mother; along with her feelings of joy and satisfaction, she may be physically exhausted, anxious about her responsibilities, frustrated over her loss of freedom, resentful of her husband for not sharing more of the duties, and, in addition, guilty about her negative feelings. Similarly, although an individual may look forward with pleasurable anticipation to retiring from employment or seeing the last child launched into the world, the actual event may carry with it feelings of pain. Again, any role change, whether primarily positive or negative, involves some degree of stress.

Role is the "behavioral enacting of the patterned expectations attributed to a position" (Merton, 1957, p. 368). "Role theory in sociology centers on others' expectations as to the behavior of the individual who occupies a given position. These expectations sustain order and consistency in human interaction. These expectations are essentially normative prescriptions for behavior" (Zaleznik & Jardim, 1967, p. 210). The more an individual engages in "anticipatory socialization," that is, orientation toward the values and norms of the new role, the sooner the individual will be comfortable (Merton, 1957, p. 265). When there are no role models available for the new role, the individual remains marginal for a longer period, as did the first women executives in American business.

Thus, a given role change can be more or less difficult (and have greater or lesser impact) depending on whether the new role is a loss or a gain, is positive or negative, or has explicit norms and expectations for the new incumbent. As Pearlin and Lieberman (1979) concluded, "It is not the tearing away from old roles that matters to well-being, but what is discovered in the context of the new roles" (p. 239).

Duration

The expected duration of the transition affects the ease or difficulty of assimilating the transition. A change that is regarded as permanent will be perceived differently from one that is viewed as temporary. A wife may be willing to tolerate the inconvenience involved in moving to a new location so her husband can attend graduate school if she believes that the move is temporary and that they will return to their former home when he has received his degree. A transition that is painful and unpleasant may be more easily borne if the individual is assured that it is of limited duration, for example, when someone enters the hospital for surgery knowing that the discomfort is temporary. Conversely, if the change is desired, then the certainty that it represents a more or less permanent state may be reassuring. Uncertainty about duration, however, is connected with perhaps the greatest degree of stress and negative effect. Chodoff (1976), talking about the psychological stresses of being in a German concentration camp, said, "A healthy personality [can] defend itself against a peril, which, though grave, is predictable and is at least potentially limited in time, but the absolute uncertainty of [the concentration camp inmate's] condition was a barrier to the erection of adequate psychological measures" (pp. 337–338). To have an illness whose cause and prognosis are uncertain may be more stressful and unsettling for an individual than to know for sure that he or she has a terminal disease.

Previous Experience with a Similar Transition

It is generally assumed that the individual who has successfully weathered a particular kind of transition in the past will probably be successful at assimilating another transition of a similar nature. Conversely, the person who has been defeated by a situation may become more vulnerable and less able to cope in the future. Past experiences to some extent determine the person's mental set, and if that past experience was unfavorable, then the mental set may be something of a self-confirming prophecy. Of course, given possible changes in the balance of assets and liabilities (discussed earlier), the correlation between successful assimilation in the past and at a later point in time is by no means perfect.

Some types of loss seem to have long-lasting negative effects. For example, Fiske and Chiriboga (1990) found that of the one quarter of their sample who had suffered an early childhood loss through death or divorce, one half belonged to the "overwhelmed" category; that is, they were preoccupied with stress. Undoubtedly, some experiences are so harrowing that many people are left permanently damaged.

Concurrent Stress

Often transitions in one area stimulate other stresses and transitions. Consider the transition faced by a middle-aged couple whose first daughter is marrying. Can we rate that transition? We would say no. Understanding the transition requires examining the impact on the middle-aged couple's life. If the daughter lives across the country and will remain there, the marriage will not have a significant impact on the daily or weekly life of the parents. Some changes may, of course, occur. If, however, the daughter who has lived away returns to the parents' city to marry, has one small stepchild and little money, comes home three times a week to do laundry, and asks the parents to baby sit, then it is a transition of much greater impact.

Assessment

An individual's view of who or what is responsible for the transition affects how that individual appraises the transition (and himself or herself and the environment). Does he or she see the divorce as attributable to the other's deficiencies, to his or her own deficiencies, to societal problems, or to idiosyncratic causes? The individual's attributions about self and situation provide a theoretical basis for many studies explaining behavior.

Situation Review

Each transition event or non-event is different. The same individual can get divorced, become a grandparent, lose a job, inherit a million dollars, or not have a baby. Each of these transitions will be different in terms of the following:

- What triggered it?
- Was it at a good time in the individual's life?
- Did the individual initiate the transition or did it happen to him or her?
- Did the individual experience a role change? Is the transition permanent or temporary?
- Has the individual had previous experience with similar transitions, and if so, were they helpful or harmful?
- Is the individual experiencing stress in other areas of life?
- Does the individual assess the transition as positive, negative, or benign?

Self

We stated earlier that every individual has both assets and liabilities/resources and deficits. In addition to the Situation itself, we now look at what the individual brings to the transition. We all hear clients who state, "I'm a pessimist and always see the glass as half empty," or "I'm usually up for change but this one has really knocked me out." It is complex to get a handle on the Self, but we have identified the following characteristics that are particularly relevant for individuals as they cope with change:

- Personal and demographic characteristics
- Socioeconomic status
- Gender
- Age and stage of life
- State of health
- Ethnicity/culture
- Psychological resources
- Ego development
- Outlook—optimism and self-efficacy
- Commitment and values
- Spirituality and resiliency

Personal and Demographic Characteristics

An individual's personal and demographic characteristics—socioeconomic status, gender, ethnicity/culture, age and stage of life, and state of health—bear directly on how he or she perceives and assesses life. Research that combines societal and individual perspectives illustrates the importance and value of an integrated approach to the study of transitions. Such research clarifies the differences we refer to when we say that research results vary as a function of age, gender, and social class. People who inhabit different parts of the social system live, in many ways, in very different contexts, have different resources, and are affected differently by different events.

Sociologists Pearlin and Lieberman (1979) interviewed 2,300 adults, both White and non-White, aged 20 to 60. Four years later they again interviewed these adults, looking particularly for "the persistent problems of everyday life" as well as the life-course transitions and crises through which they had passed in the intervening 4-year period. The researchers identified the stresses and hardships the group had experienced as well as ways they coped with them.

Pearlin and Lieberman divided life strains into those that are unexpected (non-normative, such as a serious illness), those that are expected (normative, such as getting married or becoming a parent), and those that they call "persistent role problems" (such as an unaccepting spouse or children's failure to act responsibly). They then examined the effects of these life strains (or transitions) on anxiety and depression, at the same time identifying the ways people from different walks of life experienced these different life strains. Pearlin and Lieberman reported that, by and large, "The events, transitions, and persistent role problems are not scattered helter-skelter throughout the population, but tend to be more or less prevalent among groups having distinguishing social characteristics" (p. 230); that is, the life strains seemed to depend on age, gender, and socioeconomic status.

The importance of socioeconomic status is underlined in Rubin's (1981) study of the empty nest. Women from advantaged situations can anticipate that their children will go away to college; therefore, children's departure from the home is expected, and those women engaged in anticipatory socialization. Women from working-class homes, for whom money is often a problem and children's attendance at an out-of-town college is uncertain, experienced a more difficult transition in the event of their children's departure. Rubin stressed the fact that the empty nest is not a problem for most women. What makes it a problem is when it is unplanned or when feelings about it are ambivalent (Rubin, 1981).

The effects of an individual's racial and ethnic background on his or her ability to navigate transitions are probably mediated through other factors such as value orientation and cultural norms. They should not, however, be underestimated. As noted in Chapter 1, further research in this area is needed. We hope to see an increase in studies of many populations so that insights will be gained into the differing adult experiences.

The relationship between gender and the transition process is complex. Many observers have suggested that because men are socialized to hide emotion and deny problems (whereas women are given greater freedom to express their feelings), men present a more favorable picture with respect to mental health. Despite appearances, however, women's greater capacity for intimacy and mutuality may make it easier for them to assimilate certain transitions; the example of widowhood has already been cited. Moreover, evidence suggests that women "can apparently integrate many and diverse emotional experiences. Men seem more distressed by ups and downs of emotional life; they apparently thrive either on a preponderance of positive emotional experiences or a relative lack of any kind [of experience]" (Fiske & Chiriboga, 1990, p. 97).

Wherever we look, we see gender as a critical determiner of work and family issues. Tannen (1990) investigated the different ways men and women communicate. Because boys and girls grow up in different cultures, they speak and listen from different vantage points. Tannen wrote:

> If women speak and hear a language of connection and intimacy, while men speak and hear a language of status and independence, then communication between men and women can be like cross-cultural communication, prey to a clash of conversational styles. Instead of different dialects, it has been said they speak different genderlects. (p. 42)

Her research corroborated others', showing that men like to problem-solve and women like to discuss and develop ideas. "When men and women talk to each other, the problem is that each expects a different kind of response" (p. 61). Tannen's message is even more forceful when she describes the power differences between men and women as seen through their communication. This power differential is reflected over and over in different wages, different job titles, and different opportunities. These differences in power and communication styles reflect the different worldviews of men and women, and these views in turn have an impact on how transitions are viewed.

Although there have been significant strides in reducing sex-role stereotyping, there is still a great deal of difference that results from gender. Therefore, helpers need to explore with individuals how such differences may affect their response to their transition.

Again, the wealth of data about the relation between *age* and ability to assimilate transitions precludes all but a cursory discussion here. One point that makes analysis difficult is that most experts agree that chronological age is relatively unimportant compared to *psychological age* ("the capacity to respond to societal pressures and the tasks required of an individual"), social age ("the extent to which an individual participates in roles assigned by society"), and functional age ("the ability to function or perform as expected of people in one's age bracket, which in turn, depends on social, biological and personality considerations") (Spierer, 1977, p. 10).

Another complication is that the process of aging itself constitutes a series of events that require adaptation on the part of the individual. That is, the biological and physiological changes that occur over the lifespan may themselves be regarded as transitions.

As mentioned, life stage may be a more useful concept than chronological age in examining transitions. Fiske and Chiriboga (1990) identified numerous stage differences with respect to the sources and nature of stress, the number of significant life events, and the ratio of positive to negative experiences. The younger subjects (high school seniors and newlyweds) reported more "stressor events" during the last 10 years of their lives than older subjects (middle-aged and pre-retirement couples). As was pointed out previously, in the later stages of life more subtle factors cause changes in self-perception and satisfaction: the realization that one has not achieved as much as one had planned or the shift in time perspective so that one thinks in terms of years left to live rather than years since birth.

Middle age is a period of contrasting stereotypes. One is that middle-agers are the command generation—powerful, in charge of themselves and others; another is the unhappy man or woman, bored at work and with love, in the midst of a face lift or an affair. So what is the truth about midlife?

If only we could define midlife by chronological age, we at least would have the parameters. However, there is no agreement about when it begins and when it ends. Some scholars define it as between 40 and 60, others as starting at 35 with no end, and others who specify it as the fifth decade. Neugarten (1979) suggested it is when we begin to think of time left to live rather than time since birth. Women are labeled middle aged and old before men, and those from higher socioeconomic groups begin midlife later and it lasts longer than for those in working-class and low-income groups. Chronological definitions of midlife are so variable that age, per se, is no indicator.

If only there were a midlife crisis, we could plan for it, handle it, and move on. However, the midlife crisis seems to be an artifact of the media. Pearlin and Lieberman (1979) found that despite fears that life will get harder as we age, younger people experience a clustering of work/family transitions in a relatively short period. They experience more disruptions in employment, more activity in both the formation and dissolution of relationships, and more persistent problems that accompany raising young children.

There is a wider timetable for the events and non-events during middle and old age. For example, one can lose both parents by 40, yet many in their 60s still have a parent living. This lengthened time period enables anticipation and preparation for the inevitable ups and downs connected with aging.

To test out the midlife crisis, psychologists Costa and McCrae (1980) administered a midlife crisis scale to a number of men of all ages. They hypothesized that those in midlife, whatever that is, would mark more problems than others. They discovered no clustering of crises by age. Kessler, a researcher for The MacArthur Foundation's research program on Successful Midlife Development (MIDMAC), and his colleagues found that only 10% to 12% of those surveyed reported a midlife crisis. (Kessler, Foster, Webster, & House, 1992).

As with age and aging, the individual's state of health not only affects his or her ability to assimilate a transition but also may itself be a source of stress. Ill health in itself, of course, constitutes a transition. In some cases, a person may recover quickly from an acute illness and be left relatively unaffected, with little change in self-perception. In other cases, an illness—though brief—may remind a person of his or her own mortality and thus have lasting psychological effects. In still other cases, an illness may be chronic, leading to a gradual decline in physical resources and energy level and thus profoundly affecting the individual's coping ability. Moreover, health has a subjective as well as an objective aspect. For instance, some people are health pessimists, and others are health optimists.

Both demographics and personal characteristics are important as filters and mediate whether or not an individual's life will be altered in ways basic to the particular person. As an individual's social class, gender, age, life stage, and health all bear on his or her options, perceived and real, these variables need to be explored.

Psychological Resources

Psychological resources are the "personality characteristics that people draw upon to help them withstand threats" (Pearlin & Schooler, 1978, p. 5). These include ego development, optimism, self-efficacy, commitments, and values, as well as spirituality and resilience.

People approach the same transition from different frames of reference. For example, if there were 100 45-year-old women enrolled in the same educational program, they would react according to their frame of reference and their level of maturity. Loevinger (1976) used the term *ego development* to describe this process and identified several levels of maturity. At a low level, the conformist will think in stereotypes, conform to the rules, and follow instructions without question. At a higher level, autonomous individuals are more critical and better able to tolerate ambiguity.

Knowing the level of ego development of a client can be useful to counselors in many situations. Consider such diverse transitions as navigating a divorce or a layoff. If you can identify the level at which this person operates, you may better tailor your interventions. In this schema, self-protective people are motivated to satisfy immediate needs, conformists are motivated to impress significant others and gain social acceptance, conscientious people are motivated to achieve skills and competence, and autonomous people seek to deepen understanding of themselves and others as well as to develop increasing capacity to tolerate ambiguity and uncertainty and be responsible for their own destiny.

Another way to understand clients is by knowing whether they see life as a glass that is half-full or half-empty. Thus, an individual's *outlook,* itself a result of the complex interplay of many factors, colors the way change is viewed. Optimism and self-efficacy are two critical aspects of one's outlook.

Seligman (2002) studied the qualities that enable people to rise above life's challenges, overcome adversity, resist illness and depression, and lead happier and more successful lives. His work has focused on different ways people react, especially to negative, uncontrollable, or bad events. According to Seligman, life inflicts similar setbacks and tragedies on optimists and pessimists, and optimists tend to weather them better. In other words, those who feel they have control over their lives or who feel optimistic about their own power to control at least some portions of their lives tend to experience less depression and achieve more at school or work; they are even in better health. Although Seligman was careful to point out that optimism is not a panacea, his findings supported its positive impact on achievement, physical well-being, and overall mental state. He stated that optimists actually age better, and experience fewer of the usual physical illnesses of middle age.

One study showed that men's optimism following bypass surgery positively correlated "with a faster rate of recovery during hospitalization, a faster rate of return to normal activities after discharge, and higher quality of life at six months after the surgery" (Scheier et al., 1989, p. 1034). The importance of this study is that data were collected at three points in time—before surgery, right after surgery, and 6 months later. This finding fits in with what we know about transitions: They are a process over time rather than a point in time.

Seligman (2002) suggested that the individual's explanatory style, the way a person thinks about an event or transition, can explain how some people weather transitions without becoming depressed or giving up. As many transitions are neither bad nor good but a mixture, a person's explanatory style becomes the critical key to coping. A person with a positive explanatory style is an optimist, whereas one with a negative style is basically a pessimist.

For example, we can ask a client, Steve, who has lost his job, to explain what happened. Did he blame himself and say he lost the job because he was inadequate? Did he conclude that he would always be inadequate at work? People who blame themselves for everything that happens and then generalize to think they always "foul things up" have a good chance of being depressed and passive. On the other hand, if Steve saw that he had some role in the job decision and that, in general, he handled complex situations well, he has a good chance of coping effectively with this transition.

Seligman (2002) also suggested that people's explanatory style can predict their success on a job. In a study of insurance sales people, those representatives with a "positive explanatory style" were twice as likely as those with a "negative style" to be still on the job after a year. Following up on this study, a special force of 100 representatives who had failed the insurance industry test but who had a "positive explanatory style" were hired. They were much more successful than the pessimists who had passed the test.

A related concept and one that predicts how one will negotiate transitions is self-efficacy. "Bandura has argued that, among the different mechanisms of personal agency, none is more pervasive than people's beliefs in their capabilities to exercise control over their own motivations and behaviors and over environmental demands. Self-efficacy depends on the individual's belief that he or she can cause an intended event to occur and can organize and carry out the courses of behavior necessary to deal with various situations" (Rodin, 1990, p. 2).

Related to self-efficacy is the notion of perceived control. "The illusion of control is . . . the inverse of . . . learned helplessness. . . . Although learned helplessness is the erroneous belief that one has no control to affect the outcome of a given event when contingency does in fact exist between response and outcome, the illusion of control involves the erroneous belief that one can produce a positive outcome when such a contingency does not exist" (Rodin, 1990, pp. 4–5).

Taylor (1989), a psychologist, wrote: "My task . . . is to persuade the reader that normal human thought and perception is marked not by accuracy but by positive self-enhancing illusions about the self, the world, and the future . . . these illusions [are] . . . adaptive, promoting . . . good mental health" (p. 7). Taylor described different, but related, types of positive illusions: "self-enhancement, . . . personal control, involving the perception that one can bring about primarily positive but not negative outcomes, and unrealistic optimism, namely perceptions that the future holds an unrealistically bountiful array of opportunities" (p. 6).

In her book, Taylor argued for the importance of perceived illusions and control. She demonstrated that a cancer patient's belief in a particular treatment and/or doctor can influence how the patient copes with the disease. When recovery does occur, it is attributed to a person's belief system. We do not know how many people with positive illusions die, but the very fact of having positive illusions and of being optimistic serves as a resource even in the case of impending death. Of course, self-efficacy makes a difference, as does optimism and one's style of processing the world. However, it can be a disadvantage to assume that a client with an upbeat attitude and a sense of personal power can control the entire transition. The transition model is intended to show the interrelatedness of Situation, Self, Support, and Strategies. So yes, self-efficacy and optimism are crucial, but they are not the entire story.

For instance, the style one uses to process the world is important. Some rely on intuition, doing what feels right to them. Others use their senses to gather data on the world and then process these data in a logical, systematic way, arriving at reasoned decisions. People differentiate themselves along these lines, and many counselors spend time helping their clients recognize that their styles might be different from that of their partner, boss, or friends. Acknowledging these differences can be helpful in building collaboration rather than conflict. The Myers-Briggs Type Indicator® (1977) is one way of identifying one's style.

Fiske (1980) studied men and women's changing commitments over the lifespan. An individual's major commitment, whether it lies in his or her relationships (interpersonal), in working for others (altruism), in self-improvement (competence/mastery), or in survival (self-protection), determines his or her vulnerability.

The father of a 26-year-old son who committed suicide explained how differently he and his wife reacted. He said it was easier for him because he could bury himself in work, a commitment to mastery, whereas his wife, whose lifelong commitment had been to relationships, especially in the family, was unable, even after 5 years, to reinvest in life. Clearly individuals' reactions to and assimilation of transitions are greatly influenced by their commitments—which, of course, change over time, thereby changing those individuals' areas of vulnerability. An individual's basic values and beliefs are also a factor in his or her ability to assimilate transitions. On the basis of subjects' responses to the question,

"What is the main purpose in life?" Fiske and Chiriboga (1990) developed a seven-category value typology:

1. achievement and work (economic competence, rewards, success, social status)
2. good personal relations (love and affection, happy marriage, friends)
3. philosophical and religious (including concern with the meaning of existence and an adherence to an ethical code)
4. social service (helping others, community service . . .)
5. ease and contentment (simple comforts, security, relaxation)
6. seeking enjoyment (recreation, exciting experiences . . .)
7. personal growth (self-improvement, being creative) (p. 216)

A value system that contributes to assimilation at one life stage may be dysfunctional at another. People at different stages tend to emphasize different values. The specific content of a person's religious beliefs, and the cultural norms associated with particular religions, should also be considered. For example, a woman from a Catholic background facing divorce may find her distress exacerbated by the church's strictures against divorce. A man from a Protestant background who has grown up with a strong commitment to the work ethic may find forced unemployment especially hard to take, quite apart from the financial strain it entails.

Another concept to consider is spirituality, which is closely related to religion, yet can be understood as a distinct phenomenon (Young, Cashwell, & Shcherbakova, 2000). Although religion can be part of spirituality and serve as an expression of spirituality for people, it does not encompass the broader concept of spirituality that runs through all religions and cultures. Religion generally refers to an integrated set of beliefs and activities, whereas spirituality is central to a sense of meaning and purpose and has been conceptualized as the meaning gained from life experiences (May, 1982; Myers, Sweeney, & Wittmen, 2000). Spirituality is an especially important area of exploration when one works with clients and may be an area that is overlooked. We are most likely to hear spirituality expressed through our clients' subjective, personal experiences and through their need for connectedness, meaning, and transcendence (Burke & Miranti, 1995; Burke et al., 1999; Polanski, 2002). Incorporating spirituality in the counseling process is a holistic approach that addresses body, mind, and spirit and may actually enhance and deepen the counseling process. By delving into questions regarding how our clients find meaning and purpose in their lives we may also tap into a hidden resource for coping with transitions. A growing body of research has documented spirituality's relationship to both physical and mental health as well as to coping ability. For example, studies have found that people with a positive spiritual identity cope more efficiently with stress, heal faster, and establish healthier lifestyles (Bergin et al., 1994). In a recent workshop, "Coping with Retirement," many of the participants said that their faith, their spirituality, enabled them to cope with this major set of transitions.

Beyond the concepts of religion and spirituality, strong commitment to an ideology or cause may be a necessity in some situations. Thus, those draft dodgers who moved to Canada not to escape from some difficult personal situation or to seek adventure but for ideological reasons, because they believed the Vietnam War to be immoral or regarded themselves as political refugees from an oppressive system, were more likely to adapt to the new situation (Levine, 1976). Concentration camp victims who saw themselves as surviving for some greater purpose were able to mobilize their coping resources more effectively (Frankl, 1963).

People face transitions, problems, and joys with characteristic psychological patterns and resources. These vary according to ego development, outlook, commitments, and values.

When counseling adults in transition, it is important to look at resilience. Resilient people have been described as those, "Who are able to weather a storm in their lives, bounce back from adversity, or grow stronger in the face of adversity" (Bosworth & Walz, 2005, p. 1). The term *resilience* is related to its use in physics as the ability to return to an original form after being "bent, compressed or stretched" (p. 1). An interesting analogy was made by these authors in their description of why they chose a blooming cactus for the cover of their book. They state that the cactus, "is noted for its ability to overcome extreme environmental deprivation (i.e., drought) for extended periods of time and still display both beauty and strength. . . . This ability parallels what the resilient person is able to do" (p. ii).

In the literature, resilience is not narrowed down to a specific characteristic but rather includes a blend of characteristics in an individual. These may include characteristics such as positive, focused, organized, proactive, and flexible (Barrett, 2004). A related concept is hardiness, which has become an established aspect of counseling psychology over the last 20 years. When considering hardiness we might look at individual differences, for example, how stressful changes may be debilitating for some people but developmentally provocative for others (Maddi, 2002). According to Maddi (2002), three attitudes combine to form hardiness: commitment, control, and challenge. Through these attitudes people may learn to exemplify what he termed *existential courage* when facing difficult situations.

Review of the Self

Every person brings different assets to a transition. The following are some ways to assess clients.

- Are they able to deal *with* the world in an autonomous way? Can they tolerate ambiguity?
- Are they optimists? Do they see the glass as half-full or half-empty?
- Do they blame themselves for what happens?
- Do they feel in control of their responses to the transition?
- Do they believe that their efforts will affect the outcome of a particular course of action?
- Do they have a sense of meaning and purpose?
- Do they have characteristics that contribute to resiliency?

Support

Social support is often said to be the key to handling stress. Support, however, needs to be defined operationally because it comes in many sizes and shapes and can be for better or for worse.

Types of Support

The types of support people receive are classified according to their sources: intimate relationships, family units, networks of friends, and the institutions and/or communities of which the people are a part.

With respect to the first of these four types, Lowenthal and Weiss (1976) maintained that "intimate relationships—involving trust, support, understanding and the sharing of confidences" (p. 12)—are an important resource during stressful transitions. There are gender differences. Some suggest that the death of a spouse may be more traumatic for men than for women, in part because men may have more difficulty forming intimate relationships. Men's difficulty in forming close ties with other people may also contribute to their shorter life expectancy.

As a further indication of the power of intimate relationships, Lowenthal and Weiss (1976) suggested that "former intimate relationships, disrupted by death, distance, or interpersonal conflict, may continue to be a resource in terms of crisis, chronic and acute, throughout the life course. . . . Knowing through past experience that one is capable of having an intimate relationship, romantic or otherwise, may prove nearly as important a resource in difficult life situations as actually having an intimate at the time of crisis: a former relationship is reinforcing, and at the same time sustains hope for a future one" (p. 14:7).

The family unit has long been a subject for study by sociologists and others, many of whom have attempted to define those qualities of the family that contribute to its ability to adapt to a crisis or to ease the process of adaptation for one of its members. For example, the already mentioned study of draft dodgers and deserters who fled to Canada during the Vietnam era (Levine, 1976) indicated that those who received parental support for their move adapted better to the new situation than did those whose parents disapproved of their action.

An individual's network of friends is also an important social support system. One of the most stressful side effects of divorce is the loss of friendships that were based on couple relationships. Loss of the network of friends may also result from a residential move or from the death of a spouse, thus exacerbating the difficulties of those transitions. Conversely, the presence of friends can cushion sudden shock.

The fourth type of support involves those organizations individuals can turn to for help, such as religious institutions, political groups, social welfare or community support groups, and other more-or-less formal agencies. As discussed in Part III of this book, the need for such agencies has become more widely recognized. There has been a proliferation of programs, which may take the form of seminars, lectures, workshops, or simply discussion groups, aimed at people experiencing particular transitions: midcareer change, divorce, retirement, or a return to school.

Functions of Support

According to Caplan (1976), support systems function mainly to help "the individual mobilize . . . psychological resources and master . . . emotional burdens; they share . . . tasks . . . they provide . . . extra supplies of money, materials, tools, skills, and cognitive guidance to improve . . . handling of . . . situations" (pp. 5–6). Developing this concept even further, Kahn and Antonucci (1980) identified the functions of social support as an incorporation of one or more of the following key elements: affect, affirmation, and aid. Affect refers to expressions of liking, admiration, respect, or love; affirmation refers to expressions of agreement or acknowledgment of the appropriateness or rightness of some act or statement of another person; and aid (or assistance) includes the exchange of things, money, information, time, and entitlements (pp. 267–268).

In addition to the functions of affect, affirmation, and aid, we include another—honest feedback. This refers to reactions offered that might be negative as well as positive. For example, if a parent is complaining about a teenager's behavior and telling how the teenager is going to be punished, a counselor might suggest the coping strategy of selective ignoring, or if the parents always selectively ignore, a counselor might suggest providing more structure.

Measurement of Social Support

Robert Kahn (1975) introduced the concept of the "convoy" of social support, "the idea that each person moves through the life cycle surrounded by a set of significant others related to him [or her] either by the giving or receiving of social support" (p. 1). Two notable features of this concept are, first, that it implies movement and change, and second, that it emphasizes "the giving as well as the receiving of social support . . ." (p. 1).

Kahn used several methods to measure social support, based on some operational definitions. "Convoy is a person-centered network; each convoy is a personal network of social support, defined around a focal person whose activities and well-being we wish to understand. . . . The network stops with that set of other persons with whom the focal person has direct relationship of support-receiving or giving. . . . The convoy structure is the delivery system" for social support (p. 278). An individual's convoy includes those who are stable over time and not role dependent, those somewhat role related and likely to change over time, and those "tied directly to role relationships, and most vulnerable to role changes" (p. 273).

Figure 3.2 illustrates a convoy with the focal person in the center. The first circle around the person represents his or her stable supports, irrespective of roles; the second circle represents the group that is somewhat role dependent; the outside circle represents those supports most likely to change. Techniques for using the convoy are discussed later in the book.

Kahn recommended a procedure to measure support, based on the convoy model. Adults in transition identify people close to them, placing them in categories such as family, coworkers, other organizational members, neighbors, professionals, and friends. The adult then rates each person listed in terms of the social support offered. Three measures are thus obtained: one for affect, one for affirmation, one for aid (pp. 279–280).

Support Summary

In summary, to take stock of their clients' supports counselors can ask the following:

- Is this client getting what he or she needs for this transition in terms of affect? Affirmation? Aid?
- Does the client have a range of types of support—spouse or partner, other close family or friends, coworkers? Colleagues? Neighbors, organizations, strangers, and institutions?
- Has the client's support system or "convoy of social support" been interrupted by this transition?
- Does the client feel the support system for this transition is a low or a high resource?

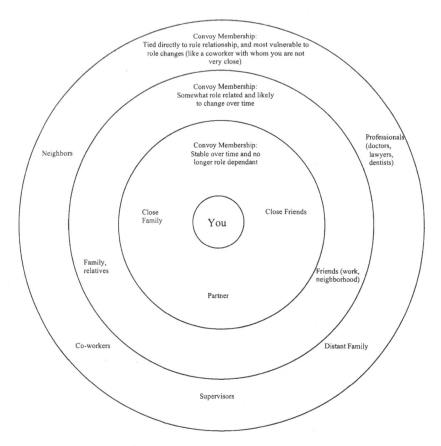

Figure 3.2   Convoy of social support.

Strategies

"By coping we refer to the things people do to avoid being harmed by life strains" (Pearlin & Schooler, 1978, p. 1). Another definition is that "coping is the overt and covert behaviors individuals use to prevent, alleviate, or respond to stressful situations. . . . Coping can occur before, during, or after a stressful or challenging situation" (George & Siegler, 1981, p. 37). And yet another view: "In my view, stress itself as a concept pales in significance . . . compared with coping. . . . Stress is ubiquitous, an inevitable feature of normal living. . . . What makes the difference in adaptational outcome is coping" (Lazarus, 1980, p. 52).

Pearlin and associates identified major life strains and the coping strategies people use to deal with them. Coping "represents . . . concrete efforts to deal with the life strains they encounter in their different roles"; that is, those things an individual does in his or her own behalf (Pearlin & Schooler, 1978, p. 5). The researchers distinguished three types of coping:

1. "Responses that modify the situation" (such as negotiation in marriage, discipline in parenting, optimistic action in occupation, and seeking advice in marriage and parenting)
2. "Responses that . . . control the meaning of the problem" (such as responses that neutralize, positive comparisons, selective ignoring, substitution of rewards)
3. Responses that help to manage stress after it has occurred (such as "denial, passive acceptance, withdrawal, magical thinking, hopefulness, avoidance of worry, relaxation"). Specific mechanisms include "emotional discharge versus controlled reflectiveness, . . . passive forbearance versus self-assertion, . . . potency versus helpless resignation, . . . optimistic faith" (pp. 6–7)

Coping strategies are related to people's "psychological resources of self-esteem and mastery" (p. 5). With chronic unemployment, damage to the ego can limit the individual's flexibility in selecting coping strategies. In discussing chronic unemployment, a physician commented on her unemployed husband's shattered ego. Despite the fact that they tried to manage the stress, redefine the situation, and change the situation, there were some lasting and damaging effects on their marriage. Members of another family—the wife a nurse, the husband an unemployed air traffic controller—reported feeling at the end of their rope. They did not know how to change the situation, redefine the problem, or manage their stress. Counseling could help them develop strategies in one or all of these areas.

Of course, the question arises as to which coping strategies are best in different situations. Pearlin and Schooler (1978) reported that there are many options for people to use in every area of their lives and that certain strategies do reduce stress in certain role areas, but they also reported that individual coping has the greatest chance of being efficacious with interpersonal problems rather than work-related problems. They further cautioned against assuming that coping efforts will work in all settings. It is important to see coping in a broader context. In some cases, collective coping, that is, helping people share in a problem they cannot undo individually, is essential. Structural unemployment is just such a case, for it needs to be addressed collectively and politically. Some people, however, are clearly going to cope more effectively than others, and those with a repertoire of responses relating to their various roles will most likely handle the strains of life more effectively.

The coping strategies identified in the Pearlin and Schooler (1978) study "constitute but a portion of the full range of responses people undoubtedly call upon in dealing with life-exigencies" (Pearlin & Schooler, 1978, p. 5); nevertheless, they indicate a systematic way to think about strategies. The following outline is adapted from the study; questions or descriptors illustrate each strategy or coping response. The items for the responses are taken from Appendix 4 in "The Structure of Coping" by L. I. Pearlin & C. Schooler, *Journal of Health and Social Behavior,* Volume 19, 1978. (Reprinted with permission.)

1. Responses that modify the situation and are "aimed at altering the source of strain." (p. 20)
   - Negotiation. "How often do you try to find a fair compromise, . . . sit down and talk things out?"
   - Optimistic action. "When you have difficulties in your work situation, how often do you take some action to get rid of them, or to find a solution?"
   - Self-reliance versus advice-seeking. "In the past year . . . have you asked for the advice of friends . . . relative . . . doctor . . . or other professional?"
   - Exercise of potency versus helpless resignation. "How often do you decide there's really nothing you can do to change things?"

2. Responses that control the meaning of the problem to cognitively neutralize the threat. (p. 6)
   - Positive comparisons. "A device . . . [to enable] a temporal frame of reference, . . . captured in such idioms as count your blessings."
   - Selective ignoring. A "positive attribute . . . within a troublesome situation. When you have difficulties in your work situation, how often do you tell yourself that they are unimportant [and] try to pay attention only to your duties and overlook them?"
   - Substitution of rewards. "Hierarchical ordering of life priorities . . . to keep the most strainful experiences within the least valued areas of life. If I have troubles at work, I value other areas of life more and downplay the importance of work."

3. Responses that help the individual manage stress after it has occurred to help "accommodate to existing stress without being overwhelmed by it." (p. 7)
   - Emotional discharge. "Expressive ventilation of feelings: How often do you yell or shout to let off steam?"

- Self-assertion. "When you have differences with your spouse, how often do you fight it out?"
- Passive forbearance. "When you have differences with your spouse, how often do you keep out of his or her way?"

Pearlin and Schooler relate the selection of coping strategies to the individual's psychological resources, which we discussed earlier:

Coping, in sum, is certainly not a unidimensional behavior. It functions at a number of levels and is attained by a plethora of behaviors, cognitions, and perceptions. It is useful . . . that coping responses be distinguished from what we have identified as psychological resources for coping, those personality characteristics that minimize threat to self . . . we cannot completely understand coping without: looking beyond the personality attributes of individuals to the specific responses to problems in different social roles. (pp. 7–8)

Pearlin and his associates identified a number of coping strategies. None contains magic; rather, effective coping means flexible utilization of a range of strategies as each situation demands.

Like Pearlin and associates, Lazarus and Folkman (1984) see the coping strategies a person uses as more relevant than the event, hassle, or strain and the person's appraisal of the situation as more central than the event. As we described earlier, the key is the way the person sees the strain, stressor, or event—whether it is perceived as harmful, benign, or challenging. Lazarus and Folkman classified coping in two major ways: instrumental or problem-focused behavior that aims to change the situation, and palliative or emotion-focused behavior that aims to help minimize emotional distress.

Whether individuals want to change their situation or reduce their distress, they can choose from among four coping modes: information seeking, direct action, inhibition of action, and intrapsychic behavior. The first three seem self-explanatory; the last one (intrapsychic) refers to the mind sets individuals use to resolve problems that arise. These mind sets, which include denial, wishful thinking, and distortion, enable people to carry on. Lazarus (1980) found that "effective copers use both direct action and palliative coping modes" (p. 54). Similarly, Pearlin and associates identified "selective ignoring" as an adaptive strategy.

Lazarus emphasized the fact that selection of a coping strategy depends on whether or not the situation can be changed. If it can be, then problem-focused instrumental strategies will be used; if not, then emotion-focused, palliative strategies will be employed.

An important point for helpers to remember is that effective copers are flexible and utilize a number of methods. Ability to cope is not a trait, but a dynamic process constantly in flux throughout the continuing process of appraisal. For example, Cohen (1980) looked at ways people coped with surgery. She reviewed studies based on a theoretical framework suggesting that people's appraisal of a situation determined subsequent emotion and behaviors (p. 376). She studied 59 patients undergoing hernia, gall bladder, and thyroid surgery on the night before their operations and rated them on a continuum from avoidance (avoid information and knowledge about surgery and outcome) to vigilance (seek out information about surgery). Then she measured recovery on a number of dimensions. Contrary to expectation, neither age nor life change score was a factor in recovery, but the coping strategy of denial was. Those who knew the most had more "complications and a longer hospital stay" (p. 377). In this kind of situation, too much knowledge can lead to panic. Furthermore, trying to be in charge in a situation that the individual is unable to control can lead to frustration. Although, in general, most of us will work to help people take control, in some situations this strategy is counterproductive.

How effective such strategies are overall is a complex question. For example, some theorists and counselors focus on outcomes. Was the client accepted into an apprentice training program? By focusing only on outcome, however, we may overlook a client's coping effectiveness. A client may employ many strategies flexibly but still not be able to achieve the stated goals. Just as being assertive doesn't guarantee "winning" and using flexible coping strategies does not always guarantee the desired outcome.

Summary of Coping Responses

In the preceding section we described the ways several researchers have conceptualized and studied coping. According to Pearlin and Schooler (1978), most individuals when faced with a transition try to control the situation (for example, by publishing a great deal to ensure promotion), control the meaning of the situation (by seeing promotion as irrelevant), or control the stress (by jogging to release tension caused by promotion worries). Lazarus and Folkman (1984) identified two major coping orientations—changing the situation (instrumental) or relaxing oneself (palliative)—and suggested four possible modes of coping: direct action, inhibition of action, information seeking, and intrapsychic.

ASSETS AND LIABILITIES: ANOTHER LOOK

An individual's ability to cope with transitions depends on the changing interaction and balance of his or her assets and liabilities. Thus, to study or understand an individual's balance, we need to ask questions such as these:

- What are the variables characterizing the particular situation in terms of timing, assessment, and duration?
- What are the personal and demographic characteristics of the individual at the time of the transition—the Self?
- Is the client sick or well?
- What is the client's level of ego development, personality, and outlook?
- What coping strategies does he or she use?
- What types of support does the client have?
- What are his or her actual and perceived options?

These variables could also be scored as to whether the individual sees them as assets or liabilities.

An effective coping strategy may be effective in one situation but not in another, especially if the person perceives the situation as controllable (Folkman & Moskowitz, 2004). Hobfoll (2001) developed a theory about coping that emphasizes loss experiences. Significant losses are those that threaten one's sense of self or challenge one's security. According to Hobfoll, many life events are positive; it is when there is a major loss attached to the event that one feels stress. Hobfoll named his theory Conservation of Resources, suggesting that when individuals experience loss, in whatever form, they tend to act in ways to conserve their resources. Resources are defined as what people value or find important. This includes material possessions, situations such as marriage or job status, personal characteristics, or time and energy. According to this theory, resource loss can be a predictor of distress, and some research has supported the fact that people tend to view what they have lost as more important than what they have gained. However, Schlossberg (1994) found in her transition studies that people are stressed even when events are positive. If the transition changes all aspects of a person's life—their relationships, routines, assumptions, and roles—then the individual is forced to deal with many unsettling aspects of life.

People rarely are faced with only a single type of stressful transition; rather they more than likely face a variety of stressful events resonating through many life areas that intersect with the transition. Studies on coping flexibility (Cheng, 2003; Schmidt, Nachtigall, Wuethrich-Martone, & Strauss, 2002) show that individuals differ in their ability to handle stressful situations depending on the specific situational demands. Also, individuals formulate flexible or inflexible coping strategies across their stressful situations, with some people varying their strategies as they face different situations, and others using the same strategies regardless of the situation. Cheng and Cheung (2005) explored individual differences in appraising and dealing with stressful situations. The participants of their study were 127 Chinese university students. They found that individuals who cope more flexibly tend to differentiate stressful events in the way that they perceive the controllability and impact, and thus deploy more integrated strategies in dealing with stress. In other words, they would use more strategies to deal with controllable situations, and use fewer strategies when confronting uncontrollable situations. Individuals with less flexible coping flexibility tended to perceive all stressful situations as similar. Cheng and Cheung (2005) concluded that managing stress is improved when people have diverse, flexible strategies to meet differing stressful situations.

Often clients ask, "Should I initiate a change?" "Should I go back to school?" "Should I get a divorce?" "Should I move?" Or they may wonder, "How can I weather the transition imposed upon me?" To answer these questions, one rates the client's 4 S's—the variables characterizing the Situation, the Self, the Support, and the Strategies. From these ratings, a balance score can be derived that will indicate whether or not the client has many or few resources. Further, the client can determine where his or her liabilities lie (Kay & Schlossberg, 2006).

Now that the framework, which conceptualizes the way an individual copes with transitions is in place, we move to a discussion of transitions from clients' points of view. We will hear their views of the balance of their liabilities and assets. Then in Part III of the book we consider how that balance suggests to helpers the areas in which they can be most effective in providing motivation, support, and resources to help adults who experience disabling problems with love, work, or play.

PART II

What Are We Likely to Hear?

INTRODUCTION

In this section we move to a discussion of what counselors are likely to hear as they deal with adult clients anticipating or experiencing transitions. As you read this section, we hope you will visualize the clients whose stories we tell you. More than that, however, we hope that these stories will be a trigger for you, encouraging you to think about adults you know—yourself, friends, family, coworkers, as well as clients—who are by choice or necessity in the process of reshaping their lives.

Assume that you are the unseen audience, watching, listening, and interpreting what goes on in the counselor's office. It may help to imagine that you are observing through one-way glass, as in a practicum laboratory. Many of these stories are ones we have heard directly from clients, students, and friends calling somewhat desperately and even seatmates on airplanes. Whatever the source, the stories are often poignant as they illuminate the struggles and challenges of adults navigating transitions. They are designed to help you understand transitions from the client's point of view.

This section is divided into three chapters that focus on different areas of life in which we experience transitions—internally, in relationships with family and other intimates, and in our work lives. Clearly the classifications used here are somewhat arbitrary. For most people there will be considerable overlap among the categories. Almost always a transition in one area of a person's life has an impact on other areas of that person's life, as well as on the lives of the person's significant others.

Chapter 4 focuses on transitions that are mainly intrapersonal in nature. Although decisions made by the individual may ultimately have a dramatic effect on others, the basis for the transition is an internal one. Recurring issues here deal with questions of identity, autonomy, and making meaning of one's life—often related to spirituality.

Chapter 5 deals with close interpersonal relationships, often but not always within families. Transitions may take the form of events or nonevents as people couple or uncouple, have children or decide not to, and become grandparents or realize they will not. Here, too, adults face changes in relationships with lovers, siblings, close friends, and aging parents, as well as the fear of losing people close to them. Recurring issues in this chapter are intimacy, mattering, and belonging.

Chapter 6 surveys the place of work in our lives and the many transitions that occur in this arena. Adults constantly reexamine where they want their careers to go and where they want to invest their energies. Counselors see people looking for their first jobs, some as teenagers and others as mature adults; they also deal with people wanting to change careers, "fix" their present jobs, or leave the paid workforce. Recurring issues here deal with work salience (the centrality of work in people's lives), resilience (career adaptability), mastery (self-efficacy), and balance.

In each of these chapters, we include several case studies and a discussion of the types of transitions that may bring adults to a counselor. Using the transition model explicated in Part I, we listen for what clients tell us about their resources for coping with these transitions, that is, their 4 S's: their Situation, Self, Support, and Strategies.

CHAPTER 4

Individual Transitions

Jack Williams, a man in his late 30s, tells you the following:

I woke up one morning a few months ago, looked in the mirror to shave, and saw my father. I don't mean that I hallucinated. I knew it was me, but I looked just like him—colorless, tired, bored. It scared me half to death. I don't want my life to be anything like his. He's retired now and bored to tears, but even when he was working, he always seemed bored. I don't remember his ever being excited about anything. It's like he went, and still goes, through the motions of living without enjoying it. I can't face a lifetime like his.

I've been married for 18 years. My wife and I have two darling kids, a girl 15 and a boy 13. They have their whole lives ahead of them, and I find I'm kind of envious. There is so much they can do, experience, try. My daughter now has a chance for a basketball scholarship. I'm excited for her, but again, I'm jealous. My job is OK. I am the manager for Roberts' furniture store in our small town about an hour and a half outside of the city. It's a job I do well, and I enjoy the contact with everybody I see all day. But all I can think about is if this is all it's going to be for the rest of my life? Is it enough for me?

When I was a teenager I had such dreams. I was the star pitcher on the baseball team in high school, in the same town where I now live. I expected to get a college scholarship. But then I injured my arm, and it didn't happen. There wasn't money to send me to school, and to tell you the truth, I wasn't that interested in more education.

I worked a couple of years at the furniture store where I continue to work, married my high school sweetheart, and settled down. I've done well at the store, moving from stock boy to manager in the last 20 years. I've been involved in the community, done all the "right" things. My wife's and my families live in town. We've been lucky that everyone is still healthy. We spend most Sundays with either my parents or hers. I've coached little league and gone to Rotary luncheons. I've been an active member of our church, even taught Sunday school for a few years, but haven't felt any real comfort from my faith. Nevertheless, it sounds like the good life, doesn't it? So why am I so unhappy?

I've had fantasies about having an affair. It might bring some excitement into my life. But I wouldn't even know how to go about it, and anyway it wouldn't be right. But if I don't do something, I think I'll just wither away.

I've always been the "good kid." My older brother was wild when he was a teenager, but I was always solid Jack—the one you could count on. I still am. I shovel my parent's and in-law's snow in the winter; I'm a volunteer fireman; I always call if I'm going to be late for dinner— though even that much change of routine rarely happens. Good old solid, boring Jack.

I thought if I waited a bit, this feeling would pass. But it hasn't. Sometimes I don't even know who I am. I'm Roberts' store manager, Susan's husband, Cindy's and young Jack's father, the Williams' son, the Paine's son-in-law; you get the idea. If none of those people existed, would I? I think I've just drifted to where I am, and don't have any sense of the future except bleakness. What will it all matter in 100 years?

I've tried to talk to my wife about some of this. (Except the idea of the affair, of course.) She says everyone goes through these times of doubt and it will pass. But it hasn't. And I'm finding it harder and harder to get up in the morning. I can't face that face of my father's in the mirror.

Jack Williams' poignant story describes his confrontation with several event and non-event transitions that often occur in midlife. His children are getting close to graduation from high school, and he is anticipating their leaving home. He is asking himself, "Is this all there is?" The peace and joy he expected to find in his middle years have not happened. Clearly, it is a rare individual who lives in a vacuum; relationships and work are almost always an important part of life. But in this chapter, we will use Jack's story to clarify transitions—events and non-events— that pertain primarily to the individual.

We will focus on what counselors *hear* from their adult clients about intrapersonal transitions, interweaving Jack's story with illustrative literature. We will show how individuals experience their transitions in a unique manner, depending on their particular Situation, the aspects of Self that come into play, the Support they have available, and the Strategies they are currently using.

SITUATION

What makes Jack's situation similar to and different from other people's transitions? In this section we will first discuss the triggers to internal transitions, some of which may come from internal awarenesses and some of which may be stimulated by external events. We will then turn our attention to the timing of these transitions. Are they off time or on time? Do they come at a time of relative peace in the person's life or at a time of turmoil? Next we will talk about the duration of the transition, and, finally we will address the source of control—or perceived control. As we discuss these general questions, remember that as people's answers differ, their experiences are unique.

Triggers

Jack has come to see a counselor to talk about his malaise—his discomfort with his life. He is experiencing a transition in how he views himself; indeed it seems that he is looking at himself in a conscious way for perhaps the first time in his adult life. What has triggered this transition? On the surface, seeing his father's face in the mirror is the primary trigger. And he sees his aging father leading a sterile life, one that he wants to avoid. But what caused the experience? Jack seems to be confronting a change in perspective from seeing life as time spent to seeing life as time left. He worries, wondering, "Is now forever?" He fears that his future will continue in the present pattern and does not like what he sees. It was all right as long as he could imagine a different future. When that seemed unlikely, he became terrified.

Newman and Newman (2003) stated that during the stage of middle adulthood, people encounter many complex challenges for which they may not be fully prepared. Midlife has been described as an evolving concept, and as life expectancy increases, the definitions and attitudes about midlife continue to change (Howell, 2001). When one of the authors of this volume (Goodman) did a workshop for women in midlife, the self-selected participants ranged in age from their early 30s to their late 60s. Clearly, there is not general agreement about what constitutes midlife! According to Sheehy (1995), there is a revolution going on in the lifecycle. She stated that there has been a fundamental shift regarding the stages of adulthood, as age continues to be pushed forward and lifespans continue to increase. And research suggests that people grow older in very different ways, with striking variations between people as they age, the fanning out phenomenon described earlier (Neugarten, 1982). Isenhart (1983) compared the midlife transition to river rafting. She stated that (a) the current of the river is like adult development. It can be anticipated but never completely controlled. (b) Submerged rocks below the surface of the river are like stressful periods in the transition that often present themselves first as smooth nonevents, and (c) the circular currents of water reflect the sense of limitless time when no progress appears possible. Jack seems to be stuck in this time of circular water. And his perspective of the future has changed.

This change in perspective can be brought on by an external event, such as being called "sir" or "ma'am" for the first time; it can be caused by a consciousness of the changing physical self, such as a twinge in the knees, needing bifocals, or that first gray hair. For people whose self-esteem is closely tied to their appearance, the awareness of aging may be very painful. For people whose work roles require a youthful appearance, for example, models, this transition may be an important one. In the American culture, women are probably affected more strongly than men. We are more accepting of aging actors than actresses. Gray sideburns make a man look distinguished, but graying hair is seen as making a woman look less desirable.

For some women, the onset of menopause is the trigger that begins their internal transition. Raphael (1994), a therapist who ran self-discovery groups for mature women, described her own experience:

> Beginning menopause also signals getting older, and, like it or not, our physical appearance is a large part of how we view ourselves. Distasteful as we may find the leers and come-ons that youthful beauty attracts, becoming invisible is no better bargain. I had no trouble getting older until it showed. In my early fifties, I would brag about my age, confident of hearing, "but you don't look it." The absence of that response can still feel chilling. I don't like being addressed as "Ma'am" and I don't like reminding grown people of their grandmothers. But it is all part of the process. One cannot sort through the various accumulated labels, judgments and programs of one's lifetime without looking inside. And this kind of self examination is actually facilitated by the kind of invisibility that accompanies midlife in our culture. Menopause really is a Change of Life. It is about becoming your own person. I am healthier, happier and more energetic now than at any previous time in my life. (p. 10)

Although Raphael bemoans some aspects of aging, her conclusion is a positive one.

Clients describe many triggers including an impending high school reunion, eligibility for the American Association of Retired Persons or senior discounts, ineligibility for a management training program or the junior league, being offered a seat on the bus or presented with a face cream for mature skin. The death of one's last parent creates an awareness for many of now being "the older generation."

Whether internally or externally triggered or sudden or gradual, the realization of aging can be disturbing. In Jack's case, the trigger included his awareness of his children's growing up and the lives he sees them having *ahead* of them. Different cultures may have differing systems for recognizing aging. Some East African tribal societies organize their population into age groups. "Men in their prime may resist initiating a new cohort of young warriors. The entry of a new cohort automatically advances those above it by one grade and so places the senior men into the respected—but terminal—grade of elder" (Plath, 1980, p. 117).

Furthermore, awareness of time left often includes for the first time a personalization of death. The author William Saroyan is reported to have said on his death bed, "I knew everyone had to die sometime, but I always thought I'd be the exception." Decade birthdays often stimulate this kind of awareness. Card shops sell a variety of paraphernalia with the theme, "over the hill." Although meant to be humorous, this message implies that one is on the downside of the hill—with death at the bottom of the slope. Consider this line from a middle-aged character in the play *Change of Life* (Dubin, 1994), "People always said, 'You have your whole life ahead of you.' Well, my life isn't ahead of me anymore." Even the daily comic strips show an awareness of this phenomenon. The following conversation took place in *For Better or Worse* (Johnston, 1994):

> *You know, Connie . . . I thought I'd never get old. Other people got old, but not me.*
>
> CONNIE: *Yeah.*
>
> *Then suddenly you realize that it is happening. I* **am** *following my parents, as my parents followed their parents. The laws of nature apply to* **me** *too! . . . It's scary.*
>
> CONNIE: *Yeah . . . we're on the great conveyer belt of life, and from this point you can look up and see the end.*

For some, the realization of the finiteness of life can lead to a determination to live life fully, to appreciate existence, to, in the words of the cliché, pick more daisies. For others, the awareness can lead to depression or panic, occasioned by a sense of urgency to "do it now!" As will be discussed in Part III, the challenge for counselors is to help reframe this awareness into appropriate goal setting.

Jack's transition is a complex one. It includes the *events* of his children getting ready to leave the nest, his own aging and what he sees as diminishing opportunities for himself. His recognition that he has advanced as far as he is probably going to at work and that he really never will achieve his dreams of sports stardom are *non-events* affecting his life at this point. (Even though he may have grieved in the past for his injury and the lost scholarship, his current recognition is different in that it encompasses the future.) Jack seems, in Hudson's (1991) words, to have "run out of dreams and . . . [to] lack the ability to envision new ones" (p. xii). . . . [He feels] "vulnerable instead of visionary, trapped instead of empowered" (p. 13).

Timing

In Jack's case, his transition is created by the stage in his life in which it is happening. He is established in his career, in his community, and in his family. He is close to the statistical midpoint of life. He sees his children heading off to partake of opportunities he feels he missed.

Jack is also at a time when he has some freedom to be introspective. His children are "on track," his place in his marriage, his work, and his community are secure. One might speculate that it is because of this secure base that he feels safe enough to risk looking at his life in this way. Maslow's (1954) hierarchy indicates that basic needs for physiological and psychological safety precede the need for belongingness and self-esteem, and later, the search for self-actualization. The internal transition of meaning-making, seems to be such a search. This would indicate that this sort of midlife transition is a phenomenon of the comfortable. It seems unlikely that the homeless or others desperately struggling to survive have time or energy to ask meaning-making questions. But there is little research on the psychological aspects of that population.

Age is an important, but not the only, determinant of a typical adult's midlife awareness. Internal or external triggers may precipitate this awareness at a variety of ages and invite the existential question, "Is this all there is?" And age may also have an effect on how an individual reacts to a transition event. A classic example comes from a study of men aged 37 to 67 who were hospitalized following heart attacks (Rosen & Bibring, 1968). Whereas the younger men were generally cheerful and the 60-year-olds fatherly and easy going, the 50-year-olds were hostile, withdrawn, depressed, and difficult as patients. The authors interpret these age differences as follows: Those younger than 50 simply denied the seriousness of their condition, those in their 60s accepted it as an on-time event, but those in their 50s experienced "open conflict from the active orientation of youth. . . . A heart attack theoretically accentuates the very issues with which the [middle-aged man] has been actively struggling" (p. 207), that is, with his anxiety about aging and his reluctance about shifting from an active to a passive role.

Different cultures may attach different meanings to certain ages. The definition of *old* is changing as today's generation ages with greater health and longevity than previous generations. Gloria Steinem's classic statement, on being told she looked young for 40, "This is how 40 looks!" reflects this. Yet, in American culture there is also the paradox of the worship of youth. For women, this is particularly poignant. Fashion magazines rarely portray older women in either editorial or advertising photographs. Television advertisers consistently use young models to sell their wares.

Niemela (1987) studied Finnish women aged 49–55 and found that

> The 50th birthday had shaken up these women, starting a process of rethinking and reevaluating their total lives. If middle-aged women no longer reflect the cultural image of the ideal woman as a young, attractive sex object, what can they be? My study showed that they start thinking about what they really are; get more in contact with their real feelings and thoughts, needs and wishes. The older women of the study expressed more independence. They felt they were more in the center of their own lives, more responsible for themselves. . . . "Instead of material goods, I have started evaluating other things. I have started valuing health and small joys." (p. 5)

Further in the same piece, Niemela speculated about why an artificial event such as a birthday can lead to such profound changes in a woman's life, and in particular, how it becomes an impetus to individuation. She stated, "It is not the age per se, but the woman's awareness of being 50, which starts the developmental processes. The 52–55 year old women had worked through life matters which the 49–51 year olds had only started to confront." (p. 5)

Counselors need to be alert for client comments that demonstrate concern about aging, fear of future limitations, or more positively, excitement about future possibilities. We need to be alert for artificial barriers to change that may be revealed by statements such as, "You can't teach an old dog new tricks." Clients who feel hopeless about their abilities to manage a transition may say things like, "It's too late for me to change; I'm too old." Sometimes a humorous interchange like the following may help break that cycle:

> CLIENT: *I can't train for a new job, it would take me 5 years and I'll be 55 by then.*
>
> COUNSELOR: *How old will you be in 5 years if you don't take the training?*
>
> CLIENT: *Fifty-five. . . . Oh . . .*

The insight represented by that, "Oh." can be the beginning of a new view of life's possibilities.

Pearson and Petitpas (1990) examined the unpredictability of athletes' careers, which often make their transitions off time. They cited Mihovilovic's (1968) finding that 95% of professional soccer players leave the sport against their will, usually by not making the team or being injured. As we saw with Jack, this loss may stay with a person for many years. According to Pearson and Petitpas, when ". . . a person's identity and activity increasingly center on athletics" (p. 7), the transition becomes even harder to manage. The *macho* tradition that makes it difficult for athletes to ask for or accept support complicates the issue. Counselors may see athletes who come in for help with career planning or for marital counseling, who also, or perhaps primarily, need to deal with their transition from athletics.

Similarly, older actresses, no longer able to secure ingénue roles, or actors, forced to change from leading man to character actor, must, because of an *external* trigger, change *internal* assumptions as they change roles. The performer who tries to retain a youthful appearance by cosmetic surgery and excessive make-up has become a commonplace butt of comedians' put-downs. But the real limitations in possible roles created by aging are no joke to the performer.

Duration

The duration of an individual transition is not always obvious. The time it takes for the new self to be accepted and integrated varies widely from individual to individual. The menopause process, for example, can last 10 years. Some questions that may help a client gain a better understanding of duration are: Is it perceived as permanent, temporary, or unknown? Does the individual assess it as positive, negative, or mixed? Is it of great salience to the individual? For example, waiting one year to take one last class to complete a degree may be agonizing to person A and a minor nuisance to person B.

In one study, 50 clerical workers were questioned about ways they coped with transitions. One woman selected remarriage as the transition of most recent impact. When asked whether she saw the remarriage as permanent or temporary, she thought a moment and said it was too hard to answer. She would like it to be permanent, but since she was married to her *fourth* husband, she would probably have to say temporary (Charner & Schlossberg, 1986).

Health crises are an example of internal events with varying durations. A person may be temporarily immobilized by back surgery or permanently disabled due to a spinal injury. Someone may have to restrict activities owing to a bout of pneumonia; another may have to lead a permanently quiet life because of a heart condition.

Even health events with temporary durations, however, can trigger a more lasting transition. If the health crisis leads to a redefinition of self or a sense of vulnerability or frailty, it may affect future goals and plans or lead to a different lifestyle. Of course, some health events may be of unknown duration, for example, knee surgery or cancer treatment. Counselors will hear some people with orthopedic problems complain that the athletic side of their lives is over; they will hear others investigate what kinds of braces to wear as they resume their sport or look into what sports they can play with their new deficit. Some tennis players, as their knees and backs give out, make the move from playing singles on a hard court to playing doubles on a clay court; others, with the same level of deficit, quit the game entirely.

Although some cancer treatments are so devastating that one can barely manage one's daily life, others allow more freedom. However, helpers hear adults in similar circumstance describe their health transitions in widely different ways. The duration, uncertain, is the same for all; the interpretation is again quite different. Some of the reasons for these different interpretations will be discussed below in the sections on hope and selective denial.

The duration of non-events is even more difficult to assess. As one woman, bemoaning what she saw as a static life, said, "I thought this was to be the 'Change of Life,' but nothing has changed!" Perhaps the duration of non-events is more appropriately considered as the length of time it takes people to accept as permanent a condition they thought was temporary. When concern about the non-event ceases to take center stage, the transition can be thought of as integrated into one's life.

Source of Control

The source of Jack's transition is internal, although fed by external factors. Having a sense of control is often critical to success in managing transitions. Many self-related transitions have an internal genesis and therefore an internal locus of control. Some, however, are a combination of internal and external factors. Health problems are a good example. If your asthma is aggravated by smoking you have some control over the course of the disease. If you have a bad back, it may be improved by appropriate exercise. Careful management can allow a person to control diseases such as diabetes or high blood pressure. Many believe that our minds have great influence over the state of our health in general (e.g., Wittmer & Sweeney; 1992).

Garrett and Carroll (2000) described the mind–body connection as seen from a traditional Native American perspective.

> Life . . . is viewed as a series of concentric circles that emanate from one another like the rippling waters of a lake. The first circle is the inner circle, representing that which is within us, being our spirit, the culmination of all of our experiences and the power that comes from the very essence of our being. The next circle is family/clan. Family might be blood relations, and it might be family of choice or adopted family (family in spirit); this circle also includes tribe/nation/community because this is the social context in which we live and represents a different sense of belonging. The third circle is the natural environment, Mother Earth, and all our relations. A fourth and final circle consists of the spirit world, which encompasses all of the other circles, along with all our ancestors and other spirit helpers/guides. Therefore, circles of life energy surround us, and make up the many relationships of our existence. In all, we each have a circle of self, comprising the many facets of our own development (e.g., mind body, spirit, and surroundings); a circle of immediate family, extended family, tribal family, community, and nation; a circle consisting of all of our relations in the natural environment; and a circle of our universal surroundings. (pp. 380–381)

The concept of wellness is increasingly being studied in medicine, psychology, and religion. This concept centers on a holistic view of human functioning, and the focus is on improving human functioning through the integration of body, mind, and spirit (Myers & Williard, 2003). The goal of current wellness models is to maximize the potential through which people make choices for a successful existence. Myers et al. (2000) defined wellness as a way of life orientated toward optimal health and well-being, in which body, mind, and spirit are integrated by the individual leading to living life more fully.

Models of wellness address the myriad factors that create healthy functions (Hattie, Myers, & Sweeny, 2004). A paradigm of wellness has evolved as an alternative to the traditional medical model for the treatment of physical and mental disorders (Hattie et al., 2004; Myers et al., 2000). These models represent new directions in health care and have come out of the physical health professions that focus on the physiological aspects of development (Myers & Williard, 2003).

Myers et al. (2000) developed a Wheel of Wellness, which is a holistic model with 16 characteristics of healthy functioning. They based their model on cross-disciplinary research that identified healthy behaviors that contribute to longevity, quality of life, and well-being. They concluded that spirituality is the core characteristic of healthy people.

These researchers emphasized the characteristics of healthy functioning as a major component of wellness and outlined five major life tasks that can be identified with each component of the Wheel of Wellness. Life Task 1 relates to spirituality, which they define broadly as "an awareness of a being or force that transcends the material aspects of live and gives a deep sense of wholeness or connection to the universe" (Myers et al., 2000, p. 253). They refer to specific components of spirituality as resources: positive thoughts, hardiness, generalized self-efficacy, and optimism. All of these factors have been strongly correlated with well-being and resistance to stress in the literature relating to the relationship between psychological resources and wellness (Lightsey, 1996). They point out that a clear correlation between subjective well-being and optimism is related to spirituality and the mediation of stress. They also relate the concept of tasks to Adler's (1954) major life tasks of work, friendship, and love and concluded that spirituality is central to achieving these tasks. Sweeney (1998), expanded Adler's tasks by adding the task of *self-direction,* which relates to how people regulate and direct their daily activities in pursuit of their long-term goals.

Counselors may hear adults bemoan the fact that they have lost control to the medical establishment. Many are determined to influence their treatment; others find letting go of control can lessen the stress of the situation. The accessibility of medical information on the Internet has compounded this dilemma for many adults. Amid the enormous amount of information available, individuals may become even more dependent on their doctors to sort out what is true, untrue, or unproven. In the first section of the *New York Times,* on Sunday, August 14, 2005, several pages were devoted to this quandary (pp. 1, 16–17).

Two women known to the authors developed emphysema and needed to adapt to a future with limited mobility. One sat in her chair and rarely moved. She saw the illness as not only permanent but also one over which she had no control. Another used portable oxygen, acquired a good backpack to carry it, and took walks with her family. Even if the walks were slow, she was able to be outdoors and participate in activities she had enjoyed previously. For both of these women, the limitations imposed by the disease were similar, but the two women took different amounts of control, and therefore the amount of change created by the event differed.

A difficult decision for many gay, lesbian, or bisexual persons is whether or when to "come out" to family, friends, or work colleagues. Although individuals control the decision, they cannot control others' reactions. Sometimes a partner forces a revelation; sometimes a person is "found out" by being seen in a gay environment or by contracting AIDS or having a "roommate" contract AIDS. Some people make an active decision to let those close to them know about their sexual orientation but not to tell the world in general. Regardless of the etiology, the transition from secret to public is an important one to the individual and those close to that individual. A mystery novel by Alison Gordon (1990) dramatized the pain and loss of privacy when teammates and press responded with great hostility to a baseball star's coming out. The shock of his teammates and the sports world that an athlete could be gay provided a dramatic illustration of the misconceptions of many about homosexuality. The coming out process, and other issues related to the Gay Lesbian Bisexual Transgendered identity is discussed extensively in Croteau, Lark, Lidderdale, and Chung (2005).

SELF

In this section, as we focus on the self issues related to internal transitions, we will look at issues of identity, autonomy, meaning-making, and self-efficacy. These add to the personal, demographic, and psychological characteristics of the individual presented in Chapter 3.

Identity

It is tempting to assume that most self-transition issues relate to identity. The answer to "Who am I?" changes as life situations change. For Jack Williams, the old answers no longer satisfy. For a person with a chronic illness, "I" has changed. Perhaps even more importantly people often ask, "Who will I be?" With help, they may find the answers to be different than in the past. Many young adults believe that they will find out who they are one of these days. They see older people seemingly knowing this and make an assumption that this kind of wisdom comes with age. They retain the childhood wish of someday being and feeling "grown up," with its attendant assumption of self-knowledge. Perhaps one of the triggers to a midlife self-transition is the recognition that this "grown-upness" may never happen, that it is a myth. Perhaps at the same time comes recognition of ultimate aloneness—the so-called existential awareness that we have mentioned earlier.

Older people, on the other hand, may be asking themselves, "Who was I?" Counselors hear older clients reviewing their lives, looking at the past as a way of assessing the present. Erikson (1950) discussed the developmental crisis of old age as being one of integrity versus despair. Integrity is found by assessing one's life as having been meaningful. Butler (1963) theorized that an internal life review was a universal occurrence. Counselors often hear older clients asking questions such as, "Was I successful as a parent, spouse, worker, citizen, friend?" and "All in all, has it been a good life?" They may also be making summary statements such as, "Given where I started, I've done OK." or "Nothing I've done has worked out. I guess you could say my life has been a failure." Counselors need to be alert for these types of statements so they can foster appropriate follow-up exploration.

For some, issues of identity are non-events. If my dreams of being a spouse and parent, or grandparent, chair of the board, or chief steward do not happen, my identity changes. Although Erikson (1950) talked of identity formation as a task of young adulthood, midlife adults often recapitulate this issue. Counselors may hear people simultaneously grieving for the loss of a planned identity and questioning how they can reshape their dreams (Schlossberg & Robinson, 1993). If my desire to be a parent, as it often does, comes out of my need to be nurturing to the next generation, I may talk about volunteering in a child care center, being a Big Brother or Big Sister, spending more time with my nieces and nephews or becoming a foster grandparent.

Sometimes people use humor to help in their struggle to accept the non-event. Tom Lehrer, mathematician, satirist, pianist, and folk singer, once said, "It's a sobering thought to think that when Mozart was my age, he had been dead for 10 years" (Lehrer, 1990).

Judith Viorst's (1976) poem, "Facing the Facts," lists all the things she would probably never do, such as cure the cold, paint a Picasso, or advise presidents, and ends with, "I must still face the fact that they'll never be able to say, 'and she did it so young'" (p. 53).

One's past experience is clearly a central component of identity and often determines how a person approaches a current transition. Counselors may hear, if they ask the right questions, stories of previous challenges faced by their client. When these stories describe a track record of successful coping, clients are usually more prepared to take risks and confront their current transition with verve. When these stories are largely descriptive of negative outcomes, clients may be afraid to trust their own instincts and will ask for solutions from the counselor. Counselors can help people recall positive coping experiences and look for the skills they used in making them positive.

Autonomy

Autonomy is defined as independence or self-directed freedom. A great deal of research substantiates the fact that life satisfaction depends on the perception of autonomy. Whether you believe the autonomy is real or an illusion may not matter. People who feel in control of their lives tend to describe their lives as happier. Autonomy is generally considered to be a Western value and is, in fact, a meaningless concept in many cultures. Happiness is culturally embedded. We must remember, in addition,

Gilligan's (1982) work on women's development. She states that, "Illuminating life as a web rather than a succession of relationships, women portray autonomy rather than attachment as the illusory and dangerous quest" (p. 48). She poses autonomy as an aim in conflict with compassion and connection, a narrower definition than that we are using. We suggest that personal autonomy can include the choice, but not the compulsion, to be compassionate and connect. We take the androgynous position that intimacy and autonomy are desirable for men *and* women to lead satisfying adult lives.

Kincade (1987) suggested that individuals develop along the following lines: (a) The young child is *dependent* for all its needs on a nurturing parent. With growth, comes a period of (b) *counterdependence,* a time of rebellion during which individuation and autonomy take place and then a period of (c) *independence* during which the individual leads or attempts to lead a completely separate life. Many individuals stop developing at this point, but Kincade suggests that fully mature individuals move to (d) *interdependence,* during which there is a recognition of the connections and mutuality suggested by Gilligan (1982). It is the authors' position that this interdependence expresses a true autonomy. One cannot fully participate in an interdependent relationship without being at first an independent, autonomous person. Adults who believe that they are able to function independently can willingly join with another in true mutuality. Adults who believe that they need another to survive will not be able to be a true full partner in the relationship—the risks are too great.

Levinson (1986) supported this position. He stated

> One developmental task of this [midlife] transition is to begin a new step in individuation. To the extent that this occurs, we can become more compassionate, more reflective and judicious, less tyrannized by inner conflicts and external demands, and more genuinely loving of ourselves and others. (p. 5)

Clients may talk about fears related to loss of autonomy or expectations of increases in autonomy. People may be afraid that changes in relationships, such as marriage or childbearing, or changes in work, such as joining a large corporation, may have a deleterious effect on their autonomy. They may see other transitions, for example, getting divorced or having children leave home, becoming self-employed or retiring, or an increased sense of interiority, as leading to more autonomy. And to further complicate matters, some people may *fear* increased autonomy. (We never promised you this would be simple!)

Many faced with retirement feel they have lost control of their lives The CEO mentioned in Chapter 2 who was forced into retirement was asked who he was by a passport clerk. The man said, "I know who I was. I don't know who I am" (Schlossberg, 2004, p. 29). He had had one identity—a top executive and father. All that had changed, and he no longer knew who he was.

An important element of many midlife transitions is the need to make meaning of the transition and of life itself. Certainly Jack is questioning his values and his purpose in life. And surely his hope and optimism are shaky. Transitions often shake spiritual sureties as well. All we know about Jack's spiritual life is that he is active in his church, but we might suspect that he is questioning that church as he is everything else in his life. Counselors frequently hear middle-aged clients moving away from organized religion, particularly if they have been involved "for the children" who are now grown up. But they also often hear a commitment or recommitment to spirituality, defined more broadly than when the adult was younger. It now often includes belief in a higher power; hope and optimism, worship, prayer and meditation, purpose in life, love, and moral values.

Spirituality

Jung (1933) integrated the spiritual dimension with human development in his theory and conceptualized spirituality as a process of *achieving wholeness*. According to Jung, life is a journey and, particularly in the second half of life, it can become a spiritual process. Jung viewed the spiritual search for meaning as an integral part of midlife. He believed that, as people reach this stage of development, they become increasingly centered and more deeply connected to their spiritual selves.

Howell's (2001) research supported the idea that midlife can be a process involving a powerful spiritual awakening. According to Howell, a central influence on quality of life at midlife is an awareness of one's own values and motives, along with achieving agreement of these unique values with circumstances and behaviors. Hudson (1991) stated that as individuals move through midlife, their sense of purpose is likely to shift from ego-driven issues to more spiritual ones. For midlife adults, meaning and purpose become concerns as they address issues around mortal limits, death, and time left to live. This is not a morbid preoccupation; this awareness prompts adults to consider their deepest values.

Gerzon (1996) provided a metaphor for midlife. He stated that as people approach the second half of life, their old compasses no longer work, and the new compass must be read, not with their minds alone, but with their souls. At this time of life, according to Gerzon, people yearn for wholeness, and each must find his or her own way. Campbell (1988) believed that the quest for wholeness in the second half of life is ancient and universal, with the world's myths describing a quest for meaning and transcendence in adulthood. Although the word *midlife* often produces an adverse reaction in our culture, the crisis is in fact a spiritual one and can actually be a process of transformation (Gerzon, 1996). This is congruent with Bloch's (2004) ideas on phase transitions. According to Bloch, living beings are in a dynamic state, moving between order and chaos. She compared these phase transitions to the movement of water among the three phases, liquid, solid or ice, and gas or steam. She stated that phase transitions, whether sought or not, present the opportunity for creativity and the emergence of new forms (Bloch, 2004). According to Hudson (1991), as adults move through midlife, meaning and purpose become central concerns. This theory resonates with Campbell's (1988) conceptualization of the second half of life as a process of questing for meaning and transcendence.

A central theme in the literature on spirituality is its association with healthy development and functioning, along with increased adaptive capacities for dealing with distressful situations (Hodge, 2001; Larson & Larson, 2003; Paloutzian & Ellison, 1991; Pargament, 1997; Walsh, 1998). Graham, Furr, Flowers, and Burke (2001) concluded that spirituality may involve resources that include finding meaning and purpose in life. According to Myers and Williard (2003), spirituality is an essential component of wellness, acting as an integrative force that motivates and shapes the physical, psychological, and emotional functioning of human beings. Savickas (1997) asserted that it is meaning that breathes life into a situation, energizing and orientating people toward self-completion. He described spirituality as facilitating movement forward, thus increasing adaptive capacity.

Anderson (2005) looked at the concepts of spirituality and coping in her study of midlife adults experiencing a work transition. She found that levels of spirituality were significantly associated with the levels of coping for people experiencing a work transition. Existential spirituality, in particular, as distinguished from religion per se played a role for midlife adults in coping with stressful work transitions. The existential aspect of spirituality relates to meaning and a sense of purpose.

Finding one's life mission often relates to spirituality. This can relate to finding work that is meaningful in a deeper sense, but many people seek their life mission in other arenas of life. For example, one woman's search for meaning stemmed from a divorce. She took a 6-month leave from her job and spent time on an island near Singapore where she worked with a United Nations team providing mental health services to Southeast Asian refugees. While there she met two young Vietnamese refugees. After her return to the United States, she became their sponsor there, and in the process changed her views about what was important in her life. This example illustrates the intertwining of internal and external triggers that invited one adult to search for life's meaning in a new way. Her divorce and her children's becoming adults and leaving home provided both the spur and the possibility of a creative way to look for "more" out of life.

There is no right way to find meaning. Another woman quit a good professional job to spend a year in South America, doing things she had always wanted to such as swimming with dolphins and exploring more fully her own inner life. These "quests" are another way that some, whose life circumstances and financial means allow, seek to find meaning in midlife. Quests have a long tradition in many cultures. Sometimes relegated solely to the young, many cultures encouraged the middle-aged or old among them to seek meaning in exploration, e.g., American Indian vision quests. Many Catholics see a visit to a shrine, for example, Lourdes in France, Fatima in Portugal, or Guadeloupe in Mexico, as fulfilling a lifetime dream. A Moslem's trip to Mecca is considered an important component of spiritual health.

Weenolsen (1986) conducted a study to investigate empirically some of the ideas contained in existential philosophy, fiction, and psychology. Using the concept of transcendence, she described her paradigm thusly:

> The central thesis of the loss and transcendence paradigm is that we are in a continuous process of creating our lives and our selves. Our lives are the external aspects of our identity; our selves are the inner aspects. This creation of lives and selves . . . [includes] loss and transcendence. Loss is defined very broadly: it is any event, thought or feeling that destroys some aspect of one's life and/or one's self (the one cannot be affected without the other). This can be the loss of a loved one, a job, a material possession; it can be a loss of will, freedom, control, plans, expectations, hopes, ideals, or illusions. It can be a loss that is chosen or imposed, originating within the individual or without. Transcendence is the overcoming of loss and the re-creation of the life-self. There is no human activity, major or minor, that does not represent a loss and a transcendence of some kind to the individual experiencing it. (p. 2)

Weenolsen interviewed 48 women aged 25–67, asking open-ended questions related to the meaning of life. Although she found that 38 of the 48 women in her study believed that life has meaning, there was a distinction between those oriented to loss and those oriented to transcendence. In telling their stories, "The loss oriented answered in terms of what they did not have, whereas the transcendence oriented replied in terms of losses overcome" (p. 6).

Most women found meaning through conducting a life review. Although usually discussed as a later life phenomenon (cf., Butler 1963), Weenolsen (1986) found that 71% of her middle-aged interviewees reported frequent or occasional life reviews, and only one individual reported that she never engaged in such an activity. Clearly then, counselors can encourage life review activities for clients at all ages. This strategy can be encouraged or expanded upon as clients face new challenges. Weenolsen found four primary ways in which people find meaning: (a) as being preordained and coming from God; (b) as part of a process of personal and spiritual growth; (c) as a specific individual purpose such as being productive or helping others; and (d) as a more general personal purpose such as being loving or sharing joy. The women who believed that God has a divine plan for them believed that they would find life's meaning in that plan. The majority of subjects, however, believed that meaning could be created.

Weenolsen's proposed process of creation and renewal includes the stages of grieving, searching, replacing, and reintegrating. As counselors we want to listen for statements that reveal where a person is in this process and how a particular client makes meaning. We can then plan interventions to help individuals find meaning as they manage their transitions.

An interesting example of using the life review process to find life meaning is found in *Inscape: A Search for Meaning* (Young, 1983). This memoir ". . . records the backward look over a personal journey, a search to discover in the changing circumstances of my life, over a period of eight decades, my own meaning" (p. 1). Young comments near the end of the book that, ". . . the voyage of discovery consists in seeing with new eyes all that has woven the tapestry of one's life" (p. 98). Not everyone will write a book, but many can benefit from the introspective process used by Young.

Past Experience

One might make the case that having a past is the only universal experience of adulthood. All adults have both successful and unsuccessful coping experiences "under their belts." Past experience often determines how a person approaches a current transition. It is closely related to an optimistic or pessimistic viewpoint, transcendence, and self-efficacy.

Self-Efficacy

Counselors hear self-descriptions that run the gamut from confident to inadequate. Bandura (1982) coined the term *self-efficacy* to describe the belief that one can make a difference in one's own life and have an impact on one's environment. Self-efficacy enables a person to tackle a new problem with an optimistic expectation that it will be solvable, in other words, that one can cope effectively with it. Folkman et al. (1991) created an intervention strategy that included the person in the context of the environment. Two aspects are central to this model: (a) individuals' appraisal of the situation (Does it exceed or is it within their resources?), and (b) the coping response "through which the person alters or manages the person-environment relationship" (p. 240).

Lazarus and Folkman (1984) stated that an individual's appraisal of every encounter is shaped by the perceived harm, threat, or challenge found therein. And, both the quality and intensity of people's appraisal are affected by their self-efficacy beliefs. Newer research regarding the role of positive emotions and coping with stress has been prompted by evidence that both positive and negative appraisals/emotions co-occur throughout the process (Folkman & Moskowitz, 2004). As counselors, we hear a mix of feelings and cognitions, and it is imperative to listen for the positive as well as the problematic when working to increase self-efficacy in our clients.

Consider Sylvia, a 55-year-old divorced teacher who had been offered an early retirement package from her school district. She sought counseling help to decide whether or not to accept the offer. In describing her dilemma, she discussed her fears that she will be bored, that she will have no social life, which currently is made up mostly of school-related events, and that she will "wither away." She also talked about opportunities for visiting her children and grandchildren who live in distant states and for spending more time on her crafts and hobbies. She explained that she has made many bad decisions in her life, has no confidence in her ability to make this one, and is feeling panicky over its irrevocacy. Clearly her appraisal of the situation includes both present threat and fear of future harm, as well as possible challenge. This mixed bag, common to stressful situations, is coupled with low self-efficacy estimates.

Counselors can intervene in each of these arenas—evaluating the harm and threat, reinforcing the challenge, and changing the client's beliefs in her self-efficacy by helping her to explore past successes and current resources. As we get to know about the balance of Sylvia's assets to deficits, we need to consider not only the situation she faces and the areas of her self that impinge on that situation, but also where else she can get assistance to face her current challenges.

SUPPORT

When individuals hear the word *support,* they usually think of other people. Counselors, with judicious questioning, can find out the shape, size and range of a person's support system—who is in it and what function each person plays in the system. During times of transition, we often hear of great disruptions to a support system. An important first step in planning ways to enhance a system is to learn about its present status. We will discuss methods for improving support systems with individuals in Chapter 7 and with groups in Chapter 8. In this section we will describe what counselors may hear as clients describe their "people" supports. As with all of the discussions in this section of the book, our purpose here is to heighten readers' awareness of issues brought to counseling by people in transition. It is our hope that this heightened awareness will enable you to listen more productively as you help your clients explore their lives.

Types of Support

Waters and Samson (1993) used Pearson's (1990) research to provide a list of typical support needs. They included (a) acceptance, (b) self-esteem, (c) love and physical intimacy, (d) personal and work connections, (e) peers (people like one in a particular arena, e.g., other parents of adolescents), (f) stimulation and challenge, (g) role models, (h) guidance (mentors or sponsors), and (i) comfort and assistance.

Let us look at one of the needs listed above, role models. In Jack's case, the potential of his father being such a role model is lost. He portrays an extremely undesirable future. Although positive role models can be important components of support, Jack's father is a negative role model—helpful only in that in clarifying for Jack what he doesn't want to be—a future to be avoided. Jack's counselor will want to help him think about who else have been or could be role models for him. The counselor and Jack may also want to think together about whether there are *any* positive aspects of his father that he could use as a pattern for his own adult life.

As you elicit the stories of your clients in transition, listen for support issues such as having very few people filling many functions, having areas with little or no support, or statements such as, "I don't need support." or "Grown men don't depend on others." Often you can help people to feel more comfortable accepting support if you remind them of the times that they have supported others and encourage them to think of times in the future when they will again be able to be givers. It may also help to remind them of the pleasure they get in giving to others. When they do not let others assist them, they deprive the people they care about of the opportunity to be givers.

A man attending a party saw a list of emergency numbers next to a friend's telephone and asked, with some dismay, why he wasn't on the list. The unstated messages of: "I thought you knew you could count on me in an emergency" and "I want to be able to help you out when you need it" were expressive of this desire to give. Many clients do not recognize the supportive function played by people in their lives. Sometimes a delightful serendipitous outcome of exploring support systems is that clients share this awareness with those closest to them—who are generally very flattered and pleased.

People often receive support from belonging to a group designed specifically for its supportive functions. A plethora of groups have arisen, both self-help and professionally led, to provide a forum for adults with specific problems. These include support groups for people who have lost breasts or colons, groups for people who are newly divorced or widowed, or groups for new parents or those who have decided not to have children. These groups, which will be discussed more fully in Chapters 8 and 9, have the potential to offer information and support, and, with luck, help individuals to both acquire and perceive more control over their situation.

STRATEGIES

Part III is dedicated to counseling interventions—things we can do to help our clients develop strategies that will help them move forward in their lives. The goal of the strategies section of this chapter is to help you identify what you may hear from clients about strategies they currently use. We have found that it is usually easier for clients to do more of what they already know than to learn new things. Thus, finding out in some detail what successful strategies clients already use is a productive aim of counseling.

Reframing

Hackney and Cormier (2005) suggested that reframing helps develop an alternative meaning that is, "totally credible and believable" (p. 200). Counselors need to listen for statements that can be reframed. One woman we know, in the depths of despair over a painful divorce, talked about her pride in being able to care so deeply. In doing so, she reframed at least some of her pain into hope for a future deep relationship. Another woman described her graying hair as a "free frosting."

Two men were forced into early retirement by companies that were "right-sizing." One reframed it as an opportunity to spend more time with his family and to pursue several hobbies. Another overgeneralized and saw it as a total condemnation of his worth. He felt that if he was not valuable enough to the company to keep, then he was valuable to no one. He gave up his volunteer activities, quit his golf league, and retreated to his den where he watched television and generally exhibited symptoms of depression. He was not able to separate the causes of his lay-off—economics, not a comment on his work performance—from his total worth as a person.

Bandler and Grinder (1975) discussed this process from the perspective of linguistics as well as psychology. They describe three processes through which we narrow the real world into our perceptive world. They are (a) *generalization,* in which we apply learning from one situation or experience to others we deem similar, (b) *distortion,* in which we change what we think, see, and feel about the world to match our internal perceptions, and (c) *deletion,* in which we selectively screen out parts of our perception, again often to match some internal sense. Counselors need to listen to their clients' uses of each of these processes to determine whether the use is self-enhancing or self-destructive.

Let us look in more detail at the case of the depressed laid-off man described above. He extended his negative feelings about his work abilities to include his feelings about all of his abilities—*overgeneralization.* It is likely that he distorted what he heard from the personnel office. Perhaps he was told that they had to let a certain number of people go and chose everyone earning above a certain amount. Or perhaps he was told that his department was being absorbed by another and that all the managers in his had to be let go. But our hypothetical man probably already had fairly low self-esteem, perhaps based on a lifetime of negative thinking, so he *distorted* what he heard to match his internal perception of his value. Perhaps he was even told by the personnel office that the company was sorry to lose a good worker and would be glad to give him excellent references. Because he did not, deep down, believe that he was worthy, he "didn't hear" or *deleted* the positive message. Whenever any of these processes become evident to a counselor, the stage is set for reframing.

The adage that, "Every cloud has a silver lining" is well known. Another view of this situation is found in the Japanese word, *mono-no-aware,* defined as appreciating the sadness of existence. An example of the use of this word is, "You see the cherry blossoms on the trees in Kyoto in April and you love them, but you love them most of all because you appreciate, so sadly, that soon they will all be gone (Moore, 2004, p. 9). A negative example might be the so-called Murphy's law: If anything can go wrong it will. Counselors can listen to a client's abilities to reframe positively so they can reinforce, modify, or teach this coping strategy.

Selective Denial

The technique of selective denial is closely allied to reframing. Counselors can listen for the ways that people "forget" parts of their situations. A 60-year-old man had surgery for cancer. Although his odds for recovery were about 50–50, he believed that his cancer was all gone. He took the recommended chemotherapy and followed other medical recommendations, although he believed they were unnecessary. His selective denial allowed him to enjoy life during this unpleasant time, and if we believe researchers such as Siegel (1986), increased his chances of complete recovery. The difference between healthy and unhealthy denial in this situation is that an unhealthy denier might refuse treatments. People can deny facts, as in the above example, deny the meaning of a situation, deny the fact that the situation applies to them, or deny that the situation is pervasive or will be long lasting.

A client moved across the country by herself to a place where she knew nobody. She stated that she didn't consider herself alone or lonely. She enjoyed her own company, she said, and knew that eventually she would meet people and form new friendships. This denial of the possible ill-effects of her move might have gotten her in trouble if she did not then reach out to others in her new community. But at the moment it gave her the energy to focus on settling into her apartment and finding a job.

People who deny that their own aging means slowing down, even if it means so for others, may be the same people we see competing in the "over 80" field in a marathon, triathlon, or swim meet. Selective denial for these athletes creates a true change in the reality. Unhealthy deniers might continue to compete when it is causing permanent harm to their knees or even their hearts.

Denying the pervasiveness or long lastingness of the situation is the last type of selective denial. Counselors will hear people making pronouncements such as: "It was only my job, not my life." "This will feel like home in a few weeks." "I may look old on the outside, but inside I'm still a lad of 21." Counselors can be alert to the coping strategies related to selective denial currently being used by their clients. They can then support the ones that are functional and help to redirect those which are less so.

Hope and Optimism

It has been said that *hope* is the passion for the possible. According to the dictionary hope is "the feeling that what is desired is also possible and that events may turn out for the best." According to the same dictionary, *optimism* is "a disposition or tendency to look on the more favorable side of happenings and to anticipate the most favorable result." Hope only exists when there is also doubt—otherwise it is expectation. Take the case of Marie, who had two adult children. She expected that her children would marry, and she would become a grandparent. However, one daughter became emotionally unstable and was in and out of hospitals and the other daughter married but postponed having children. As the possibility emerged that she might not have grandchildren, her hope increased. In other words, when she fully expected to be a grandmother, there was no need for hope. As the possibility became ambiguous, hope became her "powerful ally." After her daughter announced that she and her husband had decided never to have children, hope went out the window. She became despondent, and she gave herself time to grieve over the loss of what might have been. Finally, she modified her dream by becoming a foster grandparent.

As mentioned earlier, Seligman (2002) addressed this issue in his book *Learned Optimism*. After much research, he concluded, ". . . the remarkable attribute of resilience in the face of defeat need not remain a mystery. It was not an inborn trait; it could be acquired" (p. 30).

According to Hof (1993) hope is an important and often overlooked aspect of the therapy process. Reviewing the literature in family–couple counseling from 1975 to 1992, he found only two mentions of hope. He says that, "One of the first tasks of the therapist is to uncover hope, to help create hope, or to instill hope" (p. 223). Counselors often find that people in transition can be divided among those with hope, those without, and even some, those he calls Paul or Paula Pollyanna, who may have so much that they fail to appropriately avoid danger. Some people come to counseling as a last hope!

What is it about hope that is so important in a transition? Again, we see the intertwining of experience and emotional state. Naturally hopeful individuals can lose this worldview during times of crisis but can regain it afterwards. Naturally gloomy individuals may struggle even harder to cope with difficult times. We recall an experienced school counselor who found himself stultified in a job he did easily and had done for a long time. He returned to school for an advanced degree solely to energize himself in his profession. He described the experience with enthusiasm, both for his own learning and renewal, and for the renewed empathy he had for his students' academic tribulations. This man clearly believed he had the ability to change his life through his own efforts—an optimist. We recall another man, also bored with his work in education, who counted the days to retirement for several years, and withdrew more and more into a cocoon. He felt helpless to change his situation and believed that he had to suffer in silence—a pessimist.

As we discussed in Chapter 3, Seligman (2002) described several components of optimism–pessimism. Counselors can listen for the following aspects of their clients' explanatory style: their habitual way of explaining both bad and good events. Explanatory style has three dimensions:

1. Permanence: Whether you believe causes are permanent or transitory. Optimists believe causes of good things are permanent and bad things are transitory; pessimists believe just the opposite—that causes of bad things are permanent and good things are transitory. Counselors need to be alert for words such as *always* and *never* and the contexts in which they are used.

2. Pervasiveness: "The optimist believes that bad events have specific causes, while good events will enhance everything he does; the pessimist believes that bad events have universal causes and that good events are caused by specific factors" (pp. 47–48). Pervasiveness can determine whether people who experience a painful transition will allow that event to spill into all areas of their lives or whether they will contain the event into its own "box." Counselors need to listen for "catastrophizing" statements as they listen for the pervasiveness dimension. The same process holds for positive transitions. Counselors need to listen for whether people will allow the event to permeate their entire sense of self. Transitions relating to the self are particularly subject to pervasiveness *because* of their internality. It is hard to see "angst" or joy as anything but pervasive. A person who declares, "I really seem to have a new sense of who I am and what matters to me" is unlikely to keep that feeling in a small box.

3. Personalization: The third dimension of explanatory style refers to whether one takes responsibility for one's own successes and failures or attributes them to others. Optimists take responsibility for their successes and blame others for their failures. A middle-aged optimistic man with healthy teeth said he had worked hard all of his life to keep them that way—flossing, brushing, getting regular check-ups, etc. The pessimistic man with similar dental health said it was because his parents and then his employer made him go to the dentist regularly and that his dentist was a genius. The middle-aged optimist with bad teeth absolved himself from responsibility saying that it was because his employer had not provided dental insurance and his parents had not taken him to the dentist as a child. The middle-aged pessimist, also with poor dental health, said it was his own fault for not paying attention to oral hygiene and being lazy about visiting his dentist. This dimension of explanatory style is closely related to locus of control.

Researchers Kobasa and Maddi with others have been studying what they call *hardiness* and others call *stamina* for several years. They questioned the oft-quoted connection between stress and illness and found that hardy people handled stress better and were healthier than the non-hardy during stressful transitions. In an article written with Kahn (Kobasa, Maddi & Kahn, 1982), they defined hardiness to include commitment, control, and challenge. These are defined as follows:

> The commitment disposition is expressed as a tendency to involve oneself in (rather than experience alienation from) whatever one is doing or encounters. . . . The control disposition is expressed as a tendency to feel and act as if one is influential (rather than helpless) in the face of the varied contingencies of life. . . . The challenge disposition is expressed as the belief that change rather than stability is normal in life and that the anticipation of changes are interesting incentives to growth rather than threats to security (pp. 169–170).

Sholk (1983) described bamboo in a poem, saying

> There is a stamina within that somehow has been
>> transferred to me.
> Boughs will bend before they break.
> Stability in a swaying mobile grassland.
> Versatility.

The hardiness model provides counselors with additional clues to their clients' state of mind. One person may describe his or her awareness of life's finiteness as a time to fulfill dreams, experience more, set new goals, or make more careful choices about how time is spent. This person may come to seek help in implementing these plans or in managing other's reactions to new lifestyle choices. A person at the other end of the commitment continuum may describe group self-hatred, saying things like, "I don't want to spend time with all those old people." Still another person may cling to the past by dressing in the clothing of his or her youth, reading nothing written after a certain date, or refusing to acknowledge changes in the world and its customs.

Listening for the control dimension may help counselors be alert to statements such as, "I've handled other tough situations, I'm sure with a little help I'll be able to handle this one, too"; or "There's nothing anyone can do. I guess I just have to suffer." Kobasa et al. (1982) stated that control "does not imply the naive expectation of complete determination of events and outcomes but rather implies the perception of oneself as having a definite influence through the exercise of imagination, knowledge, skill, and choice (p. 169). In addition to managing transitions better, people who perceive that they have more control over their lives experience fewer of the deleterious effects of stress.

In popular culture the challenge disposition is described with adages such as, "If life gives you lemons, make lemonade," or, "When you get to the end of your rope, make a knot and hang on." Kobasa et al. (1982) stated

> Challenge mitigates the stressfulness of life events on the perceptual side by coloring events as stimulating rather than threatening, specifically because they are changes requiring readjustment. In coping behaviors, challenge will lead to attempts to transform oneself and thereby grow rather than conserve and protect what one can of the former existence (p. 170).

We are reminded of the man who saw turning 60 as an opportunity to increase his chances of winning tennis tournaments as he would then be one of the youngest in his new age group. A similar positive view is expressed in a poem found in a book with the delightful title of "When I Am an Old Woman, I Shall Wear Purple." In the poem from which the title, "Warning" (Joseph, 1987), is drawn a woman describes how her age gives her the freedom to be nonconforming.

Counselors will hear statements from clients in transition that give clues to their optimistic or pessimistic outlook on life. Perhaps one of the most important interventions we can apply is to help a person establish or reestablish hope.

CHAPTER 5

Relationship Transitions

The first client you are observing today is Martha Smith. All you know about Mrs. Smith from the intake interviewer is that she is 48 years old, married with two children, and employed by an insurance company. She is smartly dressed in a gray suit with a bright print blouse and contemporary jewelry. As soon as you introduce yourself and explain a little bit about how you work, Mrs. Smith, who says most people call her Marty, launches into the following story.

> *I was out of the workforce for a number of years while the children were young. My first husband wasn't around a whole lot even when we were still married. So in some ways I was both mother and father to the children. They are both out of the house now. My son had some trouble "finding himself"—isn't that the phrase that young people use?—but he's now at the community college and living with two friends in an apartment. He still comes back all the time to do his laundry and get some home-cooked meals. And we do help him a little financially.*
>
> *My daughter is married, has two little children, and lives in another part of the state. She calls almost every week and asks if I can come for the weekend. I'm glad that she wants me, and I do love to spend time with my grandchildren, but my husband wants me to be here with him and his widowed mother who lives near us and needs a lot of help. She counts on me to do her shopping and take her to the doctor and the beauty parlor. She's a really nice lady, but I don't know why she calls me all the time instead of her other daughter-in-law who has been in the family for 20 years. She hasn't said anything directly, but I think she'd like to move in with us. She has commented on how we must rattle around in the house since the children have left.*

My husband's two children are both married and live nearby. They drop in with the children at least twice a week. They're nice kids, but they do make a mess. I know I should be flattered that they want to spend time with their stepmother. And I am. But they do tire me out. So you see why I say I should be happy. I've always wanted to be needed and I am. But sometimes I feel like an octopus, with everybody pulling on one of my tentacles.

Even at work, I'm very involved. I started as a clerical worker, and I've received several promotions. When I first went back to work, before I met my present husband, the social life I developed with the other people at work was very important to me. Some of them are really nice and included me in many of their activities. I'm also the oldest woman in my group, and the others sort of count on me to arrange the birthday celebrations, Christmas party, and other social events. Lots of them also come to me to talk about personal problems.

My boss has offered to send me to Dallas for a 2-week training program, which he says will make me eligible for a substantial promotion. I'm really excited about the prospect, but when I told my husband he looked startled. He tried to say how nice for me, but I could tell he didn't like the idea. Now isn't it silly that with all this good stuff going on in my life, I feel so unsettled?

Given what we know about adult development, it really isn't "silly" for Marty to feel unsettled. She has experienced a number of transitions in recent years—being divorced and remarried, becoming a stepmother and a grandmother, and launching a new career. The transition she is currently grappling with is whether to take training and go for advancement at work, given her complex family situation. If she were our client, we could help her make that decision, using the transition model to help her analyze her resources and deficits in each of the 4 S's.

In terms of the Situation, Marty's transition decision has to be made in the context of multiple demands on her time. Given the many stresses in her life, it may not be the best time for her to make a major change in her work role. At the same time, she may see it as a "now or never" offer. With respect to Self, we could help her explore her values concerning work and family. On the surface, she seems to be healthy, economically secure, and in a positive marriage. We could also jointly explore her spirituality, especially in regard to what aspects of her life hold a sense of purpose and meaning for her.

Marty's Support system, including her husband, blended family, friends and coworkers, seems to be both an asset and a burden. We don't know much about her coping Strategies, other than that she managed to cope with a poor marriage, a divorce, a remarriage, and a return to the work force and seems to make friends easily.

Marty's story suggests a number of recurring issues that clients bring to a counselor's office. She is experiencing a new sense of intimacy or attachment, which she apparently treasures; she certainly belongs in her new and old families and in her work place; and she "matters" to many people. In fact, the presenting problem may be that she matters too much.

In this chapter, we first discuss various types of relationship transitions, of which Marty's is only one example, that bring adults to counseling. We then review the major recurring issues mentioned above: intimacy, belonging, and mattering. In the final section, we consider ways to utilize the transition model to help us evaluate Marty's case and those of other adults facing relationship transitions.

Throughout this chapter it is important to remember Howard's (1978) statement, "The trouble we take to arrange ourselves in some semblance of families is one of the most imperishable habits of the human race" (p. 15). Although definitions of what constitutes a family change over time and differ from one culture to another, family units are the basic units of society.

While listening to client's stories, counselors also should remember that many people, particularly women, think of their lives in terms of relationships and key family events. Hagestad (1986) stated: "We place ourselves on the axis of chronological time by orienting ourselves to key transitions: when we graduate, marry, have children. In such temporal construction and reconstruction, family members play key parts: 'It was the year Pete started school, so it must have been. . . . 'In the work of creating an autobiography we need the help of family consociates" (p. 691). Plath (1980) also talked of the key role of consociates, those with whom we have close contacts over long periods of time.

TYPES OF TRANSITIONS

One of the most common reasons for adults to seek counseling is that they are contemplating, experiencing, or having trouble adapting to transitions involving family or other close relationships. Often clients lend support to Bridges' (1980, 2004) view that transitions begin with endings, as we are more apt to hear about relationships that are "going sour," needing to be redefined, or already over, than about new loves.

As counselors, we may be asked to help our clients sort out their feelings about the unpredictability of family relationships today. Families come in many different shapes and sizes; there is no longer a "typical" family. Many young girls, some married, many not, have babies during their teenage years while other women delay childbearing until their late 30s or 40s. Therefore, first-time grandparents can be 40 or 70.

An increasing number of adults, mostly but not always women, are responsible for parent care. But, once again, there is no specified age at which this occurs, no designated length of time that pinpoints how long parent care is necessary.

Today multigenerational families are common, and the term *sandwich generation* has crept into the popular vocabulary. The term refers to people in midlife who are caught between the needs of children and aging parents. As people live longer, and the number of generations increases, the metaphor becomes a *club sandwich*. For the first time in history, the average married couple has more parents than children (Hagestad, 1986). This development represents the potential for many years of closeness and many changes in relationships. Following is a discussion of some of the more common transitions involving close interpersonal relationships.

Partnering Relationships

For many adults, having one committed relationship is a primary life goal. This relationship, if obtained, may be marked by satisfaction and/or conflict requiring continuous renegotiation. An insightful man commented that he'd had one wife but several marriages. Talking of people in their 50s, Bergquist, Greenberg, and Klaum (1993) asserted that:

> The relationship that is most likely to be sustained in this period of reinventing ourselves is perhaps, surprisingly, with our spouse or significant other. While our children have often left home by the time we reach fifty and our friendships have changed and become fewer, our partner is often still there to support us and be our companion. This central, intimate, relationship can be a major source of generativity. . . . When couples fail to develop a new intimacy in these years the problem is usually that they find they no longer have any common interests. They discover new time together in their fifties but have nothing to share in that time. (pp. 80–82)

For some individuals who seek counseling, a basic concern is "Will I ever find the kind of partner I want?" and more significantly, "What will happen to me if I don't?" As adults contemplate marriage or other committed relationships, they may ask transition-related questions such as, "How will my life change?" or "He wants me to move across the country, but how do I know if I can manage without all the supports I have here?" "We both have good jobs, but in different cities. Can we manage a commuter relationship?"

Different value systems can create serious problems around the decision to marry. A woman recently said, "I think we should live together for a while before we marry, but he says his family will disown him if we do."

Her desire for a trial period reflects her concern about not wanting to make a decision without being really sure, while his reluctance may stem from family or religious scruples about living together "out of wedlock."

Gay and lesbian couples may experience even more value conflicts, both their own and those imposed by an often disapproving society. One man in considerable anguish recently said, "My partner wants me to take him to our company Christmas party. He accused me of being ashamed of him and of our relationship. Of course I'm not, but the truth is I don't know how my co-workers would react. I'm not sure they know I'm gay."

For gay men and lesbians, as for heterosexuals, the presence of a committed partner can be a source of satisfaction and a buffer against stress. When the relationship is longstanding, partners can draw on a reservoir of shared experiences and patterns of relating to each other. However, problems may arise when one member of a gay or lesbian couple is hospitalized or needs long-term care because that partner may not be perceived as "family" by the bureaucracy or the family of origin. Although this situation is slowly changing, in many cases both the ill person and the partner may be denied opportunities to support each other, to enjoy continued intimacy, or, with terminal illness, even to say good-bye. An additional problem for gay and lesbian couples is the scarcity of societal rituals for someone whose same-sex partner leaves or dies. Yet the pain and loneliness are every bit as intense as those for heterosexuals. Furthermore, individuals from the gay culture may be leery of counseling with "straight" mental health professionals.

Divorce

In a study on the experience of divorce, the impact of divorce on midlife adults was examined. In this particular sample, 73% of adults divorced in their 40s, 22% in their 50s, and 4% in their 60s. More than half (56%) remained divorced or separated, 5% were widowed, 31% remarried, and 9% were living with a partner. At the time of divorce, 76% had children, most of whom were younger than age 18. Difficulties associated with the divorce included uncertainty (40%), loneliness or depression (29%), feelings of desertion or betrayal (25%), and a sense of failure (23%). Common fears included failing again, having financial troubles, and not finding someone to marry. Yet most of these participants coped fairly well overall with their divorce (Montenegro, 2004). In another study, the longitudinal effects of continuity and transitions in marital status were examined regarding psychological well-being. Although marriage continued to be associated with well-being for both men and women, in some cases single individuals fared better than married individuals in regard to autonomy and personal growth. Midlife adults evidenced more psychological resilience than young adults in facing the challenges of a marital transition or in remaining single over a longer period of time (Lambert, 1998).

In many counselors' offices, coping with divorce is the most frequently discussed transition. Despite the fact that approximately 50% of marriages currently end in divorce (U.S. Department of Commerce, 2004), it can be among the most painful of life's experiences. Whether your client is the instigator of the divorce or the partner being rejected, he or she is likely to describe a sense of failure. For some the pain of rejection is uppermost in their minds; for others the guilt over what they are doing to other people is paramount. What clients tell you may also depend on where they are in terms of stages of the divorce transition.

One particularly difficult stage, characterized by lack of clarity, has been termed a *limbo loss* by Colgrove, Bloomfield, and McWilliams (1991). During this stage, counselors may hear statements such as "I do all right alone, and better together, but I do very poorly when semi-together" (p. 5). A similar angst is expressed in one of the writers' poems:

Limbo losses often feel like this . . . this slow erosion from below

—or within—

it's me falling down around my life because you're still in that life—but not really

And you're out of that life—but not quite. (p. 4)

From *How to Survive the Loss of a Love,* by Melba Colgrove, Ph.D., Harold H. Bloomfield, M.D., and Peter McWilliams, © 1991, published by Prelude Press, 8159 Santa Monica Boulevard, Los Angeles, CA, 90046, 1-BOO-LIFE-101. Used with permission.

One woman in her late 40s recently told a counselor, "My marriage doesn't do it for me anymore, but I don't know if I have the guts to leave. What will happen to me? To him? To the children? To our dream of being grandparents together?" Another woman said between her tears, "I think my husband is having an affair. Shall I confront him or just hope it will play itself out? Is this his midlife crisis?" Both these women are grappling with a major decision as to whether to initiate a divorce, thus embarking on a major transition. They probably need help in examining their resources for coping, regardless of the decision they make.

Alcoholism or other substance abuse is often involved when one or both partners are considering divorce. Counselors may hear heart-wrenching stories from people who are uncertain as to whether to believe their partner's statements that "they really are going to stop." Women married to alcoholic or substance-abusing husbands are more likely to "stick by" their husbands than are men married to alcoholic women

(Covington, 1994). However, one of the reasons why alcoholic women often get into treatment late in the course of their disease is that their families have engaged in an elaborate cover-up to avoid embarrassment. Peluso and Peluso (1988) stated that "For every woman drug addict hiding in a closet, there are usually several family members leaning against the door (p. 7)."

Widowhood

Much has been written about the major life transition of widowhood. The authors of books for the bereaved person such as *Living with an Empty Chair* (Ternes, 1984) and *How to Survive the Loss of a Love* (Colgrove et al., 1991), as well as books for professionals (e.g., Kalish, 1985; Lopata, 1987; Worden, 1991), discuss the devastation and mix of intense feelings that may be experienced, and of the fear of many people that they hurt so much they must be going crazy.

Didion's (2005) especially moving memoir of grief, *The Year of Magical Thinking,* provides an intensely personal experience of loss following the death of her husband of 40 years. She describes a life-changing event occurring on an "ordinary day." She was mixing a salad at one moment, lighting the candles, and moments later found her husband sitting motionless in a chair. He was pronounced dead shortly after. She was suddenly propelled into a grief that came in waves, along with what she termed *magical thinking* that she described as a dislocation of "body and mind" that brings a sense of alienation and disorientation. For example, she couldn't get rid of his shoes, because he needed them to come back to her. Didion's honest portrayal of her grief process was her way to give meaning to the experience, and provides us with a personal account of the impact of grief.

Counselors hear statements such as, "I don't think I can live without him," or "We always thought I'd die first." This is not an unusual reaction on the part of widowers as both demographics and conventional wisdom show that wives usually outlive their husbands. A review of research supports the belief that generally men suffer more than women following bereavement (Stroebe, Stroebe, & Schut, 2001). Early studies by Neugarten (1968) indicated that a major difference between the sexes is that women are more likely to rehearse for widowhood. This has been attributed both to differences in life expectancies and to the greater emphasis women put on connectedness in their thinking about and planning their lives (Belenky, Clinchy, Goldberger, & Tarule, 1986; Gilligan, 1993). An interesting finding by Bennett (2005), however, disputed the emphasis on gender: The more recent the widowhood, the more the reduction of morale, social engagement, and psychological well-being.

Another key influence was age at the time of bereavement, with increased age also associated with poorer psychological well-being. Further studies looking at both age and gender were suggested.

The effects of rehearsing may depend on the kind of rehearsing that is done. Although behavioral rehearsal (e.g., planning and making decisions, beginning to assume control of family finances, and making new friends) was helpful in the adjustment to widowhood, cognitive rehearsal, defined as the "work of worrying," was associated with increased emotional disruption (Remondet, Hansson, Rule, & Winfrey, 1987). Counselors can help both widows and widowers think about which rehearsal techniques will help them the most.

Clients whose spouses are suffering from a long-term serious disability are clearly grieving but may be unclear about "how to do it." One woman whose husband had a serious stroke and was unable to talk said, "I know I'm grieving but I'm not sure for what." There are no clear rituals, such as funerals, to assist people in this limbo status, so counselors may want to help clients develop their own. Lustbader (1994) told a moving story of a woman whose husband's personality and behavior had been altered by a major illness. The woman explained to her counselor that "I had to divorce him in my mind and marry him again on new terms." Bonanno, Wortman, and Nesse (2004) suggested that the factors surrounding one's loss are crucial to how people grieve over the death of their spouse. An unexpected finding was that participants evidenced depression before the loss followed by marked improvement after the spouse's death. For these caregivers of chronically ill partners, the death was experienced as the end of a chronic stressor.

Counselors may also hear poignant statements such as "We did everything together," or "Why did I leave the running of the house to my wife or husband. I have no idea how to. . . . ." "How-to's" can refer to handling everything from finances to household chores and social arrangements. A principle role of counselors in working with widowed persons and people whose spouses are severely disabled is to assure them of the normality of their intense and often vacillating feelings. Referrals to support groups as well as attorneys, financial planners, and other advisors may also be helpful.

Some widowed persons complain that they are being ignored, or they hesitantly express resentment that everybody else seems to be just going along with their lives. At the approach of one holiday season, a widow asked with much pathos, "Will I ever be happy again?" When confronted with such questions, counselors may be able to help widowed persons see that although they will never be their "old selves" again, they can become reasonably comfortable "new selves."

Alternatively, other widows may express feelings such as "I'm tired of people feeling sorry for me. I guess I should be grateful, but I can't stand it when people talk to me as if my life must be over." A widowed friend recently explained, "Sure I miss Joe, but I really do have a full life now, with many friends and interests."

Differences among widowed persons may reflect not only their personal styles, but also the social context in which they life. Comparative studies of widows in different communities in the United States and Canada revealed "tremendous variation in life frameworks, social roles and relations, support systems, life-styles, and self concepts" (Lopata, 1987, p. 273). A major role of counselors may be to listen carefully for information about those aspects of a widowed person's life. Such attention may provide clues, for example, as to whether the person's primary need is for self-esteem building, help in finding or utilizing informal supports, or referral to formal community resources.

Members of some social groups in this country may be effectively deprived of services because they do not understand their availability and/or do not think it appropriate to ask for such assistance. In this situation, as in many others, counselors working with individuals from a different cultural group than theirs need to educate themselves about that culture, refer the client to a counselor more familiar with that group, or else seek consultation.

Remarriage

For some widowed persons, particularly those who have spent many years in caregiving, the idea of remarriage holds no appeal. For others it may be a primary goal or emerge as a surprising opportunity.

Counselors may hear comments ranging from, "I hate the thought of living the rest of my life alone, but how can a woman my age ever find another husband?" to "My wife has only been dead 3 months, but I really want to get married again. What will people say? What will the children think?" Divorced persons often talk about being "gun shy," or fearful of making "another mistake."

Gender differences with respect to remarriage are significant. A frequent finding in the literature on remarriage is that women are more likely than men to be widowed but are less likely to subsequently remarry. An explanation that has been proposed is the longer lifespan of women, along with a tendency for men to marry women younger than they are. This results in a larger pool of potential spouses for men. An alternative explanation is that marriage may benefit men more than it does women (Gentry & Shulman, 1988). For many men, particularly those whose business responsibilities involve entertaining or whose ability or willingness to perform household tasks is limited, the thought of being without a wife may be too difficult to contemplate. Given the high ratio of widows to widowers among most social groups in this country, such men may be able to find another wife with relative ease. Women seeking remarriage may need to take more dramatic steps. One woman we know who was widowed in her 40s thought about where she had the best chance of finding a second husband and decided to take flying lessons. She was indeed the only woman in her piloting class, and her quests for a pilot's license and a husband were both successful!

In a study of 4,449 adults, aged 55–89, researchers in the Netherlands concluded that repartnering is a stressful life event that is incompletely institutionalized. They reported that more repartnered older adults choose unmarried cohabitation than remarriage. When these partners came together, their social networks expanded more than those of separated older adults. Yet the quality of the relationships with their children was negatively affected. Those who opted for unmarried cohabitation tended to have the weakest bonds with their children (De Jong Gierveld, & Peeters, 2003).

A growing interest in the literature is the effect of remarriage on adult stepchildren. Clinical observations suggest an increase in the number of adults coming to counseling when adjusting to parental remarriage that is taking place later in the family's developmental lifecycle. These adults present dilemmas that they are experiencing due to the reorganization of their families. Part of the challenge facing adults and their transition to stepchildren is the lack of social guidelines for their stepchildren roles. With the greater frequency of remarriage and the complexity of the issues facing stepfamilies, counselors need to be sensitive and tailor interventions specifically to these family's needs (Corrie, 2002).

On the other hand, many widowed persons have no desire for remarriage. Lopata (1987) found that some widows engage in what she labeled "husband sanctification." When deceased husbands are idealized to this extent, no real person can measure up. If counselors hear such themes, they have to decide whether gentle confrontation would be helpful.

Whether their clients are divorced or widowed, counselors may hear a variety of questions—logistical, emotional, and financial—relating to remarriage. For example, "How will we deal with all those children and grandchildren? How will we decide where to spend vacations and holidays?" "Do we live in his house, my house, or start all over?" "How do we deal with the "exes"? Sometimes emotional and economic issues may be interwoven. "He says he loves me, but I'm worried he is really just interested in my money." "I'm not sure I love him, but he could certainly support me and make the rest of my life more comfortable." Or "Will she think I don't trust her if I ask for a prenuptial agreement?" In many such discussions counselors can help concerned clients explore their values, their resources, and their deficits. Discussions of life meaning may also come into play with respect to transitions involving a very different relationship, that of parenting.

Parenting Issues

Parenting, like many other intimate relationships, can be a source of utter delight or unbelievable frustration. Counselors will talk to clients dealing with a host of issues, such as whether or not to have children, how custody should be arranged, or what child-rearing techniques are most effective. Parents of older children may have questions about how to encourage children to leave home or whether to allow them to return. Sometimes parents wonder how to deal with their disappointment over non-events, such as when children do not do what the parents expected.

All such decisions are complicated by the fact that many people and many dimensions of a person's life are affected. Consider the dilemma of a woman on the fast track at work who says, "My husband really wants to start a family, but I know I'd have to be the one to stay home when the baby is sick. I'm not sure I'm willing to sacrifice my career."

Counselors may hear considerable talk about the ticking of the biological clock. Some couples, particularly those with professional careers, may postpone childbearing, but there comes a time when partners must face questions such as: "Do I really want to have children, and if I do, how will it change my life?" "If I don't, am I letting my parents down? I know they are eager to become grandparents." "If I decide now not to have children, will I be sorry later?" Sometimes the difficulty of the decision is masked with humor, "If we have a baby and then change our minds, can we return it to the store within 5 years?" The decision as to whether or not to have children may be one of the few irrevocable decisions many people ever make.

For some groups, the decision about parenting may be especially difficult. Counselors working with gay or lesbian clients may hear statements such as, "Just because I'm gay doesn't mean I wouldn't make a good parent," "I'm thinking about fathering a child for my lesbian friend who wants to be a mother," or "My partner and I really want to raise a child together. We're trying to decide if one of us should be artificially inseminated or whether we should look for a baby to adopt. Apart from the logistics of how to do it, we wonder if it would be fair to the child. What would its friends think?"

If an individual or a couple decides to have or adopt a baby, it is only the first of many transitions they will face. Kimmel (1990) summarized a number of studies on the impact of becoming parents and found such a step to be a profound transition, leading to changes in individuals' views of themselves as well as the couple's relationship.

The myriad of child-rearing issues that arise for married couples, single parents, divorced couples, and extended families are beyond the scope of this book. Issues such as finding appropriate day care, selecting schools, permitting dating, or fostering healthy sibling relationships, however, are often the subjects adults in transition most want to discuss. Counselors of adults are likely to hear about the triumphs and travails experienced by their clients in their role as parents, and, life not being tidy, such experiences undoubtedly affect other aspects of their clients' lives.

Grandparenting Issues

For most people, becoming a grandparent is an exciting and heartwarming experience. For others, however, it may be an unwanted confrontation with their own aging or a mark of their children's "problems." Becoming a grandparent serves as a reminder of the continuity of the generations and provides an opportunity, to varying extents, to again help shape a young life. Conversely, the realization that one will not become a grandparent may be a prime example of a ripple non-event (Schlossberg & Robinson, 1993). When an adult child informs his or her parents about a decision not to or an inability to have children, this event can lead to unfulfilled expectations that alter the roles, relationships, and assumptions of the older person. A very disappointed "non-grandparent" may need to discuss this sadness.

Grandparenthood has become a focal point for researchers who have investigated its psychological dimensions, including social roles, legal rights following a divorce, and the impact of grandparenthood on mental and physical health. Some have described grandparenthood as a tenuous role that lacks clear, agreed-on behavior norms. Yet, others have stated that grandparents typically have many preconceived ideas and expectations regarding becoming a grandparent and, furthermore, that younger family members have expectations of grandparents, as well (Thomas, Sperry, & Yarbrough, 2000). Reactions to becoming a grandparent may depend in part upon the ages and life situations of the newborn's parents, as well as the life situation of the grandparent. Hagestad and Burton (1986) found that black women who became grandmothers "on time" were much more positive about their role than those who became grandparents "off time." Many who felt they became grandmothers too early said that the new role interfered with their own parenting, work, education, friendships, and romantic involvements.

Some actively rejected the role, bringing consequences to several generations.

Responsibility for raising grandchildren may be thrust upon some grandparents by a number of factors. At one time, this was a relatively infrequent situation, but the frequency of this phenomenon has increased dramatically. This situation has been attributed to both demographic trends and public health problems. Some scholars have pointed to longer lifespans, more highly active grandparents, increases in divorce and single parenting, and the rising rates of substance abuse, HIV/AIDS, and other health problems. Another topic of interest in this area is cultural norms and the frequency with which grandparents are raising their grandchildren. The frequency varies according to ethnicity, with the highest number among African American families (Thomas et al., 2000).

The clinical implications of grandparenthood were examined in several studies. Although increases in psychological well-being have been seen with grandparenthood in the traditional mode, grandparents may experience negative outcomes when they assume custody of grandchildren. This is a difficult transition, and these grandparents often experience ambivalence about the role, along with conflicted dynamics with their adult child who has relinquished the parenting responsibilities. In fact, these grandparents have higher than expected rates of depression. When their own children are abusive, incarcerated, or too ill to care for their grandchildren, these grandparents' difficulties tend to multiply. Low-income grandparents are at particular risk of decreases in physical and emotional health (Thomas et al., 2000).

The phenomenon of grandparents raising grandchildren has also captured the interest of the popular press and become the focus for support groups. *Family Circle* magazine frequently profiles "women who make a difference." One such profile (Waters, 1994), quoted a woman who captured the situation thus, "I felt guilty when some of my kids got on drugs. But now I'm gonna save my grandson." In recognition of the growth of the situation, the American Association of Retired Persons set up model programs and prepared resources for grandparents raising their grandchildren (American Association of Retired Persons, 1993).

Paradoxically, as more people become grandparents, the role becomes even less clear. Today's grandparents range in age from 30 to older than 100 and their grandchildren may be newborn or themselves retired. Some grandparents live with or very close to their grandchildren; others may be across the country or the world. One woman we know stopped complaining about her grandchildren being 300 miles away when she met a couple whose grandchildren were 3,000 miles away! Cherlin and Furstenberg (1992) identified three styles of grandparenting: companionate, remote, and involved. Companionate grandparents are affectionate, but somewhat passive in their behavior. They clearly see the child's parents as "in charge." Remote grandparents are geographically distant and thus have difficulty establishing intimate relationships with their grandchildren. Involved grandparents, in their terminology, are those who engage in active parenting. This style tends to emerge at times of crisis or transition, such as after the child's parents' divorce. If the children's mother is forced to devote more time and energy to earning a living, the grandparent may take over more of the child-rearing responsibilities.

Not infrequently grandparents may be asked by divorced children, usually daughters, if they may move back home. So-called "boomerang" children, with or without children of their own, clearly represent a lifestyle transition for all generations involved, and this may trigger a request for counseling.

Another issue that may bring grandparents to counseling is concern about losing contact with grandchildren. When parents divorce, grandparents on the noncustodial side, typically the father's parents, may find it difficult to maintain close relations with their grandchildren. After hearing rumblings about a separation or divorce in the family, a grandparent may tell a counselor, "I'm devastated for them and from a selfish point of view I'm terrified I'll lose contact with my grandchildren." Myers and Perrin (1993) noted, "To the extent that grandparents are denied access to grandchildren as a result of divorce, they may experience difficulty in resolving their own developmental issues, feel a sense of dissatisfaction with their lives, or feel that some part of themselves is missing or incomplete" (p. 64).

Counselors may help grandparents concerned about losing contact with their grandchildren by suggesting legal assistance, support groups, or appropriate reading material. In recognition of legal battles that may arise, grandparent-rights provisions are written into some divorce settlements. Some self-help groups provide information and support for people who fear or experience a major interruption in their relationship with the grandchildren. A poignant article by Lindeman (1987) entitled "Nana, I Can't Visit You" dealt with the plight of grandparents and grandchildren who are cut off from each other.

Counselors may hear of mixed feelings and values conflicts from people who become grandparents under nontraditional circumstances. One of our clients almost furtively showed pictures of a grandchild she yearned to hold but felt reluctant to visit because the child's parents were not married. On the other hand, there are grandparents who have a close relationship with the child of their gay son and a cordial relationship with the child's mother, who lives with her lesbian partner. In many families grandchildren, as well as their parents, may be highly involved in elder care, an important relationship issue to which we now turn.

Eldercare

Baby boomers have reached middle age, and their parents have become this nation's elderly (Shoptaugh, Phelps, & Visio, 2004). For many midlife adults, the realization that they are or may soon be responsible for caring for their parents can constitute a major life transition. Often the realization is triggered by the parent's sudden illness, which typically comes as a shock, even though to use Brody's (1985) now classic phrase, parent care has become a "normative family stress." The ubiquity of the problem can be understood by listening to informal conversations of people in midlife and reading the popular press and business publications, as well as by hearing concerns voiced by clients. There is even a special magazine, *Answers,* which its editors describe as "the only national consumer magazine devoted to the questions, issues, and concerns that arise when caring for an elderly parent or relative."

A special report in the magazine, *Money* (Hedberg, 1989), began with the following alert: "Face this fact: If you have a parent alive today, you likely have a crisis waiting for you somewhere down the road. Sooner or later that parent will need help. The problem . . . may be financial, medical, or emotional. Often it will be all three at once. And inevitably you will be central to the solution. However you choose to lend your support, . . . the effect upon your own life will undoubtedly be seismic" (p. 136). The warnings may be overstated, but they do point to a concern apt to be heard in many counseling sessions. Some adults who talk about feeling that they have changed roles with their parents may be helped by Silverstone's (1994) terminology. She described the change not as role reversal, but as moving from being dependent on parents to being dependable for them.

Becoming responsible for one's parents can radically change individuals' roles, responsibilities, and assumptions about themselves. Although most of us "know" that America is graying and that many older adults need some kind of assistance, it is very different when the older adult is "ours." In dealing with issues of eldercare, counselors are likely to hear a range of feelings including: love and concern for the parent, grief over the anticipated death of a parent, guilt over not being able to do enough, resentment over the interruptions in their own plans, confusion about where they need to invest their energies, or despair at realizing the situation may be out of their control.

Expectations about caregiving may be strongly influenced by the cultural background of both informal and formal caregivers. The training director of a large nursing home in an urban area talked of the difficulties that staff and family members have in understanding each other's values. The staff, who are primarily African American or foreign born, come from a culture that expects family members to take in "their" frail older adults. Therefore they assume that the families of the residents "don't really care" or else they would have their relatives at home. Many of the family members, most of whom are middle class and White, think they are making a good choice to give their relatives the best possible care and opportunities for socialization.

The baby boomers in midlife are frequently part of two-income households, and the feminization of the workforce is colliding with the need for eldercare. It is estimated that the number of employees with eldercare responsibilities range from 2% to 30%, with 20% as the most often cited figure (Shoptaugh et al., 2004). Traditionally, the vast major-ity of caregivers to the old have been women, primarily wives and daugh-ters, and daughters have provided even more long-term care than spouses. A prevalent and powerful theme in previous studies is that most all daughters and daughters-in-law accept the idea that parent care is a woman's role . . . and that they have been responsible for performing the instrumental, personal-care, and nursing tasks that are needed. The women also felt responsible for the emotional well-being of the older people. Indeed they often felt responsible for the happiness of everyone in their families (Brody, 2004, p. 79). Marty, our client, seemed to support this view. She expressed surprise, not that her mother-in-law didn't call her sons, but that she didn't call her other daughter-in-law.

In collecting data on the strains experienced by caregivers, Brody interviewed 1,500 women, 300 of their husbands, and 150 of their sib-lings. She noted that the women's problems were exacerbated by the per-sistent myth that adult children don't take care of their elderly parents the way they used to in the "good old days." "It is ironic that many of the parent-caring women themselves believe that myth . . . even though they do much more parent care than their counterparts in the past." Counselors who hear clients berating themselves for not doing enough may find it helpful to confront this misconception. Another area of explo-ration is that of role conflict, as women strive to balance their work roles with caring for their elderly family members.

Although most caregivers are women, Silverstone (1994) cautioned that we should not ignore the problems of male caregivers. Husbands and other male relatives may find themselves "odd man out" in terms of the provision of services.

Although children, particularly daughters, assume major responsi-bilities for eldercare, not all older adults have children. Special strains may come from caring for a frail relative who is not one's parent. Nieces and nephews, for example, may care for a childless relative largely out of loyalty to their deceased parents. Although older women in this country greatly outnumber older men, this is not true for all ethnic groups. Because many Chinese and Filipino men came to this country and either left wives at home or never married, there are large numbers of childless older men among these groups who have special needs and problems (Markides & Mindel, 1987). In helping clients with issues of eldercare, counselors may need to supplement their usual counseling techniques by providing case management services or making appropriate referrals.

Clients involved in caregiving may also be concerned about the impact on the rest of the family. Cutler (1985) talked about the spread of distress within a family and particularly the effect on grandchildren when an older family member has dementia. "The relationship between grandparents and grandchildren is often a close and special one, and when 'Grandpa' begins to be short-tempered and inappropriate, it can be devastating for the grandchildren" (p. 53). When a grandparent becomes incapacitated or dies, midlife adults may need to cope with their own grief as well as be a support to their children.

Death of a Parent

In terms of grief, counselors may find midlife adults surprised and confused by the extent of their reactions to the death of a parent. "Why am I so devastated when we knew it was coming?" is a common question counselors may hear. In a study of the impact of parent death, Douglas (1990) found that most of her sample reported that the death of a parent changed their outlook on life. They confronted their own mortality, and at the same time they grappled with feelings of being alone and orphaned. Respondents also noted that the death of a parent was often a trigger for personal growth as it inspired them to look more closely at their own lives and appreciate the relationships they had.

For many midlife adults the death of the second parent may trigger much stronger feelings than the death of the first. Upon the death of the first parent, concern and attention are typically focused on the surviving spouse. But when the second parent dies, adult children may become increasingly aware of and free to pay attention to their own loss and orphaned status. Some orphaned adults may find their new responsibilities as the older generation daunting; others may view it as an opportunity to matter in a new way. In either case, they are likely to become the primary communication channels in the family, letting others know who needs help or who is to be congratulated.

The death of a parent may drastically alter sibling relationships. In some families siblings become closer, realizing they can no longer communicate through the parent. In others, if the family has stayed together only because of the parent, siblings may drift apart. Counselors are more likely to hear about the latter situation. Discussions with friends who have experienced similar losses may be particularly helpful.

Friendships

Although the well-known saying is, "that's what friends are for," counselors may hear a wide variety of concerns regarding friends. Some adults who have experienced a major life transition worry about putting too much of a burden on their friends; others are disappointed in lack of support from friends. Some yearn for more and deeper friendships; others worry that the pressures of work and family prevent them from nurturing friendships, fearing that this neglect can have long-term as well as short-term negative effects.

In listening to clients' concerns about friendships, counselors need to be aware of gender differences that may affect the type and depth of friendships. Both research and conventional wisdom suggest that women do more self-disclosing and have more intimate relationships with same-sex friends than men. Rubin (1986) distinguished between male bonding, which arises from shared experiences and common physical or intellectual exploits, and male intimacy, which involves open expressions of thoughts and feelings. Male clients who do not understand this distinction may be surprised at their feelings of isolation, despite the presence of friends with whom they share interests.

In their study of patterns of friendship among male graduate students older than 35, Busse and Birk (1993) found that competitiveness was inversely related to self-disclosure. In addition, men who engaged in more self-disclosure perceived their friendships as being closer than those who disclosed relatively little. The authors suggest that counselors may help their male clients by making them aware of gender stereotypes and teaching them new ways of expressing feelings.

Friends are important to us throughout our lives. The crucial role of peers in the lives of adolescents is both a developmental task and the bane of many parents' existence. To adults, friends are often the people with whom they can "be themselves." In his definition, Peter (1978) said, "You can always tell a real friend: when you've made a fool of yourself, he doesn't feel you've done a permanent job" (p. 206). Going beyond the humor, our friends are often the people who help us keep our lives in balance and our sense of perspective in place.

Many transitions including geographic moves, job changes or retirement, divorce, or widowhood can lead to drastic changes in friendship patterns. As people look at the balance between their resources and deficits, friends may move from one column to the other as they become harder to access. In interviews with people in their 50s, Bergquist et al. (1993) found that many people treasured long-term friendships and believed there was not sufficient time to develop new deep relationships.

Quite a different view of late-life friendships is presented by Kidder (1993), who studied residents of a large long-term care facility. He talked enthusiastically of Lou and Joe, two men who had been assigned as roommates and became great friends. "The crucial thing about Lou and Joe is that they remain very good friends, better friends every time I visit. They present an antidote to despair, which is connectedness, and for me, I learned it is only the connectedness of the human tribe that can hold despair at bay" (p. 55).

Different groups of the population may have different friendship patterns. Lipman (1986) cited several studies showing that both older gay men and older lesbians have more friends than do heterosexuals of similar age. Such strong friendships may supplant or supplement traditional kinship support.

Sociologists have observed what they have termed as a distinct new phase in the life course regarding the transition to adulthood. This phase is characterized by movement in and out of independent living arrangements, including living with friends. Popular phrases have brought about newly coined terms such as *kidulthood* or *adultescence,* suggesting the blurring of youthful and adult roles. This shift has been attributed to the intensification of friendship networks among single people, including the greater significance of platonic (nonsexual) friendships. According to Pahl (2000), these friendships are increasingly part of the "social glue" of our contemporary society. He stated that these networks of friends act as a "social convoy" for support and self-identity into the 20s and 30s. As people continue to remain single for longer periods of time, friendship networks are taking on increased importance in their lives, often conceptualized and referred to as *family of choice* (Heith 2004).

In a study of older adults, Depner and Ingersoll-Dayton (1988) found gender differences in friendship. The men in their study were less likely to include friends as sources of social support, and therefore received less emotional support from friends and named fewer friends that they respected. Another key gender difference they found was that women reported receiving more emotional and health support from their adult children. They also found, however, that women younger than age of 65 were more likely to report having a confidante and that isolation increased as they grew older. By age 75 the women were actually more isolated than the men in this study.

Other studies suggest that friendships and partners meet different emotional needs. After studying couples who moved and individuals in Parents Without Partners, Weiss (1976) concluded that both people with partners, who have a limited network of friends, and people with large support networks but no intimate partner, can be lonely. People seem to need to be part of a social network to not experience social isolation;

people need intimacy to avoid experiencing emotional isolation. When counselors hear about either kind of void, they need to listen carefully for what clients are saying, perhaps unconsciously, about themselves. Such statements may be a signal that it is time to explore one of the recurring themes of adulthood.

RECURRING ISSUES

Marty, the client whose story started this chapter, expressed a number of concerns about herself and her values. She is involved in a new relationship, enmeshed in a blended family, and active in a work group. These relationships probably meet her needs for intimacy and belonging. In fact, she may be overcommitted and matter too much. Each of the major issues embedded in her story—intimacy, belonging, and mattering—is discussed below.

Intimacy

Intimacy is a major concern during the adult years. We may be intimate with a spouse, lover, parent, child, or friend as the term covers a wide range of close human relationships. The Random House Dictionary (2000) defined *intimacy* as "a close, familiar and usually affectionate or loving personal relationship with another person or group." Different people may describe intimacy differently, but the concept commonly involves relationships marked by strong caring, mutual support, openness, and a sense of being able to "be oneself" with another. Most people find a sense of intimacy to be an essential part of a complete life.

Concerns about intimacy—how to get it, keep it, or replace it—are issues frequently brought to counselors. We may see people who "glow" because of a new intimate relationship that adds warmth and color to their lives. Or we may see people whose lives look full, but who experience a void because they do not have a special person or persons with whom they feel really close. Many different kinds of transitions can trigger issues of intimacy. For example, loss of a relationship through death, divorce, a move, or a change in commitment, can cause adults a great deal of anguish. So can the realization that one is missing an important piece of a full life.

Adults experiencing similar transitions are likely to see very different options for themselves. An open discussion with three 60-year old widows illustrated this. One said, "I don't care about men. It's finding a man or woman with whom I can be close. I figure I have more chances with women." The other two disagreed, saying they care about men.

One said, "The demographics are against me. I'm miserable because I know I won't ever have another close relationship again." The other said, "I know I'll meet men—even if I have to run an ad in the local paper." Regardless of where they saw their options, all were discussing the pain of losing an intimate partner and were questioning how likely they were to be able to "reinvest" or replace their source of intimacy. Others may express doubt about whether a search for a replacement is worth the effort saying, "I don't ever want to hurt that much again."

According to Erikson's stage theory, achieving intimacy (vs. isolation) is a developmental task of young adulthood (Erikson, Erikson, & Kivnick, 1994). Experience suggests, however, that concerns about intimacy, like the other conflicts identified by Erikson, can surface or resurface at any stage of life. Hudson (1991) summed it up by stating, "In today's world, intimacy is a series of bonds and attachments, not merely a significant other" (pp. 11–12). The importance of close interpersonal relationships can hardly be exaggerated. To many people, the character of their relationships is what determines their level of happiness and/or life satisfaction. Close relationships have been found to be a significant buffer against the negative effects of stressful situations (Berkman & Syme, 1979; Pearson, 1990). Parkes (1982) observed that people without significant attachment or intimacy are often considered at risk, whereas those who have such significant relations are better able to cope with transitions. Moreover, intimacy and attachment are often what add zest to a person's life.

There seem to be significant gender differences in the ability to form intimate relationships. In their longitudinal study of adults, Fiske and Chiriboga (1990) reported, "One of our research-based observations is that losing a spouse is often more traumatic for men than for women because men are less likely to have really close relationships with anyone but their wives . . . men name their spouses as confidants far more often than women do" (p. 255). Thus, when a man's wife dies, he often loses his best friend along with the person who was responsible for his social life.

Despite increased attention to "men's issues" and the formation of men's support groups, (e.g., Bly, 1990; Doerr, 1993; Rubin, 1986), male friendships are often based on common interests and activities. However Bergquist et al. (1993) reported:

> By the time they reach midlife . . . men find themselves increasingly concerned about connectedness rather than differentiation . . . as they move into their fifties, men often try to establish a community. . . . They want to feel as if they belong and begin paying attention to their voices from other rooms that speak about increased sociability . . . or the importance of intimacy and interpersonal commitment. (pp. 58–59)

Women's investment in establishing close relationships is documented in the research of Bergquist et al. (1993), who observed that women define themselves in a context of human relationships. Such relationships are clearly involved in a sense of belonging, another major theme of adulthood.

Belonging

By the time we met Marty at the beginning of this chapter, she belonged in many places; that is, she was a part of a number of groups: home, family, work, in-laws, and so on. She had apparently worked hard after her divorce to make sure she belonged to her work group. For many counselees, however, lack of belonging can be a major problem. Consider the following statements that a counselor is apt to hear.

> "I've joined a new church, but I don't really feel like I belong. It sure is different from the church in our old neighborhood."

> "Joe and I belonged to a couples group that met once a month for dinner. We rotated from one house to another. After he died, I didn't know whether to stay with the group or not. A couple of people asked me to, but I wasn't sure they really meant it. Maybe they thought they had to. I went once and felt like a fifth wheel. I'm really more at ease when I'm with other widows or even just the wives. There is another dinner coming up next week and I just can't decide."

> "I just moved out of my girlfriend's house where I lived for 5 years. I really thought we'd get married some day, but it just didn't work out. Now I feel lonely and rudderless."

> "The holidays are coming up and I don't know what to do. I wish I could get in bed and stay there for about a month. Before my son and his wife got divorced they used to come to my house for almost all the holidays and I loved it. Now my son is married to someone else. My stepdaughter is nice but she has her own family. She asked me if I wanted to come for Thanksgiving but I don't feel like I really fit."

The clients above seem to be questioning where they belong. Their transitions have placed them in an unclear situation between belonging and marginality or, stated differently, between being central or peripheral to a particular group. Every time individuals move from one role to another or experience a transition, they risk becoming marginal. The larger the difference between the old and the new roles and the less knowledge people have about the new role, the more marginal they may feel. Counselors who can discuss this phenomenon with their clients may help them better understand their concerns about not feeling "part of it." Counselors can also help clients realize that this sense of marginality may be only temporary.

Societal changes also can affect an individual's sense of belonging. Increasing mobility and increasing divorce rates have meant that in many families, parents and children live far apart. The sense of not belonging experienced by many adults whose children have moved away is reflected in the title of an organization formed by an innovative religious organization. Members of the "Orphaned Parents Group" get together to discuss their concerns and provide support for each other and to hold group holiday celebrations so people have somewhere they belong.

While the orphaned parents are meeting in one city, their children may be feeling equally lonely in another part of the country, where they, too, may be working to build friendship groups or families of choice with whom they can share holidays. Such groups may include courtesy "aunts and uncles," close family friends who are given honorary titles that may make them feel more a part of the family.

Societal changes can have a particularly negative effect on older adults. Difficulties may stem from a combination of internal and external factors. The pervasiveness and the debilitating effects of loneliness have been pointed out in research. The focus of this research tended to be on personality factors and/or social contacts (Rokach, 2002). For example, in a study of loneliness and adjustment to old age, Hansson, Jones, Carpenter, and Remondet (1986) found that loneliness was related to both poor psychological adjustment and to dissatisfaction with family and social relationships. They noted that loneliness can stem from "an underlying lack of skill in living, perhaps including social skills, planning, and control over actions and internal thoughts . . . or loneliness may interfere with effective interpersonal functioning resulting in unpleasant and self-degrading emotional experiences" (p. 51).

Social and spiritual isolation are growing issues for those aging in a society that places high value on autonomy and independence (MacKinlay, 2001). For example, in a cross-sectional study of depression in old age, loneliness was reported by 29% of the sample and 16% felt lonely often. Frequent loneliness was reported as one of the strongest associations with pervasive depression. Women were 19% more likely to be lonely than men, and participants older than age 82 experienced higher rates of loneliness (Prince, Harwood, Blizard, Thomas, & Mann, 1997). In a study of the elderly in North America and Portugal, results indicated that cultural background influences the manner in which elderly people cope with loneliness. The North Americans reflected on, faced, and accepted feelings of loneliness. On the other hand, the Portuguese elderly were very rooted in and surrounded by their families, had less time to engage in solitary activities and didn't consider reflection as a way to cope with loneliness. North Americans scored higher on both distancing and denial as coping mechanisms as well. An interesting finding was that the use of prayer and the sense of belonging through church services was a highly reported strategy of the North Americans, but not by secular people. Although the Portuguese elderly reported praying regularly, they did not consider it as a coping strategy, but rather a familiar way of life (Rokach, 2002).

If counselors hear concerns about loneliness, they may want to help clients explore the basis for the loneliness and consider ways to find places where they belong or matter.

Mattering

Mattering, the need to be appreciated, noticed, and acknowledged, is a concern of people at all stages of life and can strongly influence behavior. The late sociologist, Morris Rosenberg, coined the term *mattering* to describe a universal, and overlooked motive. He pointed out how critical it is to believe that we count in other's lives and feel we make a difference to them. Mattering to oneself, others, and the world is the coordinating, although not single, issue that guides our understanding of our selves: Do I know who I am? Do I appreciate myself? Do I feel competent? Are my inside and outside worlds congruent? Do *others* appreciate me? Do work and community worlds make me feel needed? Rosenberg's concept of mattering is a universal, lifelong issue that connects us all (Rosenberg & McCullough, 1981).

To whom did Mark, high school graduate, having been a lead quarterback, and Lee Bradford, former founder and CEO of the National Training Lab, voice their despair, "I don't feel important to anyone." Though of different ages, dealing with different life decisions, they had much in common the summer Mark graduated from high school and Lee Bradford retired. Mark said, "Now that I am no longer a football star, who am I, who will I become?" Lee Bradford, expecting to be treated as a senior statesman, realized when he called someone for lunch that he was a "duty lunch." Both were unsure of their identity, their competence, and their future. Both were in limbo, experiencing major transitions. Mark could not stay in high school forever, and Lee could not remain a CEO forever. Neither felt that he mattered anymore.

Rosenberg and McCullough (1981) found that nondelinquent boys differed from delinquent boys in that the former felt they mattered to parents and teachers. Some schools have taken this idea and incorporated strategies to have students feel that they matter. All adult staff, from teachers, administrators, janitors, bus drivers, and lunch ladies, are on call for at-risk students. When a student comes to the attention of the staff, one person takes that student as their own. This person then seeks out the student, asks how he or she is doing, and follows up with teachers on grades; in other words, takes an interest and shows this student that he or she *matters* to someone.

We need to look at ways people matter to others in their lives. One widow said, "I'll never be number one for any one else again." Grandchildren, whose parents are incarcerated or are addicted to drugs and who are often shifted between parents and grandparents, do not know to whom they belong or to whom they matter. This is also the plight of children in the foster care system. And once they reach the age of 18, they are then on their own. Mattering is sometimes key to survival. For example, depressed people who think they matter to family and friends are less likely to commit suicide. A rationale for pet or horticultural therapy is that having responsibility for the care of a pet or a plant helps people know they still matter.

Mattering to others in relationships is not enough. For example, talk radio offers people an opportunity to express themselves, which results in the sense that they matter, that their views count, and that they are being heard. People who choose to become politically active can also find a venue to express their opinions and to possibly make a difference.

Individuals who are unemployed or underemployed often feel they are living in a never land. Why are they not able to get jobs, feed their families, and live lives of dignity? Again, the need is to matter, to be treated with dignity, and to be noticed rather than shoved away.

The sense of mattering played out on a large scale when the hurricanes and floods hit the Gulf Coast of the United States in 2005. Many individuals were left for days in their attics or on their roofs, clinging for survival, and many felt forgotten or overlooked while they watched in anguish as their loved ones perished around them. Those in shelters experienced a similar crisis in mattering, for example, some elderly persons who were left on gurneys next to those who had already died. The nation watched in horror as witnesses to what could be termed as a *national crisis in mattering*. Many believed that they were ignored because they were poor or Black. Mattering to others and to the larger community is critical to one's sense of well-being. Yet, it is mattering to oneself, to feeling that one is centered or harmonious and can take the vicissitudes of life that is most often the bottom line.

To be sure, our client Marty may have mattered to too many people, but the opposite is more often the concern of those in transition. The rejected lover may think, "If my former partner no longer cares about me, I may not matter to anyone." What has been called the empty nest syndrome is an example of a loss of mattering. Some people—men and women alike—feel that they are no longer important after their children leave home. Others view the emptying of the nest as a transition to a potentially exciting new stage of life. If adult children return home and refill the nest, it may be another example of mattering too much.

Mattering is clearly an issue outside of families as well as inside them. Employees who talk about constant put-downs and lack of appreciation at work, as well as people who complain that their teachers do not listen to them, may feel they do not matter. Schlossberg, Lynch, and Chickering (1989) gave examples of how adult learners might be helped to feel they matter to the school, basing their discussion on five dimensions of mattering identified by Rosenberg and McCullough (1981): attention, importance, dependence, ego-extension, and appreciation. For example, adult learners are more likely to feel accepted if they have a place to put their things and receive mail and messages. Adult learners may feel important if there is evidence that someone cares about what they want and notices if they miss a class.

These same dimensions of mattering can be crucial to an adult facing a relationship transition. For example, a person who has lost a partner may experience lack of attention, feel unimportant, and think, "Nobody depends on me, is proud of my accomplishments, or appreciates what I do."

ASSESSING RESOURCES: LOOKING AT THE 4 S's

When counselors hear concerns about interpersonal issues, it should alert them to use the transition model to help clients analyze their resources for coping with the change in their lives. Each client brings to a transition a unique combination of Situation, Self, Supports, and Strategies. In discussing interpersonal transitions, clients typically talk first about the situations in which they find themselves. Counselors can then ask them to consider more carefully what they are saying about themselves. It is also important to hear what clients say about their support system and learn something about the strategies they have used in the past.

Situations

Let us take another look at Marty's situation. Marty and her husband seem to be in the throes of what has been termed the *dromedary/camel phenomenon,* or the *out-of-sync career commitment curve* (Goodman & Waters, 1985), a not uncommon problem experienced by couples in late midlife. Men who have invested themselves highly in their careers for many years come to a decision that they want to turn to other interests and spend more time with the family. Their career commitment curve, which has "one hump," like a dromedary, has peaked and is on the way down. At the same time, their wives, whose interest may have peaked earlier and then dropped down during their child-rearing years (whether or not they were working), rises again as child-rearing responsibilities diminish. Like a camel, their career commitment curve has "two humps."

In an article in the *New York Times,* Lewin (1993), referring to several studies on the impact of retirement, reported, "In many cases, husbands and wives find themselves troublingly out of sync as they approach retirement age. Husbands who have worked for 40 years may be eager to leave their job pressures behind, while wives who entered the work force late find those same pressures exhilarating." Retirement often precipitates a renegotiation of marital roles, a situation that may bring one or both members of the couple to a counselor.

In terms of the facets to be considered when examining one's situation, the trigger for Marty to seek counseling may have been her need to decide about the training opportunity. Timing is an issue because she and her husband are in different phases of their careers. If Marty takes the training and receives a promotion, it may well lead to a role change, which may affect her relationships with her coworkers as well as her view of the importance of work in her life. The duration of the transition issue is not clear. Her bosses' suggestion to send her for training is an external stimulus, but the decision about the training is hers, so it represents an internal locus of control. A counselor can help Marty assess these situational factors and decide which aspects of the possible change she sees as positive, as negative, or as benign. The counselor can also help her explore her internal resources for coping with change.

Self

Many clients find it difficult to talk about, or even identify, their internal resources. These resources include the degrees to which they are optimistic or pessimistic in outlook, able to tolerate ambiguity, or inclined to act autonomously. Helping clients know themselves and clarify their values and their assumptions about themselves is a key part of self-assessment.

Fox and Halbrook (1994) examined the changes in how low-income women saw themselves after they ended a relationship with a male partner. The women, who were between the ages of 33 and 42 and had two or more children, went through a "three-phased process . . . 1) an early phase designated by original assumptions and "happily ever after" dreams; 2) a period of disintegration of original assumptions resulting in "shattered dreams"; and 3) a final phase when [the] women were actively involved in reconstructing new, meaningful assumptions" (p. 152).

It is interesting to note that although these interviews were conducted in the early 1990s, after several decades of the current women's movement, women in the first phase consistently subordinated their interests to those of their husbands. They also subscribed to strong beliefs about what women should do, say, and feel to maintain their marriage relationships. When they reached Phase 2, shattered dreams, the women tended to blame themselves, often labeling themselves as failures because their marriages did not last. One woman whose husband abused her talked of her responsibility for his anger, explaining, "I guess I couldn't please him." As they moved to the third phase and began to reconstruct assumptions about themselves, they had to confront their own identity with the profound question, "If I am not who I thought I was, then who am I?"

Counseling interventions helped these women. The authors observed that after considerable work, "independence developed confidence; many discovered resilience and other assets which helped them cope. Their self-esteem began to expand, and they felt stronger, more in control" (p. 17).

Unlike the women in the above study, Marty came for counseling to make a choice, not deal with a fait accompli. A counselor could help Marty examine her work and family values, her sense of autonomy, her self-efficacy, and her spirituality. The counselor could also direct her attention to her support system and help her look at ways to utilize it more advantageously.

Support

As we listen to adults in transition talk about their relationships, support is often an integral part of the discussion. Indeed, providing emotional and instrumental support may be considered at least a partial measure of what constitutes a close relationship. However, such relationships can change over time. One older woman, whose close friends and relatives were suffering from many disabilities, told us in a weary tone, "My support group is no longer supportive. I still love them, but they're a drain now." Another woman joined a women's support group after her husband's death and found she had trouble being heard in the group, which tended to focus on "male bashing." In some ways Marty's support system has become a drain or a liability as well as an asset. A counselor who hears this concern may be able to help Marty understand the changing nature of her support system and consider strategies for redressing the balance between nourishers and drainers.

Social support can be a major buffer enabling adults to cope with stressful situations. It can be provided by intimate relationships, family members, networks of friends, or by institutions. A paradox of support systems is that at the very time they may be most needed, during major transitions such as divorce, widowhood, or a long-distance move, they may be most in jeopardy.

When helping adults cope with transitions, it is important to listen to their ideas of who and what serve as supports for them. Counselors may hear concerns not only about the presence or absence of supportive people but also about the way friends and family provide support. After finishing a trying course of radiation treatments, a colleague who had breast cancer wrote about what she most needed from her friends (White, 1992):

> During a recent bout with cancer, I went through all the stages of grief. In the process, I relearned the importance of receiving helpful help, and that unhelpful help can actually hurt. . . . Help came from many sources, and I feel lucky to have such a good support system. When special friends would call and tell me I sounded stronger, so they knew I was making progress, I would feel encouraged . . . [but I also received unhelpful help] from well-meaning friends of long standing. One told me about radiation sickness horror stories. . . . I asked my family to keep her posted about my progress, so I didn't have to talk to her. . . . Yet another friend seemed to have difficulty accepting my cancer, describing it as "my health challenge" while announcing that we would only speak of pleasant things. Fortunately I had enough power at the time to tell her that I needed to be with friends who would accept my need to be honest about the fact that I have cancer. While I had yet to find it pleasant, I did need to talk about it. She is still my friend but she does tip-toe up to me. (pp. 7–8)

Few clients are as clear and articulate about what they want from friends as this woman, but as helpers we can encourage clients to identify and express their needs. This is important as the needs of people in the same situation may vary considerably. Another coworker with breast cancer, for instance, wanted very different support from her friends. She chose to talk about her cancer with only a limited number of people and wanted her friends to keep her involved in social activities to the extent that her strength permitted.

Research findings support the concept that social support is one of the most effective strategies that people use to cope with stress. Social support has been generally defined as the experience of being loved and cared for and esteemed and valued, all within a social network of responsibilities, assistance, and communication. This social network may include immediate family members and other relatives, friends, and social or community links and owning a pet (Taylor, 2005; Taylor et al., 2004).

The increased attention to the concept of social support is evident within the fields of counseling and psychology. Research findings support the positive impact of psychosocial support, which has been associated with resistance to stress, increased coping ability, and overall sense of physical and mental well-being. Support can include close attachments, social support, and money. These are considered key resources for people in that they may lead to higher levels of self-efficacy and optimism (Hobfoll, 2002).

Support comes in many forms and may include tangible assistance, information, or emotional support. These types of support could range from monetary assistance to easing discomfort in facing an uncomfortable situation. Although support is helpful in both nonstressful and challenging situations, the benefits are more obvious during highly stressful periods. Assisting a person in transition could include helping him or her to better comprehend the stressful event and to select the appropriate resources and coping strategies that could be implemented. It is important to note, however, that not all forms of social support are effective but rather are dependent on matching the support to the person's needs (Taylor, 2005).

In a study of people facing elective surgery and their levels of anxiety, Krohne and Slangen (2005), found that gender played a role regarding perceived social support. Female patients with the lowest levels of support experienced the highest levels of anxiety. For these women, perceiving that they had no emotional support was a significant stressor. Culture plays a role in social support, as well. Individuals from cultures that prize interdependence view people as fundamentally connected, whereas Western cultures typically view people as independent and separate from others. For example, three studies of Asians, both in their home countries and in the United States, found that they reported less use of social support for coping with stress. It is likely that culture played a key role in this finding because of a concern with the possible consequences of seeking social support, which could include being criticized, losing face, making the situation worse, and disturbing the harmony of the group (Taylor et al., 2004). These types of studies underscore the importance of considering the effects of both gender and culture when one is working with clients experiencing transitions.

George Gazda expressed the hope that Pearson's (1990) book, *Counseling and Social Support*, will refocus counselors on "the importance of utilizing natural and social support groups in the counseling process" (p. 9). Such an orientation should sensitize counselors to listen more attentively to what clients have to say about the kind and amount of support they get from their close relationships. It may also assist them in determining whether problems with a support system stem from problems with the client or with the external sources of support. For example, a person going through a divorce may find that his or her friends feel they have to choose sides. If they choose the former spouse, the client may feel additional rejection and lack of support.

As mentioned earlier, Kahn and Antonucci (1980) suggested that we think of support systems in terms of convoys. They picture individuals moving through their life cycles surrounded by other people on whom they rely for support and to whom they provide support. As depicted in Figure 3.2 in Chapter 3, they envision a person as the center of a ring of concentric circles. This method of visualizing support enables us to see the impact of a transition upon an individual's support system. For example, geographical moves can negatively affect the relationship of husband and wife. Those wives who do not want to move, but who agree for the sake of the family, may experience deep resentment and anger. This may change their relationship from one of being close to becoming "intimate enemies." If a retired couple moves from an area with many supports to a place with no supports, the transition can be very difficult. If, however, an individual moves to an area with more support than in the one left, the transition will be much easier. Thus, an important element in listening to clients talk about their transitions is to consider the effect upon their convoy. This focus may help you to identify strengths and weaknesses in the client's support system.

Major transitions can affect not only receiving support but giving it. Pearson (1990) noted that "most long-standing support relationships are reciprocal in nature. Therefore, one of the issues a person may confront on the death or disability of a loved one is what to 'do' with the love, affection, companionship, and material assistance that had previously been expended on the lost one" (p. 31).

Losing the ability to give can also stem from one's own disability. One woman, Millie, who lost a leg to complications of diabetes, became depressed over her inability to take care of other people as she had done all of her life. After listening to the woman and talking with various volunteer centers, her counselor was able to help her find a telephone job with a local hospital. She called newly discharged patients who lived alone at regular intervals to make sure they were all right. This was a win-win situation: Millie was helped, and the discharged patients felt that they mattered.

Another perceptive woman, temporarily immobilized by a hip problem, said, "I think I've always gotten support, and felt good about myself, by being a support. Now that I'm having to stay off my feet for several months, I'm finding it really hard to ask for help." It helped her to learn the meaning of the term *cosmic accounting* (S. Uhle, personal communication, 1988), which refers to the need for people to be in relative balance in terms of the amount of help they give and receive. She realized that her reluctance to ask for help deprived members of her support system of the opportunity to assist her. As a result, she began to work on a new strategy to deal with her, she hopes, temporary transition to the state of invalid.

Strategies

Here is the list of coping strategies. In the first column, check off the ones you are now using for your transition. In the second column, check off the ones you'd like to try out.

It is important for counselors to help people identify the strategies they have used for coping with past relationships. Counselors can ask clients how they made friends or dealt with past family tensions. By listening carefully to the answers, both counselor and client may learn about the client's decision-making styles as well as his or her experiences and feelings about intimacy, belonging, and mattering.

Possible Coping Strategies +	*Now Using*	*Will Try*
Change/Modify Situation through Problem-Solving		
Negotiating	___	___
Taking optimistic action	___	___
Seeking advice	___	___
Asserting yourself	___	___
Brainstorming new plan	___	___
Taking legal action (if needed)	___	___
Change Meaning of Situation through Reappraisal		
Applying knowledge of transition process	___	___
Rehearsing	___	___
Developing rituals	___	___
Making positive comparisons	___	___
Rearranging priorities	___	___
Relabeling or reframing	___	___
Selectively ignoring	___	___
Using denial	___	___
Using humor	___	___
Having faith	___	___
Managing Reactions to Stress		
Playing	___	___
Using relaxation, meditation, prayer	___	___
Expressing emotions	___	___
Doing physical activity	___	___
Participating in counseling/therapy/support groups	___	___
Reading	___	___

Other Strategies

_____

_____

_____

_____

Figure 5.1   Possible coping strategies.

To help clients assess their coping strategies, counselors may wish to give them the "Your Coping Keys Worksheet" (Figure 5.1). This worksheet enables clients to identify strategies they currently use, as well as others they might include in their repertoire. They can ask themselves: Are there new strategies I can use to change or modify the situation, change the meaning of it for me, or change the way I manage my reactions to it?

In working with Marty, for example, we could learn how she handled her divorce, how she related to her former husband, her children, and her friends and family and also how she reached out to coworkers as a source of friendship. In looking at the meaning of her present situation, we might ask her how she would rearrange her priorities if she were promoted. She might need to practice ways to ask for help with some of her family responsibilities. Given the tremendous pressures she is under, we might inquire about the stress management strategies she uses and suggest additional ones.

People, such as Marty, who are contemplating role changes, may find it useful to consider how they handled previous changes. For example, if they moved in the past, what did they do to integrate themselves into the social fabric of the new community? When they first became engaged, how did they relate to their partner's family? Counselors can ask questions such as these to learn more about the relationships and coping skills of their clients.

SUMMARY

In this chapter we have identified a number of relationship transitions involving role gains and role losses, discussed three major themes of adult development—intimacy, belonging, and mattering—and looked at ways to use the 4 S's of the transition model to listen more effectively to what clients tell us about how they handle relationship changes. Some people may have chosen to ignore or gloss over feelings generated by family transitions in the past; others may have always confronted them head on. People who cope effectively use a variety of strategies, and counselors need to listen carefully to their stories so as to help them identify and expand their repertoire of coping skills.

CHAPTER 6

Work Transitions

Joe Jones, a 40-year-old machinist, tells a career counselor the following:

I've been a machinist since I was 18. I learned the trade in the Army and stayed with it when I got out. I never really chose it; the Army assigned me to the training and I did well at it, so I kept at it. I'm good with my hands. I can still make a good living as a machinist, but the new technologies are changing the work. If I do have to get more training or go back to school, I don't know if I want to do it as a machinist. My boss says he'll help me pay for night school training, and my wife says I should do it. They both nag me to sign up for classes at the local community college, but I don't ever seem to make the call. I don't know what I want to do.

When I was in high school, I was more interested in hanging out with my buddies than I was in studying. I graduated and went straight into the service. I was never much of a student. I don't think I could hack it today. I got married right out of the Army, and my kids are getting ready to go to college. My oldest starts this fall. I don't want them to see me struggle with what they find easy. Also, school takes a lot of time. When I was younger I worked long hours, hardly ever saw my kids, and had little time for fun. Now I have enough seniority to work the day shift. I hate to give up the time with my family and the time for myself. I have my softball team, and I like to work in the garden. My kids are almost grown and this may be my last chance to spend a lot of time with them. I hate to give that up.

What I'd really like is to start my own business. I've always dreamed of being my own boss! My brother owns a neighborhood bar, and he'd like me to come in with him. He isn't making much yet, but with both of us working at it, I think we could do well. I've always gotten along well with people; that's one reason I'm tired of being a machinist. It's kind of lonely. I guess I don't really know what I'm good at. I just kind of fell into being a machinist. I took some kind of test in the Army, and they assigned me to machinist training.

My wife stayed home when the kids were young and went back to school a few years ago to become a nurse, her lifelong dream. She has just started working full-time and is still low seniority, working the worst shifts, and not getting paid very well. She wants me to stay in my job so we can afford the kids' college expenses. She says I make good money, and that's true, but I'm just not happy. I'm 40. Soon it's going to be too late for me to change. Maybe it's too late already. I've done the same thing my whole life; maybe I'm too old to change. I've never made this kind of major change in my life. My sister-in-law changes jobs all the time, and it seems to work out for her, but I don't know if I can do that. What if it doesn't work out? Can I handle that? I just don't know. I just don't seem to be able to make a decision. I want to be sure that I'm doing the right thing. What do you think I should do?

Joe Jones's issues are typical of those of many adults in a career transition. He is questioning not only what work he does but also the place of work in his life. He is saying that work is no longer as central, or salient, as it was when he was younger. He has a sense of mastery, or self-efficacy, around being a machinist but is unsure what will happen if he changes jobs. He wonders if he has the resilience to risk change and is unsure about how to do so, and he questions the balance between work and family life. He has changed over the years to become more family oriented, and he does not want to disturb this balance.

To understand Joe's Situation during his transition, it is important to look at the trigger, timing, source of control, concurrent stress, and his previous experience with a similar transition. As we use our transition model to analyze Joe's major issues relating to Self, we see that it is important to consider salience, balance, resilience, self-efficacy, and meaning-making. Joe's Support system includes his wife and children, his brother, and his boss. There is no mention of colleagues or subordinates, often a part of a work support system. Apparently Joe views his work as something he does alone. The Strategies Joe is using include exploring alternatives and seeking help from a counselor. Having used Joe's story to highlight the above issues, we now turn to an examination of some of the other types of work transitions experienced by adults and to the strategies they may use to manage these transitions.

ISSUES RELATED TO SITUATION

Joe is not experiencing his transition in a vacuum. The world in which he lives had an impact on what is happening to him and on the possible outcomes of his transition. His personal history makes his situation unique, as each individual's does. The following discussion covers some of the situation factors identified in Chapter 3 that are likely to play out in the life of an individual involved in a work transition.

Triggers

When people experience a work transition, especially when it is unanticipated, they may come to counseling feeling that they are in crisis. Counselors may want clients to consider their values, interests, temperaments, and the like, as they make new career decisions, but clients experiencing bad times may be too frightened to consider anything but their immediate needs for security. They may resist life planning as being more complex than they wish. The search for simple answers is a common one. Counselors have an obligation to explain the process and explain what makes effective decisions, as opposed to merely efficient decisions. In many cases there may be what can be called an *unconscious conspiracy* between counselor and client to avoid ambiguity, short circuit the process, and arrive at what has been a premature foreclosure. Lovén (2003) found that clients wanted their counselors to "fix everything," whereas counselors were trying to teach the clients self-directedness in their career decision-making. Lovén described this as a conflict, "between a post-modern view in research and international debate and a counsellor's [sic] everyday practice, which is still based in the 20th century" (p. 126).

The Bureau of Labor Statistics (1998) estimated that the average baby boomer in the United States held 9.6 different jobs from the ages of 18 to 36. Peterson (1995) stated that "most people entering the work force today will have three to five careers and eight to ten jobs" (p. xiv). According to a report in *USA Today* (July 9, 2003, p. 1B) in 2002, 85% of workers who changed jobs switched industries, up from 11% in 2001, although 66% said they would be happy spending the rest of their career with their current employer. The basic structure of the labor force has also changed. These changes are a result of the combination of changing birth rates, the entry of large numbers of women into the workforce—from 30% in 1950 up to an estimated 48% in 2050—the aging of the workforce and its increased diversity (Toossi, 2002).

Career counselors often hear from clients a sense of urgency bordering on panic. One way to diminish that panic is to look simultaneously at immediate solutions, that is, a job right now, and long-term goals, that is, work that fuels a sense of accomplishment. It is interesting to note, however, that a 1991 public opinion survey found in that only 51% of people surveyed indicated that a feeling of accomplishment was what they wanted most in a job (Elmer, 1994). To recast the old adage, you must feed a man while teaching him to fish—you can't learn on an empty stomach.

The changing workplace and his boss's "suggestion" that he upgrade his skills triggered Joe Jones's transition. He received his training as a machinist approximately 20 years ago. Technology has changed drastically in those 20 years, and he has not kept up with the changes. We heard him describe how he needs to either retrain or leave. His boss has offered to help him with tuition, but the message is clear. He must update his skills to keep his job. And he is listening to the message.

Not all workers are so foresightful or so lucky. Many workers do not heed the message and are forced into an unwanted transition when their place of business shuts down or downsizes and they are laid off. Others experiencing work transition may have very different triggers. Some may be seeking increased responsibilities or better pay. There are many triggers—what they have in common is that they create change in the life of the individual.

Timing and Concurrent Stress

Two aspects of timing have an impact on Joe's transition—the state of the economy and the time in his own life. Joe is thinking about upgrading his skills or changing jobs at a time when other things are going smoothly, but one in which he needs a consistent income—remember that college tuition! He is also responding to a future need, to have more high-tech skills or a more meaningful job, rather than a present emergency such as being laid off. One individual may have a good support system and few responsibilities; another may be a single parent living far from family and also battling a serious illness. Each of these timing and stress issues is mediated by the individual's perception of them.

We not only need to consider when a transition takes place in the life of the individual, but we also must look at the state of the economy. It is far easier to cope with a work transition during economic "ups" than it is during down times. When there is full employment, jobs are easy to find—it is a "seller's market." During recessions even highly skilled people may struggle to find new employment. We must also keep in mind that employment conditions vary greatly by locality. The ups and downs of the automobile industry are a classic example of this.

It is easier to contemplate "reskilling" when a joint union–management program prepays your tuition, your employer gives you released time, or your local adult education program is free, than it is when the costs and time are all your own. These benefits, too, often reflect the state of the economy. Joe, apparently, has some time to make his decision. He must upgrade to stay in his field, but the local economy seems to allow for the possibility of a successful small business. During a recession, neither of these options might be available.

Control/Source

Stan Popovich was a successful tax attorney, who wanted to help people as he had been helped when he had a substance abuse problem. He decided to go back to school and get a degree in counseling, specializing in addictions, planning to work in an inpatient setting in a hospital when he completed his degree. Jennifer Washington was another attorney facing a career transition, in her case because she developed chronic fatigue syndrome and could not work the long hours her job required. For whom was the transition more difficult? We cannot answer that question without knowing a great deal more about both lawyers, but we can speculate that it was easier for Stan Popovich because the decision was his. In the same way people who seek transfers, promotions, or new career areas are likely to adjust more easily than those who have change thrust upon them, depending on their other resources.

Control can be achieved in ways other than being the source of the transition. People who can do two things will find it easier to find a new job than those who can only do one; those who can do three will find a new job easier than those who can do two, and so forth. Individuals who must change jobs have more control over the situation if they are adaptable. Similarly, they have more control over the transition if they have more education, have a good network, are healthy, and are not members of a group often discriminated against in the workplace.

Several large corporations have negotiated wage and salary contracts with their unions that include higher pay for knowing more work tasks, rather than basing raises solely on seniority. This recognition of the value of flexibility reflects a dramatic change in the needs of the workplace as well as in the goals of labor negotiations.

Many career counselors recommend that all of their clients have a "Plan B" (Schlossberg and Robinson, 1996) because in today's world, it is wise to be prepared for change. Clients who take that advice when faced with a career transition have more control than those who are unprepared. Joe's foresight places him in the lucky position of managing his own career transition.

Previous Experience with a Similar Transition

Ben Franklin is credited with saying, "Experience is a dear school." The lessons from experience may be hard, but they are valuable. Consider a 60-year-old man who worked for the same company for his entire working life, who lost his job due to a merger. Consider another 60-year-old man in this same situation who has held six different positions in his working life—losing the last three to similar corporate decision-making. We might say he was unlucky to have had to handle this sort of transition three times, but we could certainly credit him with expertise in making work transitions! Furthermore, he probably has more confidence in his ability to change than man number one. After all, he has done it before.

Transferable skills are usually described as being those skills that one can carry from one job to another, such as organizational or communication abilities or the ability to read a technical manual. Perhaps a critical transferable skill in today's global economy is that of knowing how to make changes. Just as with other transferable skills, the new task need not be identical to the old. A person can learn the skill of making changes by moving, or by working in a variety of volunteer capacities, or by being involved in a workplace that is undergoing transformation. The trick is to recognize the learning and be able to apply it in the new situation. Joe has not told us about any previous experience with a similar transition except that of mustering out of the armed services and moving into private employment. With judicious questioning a counselor may find that he has had several others. If not, his change will be that much more difficult.

Summary

As you listen to your clients in transition, pay attention to what they tell you about what has triggered their transition, the timing of it in their lives and in the world situation, and the concurrent stress they are experiencing. All these will have an impact on the meaning of the transition, as well as on your clients' ability to manage it. It is also useful to keep in mind the degree to which your clients make the choice, how much control they feel they have over the transition, and their past experience with similar transitions.

ISSUES RELATED TO SELF

The transition model encourages us to gather information about clients' internal worlds—their selves. We will now look at four Self issues as they relate to work transitions.

Salience and Balance

Work is a major component of the lives of most adults, but clearly not the only component. The interplay of work, love, and play is what we mean by balance; the place of work in one's life has been called its *salience*. Super (1980) developed a widely cited life rainbow to graphically represent this idea. The rainbow includes the life roles of child, student, leisurite, citizen, spouse, homemaker, parent, and pensioner, as well as worker. He postulated that one can ascertain the relative importance (salience) of work and other major life roles "in the life scheme of the client" (p. 19).

Let us consider how the rainbow might look for a young mother, age 30, with two preschool children. The woman, an engineer, is on a fast track with her company, with the attendant demands of long working hours. One might speculate that her rainbow will have wide bands for work and parent, medium ones for spouse and homemaker, and narrow ones for leisurite and citizen. Let us look also at how the rainbow might look for a 60-year-old single female school teacher, with three grown children and no grandchildren. Her widest bands are likely to be worker, leisurite, and citizen, with smaller bands for parent and homemaker. For both of these people, work is an important aspect of their lives. But what of a young man, father of three, doing occasional part-time work and staying home with his children while his wife works to support the family? How might his rainbow look? Clearly it would have wide bands for parent and homemaker, a very small band for worker, and perhaps medium bands for citizen and leisurite. In his case, work is not a particularly salient aspect of life.

Hughes and Graham (1990) suggested that adults go through cycles of initiation, adaptation, reassessment, and reconciliation in each of six life roles, similar to those in Super's (1980) rainbow: relationships with self, work, friends, community, partner, and family. We can interpret Joe's current dissatisfaction with life as being primarily caused by his dissatisfaction with his work role. It is also important to look at his other life roles and help him assess both their current salience and his current comfort level in each, considering where he is in Hughes and Graham's (1990) cycles. Is he in the process of reassessing his place in the community? Is he perhaps in the stage of initiation in his relationship with himself? It is not uncommon for people to seek a change in one life role, even though the actual source of their discomfort arises out of another role.

People frequently come to career counselors looking to change jobs, because it is "safer" to talk about career concerns than to face personal problems. A sensitive counselor needs to listen for this kind of displacement and help adults consider whether or not they really want to make a change, and if so, in what area of their lives—internal issues, relationships, work, or all three.

Counselors may also see clients who come to their offices expressing concern about their relationships, using this to mask other issues. After appropriate trust has been established and after the counselors have had an opportunity to hear about the concern, they may find that other issues underlie the stated problem or even replace it in importance. Some clients may be experiencing a fear of aging and think that a new job would cure all their problems. Some may be avoiding their spouse's confrontation of their alcohol abuse, or they may be unhappy at work and too afraid to face the implications of that unhappiness, "blaming," instead, an unsatisfactory relationship.

In their study of adults with orthopedic and soft tissue injuries, Britnell, Madill, Montgomerie, and Stewin (1992) found persuasive evidence for the salience of work in the lives of many adults. These adults, whose average age was 35, typically wanted to and did return to work with significant pain, making necessary accommodations in their leisure and family time to do so. Interestingly, even though their injuries often resulted in lesser participation in their working roles, they did not result in a reduced commitment to that role. It is important to remember the distinction between participation and commitment when an injury or other external event forces reduced work time—when, for example, a client has to care for elderly parents or returns to school. Counselors may hear such clients' frustration with their inability to act on the work salience they feel. They may hear hopes from some that they will be able to return to full work participation in the future or expressions of grief for the permanent loss of such possibilities. It is always important to remember, however, that some, for whom work is not particularly salient, may welcome the reduced participation.

As counselors listen to clients in career transition, it is important to remember that for some, work is a major life role, whereas for others, different roles are ascendant such as home and family or leisure. Super and Nevill (1984) found that work salience was perhaps *the* important determinant of career adaptability. It is important to listen for values statements as clients describe their situations or the decisions they face. A transition may be a time to take a fresh look at values or to consider how current values may be better implemented.

In a "personal experience" article in *The New York Times,* Scofield (1993) described his own accommodation with the realization that he, in his mid-40s, probably would not get any more promotions, therefore offering him freedom from considering how each act would affect his job, freedom to speak his mind at work, and freedom to spend more time with his family. "Some would say I've lowered my goals to meet reality. I say I've exchanged career goals for a vision of life. I have never felt happier or more content. There's much more to my life today than just making a living" (p. 22). In other words, his work has become less salient, his family more so. Hansen's (1997) work on *Integrative Life Planning* is focused on this concept of looking at the balance of life roles.

Anecdotal evidence of changes in work salience in midlife is extensive. This change may be triggered by external events such as plateauing at work, as described above, by the birth of children or grandchildren, or by the retirement of a spouse. Or it may be triggered by internal feelings of boredom with work or a need to be more connected with family and community, discussed elsewhere. A 60-year-old returning student said, "I have made enough money to be comfortable. I have proved I can be a success in business. Now I want to give back. This man returned to a career in teaching he had abandoned many years earlier. A woman we know whose older husband had retired many years earlier said, "It is time to spend more time with him, to be more available for my children and grandchildren, and to play more. So I am retiring from my job." This woman stayed active in her profession, but gained the flexibility to choose her own activities and her own timetable.

There are indications that for people in their 20s and 30s, family and friends come before work. "Americans' interests have expanded, meaning time for family, themselves, and their personal pursuits, crowd and sometimes overcome their commitment to work . . . 'People's view of work is not all-encompassing anymore,' says Douglas Fraser, former president of the United Auto Workers. . . . 'The changes in the workplace in the last ten years are greater than any in my lifetime'" (Elmer, 1994). Achieving balance between work and personal life seems to be a growing need in our culture. One of the ironies we find here is that while downsizing of companies results in many unemployed people struggling to maintain themselves and their families, those left in the workplace are working longer hours, are under more pressure, and are looking for ways to reduce their work commitments.

For Joe, also, his work as a machinist has become less salient, less central in his life. But work as a whole still seems important. He needs the income and wants the satisfaction of being his own boss and being with people. Counselors often hear this sort of reappraisal from adult clients. The oft-quoted statement that no one ever said on his or her deathbed, "I wish I had spent more time at the office," is a recognition of this common adult experience.

Resilience or Adaptability

The ability to bounce back, to weather changes without major personal turmoil, has been termed *resilience*. Super and Knasel (1981) proposed a new term, *career adaptability*. The term was designed to focus on the balance each individual seeks between the world of work and his or her personal environment and ability to react to changing world conditions. The term is a response to a world in which adults make many career decisions— voluntary and forced. "One of the major reasons for the introduction of the term 'career adaptability' is that it allows greater emphasis to be given to the novel, non-maturational problems which presently confront many people" (p. 199).

Until recently, career theorists have described the development of an individual's career as unidirectional, resulting from a choice and the implementation of that choice. The phrase *career maturity* has been used to describe workers' readiness to make a "good" career decision. Today's world makes such concepts obsolete for adults, as most will return to the decision-making process many times during their work lives, making new choices each time.

In developing their instrument for assessing career adaptability among young adult blue-collar workers, Super and Knasel (1979) interviewed a number of Canadian workers. They culled seven dimensions of adaptability from these interviews:

- work values and work salience;
- autonomy or sense of agency;
- planfulness or future perspective;
- exploration and establishment;
- information;
- decision-making; and
- reflection on experience.

The interrelatedness of the concepts discussed here (salience, resilience, and mastery) is clearly demonstrated by their findings, and as we look at resiliency, we should keep this interrelatedness in mind.

Counselors are likely to hear adults facing or coping with work transitions talk about these triggers, the amount of role change experienced or anticipated, and their own feelings about the change. Again, we see the interrelatedness of all of the dimensions we are discussing.

Perosa and Perosa (1985), studying the career changes of adults returning for advanced education, found what might be called internal spurs to change:

> From the life histories of the participants, five patterns emerged: The more common pattern, 73% of the sample, was for the fit between the individual and the first career to be "good," "excellent," or "like a glove." Gradually the fit broke down as it became apparent that important aspects of the self were denied expression. For another group, 27%, the struggle was to find some other career in which they could find meaning: for them the fit had been "poor" or "terrible" from the beginning (pp. 63–64).

Other patterns included 29% of the women who were looking for careers to enhance new-found independence, 17% of the men looking for careers in which they could "relate" to people, 15% of the total who were seeking a lost dream, and a scant 4% who were pursuing an avocational interest. The retired businessman who is now a teacher had the good career fit described by Perosa and Perosa (1985) that broke down as his internal life changed. The recently retired woman had a good career fit that broke down as her external life changed.

The experience of Joe Jones, whom we met at the beginning of this chapter, could be described by several of these patterns: a "fit" breaking down, looking to "relate" to people, seeking a lost dream, and perhaps also looking for "meaning." Savickas, Passen, and Jarjoura (1988) summed up the adaptability concept by saying that it "emphasizes the interaction between the individual and his or her environment and this shifts attention from career maturity as readiness for decision-making to career adaptability as readiness to *cope with changing work and working conditions*" (p. 83, emphasis added).

Joe's transition is triggered by a change in both his internal and external worlds, but he is worried about his resiliency. He has little experience in managing work change and does not know if he can do so. We do not know whether he has weathered other transitions. That area would probably be a fruitful one for counselor investigation.

Increasingly, career theorists have focused on context as an important component of career development. Watts (2004) suggested that we help clients develop a contextual awareness to understand how their personal transition fits into the world situation. He stated that we must remember, "that all guidance services [must] reflect the economic, political, social, cultural, educational and labour [sic] market contexts—as well as the professional and organisational [sic] structures—in which they operate" (p. 3).

For example, losing one's job may be a result of local, national, or international economic events or may result from personal activities such as a lack of keeping up with necessary technological advances. Valach and Young (2004) proposed that even within clients' action planning there are three components, "manifest behavior, internal processes, and social meaning" (p. 65).

Context is a particularly important construct when one looks at people from diverse backgrounds, especially those from the nondominant culture. Whiston and Brecheisen (2002), in a review of the career development literature of 2001, cited Byars (2001), Constantine and Parker (2001), Pearson and Bieschke (2001), and Gomez et al. (2001) to make this point. As an example they summarized Constantine and Parker's (2001) assertion that "social constructionism emphasizes the importance of culture, language and socialization, which directly corresponds to the needs of African American women in transition" (p. 112).

Self-Efficacy

As mentioned previously, Bandura (1982) proposed a construct to explain certain behaviors such as persistence or the lack thereof in the face of obstacles. He called it self-efficacy, the belief that one's actions will have an impact on one's environment. He found that expectations of success or failure were important in determining motivation; there is much reason to try if you think you will achieve your goals, little reason if you think you will not. Lent and Hackett (1987) summed up self-efficacy research thusly: "With apologies to those with literary sensibilities, if you've got the skill, support, and desire, then 'thinking you can' could light your fire" (p. 377).

To bring this concept to life, let us imagine two 40-year-old women, both forced into early retirement by the new owners of their small plant, a pickle bottling company. Both women were first-level supervisors, both had high school educations, and both had worked for the company since their graduation from high school. One of the women had overcome many obstacles in her personal life. She was married in her teens, was the mother of two by the time she was 20, was divorced at 25, and had been the sole support of both children since then. She also helped raise her younger sister, who was only 12 when their parents died in an automobile accident. She always believed that she could do whatever was necessary to get along. She trusted her coping abilities. In other words, she had strong self-efficacy beliefs.

The other woman had led a life with fewer challenges and fewer successes. She felt that she held her present position by virtue of luck, and that, although she got good evaluations, she performed only minimally well. She lived at home with her parents and did not believe that she could manage on her own. She felt that nothing she did could make a difference and that she would only get new work if the job counselor found it for her. In other words, her self-efficacy beliefs were very weak. With respect to self-efficacy, the first woman thus has far better resources for coping with change than the second.

Counselors can add to their own efficacy by listening for and asking questions about clients' perceptions of their ability to make a difference in their world. Requests such as, "Tell me about past transitions and how you handled them," and questions such as, "How do you gauge your chances of being successful in finding work you enjoy?" will be helpful in assessing these perceptions.

Self-efficacy also seems to be related to salience. Layton (1984) found that for college women with high career salience, self-efficacy was an important determinant of choice, whereas that was less true for women with low-career salience. Let us look at a woman with high self-efficacy beliefs who wanted to become an architect. She faced a demanding training program but was willing to put in the work because her career was important to her. Another woman who had also expressed an interest in architecture was not at all sure she could succeed (low self-efficacy) and was not willing to put in the time and effort because work did not matter that much anyway. She therefore chose an easier program of study.

Nevill and Schlecker (1988) found that women who had high self-efficacy expectations and who were assertive were more willing to choose nontraditional occupations. Yang (1991) stated, "Women who seek traditionally feminine roles operate from an external locus of control, but, conversely, women who consider nontraditional occupations tend to operate from an internal locus of control" (pp. 353–354). Clearly, if you feel independent of other's viewpoints, it is easier to plan involvement in a nontraditional activity. Undoubtedly, socialization and culture play roles here also (cf., Evans, Rotter, & Gold, 2002).

Self-efficacy also seems to have cultural determinants. Sharify (1988) suggested that for Asian Americans to be more effective in their careers, they need to increase their self-confidence—closely related to self-efficacy—and reduce their timidity. Young (1988) suggested that Asian American librarians often hamper their career progress because they need to be more flexible (resilient in our terminology) and need to reduce their fear of failure (increase their self-efficacy in our terminology). Counselors need to be sensitive to cultural variations in the meaning of what they hear from clients whose culture is different from theirs.

Halstead (1991) suggested that we keep "one primary question in . . . mind. Would my impression and understanding of this person be different if our cultural backgrounds were similar?" (p. 26). Thus, we may see members of groups from the nondominant culture believing that they "cannot" when in actuality they are victims of discrimination. Or we may have others who gave up striving because they are tired of "knocking their heads against the wall." Still others may sound as if they lack self-efficacy when in fact they are reflecting a cultural imperative to sound modest.

Meaning-Making

As we listened to Joe Jones's story, we heard that he was feeling pressure from inside to have work that is more meaningful to him—that meets his needs for more autonomy and more personal connections on the job. Men in midlife often become more interested in relationships with people, and women often become more interested in achievement—leading to greater balance in the lives of both. The term *affective men and effective women* is more than alliterative. It aptly describes this phenomenon.

As mentioned earlier, especially for midlife adults, meaning and purpose may become central concerns. As adults grapple with their mortal limits, death, and time to live, they frequently also come to a deeper awareness of their inner values and spiritual selves. Meaning in life usually comes from multiple sources, and a key source of meaning for many people is related to their spirituality.

Many discussions in the counseling field have focused on defining and describing the construct of spirituality as it relates to career development (Young, Cashwell, & Shcherbakova, 2000). Chiu et al. (2004) found that most researchers defined spirituality with an existential dimension, referring to the concepts of meaning and purpose and to the subjective, individual experience of meaning-making. According to Carlsen (2000), to search for meaning is to search for an organizing principle, a guiding ideal that helps to give significance to actions and to structure life purpose. Frankl (1963) stated in his classic work, *Man's Search for Meaning*, that striving for meaning is a primary force in life. While a prisoner in Auschwitz, he noted that those who lost faith in the future were doomed in that that they had lost the spiritual hold that sustained them. Frankl (1963) stated, "The way in which a man accepts his fate and all the suffering it entails . . . gives him ample opportunity, even under the most difficult circumstances, to add deeper meaning to his life" (p. 76). This is congruent with the view of spirituality as a dynamic aspect of human beings, an aspect that includes its own requirements for meaning, authenticity, and unfolding (Slife & Richards, 2001).

According to Jones (1996), hope, meaning, and purpose are critical factors for mental and physical health and for psychological strength and coping. Coyle (2001) stated that the spiritual concepts of meaning and purpose are attitudes and behaviors motivating an individual to action. The spiritual theme of *connectedness* relates well to Joe's issues. Bloch and Richmond (1998) stated, "Spirituality is the ability to find communion with that which is deepest within ourselves and the greatest outside ourselves" (p. 18). According to Bloch and Richmond (1998), we are all part of a system, something larger than ourselves. They stated that this system is one of believing and seeing that "enables us to learn our purpose, to discover our wisdom, to define and redefine ourselves, to connect and reconnect to our environment, and to create our future" (p. 7).

For Joe, meaning-making and spirituality might be directly related to his work situation. Current literature reflects a growing interest in spirituality in the workplace (Ashmos & Duchan, 2000; Looby & Sandhu, 2002). It seems that, as our social context has become more chaotic and unpredictable, people are seeking answers to questions that have historically been answered by spiritual traditions: "How do I live in uncertainty, unable to know what will happen next? . . . Where can I find the courage and faith to stay the course?" (Wheatley, 2002, p. 42). This turning to spirituality and/or the religious realms fits well with research that supports their positive relationship with hope, meaning, and optimism (Ellison & Smith, 1991; Pargament, 1997). Brewer (2001) asserted that the connection between work and spirituality relates to a personal sense of life's meaning, an unfolding sense of self, and purpose that is expressed and driven by action. Most of the writing about spirituality in the workplace of the past decade addresses issues around the problem of meaning in work, both for the individual and for organizations, and a core concept related to meaning in the workplace is a sense of purpose (Lips-Wiersma, 2000). This connection between spirituality and work reflects an emerging worldview of the workplace that is rooted in holism, interconnectedness, and authenticity (Molinaro, 1997; Savickas, 1997). According to Savickas (1997), work provides the context for agency and union and is the forum for developing a sense of identity and social significance.

A related conceptual link between spirituality and work is the idea of *mission*. According to Bolles (2000), having a mission is a way of marrying our beliefs with our work, and these can work together to uplift each other. Hansen (1997) stated that people are increasingly considering their life mission, looking at what really matters, and exploring life purpose and meaning through their work.

In a study of corporate America, a unanimous agreement with the definition of spirituality was found among executives, managers, and workers at all levels in a variety of industries. This definition of spirituality had two components: a sense of connection to something beyond the individual, and a sense of meaning, purpose, and integration in life (Mitroff & Denton, 1999). Ashmos and Duchon (2000) found that corporate America is recognizing that meaningful work and connection to others is actually good for business, with the workplace offering its own kind of community as a key source of connectedness.

According to Ashmos and Duchon, for many people the inner life is about understanding one's own divine power, and extending this to a more fulfilling outer life. They stated that this quest for meaning at work is not new and that workers are spiritual beings whose souls are either nurtured or damaged by their work. Research conducted by Lips-Wiersma (2000) found that, regardless of their diverse beliefs, people shared four purposes in the workplace: developing and becoming self, union with others, expressing self, and serving others. According to Lips-Wiersma, when these purposes are fully expressed, a person is more likely to feel that his or her work is aligned with a bigger (divine) plan, and setbacks are thus reframed as opportunities for learning and development. The integration of spirituality into everyday work activities can be the spark that ignites meaningfulness and purpose within the workplace, both for individuals and for organizations (Looby & Sandhu, 2002).

Summary

The dimensions of salience, balance, resilience, self-efficacy, and meaning-making are all critical aspects of a client's work transitions. Listening for and asking about these dimensions will help counselors gain a more complete picture of a particular client's experience. One might think of them as the background of a picture, for which the client's own situation forms the foreground.

ISSUES RELATED TO SUPPORT

Counselors working with adults in transition often hear about a variety of available supports *and* the stressors that often go along with them. The following story illustrates that situation.

> *Susan Rodriguez is a 55-year-old woman who is trying to balance her work as a teacher with the demands of her husband, parents, children, and church. She went back to college and completed her degree when the youngest of her five children started school. She has been teaching elementary school for 20 years and still loves it. She managed her work and family responsibilities capably until recently, when the failing health of her mother and father led her to bring them into her home and assist them with daily living tasks. At the same time, her oldest daughter got divorced and came back home with her two children, ages 3 and 5. Susan is eligible for retirement, an option that her husband, soon to retire himself, wants her to exercise. She loves her job, however, and has just been asked to be a master teacher, leading a team of three in implementing a new third grade program in her school. She is excited about the changes in educational philosophy and is looking forward to the learning, growth, and recognition that will be a part of this change.*
>
> *Susan's support system includes her husband, who meets her needs for intimacy and love, but who does not give her much instrumental support and previously included her parents, although at this time they are demanding more support than they are giving. Her daughter also is in a needy time of her life, asking for a lot of emotional as well as financial support. Susan has several good friends but believes that they have problems of their own and do not need to be bothered with hers. She feels that she can occasionally talk to her teaching teammates, but there is nothing they can do to help. Susan has strong religious beliefs and is an active member of her church. She has talked to her priest, who encouraged her to join a support group for adult children of aging parents, but she does not think she can spare the time.*

*Susan has a potentially very effective support system, but she may not
be using her access skills as well as she could. She also does not seem
to be taking advantage of institutional support, such as agencies that
might help her care for her parents.*

Counselors often hear adult's speak as Susan does, about needing to
do everything themselves or not wanting to lean on others, appear needy,
or "air their dirty laundry in public." Many ethnic groups have their own
version of this mindset. Keeping a stiff upper lip is not confined to those
of Anglo-Saxon origin.

Goodman and Hoppin (1990) identified some support needs particularly relevant for work transitions. They included the following:

- feeling positive about yourself (provided by people who like you
  and know what you can do);
- encouragement (provided by people who expect you to succeed, can give you positive direction, and have an optimistic
  outlook);
- information (provided by people, books, and resource materials
  that teach job-hunting techniques and provide information on
  jobs and employers);
- referrals (provided by people and agencies who know of help like
  health care or financial support available to laid off or unemployed
  people);
- door-openers (provided by people who are willing to make contacts
  for you); and
- practical help (provided by people who will baby sit, loan money,
  provide transportation, or type a letter or resume).

The support systems of people from other cultures may be quite different. Martin (1991) listed the following traditional supports for
American Indians, ". . . the family, the tribe, religious beliefs, and the land
itself" (p. 277).

Counselors often hear people describe very limited support—like
Joe's. Those who lose their jobs frequently feel that they have lost much
of their support system at the same time. Statements such as, "Most of
my friends were from work. They can't help me; they've lost their jobs,
too," are common. Clients often see support only in terms of individuals
who can meet all of their needs—a rare breed indeed. Counselors should
encourage clients to think about individuals who meet some of their
needs, as well as about non-people supports, such as job training centers,
the public library, their faith, or their pets. Support tends to be an area in
which counselors hear little and can do much.

ISSUES RELATED TO STRATEGIES

What coping strategies are Joe and Susan using? Joe is tentatively beginning the process of exploring alternatives. Susan is using the coping strategy that has worked for her in the past—doing everything herself. Clearly we have identified an area for further exploration and assistance. Counselors will want to make sure they hear about a person's past record of coping skills as well as about current strategies. Both Joe and Susan have wisely chosen the strategy of seeking help from a counselor, but their counselors are not hearing much about the strategies already under way.

Some of the strategies that counselors will hear from other clients were listed in Figure 5.l, Your Coping Keys Worksheet. Counselors also may hear strategies designed to change or modify the situation through problem-solving, such as negotiating. They may hear strategies designed to change the meaning of the situation through reappraisal, such as developing rituals. And counselors may hear strategies designed for managing reactions to stress, such as doing physical activity.

MOVING IN, THROUGH, OUT, AND BACK (AGAIN) INTO WORK

Counselors listening to clients engaged in managing work transitions will benefit from having a framework they can use to listen to and understand what their clients are experiencing. The following model takes an individual through a work lifecycle (see Figure 6.1). A newly employed person is said to be *moving in;* a person who is fast tracked or plateaued is said to be *moving through;* a person who has been laid off, retired, or is making a voluntary career change is said to be *moving out,* and an unemployed person is said to be *trying to move in again.* As counselors listen to clients' career concerns, they need to listen to:

- The focus of the career concern. Is the client trying to figure out how to *move into* a job or school? Is the client trying to hang in there and balance competing demands? Or is the client *moving out* of the job, school, or the workforce? In other words, where the client is— moving in, through, or out—influences underlying concerns.
- The way the client handles moving in, through, or out depends on his or her resources. What comprises the client's Situation? Self? Support? Strategies?

What then, do counselors hear from their clients during these times? In the following discussion, we will examine these issues for individuals as they cycle, or recycle, through the various stages.

Work Transitions	Issues for Individual

Moving In:
 • New employees
	"Learn the Ropes"
	 • Expectations regarding
	  - job
	  - culture
	
	 • Explicit and implicit norms
	 • Marginality, at the edge

Moving Through: • Fast track • Plateaued • Caught in between	*"Hang in There, Baby"* • Loneliness and competence • Bored, stuck • Competing demands
Moving Out: • RIF • Retirement • Career change	*"Leaving, Grieving, Striving"* • Loss and reformation of goals • Articulation of ambivalence
Trying to Move in Again: • Unemployed	*"Falling Through the Cracks"* • Frustration • Despair

Figure 6.1 A Model of Worklife Transitions—Nancy K. Schlossberg.

Moving In

When clients secure a new job, another transition must take place. Many employers fail to provide a true orientation to new jobs. Partly as a result of this failure, as many as 50% to 60% of all new hires leave their jobs within the first 7 months (Leibowitz, Schlossberg, & Shore, 1991). The transition to a new job requires the worker to understand the expectations of peers, subordinates, and supervisors and also to learn the company's formal and informal norms. It often requires learning new skills and almost always requires learning new ways of using old skills. It can result in clients feeling marginal—the feeling that they are at the edge, on the fringe. For many bicultural individuals, of course, marginality is a way of life. All of us, whether rich or poor, minority or majority, feel marginal when we move into new roles. We are not what we were, nor are we clear about who we should be and what is expected of us.

All of this comes at a time when both the individuals themselves and their families expect them to experience unadulterated joy at having a new position. One woman we know had finally moved to a long sought-after position. She loved the new work and her new colleagues but was puzzled by her resistance to a new computer system. All of her feelings about the change had become displaced onto the unfamiliar machine on her desk.

When she was finally able to recognize the magnitude of the change she had made, she was easily able to learn, and even embrace, the new system.

Moving Through

Moving through work has changed drastically in the past few decades. What was formerly a predictable series of stages (see Super's, 1980, stages of establishment, maintenance, and decline), has become an unpredictable course, described by Gelatt (1993) as similar to the turbulent white water one encounters while river rafting.

Counselors may well hear clients' confusion and distress over navigation in the new white water and may also hear concerns about plateauing. Moving unpredictably is frightening for many, but many others are afraid of staying stuck in a dead end job—plateauing. Bridges (1980) suggested two major strategies for helping employees through that confusing, conflicting middle period. "The challenge is how to provide an interim system of temporary policies, procedures, responsibilities, and authority structures to get people through . . . creating temporary policies . . . encouraging cohesion . . . expecting old issues to surface" (pp. 62–63).

The issue of plateauing was also addressed by Land and Jarman (1992) in their book, *Breakpoints and Beyond,* in which they look at the process of renewal for both individuals and organizations. The researchers described a cycle of change that begins with *forming,* a period of exploration, innovation, and invention. Using examples from the physical world such as the transition of water to ice when the separate molecules forming the liquid "suddenly" line up and form a solid crystal, they postulate that after this phase a massive shift occurs, which they call *breakpoint.* A person or organization then moves into a second phase, *norming.* This phase encompasses extending and improving what has gone before; the crystal grows, but does not change its nature. It is in this phase that many get stuck, plateaued one might say. If the individual or organization does not actively move into the next phase, *fulfilling,* the third phase will be a diminishment or a disintegration.

To move into a successful third stage, one must integrate the new and different. This results in a transformation that is necessary for successful fulfillment and leads to reinventing the future. If reinventing does not happen, and they argue that it usually does not, gradual decline is the norm. As an example, they remind the reader that the development of the airline industry was not done by the railroads, which were then at the height of their success and logically placed to be leaders in the new transportation industry. The railroad industry ignored the possibilities in the infant science of flight and was left in the dust as far as passenger travel was concerned.

The parallels for individuals at midlife are obvious. Counselors often encounter adults at the breakpoint between norming and fulfilling. What they hear is discomfort, distress, and a desire to cling to the comfortable norm even while the individual recognizes that it no longer serves its purpose. They hear confusion about what to do next and how to deal with changing demands. An understanding of the process of change itself may be useful to such clients for managing their transition, after which they will be in a better position to move back into work, at the same or a new job with renewed commitment.

Moving Out

Bridges (1980), conducting a workshop for people in transition, found that although the nature of their transitions varied widely, all the seminar members shared the basic experiences of (a) an ending, followed by (b) a period of confusion and distress; leading to (c) a new beginning, in the cases of individuals who had come that far. For work transitions, that ending, whether voluntary or involuntary, usually involved leaving the job.

Counselors frequently first hear about the grief that accompanies the moving-out phase. Even when a job change is voluntary, there is a process of mourning for the old ways. There may be ambivalent feelings that make it hard to acknowledge the sense of loss. When the change is involuntary, that is, when the worker is laid off, fired, or forced into retirement, the pain is often intense. A grief period can ensue, much like that identified by Kübler-Ross (1969) in relating to the death of a loved one.

In a study of men whose jobs were eliminated Schlossberg and Leibowitz (1980) confirmed the notion that a transition can be an opportunity for either growth or deterioration. Reactions changed over time. They identified five phases—disbelief, sense of betrayal, confusion, anger, and resolution—as marking the movement in a transition process from disequilibrium following the transition to a new state of equilibrium. When the reduction in force (RIF) was first announced, many of the affected men reported feeling a sense of numbness and disbelief: "Why me?" One man said that when he was called into his supervisor's office, he thought he was going to be commended for his work or else receive a challenging new assignment; the news of the RIF stunned him. Several of the men refused to accept and incorporate the loss. Instead, they felt an unrealistic hope: "Maybe it's not true."

A sense of betrayal often accompanied the initial disbelief. Most of the employees said they felt they had entered into a psychological contract with the organization, the terms of which were, "If I am loyal and competent, the organization will take care of me." The RIF represented a breach of that contract, a "slap in the face," a "kick in the pants."

One man who was within 3 months of being a career veteran was especially bitter about the betrayal: "If a RIF must be done, it should be based on a man's production."

Once they had recovered from the initial shock and their immediate sense of having been dealt with unjustly, the men began to accept the reality of the situation. At this point, many began to panic: "'What do I do now?" They tended to be immobilized, waiting for some "magical" solution to occur. Around this time, a special program of career assistance was started, giving rise to some ambivalence. On the one hand, the men were dismayed at being fired; on the other hand, they were grateful to the organization for the help and support it offered. They wanted to be able to put the blame somewhere but could not find a suitable object. Their emotions fluctuated from anxiety and anger to excitement and anticipation. Some men contradicted themselves in a single statement. For instance, one man began by talking about the problems created by the reduction in his income, but then immediately after spoke with great excitement about his plans to move to Florida.

Among those employees who could not resolve their confusion, the natural progression was to *anger,* usually directed at themselves or at the organization. Often, the anger was expressed in inappropriate ways by "bad-mouthing" or "dumping on" the organization. In other cases, anger was directed elsewhere, for instance, at the veterans-preference provision in the Civil Service regulations or at the computer, which had been used to actually select the men to be fired. Sometimes the anger took a very concrete form: 14 of the 53 employees affected by the RIF filed formal grievance complaints against the employer. One man articulated his anger by saying, "I'm going to appeal this case and become a thorn in somebody's side."

By the time of the 3-month follow-up interviews of the 53 men, 19 had been reassigned to other jobs in the organization, 9 had decided to retire, and the remaining 25 had found new jobs. In virtually all cases, they seemed to have resolved their reactions to the transition.

It is important to note that these positive reactions resulted from the fact that the men were all helped to obtain new jobs. This positive resolution was not as easily achieved during the late 1980s and early 1990s, when the increasing number of job losses was coupled with the decreasing number of jobs. Job loss during that period often resulted in continued anger and increased depression.

Spencer and Adams (1990) provided a useful description of the grief process. They identified a series of stages that included losing focus, sinking into "the pit," and a search for meaning. Of particular interest to counselors working with the newly unemployed is the pit—a time when adults experience paralysis and even hopelessness of ever emerging from their despair. Counselors often hear tales of depression or inaction from adults in the midst of the job search that counter the logical expectations of maximum effort. Clients themselves may be as puzzled as their family members as to why they are not "looking harder." Some people may spend months in the pit! Counselors often find that all they can do for these clients is listen, be supportive, and help them begin to visualize an end to their pain. Developing job search strategies is probably premature in this situation.

The study of Schlossberg and Leibowitz (1980) did not address the issue of making meaning of the pain caused by the RIF. Scofield (1993), who wrote the personal article in the *New York Times*, and the student who left his business to return to teaching, are good examples of that search for meaning. Scofield found it in spending more time with his family; the student found it in doing work that he felt mattered. Adults who tell counselors that they have used their involuntary leisure to develop closer relations with their families or who now volunteer their time to help other newly unemployed people, illustrate this principle.

Moving In Again

Families of the unemployed may also develop useful strategies for coping with job loss. In one family in which the husband had been unemployed for 18 months, the wife used three major coping mechanisms. First, the family kept trying to modify the situation by continuous, systematic job hunting. In fact, their phone bills averaged $400 a month, indicating that the husband was working on networking and contacts. Second, they tried to control the meaning of the problem. They joined a support group, made up of others with the same problem, which focused on the economic aspects of structural unemployment as well as job search strategies. They also identified the positive aspects of the situation; for example, the father was now able to be involved with the children on a more regular basis. In this way, they took the blame away from themselves personally. Third, they utilized responses that helped to manage stress by keeping busy with a rental property, running, and gardening. Obviously, moving out raises many issues for counselors to attend to. What about moving in?

When we examine moving in again, we can benefit from research done by Peterson, Sampson and Reardon (1991) on the needs of career decision-makers. In developing a system for helping students at their career center, they discovered that they could divide clients into three groups of people, each of whom presented themselves with differing "stories" that led to different helping strategies.

They found that some clients who came to their center were decided—that is, they knew what they wanted to do and only needed help in knowing how to get there. Those people would tell counselors that they needed academic advising, job search assistance, resume writing, and so on. For those students who needed instrumental assistance and information, workshops could be offered to address specific needs. A series of workshops on job search, for example, might include networking, writing a cover letter, writing a resume, identifying job openings, learning how to "ace" an interview, and learning follow-up techniques.

Another group of students were undecided. They talked about the pros and cons of various possibilities and wanted assistance in sorting out their priorities, interests, and values. These students could also be served in a group format through a structured career development program. The group discussion could focus on identifying values, interests, and temperament; learning about the world of work and labor market information; looking at lifestyle choices; learning decision-making strategies; and developing an action plan.

A third group, most challenging for counselors, was those who were indecisive. These students presented more complex issues and often had some personal issues that blocked their ability to make decisions. Like Susan Rodriguez, they may have been in too great turmoil to focus appropriately on career decision-making. For these students, individual counseling was usually the treatment of choice. Each student had to be helped to work through individual issues before they could move to make career decisions. A successful outcome of counseling for those students might be to move into group one or two.

Gender Differences

Many researchers have looked at gender differences and work, considering differences on such variables as attitudes toward job and career, drive to achieve, and work-related behavior. Often such approaches involve analyzing these differences on the basis of early socialization patterns.

Notwithstanding changes in recent years, many girls in our society are still brought up to be passive, dependent, and nurturing, whereas boys typically are brought up to be active, independent, and aggressive. Thus, many women come to be inculcated by the "vicarious achievement ethic" first identified by Lipman-Blumen and Leavitt in 1976. Such women define their identities not through their own activities and accomplishments but through those of the dominant people (usually men) in their lives: at first their fathers, later their husbands, and still later their children. As a corollary of this tendency, many women perceive themselves primarily in roles such as wife, mother, and homemaker; even those with jobs outside the home may devalue or deemphasize their role as worker. Men, on the other hand, are governed by the direct achievement ethic and tend to base their identities on their career achievements. They are "success objects," whose value as human beings is measured by their ability to provide for their families.

There has been increasing attention in recent years on women's career development (e.g., Astin, 1984; Betz, 1989; Fitzgerald & Harmon, 2001; Fitzgerald & Weitzman, 1992; Hansen, 2001; Moradi, 2005). Gutek and Larwood (1989) summarized the research and stated the reasons why they believe women's careers are now, and will remain for the near future, different from men's:

- There are differential expectations for men and women regarding the appropriateness of jobs for each sex.
- Husbands and wives are differentially willing to accommodate themselves to each other's careers, with wives more willing to move or otherwise adapt to a husband's career needs than vice versa.
- The parent role is differentially defined for men and women; the mother role requires substantially more time and effort than the father role.

Compared with men, women face more constraints in the workplace, including discrimination and various stereotypes detrimental to career advancement (p. 10). Women face two kinds of barriers to success in work: external and internal. Although the situation is improving, women do not yet receive pay equal to that of men for comparable jobs. Neither is there yet full access to certain occupations or certain levels of responsibility—the so-called glass ceiling effect.

Some of these patterns were reflected in a classic study of women in middle management and top executive positions (Hennig & Jardim, 1977). Most of the women in the sample had made their career decision (defined as "a conscious commitment to advancement over the long term") 10 years later than is generally true for men. For some of these women that decision was in a certain sense a passive one, something that "just happened" when the woman suddenly realized that she was probably going to be working for the rest of her life. These managerial women were inclined to attribute their success to luck or to the kindly intervention and encouragement of a superior. Nonetheless, most of them believed that further advancement would come about through their own efforts at self-improvement and their development of competence on the job. What these women lacked, according to Hennig and Jardim, is "a sense of the organizational environment—the informal system of relationships and information sharing, ties of loyalty and of dependence, of favors granted and owed, of mutual benefit, of protection—which men unfailingly and invariably take into account" (p. 12).

This difference is attributed in part to men having learned early in their lives to play games such as football, which involve teamwork, the long-range goal of winning, and the use of short-term strategies with a view to reaching that goal. Women have little exposure to such team sports, concentrating instead on activities such as swimming, tennis, and gymnastics that focus more on the display of individual competence and do not involve working with team members. Women's failure to recognize the team sport aspects of the managerial career may lead them to behave in certain ways that decrease their chances of success in the organization.

Hennig and Jardim specified the following behavioral differences between men and women in management. First, the sexes interpret "risk" differently: women see only the immediate negative aspects (the danger of failure) and men see not only negative but also long-range positive aspects (the opportunity for success and advancement). Second, in deciding on what style to use in playing the role of subordinate helper, follower, junior colleague, equal, friend, men are more aware of the expectations of others, especially the boss, and choose a style that will satisfy those expectations, whereas women are inclined to adopt a take-me-as-I-am attitude. They are less skilled at dissembling than men are, again because they lose sight of the long-range goal of winning the (career) game. Finally, men take a more instrumental view of human relationships in the corporation and are thus more willing to work with people whom they may not like personally. On the other hand, women often view human relationships as an end in themselves; they cannot accommodate themselves so easily to the demands of working with people they don't like and thus open themselves to the charge of "overemotionalism" on the job.

Although this study is old, we suspect that many of the gender differences discussed hold true even today. Indeed, more recent research indicates that similar variables are still influential in women's lives. Roberts and Newton (1987) described what they called women's "split dream," in which the focus shifted between careers and family—for some women career first then family and for others family first then career. Many researchers have described this difference in career sequencing between women and men. Goodman and Waters (1985) described it as the out-of-sync career commitment curve.

As we have already noted, Gilligan (1993) made the point that though sex differences are identified and discussed, they are not incorporated in most models of human development. We must recognize that gender differences are critical in understanding the transition process.

SUMMARY

We have presented a multiplicity of issues related to the kinds of experiences, thoughts, and feelings that have an impact on adults engaged in work transitions. We have discussed what counselors might hear from the perspective of the 4S transition model and have added to that the proposition that all transitions involve moving in, through, out, and back in again. We hope you keep these examples in mind as you read Part III, What Counselors Do.

PART III

What Can We Do with What We Know and Hear?

INTRODUCTION

In the last section we looked at transitions from the perspective of clients as they tell us about their individual, relationship, and work transitions. We intended that those chapters would prompt you to ask questions about what you can do to help clients cope more effectively. This section is designed to respond to some of those questions. Written from the counselor's point of view, it is intended to give you ideas and suggestions for helping clients expand their coping resources.

As you read this section, remember that counselors have differing theories and approaches to individual and group counseling. A discussion of those theories and approaches is beyond the scope of this book, but there are many counseling texts that cover this content. Remember also, that to be effective, you will have to adapt the ideas we present to fit your own style and approach. You will also need to consider issues of cultural diversity as you work with clients whose cultural background is different from your own.

We will discuss techniques for using the transition model to facilitate change in clients individually, in groups, and through other means. We revisit some of the clients whose transitions were described in Part II and consider what we can do to help them and other adults improve the balance of their resources to deficits.

Chapter 7, which focuses on individual counseling, blends the transition model with the process guide to helping, developed by Hackney and Cormier (2005). Chapter 8 begins with a discussion of the value of group counseling in providing both information and support for adults in transition. It draws on the classic work of Irvin Yalom (1985) in identifying curative factors in group therapy and the research of Robert Weiss (1976) who developed a model of groups for people in transition. In addition to seeing adults in transition individually or in groups, counselors may also be involved in noncounseling arenas. In Chapter 9 we invite readers to look beyond their office doors at professional activities that include consulting and developing programs and workshops to assist adults in transition. In the final section we consider the role of counselors as advocates, helping to effect changes in organizations and society, which may make the environment more supportive for adults in transition.

CHAPTER 7

Individual Counseling

The transition model provides a framework, a conceptual lens if you will, for counselors to use as they help their adult clients look within themselves, their relationships, and their work. Our approach is simple: help clients enhance their resources for coping by assessing their Situation, Self, Support, and Strategies.

Levinson (1978) described a successful outcome of a midlife transition in his case study of John Barnes, biologist:

> He had given up the image of himself as a youthful hero going out to save the world but had not yielded to the threatening specter of the dried up, dying old man. He accepted himself as a middle-aged man of considerable achievement, experience, and integrity and of serious shortcomings. He felt privileged to be able to do work he enjoyed, and he was content to make a modest social contribution as parent, concerned citizen, scientist, teacher, and mentor to the younger generation. He had a sense of well-being (p. 277).

How can we help other adults in transition achieve the same peace? Hackney and Cormier (2005) presented a particularly useful road map for counselors to follow when helping clients work through problematic transitions. We clearly cannot in one chapter present all that you need to know to become a counselor, but the following overview should provide a way to tie your counseling knowledge to the framework of the transition model.

HACKNEY AND CORMIER'S COUNSELING MODEL

The Hackney–Cormier model is based on the premise that the counseling relationship is developmental in nature. Although each of their five stages is not truly discrete from the others and clients and counselors may move

179

back and forth among the stages, the process can be described in a linear fashion. The stages are (a) rapport and relationship building, (b) problem assessment, (c) goal setting, (d) initiating interventions, and (e) termination and follow-up. We will discuss each of these stages briefly and then concentrate our attention on what we call the action stages—assessment, goal setting, and interventions.

Relationship Building

The first stage, relationship building, is when the counselor develops rapport with his or her client. This stage requires the counselor to demonstrate what have been called the "core conditions" of empathy, genuineness, and unconditional positive regard or respect (cf., Rogers, 1957). It has been said that the counselor's goal is to demonstrate respect and the client's goal is to demonstrate trust. Respect should be a given; trust has to be earned. Most theorists, even if they are not proponents of Rogerian person-centered therapy, agree that these conditions are useful in developing a positive relationship with the client. To demonstrate these conditions and in general to help clients see that you are interested in them and able to help them, you need to use certain skills.

As Hackney and Cormier (2005) presented these skills, they reminded us of the issue of cross-cultural differences in how clients and counselors communicate. For example, eye contact, considered a necessity of communication in Western middle-class society, is considered intrusive by some groups. Comfort with physical proximity varies greatly among cultures. The authors stated that counselors must "embrace the *client's worldview.*" This incorporation includes the client's ethnic and cultural sense of self, as well as other aspects of the client's life experiences that have shaped his or her worldview and his or her wish to change (p. 51)." We would add that even seasoned counselors must stay alert for multicultural issues, especially when their clients are from a group with whom they have had little experience. All counseling relationships depend on the following:

1. Demonstrating empathy: Counselors can use nonverbal attentiveness, verbal attentiveness, paraphrasing and reflecting client messages, and reflecting client feelings.
2. Conveying genuineness: Counselors can use supporting nonverbal behaviors such as direct eye contact, smiling, interested facial expression, and leaning toward the client while seated. Counselors can also use congruence, openness, and self-disclosure. One way to manage potential cross-cultural differences in expression of genuineness as well as the other core conditions is to use "nonverbal

behaviors that parallel or are in synchrony with the client, particularly in the initial stage of helping" (Hackney & Cormier, 2005, p. 57).

3. Conveying positive regard: Counselors can use nonverbal behaviors similar to those used in conveying genuineness. Again, it is important to be cognizant of the client's cultural background to assure that the message communicated is the one you want to send. The authors give as an example the fact that different cultural groups vary in their degrees of comfort with silence. Counselors must therefore not only be sensitive to these differences but also perhaps discuss them with their clients. After all, who is more expert about a client's culture than the client?

Assessment

The second stage, problem assessment, makes use of the techniques of clarifying questions—open-ended and closed. Some of the information that one might want to acquire in an intake interview includes identifying data; range of problems; current life setting; family history; and personal history—medical, educational, military, vocational, sexual, and marital. Be careful not to act as an interrogator, with one closed question followed by another. Your questions should provide information necessary to lead into a problem-definition analysis that includes (a) components of the problem—feelings, cognitions, behaviors, physical or somatic complaints, and interpersonal relationships; (b) patterns of contributing events; (c) duration of the problem; and (d) client coping skills, strengths, and resources (Hackney & Cormier, 2005, pp. 81–82).

Because assessment can have positive and negative effects on clients, it is important to use care and sensitivity during the assessment portion of the counseling interview. If assessment is well done, clients feel understood, relieved, hopeful, and motivated. If assessment is not well done, clients feel anxious, interrogated, vulnerable, and evaluated. Counselors can avoid some of these negative reactions by taking care to intersperse relationship-building techniques such as reflecting thoughts and feelings and by being sensitive to the client's reactions during the assessment phase.

Although assessment remains a key aspect of this phase of counseling, we do not view it as an initial discrete responsibility of the counselor. Rather, assessment is an ongoing process throughout the counseling relationship and is best approached in a collaborative manner with the client. Transitions involve adjustment and the assimilation of life changes, and ongoing collaborative assessment keeps both counselor and client mindful of the process. Working with the client in this way provides ongoing opportunities to adjust the focus of counseling, affirm the client's strengths, and work with liabilities.

Goal Setting

The third stage, goal setting, responds to counselors' and clients' need to know where they are heading. Goals have motivational, educational, and evaluative functions. Agreeing on the desired outcomes of counseling can keep the sessions on track; agreeing on how the counseling will proceed is an appropriate aspect of entering into any therapeutic relationship.

Of course, both outcome and process goals may change during counseling. As counselors help clients deepen their understanding of themselves and their situations, they may abandon earlier goals and set new ones. The important point is to make these changes as explicit as possible. Often the client's stated goals—the so-called presenting problem—are a way for clients to test the counselor and the process. The stated goal is usually real but not always the most important. This phenomenon is particularly common when clients come to counselors with career issues. This "safe" topic often gives way, after trust is established, to concerns about relationships or the clients' own internal feelings. Changing or deepening of goals may also occur in situations in which the counselor's culture is different from that of the clients. In that situation, the question, "Can I trust you?" may be especially salient. When setting goals, counselors may also use the techniques of confrontation, imagery and visualization, and role enactment. Language work such as completing sentences such as, "I want . . ." or "I do not want . . . ," may also be useful at this stage.

Interventions

Hackney and Cormier's fourth stage—interventions—is clearly the meat and potatoes of the counseling meal. The selection of appropriate interventions reflects the counselor's theoretical orientation. Let us express a hope here that you will be flexible in choosing interventions, basing your choice on your client's needs as well as your own predilections and that you will consider your client's learning style and the characteristics of the problem as well as your own experience and comfort level. Most counselors adhere to one of the following four major theoretical orientations. The first, *affective interventions,* are designed to help clients focus on feelings. Some strategies used by affectively oriented counselors include listening for and reflecting feelings, focusing (cf., Gendlin, 1981), and helping clients integrate or change feeling states. Some other techniques that may be used come from the Gestalt literature, for example, the empty-chair technique or dream work. The second, *cognitive interventions* are designed to help clients change their belief system—their thinking. Strategies include (a) Ellis's (e.g., 1984) ABC process for challenging irrational beliefs, (b) transactional analysis (c.f., Berne, 1964), (c) postponement strategies, and (d) cognitive restructuring shifting from self-defeating to coping thoughts. The third, *behavioral interventions,* was designed to help individuals replace a maladaptive behavior with a more desirable one. Some strategies include: social modeling; role play and rehearsal, systematic desensitization; and self-management techniques, for example, self-monitoring, self-rewards, or self-contracting. And the fourth, *system interventions,* was designed to change the system in which individuals find themselves. These are based on the beliefs that (a) all elements in a system, for example, a family, are interrelated; (b) change in any part of a system, for example, in an individual, will lead to alteration of the entire system; and (c) systems have inertia and therefore resist change. This leads to the conclusion that it is difficult for individuals to change without a concomitant change in the system in which they are involved, usually their family. Systems interventions, or family therapy, are beyond the scope of this book, but they are often appropriate for people in transition, especially if the transition is one that involves the family, such as a job loss or the birth of a child. Some of the systems interventions mentioned by Hackney and Cormier (2005) included altering communication patterns, role playing, altering family structure, and using the family genogram. (For more information on systems interventions, see Kaplan, 2003; Minuchin & Fishman, 1981; Haley, 1982.)

Another type of intervention key to the counselor's role involves *advocacy.* Especially when working with clients who are marginalized, poor, or dealing with oppression, advocacy can be an important component of the counseling process. We discuss counselors as advocates in Chapter 9.

Termination and Follow-Up

Stage five, termination and follow-up, is a process that begins when either the counselor or the counselee decides that the counseling relationship will end soon. Reasons for termination vary widely, ranging from a projected move, to lack of funds, to dissatisfaction with progress, or to such satisfaction with progress that there is a lessening need to continue. Regardless of the etiology of the decision, progress should be assessed by client and counselor, and generalized when possible into other areas of life. Follow-up should be planned and should include referral if necessary. Finally, the relationship should end.

An alternative termination strategy uses the metaphor of the periodic check-up. Goodman (1992) suggested that the "dental model," with its expectations of regular check-ups and routine maintenance, is an analogy that can be applied to counseling. In the more traditional format, we, as counselors, often distinguish ourselves from many of our mental health colleagues by saying that we use an educational rather than a medical model. Instead of diagnosis, treatment, and cure counseling emphasizes teaching students and clients the necessary skills for developing satisfying and productive lives.

The premise behind the dental model of counseling is regular check-ups, closer together at first, but lengthening eventually, to see how things progress. In those meetings, counselors and their clients will check out the effectiveness of the maintenance activities they had agreed upon, for example, mood-altering exercises or support utilization. They would make a determination about the effectiveness of current levels of functioning, and work together to plan the future. In this model, final termination would be a rare event; rather, each check-up would include decisions about future sessions.

THE TRANSITION MODEL AND THE HACKNEY–CORMIER MODEL: AN INTEGRATIVE APPROACH

Figure 7.1 illustrates the integration of Hackney and Cormier's (2005) stages with the transition model, showing how it can be used by a counselor working with an individual in transition. In the figure illustrative counselor behaviors for each stage of the Hackney–Cormier model are correlated with each area of the transition model.

Stages in the Hackney/Cormier Model:	The 4 S Transition Model:			
	Situation	Self	Support	Strategies
Relationship Building	Counselor Uses Basic Listening Skills			
Areas to Assess	Client's Environment	Internal Resources	External Resources	Current Repertoire of Coping
Sample Client Goals	Modifying the Environment	Return to Equilibrium	Increasing Support	Developing an Action Plan
Possible Counselor Interventions	Reframing, Assertion Training	Positive Asset Search	Referral to Support Group	Problem-Solving Strategies
Termination Follow Up	Counselor Helps Client Review What Has Happened and Plan Next Steps			

Figure 7.1 Counseling adults in transition: combining the Hackney–Cormier and the 4 S transition models.

Counselors' behaviors during the relationship-building and termination stages of the Hackney–Cormier model are not likely to vary, regardless of the area of the transition model being addressed. In relationship building, counselors strive to build rapport—to get to know their clients better. During termination, counselors strive to help their clients evaluate their progress and make plans for their futures. However, counselors can enhance their work in the assessment, goal setting, and intervention stages by using their understanding of the 4 S's of the transition model. The figure can be used as follows (italicized words here identify terms used in Figure 7.1). Suppose that a counselor is at the *intervention* stage of counseling with an adult who, during the *assessment* stage, identified the *self* as an area of need and, during the *goal-setting* stage, expressed a desire to return to a *sense of equilibrium*. You might use the intervention of a *positive asset search* to help that adult rediscover strengths and identify internal resources to use in coping. The rest of the figure can be used in a similar manner. The balance of this chapter provides more detail about using the assessment, goal-setting, and intervention stages of the Hackney–Cormier model with each of the components of the transition model—Situation, Self, Support, and Strategies.

Assessment

The goal of the assessment phase is to help both counselors and clients gain a better understanding of the issues that brought the client to counseling in the first place. During this phase, they jointly assess the clients' balance of resources and liabilities. For example, Jack Williams, discussed in Chapter 4, questioned his identity and lifestyle, the lack of opportunities he saw in his small town *environment* (his Situation), his *internal resources* (his Self), his perception that his wife did not understand his current concerns and his lack of perceived *external resources* (his Support). Although the *current repertoire* of coping strategies he had considered were not likely to be effective, his willingness to confront his life and seek help represent a good beginning.

The other case studies presented in Part II also illustrate the importance of assessment. Examples include Marty Smith, who "mattered too much," Joe Jones, the frustrated and perhaps technologically obsolete machinist, and Susan Rodriguez, the master teacher in a career stage different from that of her retired husband. With each of these clients we would depend primarily on listening skills for our assessment, although with Joe we would supplement these with some formal career assessments, and we would be mindful of reassessing throughout the counseling process.

Assessing Situations

To understand a client's Situation during a transition, a counselor must explore the transition's triggers, timing, source, control, role change, and duration; the client's previous experience with a similar transition; and concurrent stress. These describe aspects of the transition that are particular to the individual. As mentioned, a dozen adults experiencing the same transition, such as getting divorced, all operate in a context that makes each of their situations unique. These areas should be discussed with clients as you work jointly in the assessment phase of counseling, bringing about a greater understanding of the nature of their transition. Let us look at two divorced women to examine how clients facing similar transitions can differ.

Shu Fen Lee, a 40-year-old homemaker, recently divorced her husband of 20 years. She worked as a receptionist in a law firm for 3 years after graduation from high school, then married and spent full time at home raising her 5 children, who now range in age from 7 to 18. Although she is receiving child support, she must return to work to support herself and help support her children.

In working with her to assess her Situation, her counselor helps her to look at the context in which the transition is happening. On the positive side, she is staying in the family home, which she now owns without a mortgage. Her ex-husband is reliable about paying his child support. Her health is good. Her elderly parents live with her, and her mother can help with childcare for brief times, if necessary. On the negative side, her ex-husband hardly sees his children, her father's health is rapidly failing and her mother will probably soon need help in caring for him, and her secretarial skills are out of date. She has never touched a computer.

Ivana Wilson, also newly divorced, came to this country 2 years ago to marry her husband, whom she met when he was working in Hungary. She speaks very little English, has never worked in the United States, and is still waiting for her citizenship papers. Her parents are dead and the rest of her family are scattered, with none living near her. Ivana did not want the divorce. Ivana's situation is clearly very different from Shu-Fen's.

Counselors can use an environmental scan as a strategy for helping clients assess their Situations. This scan is often referred to as "developing contextual awareness," that is, being aware of the context in which one lives (A. G. Watts, personal communication, June 2000).

Locke and Parker (1994) identified five areas of cultural assumptions and values for counselors to think about as they work with clients. They are the following:

1. Activity: How do people approach activity? How important are goals in life? Who makes decisions? What is the nature of problem solving?

2. Definitions of social relations: How are roles defined? How do people relate to those whose social status is different? How are sex roles defined? What is the meaning of friendship?
3. Motivation: What is the achievement orientation of the culture? Is cooperation or competition emphasized?
4. Perception of the world: What is the predominant worldview? What is the predominant view on human nature? What is the predominant view on the nature of truth? How is time defined? What is the nature of property?
5. Perception of self and the individual: How is self defined? Where is a person's identity determined? What is the nature of the individual? What kinds of persons are valued and respected? (pp. 42–43)

We suggest that you keep these questions in mind as you read the rest of this section. Be aware that you do not need to know all the answers; often the best way to find out your clients' values is to ask them. Given the variety of values within even the dominant culture, it may be important to ask such questions of all clients, as the answers may affect the meaning of their transitions.

Some clients may need to be taught how to look at the environment in which they find themselves. They may need to be encouraged to watch the news on television, listen to it on the radio, or read the newspaper, with an eye on issues related to the one they are facing. Often "news magazines" on air or in print supply the in-depth coverage that provides this kind of awareness. Others may gain an awareness of the world around them by listening to friends, acquaintances, and coworkers discuss their lives, again listening for information that will help them understand the context of their personal transition.

It is important to remember that clients' cultural environments are also a part of the context. People have differing ways of looking at goals and decision-making, defining roles, viewing the world, or valuing competition or cooperation. Both counselors and clients need to understand the implications of these cultural mediators as they strive to assess their transition situations.

For transitions related to the individual, the environment may include others engaged in similar searches for meaning. The women's and men's movements are good examples of this. Knowing that others are experiencing transitions like one's own provides a kind of emotional support. As we look at relationship issues, the relevant context may be a family situation, including the changing customs of society. Consider, for example, the difference between 1950 and 2006 in how someone might react to the transition of becoming a grandparent via an unwed daughter. In 1950, many people lied to the neighbors and refused to acknowledge the child and a few even severed relations with the daughter. In 2006, most would come to terms with the situation and maintain close ties with both daughter and grandchild.

Ivana and Shu Fen share the overall environment of the United States, but they may be in different minienvironments created by where they live or the belief system of their cultural group. Contextual awareness may help laid-off workers avoid shame at their plight and increase understanding of the societal forces that caused the company to reduce its size. In all of these examples, contextual awareness may also lead to political action, empowering clients to change their context.

As counselors help clients assess their environments, it is important to help them develop a reality base—seeing their situations as they really are, not as they perhaps wish or fear. We are reminded of a client who had lost her ability to drive because of failing eyesight. She determined that asking friends for rides was her only option, a position she found extremely demoralizing. Her counselor was able to help her discover both public and private transportation designed for physically challenged people. Because she was able to accept herself as being "one of them," she was able to expand her view of the environment in which she was now operating.

Traditional assessment techniques may also be used in examining clients' situations. In assessing Joe Jones's situation, for example, the counselor could have Joe describe his family and community obligations and have him begin to learn about the world of work and opportunities for education and training. The technique of information interviewing (see Azrin & Besalel, 1980) is an effective way for many adults to conduct this exploration. Others may find it helpful to read about occupations on the Internet or in publications such as the *Occupational Outlook Handbook* (2004–2005).

Assessing the Self

We believe that the most effective way to assess clients' internal resources is by listening as clients tell their "stories." By using the basic counseling skills of attending, reflecting thoughts and feelings, and asking open and closed questions, we get to hear these stories from the client's perspective. In the discussion that follows, we will first examine some methods of assessment, and then we will focus on three particular areas of the self: hardiness, spirituality, and self-efficacy. For any one individual, we will want to target certain areas of the self. In Joe's case, for example, one might give him an interest inventory or an ability test. These would help Joe expand his knowledge about what he likes and what he can do. Further, these kinds of instruments often tie interests and abilities to job titles, so Joe might be able to consider a wider range of opportunities. Or one might help him use a card sort technique to identify occupations of interest while recognizing the necessity to set priorities and make choices.

A career counselor could have Joe compose a work autobiography to observe his transferable skills and his past decision-making and problem-solving approaches. Systematic assessment instruments are also helpful. For example, counselors may use *The Salience Inventory* (Super & Nevill, 1985) to help understand the importance of work in an individual's life. They might use Krumboltz's (1991) *Career Beliefs Inventory* to help individuals become aware of and confront beliefs that may be blocking their progress.

Informal assessment techniques offer a nonthreatening and often enlightening way to assess clients' aspects of self. Art techniques, such as creating a collage representing the present and the future, can bring to light many aspects of a client that formal assessments miss. The processing of these types of projects can enrich the counseling sessions with deeper held meanings, values, and dreams of the client. Other informal techniques include creating a lifeline or the aforementioned genogram.

A lifeline provides a visual graph of the client's life story with a graphic detail of life's ups and downs. Working with a lifeline can help clients tell their stories in greater detail, and the counselor can reflect the strengths and life lessons the client has gained through past experiences. The life story can be divided into chapters with each chapter given a title. The overall story may have a title and a motto, as well. Processing these types of informal assessments may deepen the client–counselor relationship, while empowering clients to have a clearer vision of their imagined futures. Clients often experience these as creative outlets, and they may help clients give voice to what may not be as easily conveyed verbally during the counseling session.

A genogram is often used by those who apply a family systems approach and can be a valuable tool in assessing the Self. For example, clients can explore internalized family messages and family influences by using the genogram. Cultural values are often brought to the forefront when a genogram is processed, especially as these relate to gender, educational, and career expectations. These types of informal techniques allow for both personal and culturally held meanings, values, spirituality, and role expectations to be part of assessment process.

Some computer-aided career development programs are particularly geared to the needs of adults. They provide a way for clients to integrate their interests, values, and preferred work environment with job titles and descriptions and to gain information on required training or education for each. (It is beyond the scope of this book to describe these instruments and programs in depth; for more detailed information, see books such as *A Counselor's Guide to Career Assessment Instruments* by Kapes and Whitfield, 2002, or *Using Assessment Results for Career Development* by Osborn and Zunker, 2006.)

Hardiness. As we begin assessing an individual's ability to manage the transition at hand, we might consider looking at hardiness, a concept that provides a way of looking at an individual's stress resistance—the way people view themselves and their situations (Kobasa, Maddi, &. Kahn, 1982). Dailey (n.d.), expanding on this work, described several dimensions of a hardy person including openness to change, commitment, control, and confidence. Let us discuss each in turn.

1. Openness to change: Looking to the future rather than to the past, seeing opportunity rather than barriers, and accepting, and perhaps even enjoying, challenge. The simplest way to assess openness is to ask individuals questions such as: "What do you fear and what do you look forward to as you think about the future?" and "What positive consequences can you see coming from this transition?" It is important not to devalue clients' suffering if the transition is painful, rather the goal is to help them see that there is a future for them, albeit a different one from what they had anticipated. A new widow usually does not see her transition as positive, but she can be helped to see that her future may still contain happiness.

2. Commitment: Sense of purpose, seeing "life events as part of a self-chosen life course . . . [feeling] responsible to a larger social context or community" (Kobasa, 1980, p. 6). Clients who feel that they matter to individuals and to society usually have a stronger sense of purpose than those who do not; clients with unambiguous goals are often better able to focus on the future than those who wait for events to happen to them. Perhaps the clearest way to define commitment is to say it is related to the amount of energy the client is willing to invest in achieving goals. Counselors can assess commitment by considering factors such as whether clients keep appointments or do assigned "homework" or whether they seem willing to experience some pain in exploring and gaining understanding of their internal world. Counselors can help clients achieve commitment by identifying incentives or rewards for achieving counseling goals. Rewards can come from adding something positive to life, for example, developing talents or minimizing something unpleasant, such as reducing pain.

3. Control: Believing that one has control over how one will respond to life events is the opposite of a sense of powerlessness. One may still express deep feelings; we do not believe that keeping "a stiff

upper lip" is always, or even often, the best course to follow. One may control one's response by choosing to grieve deeply and publicly over a loved one, crying (or raging) frequently, and allowing oneself to feel and express all of one's pain. Another person may, however, choose to express his or her grief by maintaining a dignified quietness, by using the energy of grief to work for cancer research, or by becoming involved in action-oriented groups such as Mothers Against Drunk Driving or by supporting gun control legislation.

4. Confidence: feeling personally valuable and believing that rejection does not mean worthlessness. Although we should never underestimate people's insecurities, confident people approach transitions with a distinct advantage. We can assess global confidence in a variety of ways: with formal self-esteem measures; by asking our clients how confident they feel; and by looking at their nonverbal behavior and making our own estimation of confidence. We can also ask them questions that reveal how accepting they are of others, knowing that confident people accept their own imperfections and therefore tend to be more accepting of the imperfections of others. When judging confidence, we must be aware of cultural differences in how confidence may be expressed or hidden. Many cultural groups have taboos against speaking positively about oneself; others have taboos against eye contact or assertive speech patterns. It would be a mistake to assume that people who have these taboos lack confidence because their behavior differs from White Western male patterns. In addition, people often hide their lack of confidence under an attitude of bravura; counselors need to be able to see beneath such surface presentations. Not all lack of confidence is internally based and therefore "curable" through attitudinal change. A person may be reacting realistically to a situation that is indeed discouraging and perhaps beyond his or her ability to fix. Watts (personal communication, June 2000) stated that counselors have an obligation to help clients learn about the relevant sociopolitical–economic causes of their transition so that they can separate their own responsibilities from those things over which they have little or no control. An example of this is provided by You (n.d.), who discussed the problem of finding work experienced by Korean immigrants new to the United States. You stated,
"A significant number of immigrants lower their self-esteem in response to the dissonant situation of no jobs and even no vocational qualification, despite their previous work experience

and former job status. To adapt themselves to the reality of the lower immigrant status, immigrants generally have low expectations regarding their future vocational situation."

In a related vein, we are encouraged to think about Seligman's (2002) definition of optimistic and pessimistic persons. In the assessment phase, we need to listen for "half-full/half-empty" viewpoints. Seligman provides a "test" of optimism that clients can take if additional evidence is needed to determine where they fit on this dimension. Hopefully, this is an area that can be improved throughout the assessment process.

Spirituality. Another way to assess individuals' ability to handle the transition they are facing is to learn about their spiritual beliefs. Jung (1933) incorporated the spiritual dimension with human development into his theory, and conceptualized spirituality as a process of *achieving wholeness.* According to Jung (1933), life is a journey, and particularly in the second half of life, life can become a spiritual process. He viewed the spiritual search for meaning as an integral part of midlife. He believed that, as people reach this stage of development, they become increasingly centered and more deeply connected to their spiritual selves. We might hypothesize that this development is encouraged by the myriad transitions faced by most adults in midlife.

Research has confirmed the relationship between spirituality and coping ability (Pargament, 1997), self-esteem (Ellison, 1983), and the realization of personal strengths (Ventis, 1995). Spiritual coping has been seen to positively influence the amelioration of distress and to play a central role in coping with stress (Belavich, 1995; Kamya, 2000; Pargament, 1997). Spirituality has been correlated with the experience of resilience and the ability to overcome and succeed in times of distress and challenge (Walsh, 1998).

Studies have found that the more vital a person's spiritual health is, the more numerous are his or her coping skills (Graham, Furr, Flowers, & Burke, 2001). Graham et al. stated that "spirituality may involve something beyond tangible resources . . . spiritual health may include finding meaning and purpose in one's life, relying on a higher power; experiencing peace, or feeling a connection with the universe, the world, or nature" (p. 7). All of this leads us to the conviction that as we help clients assess their internal resources, we need to include an assessment of their spirituality. Similarly, self-efficacy beliefs form a part of clients' internal resources.

Self-efficacy. Bandura (1982) found that expectations of success or failure were important in determining motivation. The phrase "self-fulfilling prophecy" reflects a commonsense understanding of the relationship of self-efficacy to helping adults in transition set goals and plan their futures.

Clients who believe that their own actions can influence their environment will be more motivated to set goals and work toward them than those who doubt their effectiveness.

To assess self-efficacy, we may ask clients if they believe that they can influence their world, their situation, or their fate. Do they feel that most of the control for what happens to them comes from themselves? Do they feel capable of meeting the challenges that they face? Krumboltz's *Career Beliefs Inventory* (1991) provides the above information concerning career efficacy.

Assessing Supports

How do we help clients assess this area of their life? We need first to ask them to describe, or list, the external resources they have available to them. Who is "in their corner?" Who, in Kahn and Antonucci's (1980) term, is part of their convoy?

The people in our clients' support systems may also be the same ones who create stress for our clients. We are reminded of the dualistic concept of nourishers versus drainers. This concept is perhaps best described by using an analogy that compares our emotional sense of satisfaction to the water level in a bathtub. If we imagine life's nourishers as filling our "tubs" with water, and life's drainers as allowing the water to flow out, we can see that for our clients to be "full," they need to have or create enhanced flow in (nourishers) and diminished flow out (drainers). This may mean avoiding situations that are confidence draining, avoiding people who are negative or pessimistic, and spending more time in positive situations and with positive, encouraging people. In the assessment phase of counseling, we can determine how full our client's tub is and who and what are the nourishers and the drainers.

We may also want to assess clients' abilities to add to their support system, to make connections. This skill has been identified with hardiness, as people who know how to access support are more able to do so in times of stress. Getting a "reading" on clients' abilities to make connections will help counselors decide what strategies they may need to teach.

Assessing Strategies

Many adults have experienced prior transitions that they navigated successfully. The strategies they used then may be expanded. This is what might be called *a base for growth*. Helping clients remember past useful strategies can be accomplished in a variety of ways, some of which depend on whether you, as counselor, are primarily affectively, cognitively, or behaviorally focused. An affectively oriented counselor, for example, might ask Marty, the overcommitted client, to describe when she felt more in control of her life. A cognitively oriented counselor might encourage her to think about the irrational beliefs that led her to think she must take care of everybody and make them all happy. A behaviorally oriented counselor might encourage her to keep track of how many times each day she says "yes" to her family members and to try saying "no" to each of them twice a day.

Pearlin and Schooler (1978) delineated three coping responses that represent a systematic way to examine Strategies for managing transitions. Their list, which is reflected in Figure 5.1 (p. 136), includes:

1. Changing the situation through negotiation, optimistic action, advice-seeking, and exercise of potency, used synonymously with self-efficacy.
2. Controlling the subjective meaning of the situation by positive comparisons, selective ignoring, and substitution of rewards.
3. Managing the stress of the situation by emotional discharge, self-assertion, and passive forbearance.

We must always consider, however, those strategies that were successful in the past but that no longer are in the client's best interest. A classic example comes from the adult children of alcoholics literature (e.g., Black, 1987; Wegscheider-Cruse, 1989). A child may have become the "good kid" to help survive in a chaotic alcoholic family. That good kid may have hidden all feelings, especially negative ones, eventually not being even aware of them. Virginia Satir (1972) used the dramatic phrase, "brave response for survival," for strategies that helped one cope in childhood with difficult situations. For example, one might have learned to repress feelings to cope with the pain of being abused by an alcoholic mother. The response may no longer be useful, and the conditions that spawned it no longer in existence. Similarly, a person raised in a tough neighborhood may have had to be ready to fight at all times; that pugnacious attitude is probably not helpful as he or she faces adult transitions. Sorting out useful strategies already in our clients' repertoires from those that may be counterproductive is therefore another useful assessment arena.

Goal Setting

If we agree that a primary goal of assessment is to help the client have a basis for goal setting, then we can see clearly that the self-appraisal fostered by the above strategies is an essential starting place. Let us look then at goal setting in light of the transition model.

In Egan's (1994) terms, goal setting helps the client discover a scenario for a better future. There are three parts to goal setting: conceptualizing possibilities using questions such as, "What do you want?", choosing realistic possibilities, and turning them into viable goals (p. 31). Each aspect of the 4 S model can be considered in assisting clients in setting goals.

Goals Related to the Situation

Clients working with internal transitions may set a variety of goals—goals that help them to have a different cognitive understanding of the situation, goals that relate to a deeper understanding of their own psychological dynamics, or goals that relate to changing their behavior. Clients may set goals that change the way they perceive a particular situation, or they may want to change the situation. We call this *modifying the environment.* Clients struggling with transitions involving relationships may set goals that help them redefine the relationship, change the ways they relate to significant others in their lives, or grieve for lost relationships. Clients involved in work transitions may want to enter a particular work situation or may be forced to leave it; they may want to plan changes within a work situation or they may have goals related to formal or informal education or training. Or they may want or have to choose an entirely new occupation.

Goals Related to the Self

Even when a transition is desired or well accepted, we often still want our feelings to "return to normal." Sometimes we just want to come to peace with the transition. "Talking it out" is the commonsense phrase for what helpers know is an important process of expressing rather than suppressing feelings. Frequently clients will use a transition experience as a spur to pursue other therapeutic goals. Unresolved conflicts from earlier times in life may be addressed; long-standing problems such as depression may be brought to the counselor's office. Behavioral issues such as phobias may be confronted.

Transitions, be they events or non-events, or of short, long, temporary, or permanent duration, create a disequilibrium. In more idiomatic terms, they "upset the applecart." Psychologically as well as physiologically, human beings share with the rest of the physical world the tendency to return to homeostasis, to return to equilibrium. Clients express this tendency when they say things like, "I wish things could just stay the same," or "I wish things could go back to the way they were." Often dynamic self-understanding is the first step to a return to equilibrium.

An impetus for personal growth, what has been called the *teachable moment,* sometimes occurs during times of disequilibrium. It may be expressed by questions such as, "What did I do to get myself in this mess?" "How come I always get involved with alcoholics?" or "I seem to be overqualified for every job I get. Am I doing something wrong?"

These questions help clients set goals for change. Goals related to the self then usually involve a search for emotional relief or personal growth, in counseling terms, dynamic self-understanding.

Goals Related to Support

Generally people in transition find that their support systems either have diminished or have been overwhelmed by the new demands placed on the members of their system. These people need then to *enhance* or *increase support,* as shown in Figure 7.1 earlier in this chapter. Marty Smith exemplified an important exception. Marty, you will remember, mattered too much to too many people. What might be viewed as her support system was actually functioning more as a stress system. Marty needed to get support by adding other sources. She needed to add nourishers and to find ways to protect herself from drainers.

Former supports often fail to meet an individual's current needs. For example, many newly divorced or widowed people find that the couples who were an important part of their support system while they were a part of a couple are no longer interested in being a part of their new life. And even when they are willing, the support they used to provide may no longer be what the newly single person needs. Similarly, new parents may find that old friends, if childless, do not understand the complexity of their lives. These friends may have trouble understanding the need to plan all social events well in advance and to never be sure they will not have to change plans at the last minute.

Goals Related to Strategies

Clients often come to counseling because the strategies they have been using in the past are now not successful. Furthermore, they are often at a loss about what else to do. Helping them develop more, or better, strategies is often an important immediate goal of counseling. In reality, clients often wish to move directly to strategizing, and counselors have to "slow them down" to look at other issues before they move to action. *Developing an action plan* is an appropriate goal, after enough self-understanding has been created to make the plan likely to be a success.

A CASE STUDY

Let us use an example to make some of the preceding discussions come to life.

Chuck Danto, a 33-year-old, single, recovering alcoholic, finds himself flooded with feelings he does not know how to handle. He stopped drinking 2 years ago with the help of Alcoholics Anonymous (AA) 12-step program and thought that after 2 years of nondrinking he was "home free."

Suddenly he finds that he is reacting to everything—his family, friends, and colleagues say that he is overreacting. He sometimes feels out of control emotionally. He will react with rage to a minor irritation, and he finds himself crying at little things. The irony in all of this for Chuck is that, as far as he remembers, he never "fell apart" like this while he was drinking.

Chuck's goal is to *return to the equilibrium* he has recently been feeling, without returning to drinking. His counselor helps him articulate another goal: to develop a *dynamic self-understanding*, in other words, to get a better handle on what's happening to him. The counselor tells Chuck that it is common for drinking to be used unconsciously or consciously to stifle feelings and assures him that the flooding emotions he feels now are also common. As Chuck develops an understanding of the family patterns and personal predilections that led to his drinking, he will be able to better manage these unaccustomed emotions.

Chuck also decides to set a goal of changing some of the places and people with whom he spends time—*modifying the environment.* He is finding that his increased sensitivity makes his job as an assistant principal in a junior high school more difficult. Specifically, he finds himself empathizing too much with the students and finds that he is less comfortable imposing discipline on them. He decides to add career decision-making to his list of counseling goals. He also realizes that although he stopped seeing his drinking buddies when he joined AA, and although he still attends weekly AA meetings, he has not developed new friends. This has meant relying on his family for most of his social life, a situation that is not satisfying for him. *Increasing support,* then, has become another of Chuck's goals, meaning, in his case, looking for new relationships.

As all of these goals are developed and agreed upon, Chuck and his counselor recognize that the final step will be to *develop an action plan* that will enable him to master strategies such as reframing, selective denial, and developing hope and optimism. Using these strategies will help him complete his transitional journey.

At this point, you have worked with your clients to assess their current status and you and your client have set mutually acceptable goals for counseling. What do you do next? Your interventions will vary, reflecting both your own preferred counseling approach and the needs of your particular client.

Interventions

Individuals often need help in identifying options. The story of a 36-year-old man who became a paraplegic as the result of an automobile accident illustrates this point. After the initial physical battle to survive, he became preoccupied with how to live. Not surprisingly, at first he saw no options. Before the accident he had been a construction worker. Clearly he would be unable to continue that activity. His first attempt to build a new life was aborted when his application to law school was rejected. After exploration it became clear that this application had been a response to the influence of his mother, who was a lawyer. A year after the accident and before he clarified his vocational goals, he wrote his mother, "I want to share with you the perspective I now have on my future. Because of your love and support I am facing the future with courage, hope, and curiosity." The word *curiosity* showed that on a deep level he was going to make it, that he was going to create options, and that he was going to be in control. And, in fact, soon afterwards he applied and was accepted in a school of architecture, which continued his interest in building and took account of his disability. He created an option.

Fifty clerical workers at the University of Maryland (Charner & Schlossberg, 1986) were asked to identify a significant transition. The transitions fell mostly in the family category, followed by geographical moving and work. When asked, "Generally, in change situations, how do you perceive options?" Ninety-four percent saw more than one. However, when asked, "For this transition, how many options did you perceive?" Thirty-four percent saw only one. This indicates that individuals in transition usually see options, but under stress or when in the midst of a transition which has significantly altered their lives, they often "freeze" and can see only one option.

The concept of options also explains the difference between those who have a midlife crisis and those who experience a midlife transition. Everyone has a midlife transition, that is, a time when he or she begins to see time until death instead of time from birth. But only a few run off, as did Gauguin. Those having a "crisis" probably see limited options.

In the interventions stage we see the greatest differences among counselors who take different theoretical stances. Following is a discussion, organized around types of interventions—affective, cognitive, and behavioral—that will illustrate how those approaches can be used in helping clients work with Situation, Self, Support, and Strategy issues.

Affective Interventions

Affective interventions are often the most appropriate for those issues relating to identity, autonomy, and meaning-making. The *active listening* techniques used in establishing a relationship are useful in beginning the process of helping clients identify and clarify their feelings. Strictly client-centered therapists may use these techniques almost exclusively throughout their counseling sessions. Often the discomfort that arises from transitions involving the self stems from the fact that a person is not aware of why he or she is feeling ill at ease. Labeling the feelings and discovering their normality may provide relief. Some clients, however, will find it difficult to identify any feelings; some will be blocked only on some categories of feelings. Although it is an overgeneralization, we have found it useful to be alert for women who have trouble identifying angry feelings and men who find it difficult to recognize their frightened or sad feelings. Early socialization messages like, "Nice girls don't get mad," and "Big boys don't cry" do carry forward into adult life. These prohibitions are often so strongly internalized that the adult is not even aware of having them, let alone willing to express them.

Narrative approaches (e.g., Cochran, 1997; Peavy, 1998; Savickas, 2001) are frequently used by affectively oriented counselors. The modernist search for human truth is being replaced with the concept of socially *storied lives* (Corey, 2005). This constructivist-oriented technique, sometimes called *the storied approach* (Brott, 2001), centers on the exploration of the client's world through three phases of story development. The phases include: co-construction, deconstruction, and construction. The process involves the co-construction of the client's life stories with the counselor, disassembling the stories by looking at them from various perspectives to deconstruct them. Reconstruction of the stories can then take place through the process of re-authoring the stories. This approach is future orientated in that in re-authoring of the story, the client is empowered to make new choices.

Many other techniques have been developed to help people recognize and express feelings. These include bibliotherapy, focusing, and Gestalt techniques. Some affectively oriented helpers believe in delving into childhood experiences to explore sources of current feelings. These explorations may lead clients to change the way they feel about current events or situations.

One man experienced acute anxiety as he faced his 50th birthday. His wife encouraged him to begin financial planning for retirement, which he resisted mightily, calling it the "R" word, and refusing even to discuss it. As he explored the meaning of this birthday, he found that he felt well physically, was at a comfortable place in his career, and was looking forward to the easing of the family's financial burdens when his youngest child completed college in 2 years. His anxiety was a puzzle to him.

His counselor encouraged him to think back to his childhood and how he viewed 50-year-old men at that time in his life. He then "remembered" that his father, in his early 40s when our client, an only child, was born, had a major stroke a few weeks after his 50th birthday. His father lived as an invalid for many years after this time, and the family never expressed its grief for its loss of a healthy father and husband. The young boy came to be referred to as the "man of the family," and indeed took on many responsibilities much earlier than he otherwise would have.

This awareness enabled the client to do several things. He began to grieve for his father and for his own "lost" childhood. In the process of doing that, he was able to learn to feel and express other emotions, a development that greatly enhanced his sense of well-being and improved his relationships with his wife and children.

In addition, he now could separate his own life from that of his father, understand the care he took of his health, exercising and eating sensibly, and give credence to his doctors when they said he was at a low risk for a stroke. He could plan for the future with some confidence that he would live to have one. His anxiety was diminished, and he faced the future "with optimism."

Ivey and Ivey (2003) described one affective intervention—a positive asset search. The purpose of this intervention is to identify and emphasize client strengths. They indicated that this process is useful for clients to accept and acknowledge their own strengths and establish a positive base from which clients can grow.

Using active listening skills as a base, the counselor conducts a positive asset search by asking questions such as: "What went on this week that you feel good about?" Some clients respond well to a checklist of strengths (cf., Goodman & Hoppin, 1990) or to looking at transferable skills. Reframing, discussed later; can also be a useful tool in identifying positive assets, particularly when your clients see themselves primarily in negative ways.

An important function of affective interventions for people in transition is that of validating and clarifying their feelings. Adults often feel alone with their feelings, especially their fears. Adults in transition often think that the people around them "have it all together," and that others know what they want and how to get there. Tentative efforts to express their concerns to friends or family members may be met with sympathy, or they may be brushed off. Many of these others may be uncomfortable with feelings in general; and, if they are family members, may in addition be afraid to see weakness in someone they depend on. They may feel anxiety about a transition that could or already is affecting them.

For instance, Jack Williams's wife (from Chapter 4) may not be sympathetic to Jack just because of what his potential change may mean to *her*. Jack, however, may find relief by having a counselor truly listen to him and help him understand what he is feeling. Marty Smith, likewise, may find it helpful to list the positive aspects of her situation and look at her own strengths in that context. She may then be able to articulate her feelings to her husband in a way he can hear, but first she must be clear herself about their origin. She might find, for example, that she felt angry about always deferring to her first husband and that she is afraid that she is repeating a pattern.

Joe Jones, whom we met in Chapter 6 as he faced retraining or unemployment, will probably find it useful to express his fears of failing in school. He will also benefit from conducting a positive asset search before he decides which path to follow. Exploring his feelings may also lead him to better understand his wife's and brother's feelings and to understand why they have differing ambitions for him. He may begin to see that he is procrastinating and that in doing so he is allowing circumstances to make his decision for him. If he loses his job because he does not get the retraining he needs or if his brother gets another partner for the bar, his choice will be taken away. A counselor might help him to see that in a way he wants that to happen-to avoid responsibility. But he may also see that giving up control of his future is perhaps not getting him what he really wants.

Cognitive Interventions

Many counselors find that cognitive interventions are a useful way of helping adults navigate transitional experiences. We do not mean to imply that the distinctions are always clear. Often cognitive work is combined with affective and/or behavioral work.

Reframing can be described as the process of looking at a situation from a different point of view. The oft-used example of seeing a glass as half-empty is an example of a situation ripe for reframing. The goal in this case would be to help the client see it as half-full.

Consider the following example. A 40-year-old woman has recently been left by her husband of 20 years. After she took some time to ventilate some of her fear, anger, and grief and after the counselor had gained some information about the marriage, she was asked, "Could you imagine yourself thinking that he did you a favor?" As her life progressed and she began dating, she was finally able to reframe what she had seen as desertion and relabel it as a chance for her to create a new and happier life. Her counselor had helped her to reframe the events and therefore change their meaning.

Hof (1993) described a process of instilling hope and optimism. He said that counselors should use their full range of skills in doing this, but added suggestions for some specific hope-fostering techniques. Although geared to couples, they offer useful ideas for counselors working with anyone in transition. Five of his suggestions are presented here:

1. Counselors can provide support, nurturing, and empathy. They can also help clients see that "It is okay and normal to learn/change in steps or stages" (p. 225). Helping clients understand what they

can and cannot control can be a very powerful intervention indeed. Consider an unemployed aerospace worker who was laid off because of a reduction in the defense budget. Before this person can complete the grieving process and move on in life, the frustration around being fired must be "let go" and focus placed on what is controllable—personal decisions and planning.

2. Hof's second technique, re-labeling and reframing, can be used to turn negative views around and correct client's cognitive distortions. This may include helping clients see positive aspects of their situations, silver linings if you will. Not all events, however, have positive interpretations. For example, a man adjusting to the deaths of his wife and son in an automobile accident would be hard pressed to see anything good in this tragic event. Helping him gain hope that he can still have a positive future is appropriate; telling him that there is a silver lining would be cruel. However, a physician who had a similar experience, losing his wife and daughter in an automobile accident, said that the only thing that enabled him to cope was realizing the many lives that were saved when he donated their organs for transplantation.

3. A positive asset search (see Ivey & Ivey, 2003) is designed for the purpose of implementing Hof's third technique, "identifying . . . strengths and the expression of them, or of positive potentials" (p. 226). People undergoing work transitions may also find it helpful to look at their technical and transferable skills. (See Bolles, 2006, or Goodman and Hoppin, 1990.)

4. Helping clients identify and use their spiritual or transcendent beliefs, values, and resources is Hof's fourth technique. Because many religions, life philosophies, or ethical creeds offer encouragement and hope in times of trouble, the use of those beliefs, values, and resources can infuse some hope in a time of difficulty, pain, or even despair. Shame and guilt cause many individuals and couples to turn away from their religious and spiritual supports, just when they need them the most (Hof, 1993, p. 226). Spirituality is often enhanced or embraced for the first time in midlife. This phenomenon makes Hof's suggestion even more appropriate for counseling adults in transition.

5. Hof's fifth technique involves using absurdity, humor, and laughter. Hope can be increased when clients recapture or learn for the first time childlike playfulness and creativity. The physiological effects of laughter can be healing in themselves; psychologically, humor can help clients keep their problems in perspective.

Amundson (1996) proposed 12 reframing strategies for clients struggling with unemployment. These approaches, divided into looking at the past, present, and future, include normalization, looking at accomplishments, transferable skills, and attitudes, positive affirmation, externalizing the problem, and limiting negative thinking, which are all designed to help clients, "attain new perspectives on themselves and the labor market" (p. 161).

Seligman (2002) contended that optimism, too, is learnable. Blind optimism might be a mistake, but choice is the goal. For example, a risk analysis can help one determine whether optimism is the right course. If the risks are too great, one should perhaps be careful. (We do want our pilot to be pessimistic and de-ice the plane one more time!) But in navigating a transition, counselors can help their clients learn to choose when to take an optimistic stance—when to have hope.

Ellis (1984) proposed a step-by-step process for challenging a client's view of a situation. The process, often known by its acronym A-B-C-D-E, includes (a) discovering the Activating event, (b) identifying the client's Belief system, (c) identifying the emotional Consequences of the event, (d) Disputing the client's existing beliefs, and (e) arriving at new Effects. This A-B-C-D-E process is geared toward changing clients' thinking about events, beliefs, and consequences. A key element in this approach is the disputation or confrontation of irrational beliefs.

Using the analysis developed by Ellis (1984), Seligman (2002) proposed that people use one of the following techniques to change irrational beliefs:

1. *Distracting oneself:* Some ways to do this are the following:
   a. Think of something else: Counselors can help clients plan ready substitutes for disturbing thoughts, and clients can learn to use them. For example, one might ask newly laid off workers to practice thinking, "I am worthwhile" whenever they start to think, "I am useless." Thought-stopping, closely akin to thought substitution, focuses on not thinking about a particular person or event. (See *How to Survive the Loss of a Love,* Colgrove, Bloomfield, & McWilliams, 1991.)
   b. The imaginary umbrella stand: This technique involves leaving one's worries in an imaginary umbrella stand at the door of one's home or workplace. The premise is that it is easier to let go of troublesome ideas if they can be reclaimed when convenient. A related technique is to list disturbing thoughts to think about later.
   c. Physical reminders: Many people find it helpful to have a concrete reminder, for example, a rubber band around the wrist that can be snapped as a reminder when one starts to think troublesome thoughts.

2. *Disputation:* With this technique clients are taught to argue with their own beliefs and, we hope, win the argument. A recently divorced woman who wanted to date again but believed she was too unattractive to interest any man kept a log of any compliments she received or heard about herself. She enlisted a few trusted friends to help her and soon had a satisfyingly long list. These "facts" effectively disputed her beliefs, and she soon was able to change, or at least modify, her beliefs.

3. *Looking for alternative explanations:* It was said that the great actress Helen Hayes always felt sick to her stomach before a performance. Clients who experience nausea when anxious about an upcoming event, a job interview, for example, can tell themselves that they are preparing for a performance in the same way a great actress did.

4. *Decatastrophizing:* Going off a diet one evening does not mean being out of control forever. Nor does one bad grade mean flunking out of school. Many people need help in becoming aware that their catastrophic expectations are unlikely to materialize. Suppose, for example, you are trying to help a woman who moved across the country with her newly transferred husband. She is having trouble settling in and making friends. She says, "The neighbors are all snobs. I called on the woman across the street and she never even called me back. I know I'll never make any friends here." Assisting her to identify her irrational beliefs can help her to reopen her efforts at making friends.

Or take the adult who begins a session with her career counselor with, "This time I want to make the right decision. I want to get training in a field that I am sure will have opportunities for me and that I will enjoy and be able to stay with for the rest of my working life." Waiting for that kind of certainty—a near impossibility—could paralyze the client. Challenging the irrational belief may help the individual engage in effective career planning.

Transactional analysis (cf., Berne, 1964), another cognitive process useful in working with adults in transition, involves helping clients identify the aspects of themselves that derive from *parental* messages (often negative ones), remnants of *childish* thinking, and their rational *adult* parts. They can then make new decisions about what to think based on an understanding of what is real and true today. The recently transferred spouse described above may have been told as a child not to go where you are not wanted. This belief makes her even more prone to give up her attempts at making friends.

Cognitive restructuring is another thought-based approach in which an analysis of self-defeating thoughts and behavior is used as the precursor to changing how one deals with the world. Cudney (1980a, 1980b) proposed a system in which he invited clients to examine their self-defeating behaviors and to choose between what he called the life road and the death road—metaphors for ego-affirming and ego-destroying feelings, thoughts, and actions. Times of transition seem to call forth a particular need to rethink one's thought patterns, as previous ones may no longer fit new circumstances.

Networking, often touted but rarely taught, is another method clients can use to manage their need for support during work transitions, based on the fact that approximately 80% of jobs are found through some personal contact. In networking classes, clients are taught how to identify potential contacts, write a script, rehearse telephone calls, develop a record-keeping system, and follow-up on commitments. Learning how to network results from a cognitive intervention; actually networking is a behavioral change.

Meichenbaum (1977) used cognitive analysis to develop behavioral interventions. His stress inoculation training is based on the belief that people will cope more effectively if they understand the situation they are in and if they know and use techniques to reduce their anxiety. Ritter (1985) used Meichenbaum's concepts to help clients develop and rehearse a repertoire of self statements designed to help them prepare for, confront, and cope with stressors. Counselors can help clients formulate statements such as:

- You can develop a plan to deal with it, don't worry.
- Don't try to eliminate the fear entirely; just keep it manageable.
- One step at a time.
- Relax, you are in control; take a slow deep breath.
- Keep the focus on the present; what is it you have to do?
- It worked; you did it; it wasn't as bad as you expected (p. 43).

Behavioral Interventions

Behaviors can be defined to include thoughts, but here we will focus on overt actions. We believe behavior change is important and also that there are occasions when affective and cognitive change occur as a *result* of behavioral change.

Modeling, Role Play, and Rehearsal

These closely related techniques provide ways for clients to see others or see themselves performing desired behaviors. Imagine that you are working with a 40-year-old man who is having difficulty adapting to a new marriage. After his parents were divorced, he had little contact with his father. Twenty years of living on his own has made him unsure about how to be part of a couple. He tends to make unilateral decisions about activities and is then puzzled at his wife's resentment. His counselor suggests the following strategies:

1. Watch other couples and observe what the husband does, particularly in regard to decision making about how they will spend their time (*social modeling*).
2. Act out with the counselor a situation in which he is not sure how to behave. He will play his wife and the counselor will play him (*live modeling and role play*).
3. Act out the above scenario playing himself (*role play*).
4. Act out a real situation that he expects to face in the near future (*rehearsal*).

When using each of these interventions, the counselor needs to provide feedback about specific details of what is being done. It is also helpful to begin with easier behaviors and move up to more difficult ones. In the case described above, we might want first to have our client practice asking his wife's advice before he makes dinner reservations, and eventually discussing with her his career plans and long-term goals.

Imagery Training

A special case of rehearsal, imagery, allows people to mentally practice handling situations. Commonly used by athletes and performers, imagining oneself successfully behaving in the desired manner can be helpful in actually attaining the desired behavior. It has several advantages over rehearsal: it can be done alone, at any time; it applies in situations for which rehearsal is impractical; and it encourages clients to become self-directed, not depending on the counselor to play other roles or provide feedback.

Many people need practice in imagining a specific situation, but keep in mind that even though for the majority of people imagery is visual, for many it is auditory or kinesthetic. Ideally, it combines all three elements. Thus, a person preparing for the first day on a new job may want to "walk through" the day beforehand, imagining preparing for work, arriving there, seeing the worksite, hearing its sounds, feeling its atmosphere, performing the job duties, managing breaks and lunch, and ending the work day. Additional elements may be added as necessary and appropriate. When helping people with poor work records, for example, you may want to encourage them to imagine all the barriers that might prevent them from getting to work or completing the assigned tasks. Strategies for overcoming these barriers can then be identified and rehearsed.

Assertion Training

One way of helping clients change their situations is by teaching them some assertive skills—communications techniques that provide for the rights and dignity of others while maintaining one's own rights and dignity. Being assertive is an alternative to being passive or being aggressive. Counselors can help their clients integrate assertive approaches by examining the socialization messages they received as children. Many people heard things from their parents that they interpreted, rightly or wrongly, as, "You don't count" or "What you want doesn't matter." Or they may have heard "rules" such as "Don't make waves!", "Don't make trouble!", or "Don't draw attention to us!" People in vulnerable positions, for example women and members of some ethnic minorities, may have had such "rules" foisted on them even more firmly. People who received these kinds of messages tend to be passive more often than is useful to them. On the other hand, some people heard messages such as, "The squeaky wheel gets the grease" or "Might makes right." These people may tend to use an aggressive communication style.

Adult children of alcoholics often hear strong messages concerning keeping family secrets. Being truly assertive may require telling the truth about another's drinking or other "skeletons in the closet." It may be difficult for such clients to recognize that they have as much right to help as their family member has to the secret. In this case, assertiveness training may be a necessary prelude to any other helping interventions.

For assertion training to be useful, it must be translated into behavior. Clients are typically given an opportunity to practice difficult behaviors during the counseling sessions using roleplay and rehearsal and then are given "homework" that requests them to practice the behaviors in real situations. They then return and discuss what went right and what did not and perhaps practice again and try again in "real life." Most people who need assertion training are too passive, but there are some who clients who are too aggressive and can also benefit from it. These people, too, need new interaction skills and behaviors. Because of the increased potential for feedback, assertion training is often particularly effective in a group format.

Anxiety Reduction Techniques

Affectively oriented counselors may ask nervous clients about their feelings during anxiety-producing experiences. Cognitively oriented counselors may ask nervous clients about their thoughts. Behavioral counselors generally identify symptoms and focus on reducing the physical manifestations of anxiety or fear, often relying on progressive relaxation and systematic desensitization to help clients experience less anxiety. Although it is beyond the scope of this book to give instruction in implementing these behavioral strategies, they are often a useful beginning to any intervention in which anxiety is debilitating or blocking other change. We have found progressive relaxation often to be a useful beginning to a counseling session, allowing the client to be more fully present.

Combination Interventions

Few counselors adhere strictly to one type of intervention. Client needs differ and counselors must be able to vary their approach accordingly. Some interventions we find particularly helpful with adults in transition do not fit neatly into any of the above categories.

Problem-Solving Interventions

Force-field analysis, originally developed by Kurt Lewin in 1943, provides a method for analyzing the steps needed to reach a goal. The steps include (a) stating a goal or desired outcome, (b) identifying all of the pathways or methods you now know to reach the goal, (c) identifying all the actual or potential barriers that may prevent you from reaching your goal, (d) picturing the pathways and barriers as forces or vectors operating in opposite directions, and (e) discussing ways to increase the pathways or reduce or overcome the barriers. Many clients find this to be a helpful way to approach an action plan or solve a problem. And, as mentioned earlier, identifying barriers makes it more likely that a person will have the resources to manage them if and when they arise.

This approach was very successful with a rural displaced homemaker, Marie. She wanted to be a nurse's aide, but the community college was 60 miles away. Although she had a grant to attend school, was sure of her career goal, and very much wanted to be self-sufficient, all she could see were problems in attaining the goal. She listed innumerable barriers, including external barriers such as no childcare if her children were home sick from school, potential bad weather in the winter that might make driving difficult, and no private place to study at home. She also identified several internal barriers such as fear of failure, occasional bouts of depression, and a history of not following through on commitments.

Force-field analysis allowed Marie to visualize these barriers on paper. She then added, with the help of her counselor and a positive asset search, her ability to learn new things, her genuine delight in helping others, a new maturity, and a determination to make this change a successful one.

She identified a few new barriers also, including lack of funds for books and materials and a sister who thought she was nuts to work so hard and told her so frequently. She was then able to do the following: (a) make contingency plans for the external barriers, for example, find a neighbor who could handle child care in a pinch, (b) learn some assertion techniques to get her sister "off her back," (c) identify a person in her displaced homemaker support group to call when she got depressed or anxious, (d) investigate further grant funds from the college to help pay for books and materials, and (e) set aside a small corner of her bedroom for a private study place. Although new problems may well arise for her, she has learned a way of analyzing them.

Many people find other problem-solving strategies useful. For some, concrete, sequential, decision-making activities fit their personal style. DECIDES, the easily remembered acronym for the step-by-step approach developed by Krumboltz and Hamel in 1977, has become a classic. They suggest that clients

1. Define the problem: What is the decision to be made?
2. Establish an action plan: How will I make this decision?
3. Clarify values: What is most important to me?
4. Identify alternatives: What are my choices?
5. Discover probable outcomes: What is likely to be the result of following each alternative?
6. Eliminate alternatives systematically: Which alternatives won't fit my values and situation? Which have the least probability of success?
7. Start action: What do I need to do to make my plans a reality?

Other people suggest more intuitive decision-making approaches. H. B. Gelatt's (1991) positive uncertainty theory posits that if you wait to be sure, you will never decide; if you decide too firmly, you won't be flexible enough to change as needed. His plan was based on two attitudes: (a) accepting the uncertainty of the past, present, and future, and (b) feeling positive about that uncertainty. It includes four paradoxical principles: "(1) Be focused and flexible about what you want, ... (2) Be aware and wary about what you know, ... (3) Be objective and optimistic about what you believe, ... [and] (4) Be practical and magical about what you do" (p. 12).

Solution-Focused Brief Counseling

Another problem-solving strategy (Walter & Peller, 1992) is based on the premise that maintaining a solution focus helps clients avoid playing "ain't it awful?" (Berne, 1964) and move to looking for new thoughts, feelings, and behaviors. Clients (a) identify what they want, stating their goals in positive terms, (b) discuss what is working—exceptions to the current unproductive behavior, and (c) identify what could be hypothetically happening—if a miracle occurred.

Play Therapy

Typically considered an intervention for children, Frey (1993), however, made a case for using play therapy with adults. It is especially effective for adults who did not play much as children or for those who have reached some sort of therapeutic impasse. Because play is naturally illogical, it frees people to break away from the way things have been and see what could be. Perhaps it taps into different parts of the brain than other approaches. Regardless of the mechanism, it seems to work with many clients. Much has been written about using humor in helping, a technique closely related to play therapy (e.g., Moody, 1978; Mosak, 1987). Humor, too, used with delicacy, can help adults in transition see their problems in a new light.

Developing Rituals

Certain transitions, for example weddings, births, or retirement come with attached rituals that ease the passage. Others, such as divorce, job loss, chronic health problems, or failing to get a promotion are ignored. Furthermore, the rituals that often were a part of life before the transition may be accessible no longer. For example, three couples who were all married on the same date, in different years, developed a tradition of celebrating their anniversaries jointly, making it a special event. When one of the couples got divorced, the tradition continued with the other two. Not only did the former husband and wife lose a cherished celebration, but they also felt left out of an important ritual.

A ritual can help with the "betwixt and between period" to connect you to your former roles, assumptions, relationships, and routines, and to move you to your new ones. Myerhoff (1984) discussed the importance of rituals in helping people deal with marginal periods when they are shifting from one phase of life to another, that is, when they are in transition. Housewarming parties are a commonplace example of this. Originally these events provided a way for people to acquire the goods necessary to set up housekeeping; for most people today, they are a ritual to connect old friends with one's new locale.

Non-events, in particular, are rarely ritualized. Counselors can use Myerhoff's suggestions to help clients develop new rituals. For example, a couple that has decided not to have children may celebrate the decision with the purchase of fragile glassware and invite their friends for an "exhibition." A man who has realized that he will never be promoted to upper management may take his family on a vacation to "celebrate" the lessened work commitment that results from this awareness.

CONCLUSION

The foregoing has been an attempt to summarize some of the techniques you might use in helping an adult client cope with transitions using the Hackney–Cormier and transition models in combination with other techniques. We have discussed counselor techniques to be used in the assessment, goal setting, and intervention stages of the model, as appropriate in helping individuals increase the balance of deficits to resources in the areas of Situation, Self, Support, and Strategy. We have also indicated how counselors from different theoretical orientations might use this schema to help their clients.

CHAPTER 8

Group Counseling

Eleven years ago I totally lost my zest for life when my wife of a lifetime was killed. . . . Soon, with the help of some young people I discovered group psychotherapy. . . . The most helpful idea I found to combat acute depression came from a young woman I met through the group. She said that my pain of depression came because the "arrow" of my thrust in life, my attention, my energy was turned inward. Unless I turned the arrow around, outward, and forward in time, the pain would remain. . . . To turn the arrow around, I found, was not easy. At age 63 there is, looking back, a trodden path easy to discern, easy to reminisce about. But looking forward there is untrodden ground, new trails must be broken constantly that takes effort. (Bergman, n.d., p. 2)

In the statement above, taken from an article entitled, "Fresh Currents in the Stream of Life," the author wrote poignantly of the effects of group counseling on his search for identity and meaning in his life. He also talked of the role of the group in helping him develop appropriate strategies for coping with a major loss.

This chapter focuses on techniques counselors can use to work in groups. Groups are complex, requiring counselors to combine individual counseling and group management skills. We begin this chapter with some general information about the value of groups for adults in transition and depict a typology of groups. Then we describe a variety of groups and specific techniques designed for adults who are experiencing different kinds of transitions—some individual and others involving relationships or work and career. In that way, the three major parts of this chapter correspond to the three chapters in Part II. We then turn to an examination of the value of groups in helping people assess their assets and liabilities in each of the 4 S areas. Finally, we examine self-help groups and the roles counselors can play with this growing phenomenon.

GROUP COUNSELING AS A MODALITY

Groups have been around since the beginning of humankind and across all cultures. People have historically gathered into groups to create, achieve, and resolve matters that would be otherwise impossible (Gladding, 2003). Besides the potential to accomplish tasks, groups are sources of meaning and belonging, meeting needs for personal contact and interaction (Burn, 2004).

It is tempting to say that the keys to success in working with adults in transition are support, support, and support. Whether the transition is a temporary one or a permanent one, whether it represents a role gain or a role loss, and whether it comes "on time" or "off time," people experiencing major changes in their life often benefit from a better understanding of what they are going through, and from realizing that "I'm not the only one that's got it," and "I don't have to handle it alone." Stated differently, adults in transition need information and support, both of which can often be provided most effectively through group counseling.

Curative Factors in Group Counseling

Let us consider how Yalom's (1985) discussion of the therapeutic factors in group therapy applies to adults in transition. He identified 11 curative factors: imparting information, instillation of hope, universality, altruism, corrective recapitulation of the primary family group, development of socializing techniques, imitative behavior, interpersonal learning, group cohesiveness, catharsis, and existential factors.

Imparting Information

We can hardly overestimate the value to clients of gaining information about the transition they are experiencing or anticipating. Regardless of whether that transition involves confronting a change in family status or a career change, or whether it is an event or a non-event, obtaining information about the change helps individuals gain some sense of control. Yalom (1985) noted that information often "functions as the initial binding force in the group until other curative factors become operative" (p. 11).

Instillation of Hope

People in a group who have "been there," that is, people who have experienced a similar transition and are further along in the process of moving through it, can instill hope in people who are moving into the transition. The same curative factor can operate whether the group is designed for returning learners, dislocated workers, or people who have just learned they are HIV-positive. People who are reeling from the impact of the transition can benefit from seeing people who have begun to cope with it or who have integrated the transition as part of their lives. For example, people who fear losing their sight, or have been told that they will, can receive tremendous inspiration from watching people who are blind function. A major strength of many of the 12-step programs, such as Alcoholics Anonymous, is that at each session people who have experienced the particular problem and are in the process of "recovering" tell their stories to inspire others.

Universality

As they move into or out of any particular situation, adults can benefit from discovering their commonalities, from realizing they are not alone. Such a realization, referred to by Yalom (1985) as a sense of universality, typically comes when people in a group learn that many others have shared similar experiences and feelings.

A group of older adults, meeting at a senior center, arrived at such an awareness in an unusual way. One member of the group reported on his discomfort as he reflected on the large holiday dinner at his daughter's house the previous week. "I don't understand," he said, "why I always feel so much more comfortable when our daughter comes to our house than when we go to hers." As other members of the group reported a similar preference for being hosts rather than guests, they realized that they were seeing relocation of the holiday dinner as a signal of decreasing abilities. It became a metaphor for their fears about becoming dependent on their children. As they discussed this with their counselor, several members of the group realized that while fear of becoming a burden was an understandable and shared concern, it was counterproductive to let those fears—that anticipation of a possible future transition—interfere with current pleasures.

Capuzzi and Gross (1992) asserted that seeing one's problem as an example of a more general pattern may serve to demystify and deintensify the problem. Such a realization can also lay the groundwork for action steps to deal with the problem. It can help people mobilize their energies to help themselves and each other and perhaps seek social redress, attempting to change the situation.

Altruism

Helping each other relates to Yalom's (1985) fourth curative factor, altruism. He observed that clients benefit "from the intrinsic act of giving . . . they offer support, suggestions, reassurance, insights, and share similar problems with one another" (p. 14). When people experience major transitions, their self-esteem often plummets. The opportunity to be helpful to others by providing support and/or information may help to reverse the downward slide in self-esteem. Consider the case of a recently divorced woman who is seeing herself as an unlovable failure. If she is able to provide support to another group member and gets a smile in return, it may help her to see herself as "worth being with."

Corrective Recapitulation of the Primary Family Group

In Yalom's (1985) view, a major value of therapy groups is that they help patients relive and correct problems stemming from their original family groups. Early issues, such as sibling rivalry, can surface and become topics of discussion. Although such a "correction" can be very valuable for certain clients, most groups for adults in transition do not spend time reviewing early experiences in their family group. When such assistance seems necessary, a referral for individual or specialized group therapy is appropriate.

Development of Socializing Techniques

Groups can serve as a meaningful laboratory for learning social skills. Consider, for example, the widower who relied on his wife to make social engagements with friends and nurture family relationships. His actual or feared ineptness in such situations may keep him from reaching out for the sociability and intimacy he now needs. In getting feedback from other group members about how they perceive him, he can develop "outsight" as well as the insight that can come from individual counseling. The group can help him identify and acknowledge the social skills he does have, as well as help him develop additional strategies.

Imitative Behavior

In groups, members have an opportunity to model themselves after the group leader and/or other members. They also can learn vicariously as they observe interactions between the counselor and other group members as well as among members themselves. Pearson (1992) noted that in groups "members can 'catch' functional attitudes such as hope, perseverance, concern for others," and can also learn "specific coping strategies such as asking for help, publicly admitting failures, and substituting constructive for destructive behaviors" (p. 98). Groups for people diagnosed with a particular disease, or for their family members are clear examples of groups of adults in transition who can benefit from modeling or vicarious learning.

Interpersonal Learning

Yalom (1985) contended that group experiences can enrich the insight provided by individual counseling. He talked of the group as a social microcosm in which clients can display their maladaptive behavior, learn how others perceive that behavior, and come to take responsibility for the impact they have on other people. In groups, leaders and members can identify ways in which individuals are employing self-defeating or life-giving approaches (Cudney, 1980a). Such feedback can facilitate learning for people who are trying to adapt to life changes. For example, a woman whose child was killed in an accident while she was out of town may continue to berate herself for leaving. The group can help her identify the many things she had done for her child and try to stop her from dwelling on the "if onlys."

Group Cohesiveness

According to Yalom (1985), "cohesiveness in group therapy is the analogue of relationship in individual therapy" (p. 48). Members of cohesive groups are more accepting of each other, more supportive, and more likely to self-disclose. Such cohesiveness can be encouraged by skilled leaders who help people talk about their transitions and give each other appropriate feedback. Capuzzi and Gross (1992) suggested, "The actual benefit of self-disclosure and feedback relates to how these processes generate empathy among members. Empathy, or the actual experience of being understood by other members, is what catalyzes personal growth and understanding in the context of a group" (p. 19). Being part of a cohesive group can also supply the support and motivation that people in transition need to take constructive action on their own behalf.

Appropriate humor can add to group cohesiveness. Sometimes humor involves using a paradoxical approach. For example, a counselor can ask group members to brainstorm strategies that will guarantee that the transitions they are contemplating will lead to disaster. A paradoxical instruction might be: "Think of as many ways as possible to 'not listen' to friends, family, and co-workers!" or "What could you do to turn off people in your support system?" People who have recently assumed a management position can be asked what they could do to make staff meetings as dull as possible. Once the laughter subsides, the group can often help members develop appropriate strategies.

In the article quoted at the beginning of this chapter, Bergman (n.d.) described some of the efforts he made, including returning to school, becoming a writer, taking up dancing, and traveling to Europe by himself. Paradoxically, one of the major actions that helped Bergman cope with the transition of being widowed was embarking on several other transitions.

The support and encouragement he received from the group seemed to inspire these new directions.

Catharsis

Many people experiencing transitions have a lot to be angry, sad, or frightened about. Yet they may be reluctant to express their feelings to their family or friends for fear of further burdening them. Similarly, people experiencing some transitions may be reluctant to let work associates know of the situation, or their feelings about it, for fear they may be considered less valuable as an employee.

The movie *Philadelphia* captured the agony of an attorney with AIDS who feared telling his law firm of his disease. One woman, recently recovered from cancer surgery, had difficulty deciding what to tell potential employers about her health. She saw her recovery and desire to get on with her life as a reason she would be a conscientious and loyal employee but feared employers might view her as emotionally unstable or an insurance risk. Groups provide a safe and supportive environment in which people can share such concerns and achieve catharsis.

Group counselors must constantly make decisions about how to handle such sharing of concerns. Expressing concerns is cathartic up to a point. If the goal of the group, however, is to help people develop strategies for dealing with their transition, then counselors must be aware of when and how to redirect clients in the direction of action steps, to help them move from "Ain't it awful" to "What can I do?" How that is done may depend in part on the theoretical orientation of the counselor and on the type of group.

Existential Factors

Acknowledging that the term *existential* is hard to define, Yalom (1985) related it to "the central features that make us human—that is purpose, responsibility, sentience, will, values, courage, spirit" (p. 94). Such concepts may be helpful to adults in transition even when they are not discussed directly. For some people contemplating or experiencing difficult transitions, the realization of their own ultimate responsibility for their lives may be both reassuring and challenging.

Cautions About Group Counseling

Although group work can be extremely valuable, it is clearly not appropriate for everybody. Gazda (1989) noted that the same factors that make group counseling potent may also add risk. When several clients are present, the counselor has less control, and some clients may be ostracized or pressured by other members. Clients may also experience "sibling rivalry" and worry about breaches of confidentiality. Such concerns underline the importance of group counselors being well trained in group leadership as well as in counseling skills. These cautions also argue for a carefully thought-out selection and orientation process for group members. As part of that process, Corey (1995) suggested that group leaders warn prospective members about particular risks. For example, "members should be made aware of the possibility that participating in a group (or any other therapeutic endeavor) may disrupt their lives" (p. 34). Corey noted that even changes that are constructive in the long run may create crisis and turmoil along the way.

Another major risk of group counseling is that confrontation may be misused. "Intrusive interventions, overly confrontive leader tactics, and pushing of members beyond their limits often produce negative outcomes" (Corey, 1995, p. 36). Corey (2005) stated that skillful confrontation requires that the leader truly cares about the person and that the member needs an ample opportunity to consider and respond to what is being said. Rather than avoid confrontation, Corey recommended that leaders model effective and nonjudgmental behavioral feedback.

Gladding (2003) observed that research on the impact of group counseling is less sophisticated than evaluations of individual counseling. He summarized some of the methods that can be used to assess group members' progress on a variety of dimensions. Evaluation continues for the duration of the group and is an ongoing process. Leaders must not only appraise the movement and direction of the group, but must also teach the participants how to evaluate themselves and the group outcomes (Corey, 2005). Because groups are not the treatment of choice for all clients, we strongly urge practitioners to build evaluation procedures into their programs whenever possible.

Several authors have identified categories of people who may be inappropriate for groups including people who are paranoid, obsessively self-centered, out of touch, suicidal, highly hostile, aggressive, or in crisis. These people may not be good candidates for a group experience (Brown, 1988). When considering older adults, Burnside (1984) recommended excluding people who are disturbed and prone to wandering, incontinent, manic-depressive, psychotic, deaf, or hypochondriacal.

On a more practical level, we believe that groups are not the best method for people who are preoccupied with their own problems to the extent that they find it difficult to listen to others or to "take turns." An orientation session may provide an opportunity for the group counselor and each potential member to make an informed decision about the appropriateness of the group.

Types of Groups

There are different types of groups, each requiring both general established competencies and advanced competencies for particular areas of specialization (Association for Specialists in Group Work, 2000; Schneider & Corey, 2005). Schneider and Corey identified four types of groups: *task-facilitation* groups, which include task forces, committees and planning groups; *psychoeducational* groups, comprising well-functioning people who may need information in a certain area; *counseling* groups, in which the focus is the resolution of specific short-term issues; and *psychotherapy* groups, in which work is done to remediate in-depth psychological problems.

Gazda (1989) identified three major types of group work: group guidance, group counseling, and group psychotherapy. In his schema, *guidance* groups are designed to be preventive and growth engendering; *psychotherapy* groups are seen as remedial; whereas *counseling* groups are both preventive and remedial. All the types of groups can be helpful to people anticipating or experiencing transitions if there is a good match between their needs and the content and process of the group. Self-help groups, in addition to the above types of groups, can also be extremely valuable.

Group guidance programs could be a broader term that encompasses the psychoeducational groups outlined by Schneider and Corey (2005). Examples of psychoeducational groups that would fit into this category include those for stress management, assertion training, and overcoming perfectionism. These types of groups are generally offered in an educational format, in which a major task of the leader is to disseminate information. In some guidance groups, members have an opportunity to personalize the information, so the experience moves toward group counseling. *Group counseling* tends to address the usual, yet often difficult, problems of living that frequently bring people to counseling (Schneider & Corey, 2005). These groups, therefore, are designed for individuals experiencing problems that information alone cannot solve. Usually, the topics covered in group counseling are developmental or situational in nature. *Group psychotherapy,* on the other hand, is targeted to people who have serious problems, often of long duration. As the major goal of such groups is remediation or personality change, they are generally not needed for adults in transition unless the transition brings to the surface much deeper issues.

Adults in transition may need training in social skills. Such training can be provided by any of the above group formats, depending on the orientation of the group. For example, a stress-management program that focuses on explaining the sources of stress and giving information on stress-management techniques would be considered psychoeducational or group guidance. A group that combines provision of information about stress with opportunities for group members to practice stress management techniques with each other and to give and get feedback, would be group counseling. If the goal of the group is to "uncover" reasons members experience various events as stressful and to attempt psychodynamic interventions, the group would be more therapeutic in nature.

Pearson (1992) discussed the contribution of group counseling programs to increasing member coping resources or what he calls effective self-enhancement. In his view, this comes from a combination of (a) consciousness-raising or awareness of a need for change, (b) strengthened commitment to take action, and (c) empowerment or development of knowledge or skills required for self-enhancement.

Cultural Diversity

Although Pearson's three objectives can be a guide for group counselors in many situations, it is important to realize they may not be effective for all counselees. Although many cultures function in groups and value participation in them, what actually occurs in these groups may be quite different from the expected behaviors and norms of traditional counseling groups. For example, some members may be hesitant to become active participants or share personal information in a group counseling situation. Many cultures prohibit the sharing of personal information that will bring shame on the individual and more importantly, on the family (DeLucia-Waack & Donigian, 2004).

As indicated by Locke and Parker (1994), clients from different cultural backgrounds may also have different perceptions of themselves and different motivations. Cultural identity directly influences the way a person interacts with others as well as group process factors such as proxemics (emotional and physical distance), unconscious behavior, emotional intensity, and silence as a form of communication (DeLucia-Waack & Donigian, 2004). Working with culturally diverse clients requires that group leaders have the awareness, knowledge, and sensitivity to effectively deal with the concerns these clients bring to a group. It is not ethically possible for counselors to ignore their own or their clients' cultural background or cultural context (Schneider & Corey, 2005).

In a provocative article on cross-cultural considerations in group counseling, Newlon and Arciniega (1992) challenged counselors to consider the cultural implications of traditional counselor approaches in working with members of minority groups. They noted, for example, that "Afro-American [sic] group members may come from situations in which they feel powerless, hostile, and lacking specific direction. . . . Therefore, Afro-American members may want concrete responses from the group leaders much like they would receive from respected family members or friends" (p. 290).

Similarly, they stated that even though acculturated Hispanics may respond to traditional group counseling, "traditional immigrants, or first generation, are going to be more hesitant to accept participation in group approaches that rely on individual responsibility and abstract thinking. They will more likely respond to the group leader as an authority figure who will help interpret the system" (p. 291). They also asserted that Southeast Asians are more likely to want a leader who will "take an active, directive role and give them explicit directions on how to solve problems and bring immediate relief from disabling distress" (p. 293).

A Taiwanese student expressed frustration, explaining that his advisor thought him unqualified to be a counselor because he always held back his personal feelings in group discussions. "He did not understand that we seldom 'confess' our 'personal stuff' to someone else" (Chin, 1993, p. 2). People with this kind of a background may have difficulty with many personal growth group experiences and may benefit more from a highly structured group or from individual counseling.

Although groups offer definite advantages, there are also limitations to using group formats with culturally diverse populations. However, increasingly, counseling professionals in other countries are being trained to lead groups. As group work is woven differently into different cultures, it is imperative that the traditions of these cultures be honored, valued, and integrated into group work. An example of this is in the Native American culture, with the Sweat Lodge ceremony. This is an excellent example of how groups are used in different cultures, yet with different traditions and meanings.

Cultures are not static and an example of a culture undergoing dramatic change is China, which opened its doors to the outside world in the 1970s. In China, group work has been embraced as a tool for solving a variety of social problems. For example, there has been a growing demand for these group services to assist workers and students to identify the kind of future work and education that fits them and the needs of their society. Counselors working in this setting must be mindful of the dominant philosophical traditions of Taoism and Confucianism that guide behaviors and relationships with others and with nature. It is evident that working with different cultures demands skillful and sensitive interventions. For example, sufficient time must be allowed for processing what happened within the group and, especially, what did it mean? Processing and understanding meanings can be challenging in these types of settings, in which there are language differences as well as cultural differences (Conyne, Wilson, & Tang, 2000).

While discussing groups and cultural diversity, we must recognize that all groups, are, in fact, diverse. DeLucia-Waack and Donigian (2004) have proposed a model to systematically incorporate multicultural awareness into the group work process. This includes activities that explore cultural heritage, worldview, and background, along with confronting racism and prejudice. They also recommend a series of steps that group leaders can take to work toward multicultural group work competency. These steps include the following:

- Examine your own cultural and ethnic values and racial identity to understand who you are as a person.
- Examine your beliefs about group work and assumptions inherent within the Eurocentric view of group work.
- Learn about other cultures in terms of what they value and how this may affect their relationships in group work.
- Develop a personal plan for group work that emphasizes and utilizes cultural diversity.

Personal and professional growth in the area of diversity is an ongoing process. Addressing and honoring diversity is a challenging, as well as an enriching aspect of the group counseling experience.

Characteristics of Effective Groups

Robert Weiss did some of the earliest work conceptualizing the needs of people in transition and setting up groups to test his model. In a seminal article, Weiss (1976) described a useful system for classifying three different types of situational distress: crises, transition states, and deficit situations. He defined a crisis as a sudden, severely upsetting situation of short duration that requires individuals to mobilize their energies and resources. Examples might be a serious accident or the sudden onset of a major illness in the family. The crisis may end with a return to normal or with a changed situation. In the case of a serious illness, the individual may recover, become permanently disabled, or die. In either of the latter cases, surviving family members enter a transition state involving relational and personal changes.

The end of a transition state is usually marked by a new life organization and personal identity. If the new life situation is not satisfactory, then the individuals are in a deficit situation. For example, widowed persons with dependent children may find continuous difficulty in raising children as single parents.

In Weiss's (1976) view, people in each of the three states benefit from different forms of assistance. Individuals in crisis need both support and services to help them through the crisis; those in deficit situations need continuing, problem-focused support. Those in transition experience a void because their habitual patterns have been disrupted and they have not yet developed alternative ways of handling their lives. To help fill this void, people in transition need a cognitive framework that orders and explains their experiences and a temporary community of others in the same situation. Individuals in transition states are particularly likely to benefit from counseling as the decisions they make at this time may affect the rest of their lives.

Effective transition programs include three kinds of helpers:

- the expert who has studied the underlying issues connected with a particular transition;
- the veteran who has successfully negotiated a similar transition; and
- other group members who offer the immediate understanding that comes from being in the same boat.

In Weiss's (1976) view, each kind of helper can assist individuals in transition as they struggle to establish a new emotional equilibrium.

Weiss's research also speaks to the importance of designing groups to meet the needs of people experiencing different transitions. For example, he found significant differences in what worked for groups of separated and widowed people. Separated people found discussions of the nature of separation helpful whereas bereaved people found that discussions of the nature of grief evoked a great deal of pain. He also found that mixed-sex groups were valuable for separated people but not for widowed people. The separated people came to understand their former spouses better as a result of hearing from other men or women. Widowed persons did not share the same need to understand things from their spouse's viewpoint.

Weiss's (1976) findings on the importance of tailoring subject matter to meet the needs of different groups have wide applicability. Let us look at two groups in transition: first semester graduate students and newly promoted supervisors. Both groups can benefit from "cognitive information" about their transition, as well as from the support of veterans and peers. Information about the transition *process* would help both groups, but members of each group would need information specific to their particular transition. A major job of the expert here is to identify underlying issues that are relevant for each group.

Weiss's model can apply to intrapersonal, interpersonal, and work related groups. The following discussion begins with an examination of transitions that may bring clients to group counseling and then moves to a description of representative groups and sample activities.

GROUPS FOR PEOPLE FACING INTRAPERSONAL TRANSITIONS

Intrapersonal transitions are often triggered by existential questions such as "Who am I?" or "Where am I going?" Often these questions stem from non-events, realizations such as "I am not the person I expected to be," or "I took a long look at my life, and saw all the things that did not happen."

Intrapersonal Transitions That May Bring Clients to Groups

Decade birthdays or other marker moments may precipitate intrapersonal transitions as reflected in the following newspaper column headed, "At 40, at midday, a time for change": Coasting toward my 40th birthday. . . . I was half-listening to National Public Radio when a man mentioned the birth of a baby—"a baby," he said "at the dawn of its day" . . . the voice inside my head said, "If a baby is at the dawn of its day, where am I at 40? The light is changing in my life. Although several hours of sunlight remain, and the evening holds it own allure, my morning is gone. High noon passed and I didn't even notice" (Ager, 1994, p. F1).

Sometimes intrapersonal transitions are triggered by external events that leave individuals feeling very much alone. Such was the case of Gregory Bergman, whom we met at the beginning of this chapter, whose internal transition was triggered by his wife's sudden death.

For many adults, a major internal transition may be suddenly defining themselves as old or older. This redefinition may be triggered by seeing an "old" face in the mirror, by thinking that "I sound just like my mother when she was old!"; by receiving a letter stating that at 35 one is no longer part of the "junior congregation" at church, or by being offered a senior discount. Groups may provide a good opportunity for adults to discuss their feelings about their aging, to identify ways to seek support, and to consider strategies for garnering more control.

Illustrative Groups and Techniques for Intrapersonal Transitions

In the 1960s, prompted by the resurgence of the feminist movement, counseling centers around the country developed a variety of group counseling programs to help women—and sometimes men also—explore, understand, and cope with issues of identity, autonomy, and life meaning. Under different rubrics and with different approaches, many of these programs have continued. A sampling of personal growth workshops, some carried over from earlier years, reflects the variety of groups.

Investigation into Identity

The Continuum Center of Oakland University in Rochester, MI, originally designed a program to help women think about who they were, apart from their roles as wives and mothers, and how they could most effectively broaden their roles and their views of themselves. To encourage such exploration, through the program the women were provided with opportunities to identify personal goals, analyze conflicting responsibilities, and develop strategies for improving communication skills with family, friends, and coworkers (Continuum Center, Oakland University, 1978). Similar programs, under different names, have continued into the new millennium, and now attract men as well as women.

This program and others like it combine provision of information by a professional counselor with opportunities for participants to personalize the information in small groups facilitated by a peer counselor. Given its combination of information, group support, and role modeling of peer counselors, the program taps into many of the curative factors identified by Yalom and Weiss.

At many sessions in this program, group leaders use structured exercises to stimulate discussion. For example, the counselor may explain Virginia Satir's (1972) models of poor communication, giving examples of placating, blaming, overly logical, and irrelevant behaviors. Then participants consider which of the behaviors they are most likely to use when transitions have created stress in their lives. Group members also talk about and practice becoming more honest or, in Satir's terms, more "real."

The four S's in the transition model also provide a focus for counselors. Group members can define their particular transition, identify the resources and deficits they bring to it, and consider alternative ways to access support and develop new strategies. For example, Jack Williams, the man from Chapter 4 who is considering going into business for himself, might learn that his awareness of "time left" is understandable in terms of what we know about adult development. He would probably gain support from realizing that other group members are struggling with similar concerns, and he might become familiar with other ways to "be a man." Group leaders could help him identify the many areas in his life in which he had experienced success, urge him to consider how he had managed those, and encourage him to think of ways to utilize his skills in new arenas. He could also use the group to "rehearse" strategies he might use when talking to his family about his concerns.

Life Mission: The Essence of You

Cecilia Peters (personal communication, 1993) developed the Life Mission workshop, based on the book by Stephan (1989) that leads participants through an internal intuitive process to help them identify what they really want in life. The program examines ways to respond to a personal "calling" through a career, a pastime, a cause, or anything in between.

To help group members with self-exploration, counselors ask them to list and discuss, 25 words or more that describe themselves, preferably not in relation to other people. They are also asked to list their fears, then to recast their statements in terms of how their life would be without those fears. In terms of the transition model, these are techniques counselors can use to help people learn more about their views of themselves and their situations and to begin to identify what is supportive to them. Throughout the workshop, a variety of visualizations and meditations are used, some of which can then be recast in terms of alternative strategies. In this group, spirituality is included as an important element as members explore the meaning and mission of their lives.

In the Life Mission workshop, the leader uses the group to encourage self-acceptance and acceptance of others and sees group support as an essential ingredient of the program. In Yalom's (1985) terms, the workshop serves to instill hope and involves many of the other curative factors. Such a group may appeal to people who are "right-brained" in their approach to life and may be helpful to people who need to deal with unresolved developmental task issues, such as achieving autonomy. The workshop is, therefore, an example of a psychotherapeutic group appropriate for people in transition.

Groups for Persons with Particular Illnesses

Coping with a major illness is obviously a significant transition. Livneh and Sherwood-Hawes (1993) discussed the value of group counseling for persons who have had heart attacks and suggested cognitive, affective, and behavioral goals for participants. Cognitive goals include using information about cardiac impairment to realistically assess their strengths and limitations; affective goals focus on provision of support, relief of tension, and reduction of depression; and behavioral goals include development of skills to promote independent functioning, utilize appropriate exercise and relaxation techniques, and access interpersonal and community resources. They suggested that groups be conducted in an inpatient setting so that members can "practice strategies for coping with problems, and achieve a less complicated transition from the hospital or rehabilitation center into the external community" (p. 57). The authors recommended groups that are educationally based and focus on coping skills rather than on development of insight alone.

A special challenge with this population is that persons who have had a heart attack may deny that they have heart disease or acknowledge the presence of the disease but deny its seriousness. Three strategies that may be used to undermine the impact of denial are the raising of awareness, mild confrontation, and the inclusion of successfully coping veteran participants in group meetings. This recommendation fits well with those of Weiss (1976).

Another area of illness relates to breast cancer patients. Two decades of research on women with breast cancer has supported the theory that group therapy is effective in reducing mood disturbances and anxiety, while enhancing the quality of life and extending survival time. These findings are hopeful, in that 80% of breast cancer patients report significant distress. Groups have been successful in improving the psychological, social, and physiological well-being of these women as they undergo the necessary medical interventions for breast cancer (Gore-Felton, 1999).

Life Review Groups

Since Robert Butler first articulated the concept, life review groups have become increasingly popular as a counseling intervention with older adults (Capuzzi, Gross, & Friel, 1990; Moody, 1988; Waters & Goodman, 1990). Although people of all ages periodically take stock of their lives, often at times of transition, this activity has special meaning in old age. At that time, the existential questions people ask themselves may also involve a look backwards and become not just "Who am I?" but "Who have I been?" and "How did I do?" The answers to these questions may affect how people feel about themselves in terms of integrity versus despair, the developmental task of old age identified by Erikson (1950). Having such discussions in a group underlines the value of the existential curative factor identified by Yalom (1985).

Doing a life review can help older adults decide what to do with material and emotional legacies. Singer, Tracz, and Dworkin (1991) concluded that life review groups can encourage socialization, lead to a sense of self-worth and life satisfaction, and help alleviate loneliness, hopelessness, and depression. Sherman (1987) compared topic-focused reminiscence groups with those in which a focus on feelings was added and found that the latter had a more positive impact on the emotional quality of participants' lives. "Not only did they report that the present was enlivened by their memories, but for most there appeared to be a newer, more open, and accepting or integrative attitude toward the past" (p. 572).

Counselors can trigger life reviews in many different ways, depending on the needs of particular clients and groups. For example, if group members need to activate supports in their lives, group counselors can ask them to think about various periods of their lives and to identify the people and activities that were most important to them at each stage. Counselors can then encourage participants to think about how their support system has changed over time and what they did to access support in the past. Several techniques for helping older adults learn from their past are described in Waters and Goodman (1990).

In guiding a life review, counselors can help group members gain a sense of pride from looking at the people they have influenced and the crises they have weathered. Such recollections may also serve as an excellent vehicle for encouraging people to identify past coping strategies and to consider how they can be adapted to fit new transitions. Many different groups have developed programs for stimulating life reviews. For example, the American Association of Retired Persons (AARP) has a program entitled "Reminiscence: Finding Meaning in Memories" and offers a *Reminiscence Training Kit* (1989) for potential group leaders. Packages, which include photographs, music, stories, and old household items to use as triggers are available in many public libraries.

Although most life reviews involve talking, a variety of props, such as old magazines and newspapers, political buttons, greeting cards, or photographs, can be used to stimulate memories and discussions. People whose transitions involve a reduction in cognitive functioning may find such stimulation valuable. Music works particularly well in such cases. In many long-term care settings, older adults who have difficulty with conversations may be seen singing and dancing to songs from their past. This kind of success experience may help to strengthen the coping resources of people whose balance of assets to deficits is declining.

In discussing techniques for counseling people older than 60, Stachow (1993) urged counselors to consider the extent to which clients are experiencing fears of, or actual, loss of control over mind, body, spirit, finances, environment, or relationships. In her view, a goal of counseling is to help people realize that change is possible and worth pursuing at any stage of life. To help older adults regain a sense of mastery, she recommended asking questions such as

- How has your life changed recently?
- What do you think is happening to you?
- Have you ever felt this way before?
- How did you cope with it (or other difficulties) before?
- Why can't you do that now?
- What would you like to do about this situation?

Questions such as these can be used in individual or group counseling. In a group situation, they might provide an excellent opportunity for group members to provide feedback to each other, to share resources, and to take advantage of many of the curative factors identified above. Such factors also operate in groups for people facing transitions in their family or with other close relationships.

GROUPS FOR PEOPLE FACING FAMILY–RELATIONSHIP TRANSITIONS

When we think of groups for people in transition, those involving inter-personal relationships are often the first that come to mind. A glance at the community services section of many newspapers reveals a variety of groups for people moving into or out of relationships.

Common Transitions Bringing Clients to Groups

Relationship transitions may be triggered by one's own decisions or actions or by those of somebody else. Reflecting this difference, those in groups for divorced persons often somewhat ruefully identify themselves as "dumpers" or "dumpees"; in couples groups, some may consider themselves to be "draggers" and others "draggees." Whether a person is the instigator of a change or the reactor to it, drastic changes in the pat-tern of relationships are often the impetus for people to seek counseling.

A variety of transitions can bring to the surface recurring themes having to do with intimacy, belonging, and mattering. Adults worry about intimacy as they consider what kind of love relationships they want to establish, and wonder whether they will ever meet an appropri-ate life partner or develop friends as close as the ones they left behind. If they are ending a relationship, a major fear may be being alone the rest of their lives. Additionally, many people experience a lack of intimacy within an established relationship. Different groups are needed for each of these considerations. Thus, we have groups for engaged couples; for widowed, separated, or divorced persons; and for marriage enrichment. People who have moved and miss close friends may also want to find sup-portive groups in their new locale.

Questions of where we "belong" often surface after a transition. This can be particularly true of widowed or divorced people whose social life revolved around couple activities, but it is also true of parents who spent many hours in parent–teacher organizations and in volunteer work for their children's school. Do they still belong there after their children graduate?

Similarly, we know of one woman who developed a close relation-ship but was reluctant to marry because she did not want to give up her leadership role in Parents Without Partners. That was the place she felt she most belonged. People whose identity or sense of belonging is tied to being, say, an officer in a union or a member of a city commission, may feel abandoned if their term ends, or worse yet, if they are not reelected. Adults who have to leave a softball league or other team because of an injury may feel similarly bereft.

Immigrants from one country to another may experience serious emotional as well as geographic dislocation, clearly related to issues of belonging. Moving often takes people away from close friends and extended families. Hoffman's (1990) book, *Lost in Translation,* an account of trying to "belong" in a different language, attests to this. Although not as dramatic a change, people who move from one part of the country to another or from one neighborhood to another may also experience feelings of marginality. Many people find it helpful to discuss issues such as these in personal growth groups such as those described above, whereas others will profit more from specialized groups, some of which are described below.

The need for support is lifelong, but an individual's existing support system can often be one of the "casualties" of a major life transition. Ironically, we may have most need of a support system as we are moving into or through a transition that may disrupt that very system. Frequently this is true in cases of a geographic move. The same problem may arise when a job change, retirement, or illness takes us away from coworkers who were close friends.

Illustrative Programs and Techniques

Because there are so many different types of group counseling programs for people dealing with changing relationships, the following descriptions provide only a limited sample.

Groups for Couples and Families

Couples groups may be targeted to engaged couples, married couples, or gay and lesbian partners. Some religious groups require that couples receive counseling, often from a member of the clergy, before they can be married in the church.

Books often can provide a focus for group discussion. For example, in her book, *You Just Don't Understand: Women and Men in Conversation,* Tannen (1990) described typical gender differences in communications patterns and approaches to problem solving. Couples reading this book can often laugh at the illustrations she gives, and in the process gain a better understanding of their own differences. Corey and Corey (1982) described a number of exercises they use in couples groups. For example, group members may be asked to complete sentences such as "The thing I'd most like to change in myself or my spouse is . . ." or "My greatest fear concerning our relationship is . . ." (p. 266). The stimulus for couples to enroll in such groups may be events, such as one partner's thinking about or having an affair, or non-events, including a general feeling that the relationship could be better.

Similar concerns may bring gay and lesbian couples to counseling. According to House and Tyler (1992), gay and lesbian couples typically bring up issues such as differences in background, communication problems, jealousy, and concerns about health and finances, just as do people in heterosexual relationships. They add, "lesbian and gay couples, however, face other relationship problems related to their sexual orientation" (p. 196). For example, they may differ as to whether or when to "come out" to family, friends, and work associates. Gay and lesbian couples have fewer role models than do heterosexual couples and may benefit greatly from knowing how other couples deal with their daily lives. The authors suggested that "Because many of the issues facing gay and lesbian couples are related to being male or female in our society, same gender leaders are apt to be most appropriate for these groups. . . . Gay couples tend to experience competition as a difficulty in relationships, whereas lesbian couples frequently have difficulty with fusion and separation" (p. 196).

Sometimes family counseling is indicated because of concerns about an older member of the family. Gwyther (1986) noted that families who are dealing with a transition such as the illness of an older member may resist "therapy," but may be willing to come for a meeting or for interpretive information. She also observed that the focus in working with older families "is generally on coping, not on correcting longstanding maladaptive personality styles or relationships" (p. 42).

Lustbader and Hooyman (1994) proposed an interesting technique for delegating tasks at family meetings. Counselors ask each family member to make a "wish list" as to how they would like to see a particular situation handled. Counselors then instruct members to trade lists so they can identify areas of conflict and agreement and attempt to arrive at a distribution of tasks that seems fair to all.

Rituals and metaphors can be used in family counseling to help some families face transitions. Sand-Pringle, West, and Bubenzer (1991) described an innovative intervention using gardening activities to help a family allow a son to leave for a halfway house. He planted some seeds in the family planter to symbolize his continuing place there and took a separate planter with him to his temporary home. The mother, who needed to be empowered in the family, was cast as the master gardener.

In this case, the family was the group with many of Yalom's (1985) curative factors operating. The plants symbolized hope, the joint efforts led to some cohesiveness, and family members were able to express some of their pent-up feelings. In the typology of groups, this is an example of a psychotherapeutically oriented group.

Groups for Separated and Divorced People

Even though approximately 50% of marriages in this country now end in divorce (U.S. Department of Commerce, 2004), divorce continues to be among the most stressful of life's transitions. Whether a marriage is cut short by divorce or death, survivors must relearn skills of singlehood after they work through coping with grief and trauma. Groups can be particularly helpful to people in the process of working through that pain.

Many groups for divorced persons, such as the well-known Parents Without Partners, are self-help groups. Others are led by professional counselors. In a review of the literature on groups for separated and divorced persons, Zimpfer (1990) talked of the importance of understanding stages in the divorce process to determine which kind of group work is most appropriate for particular individuals. Recently divorced and panicky people may benefit from short-term and crisis-based counseling, whereas people who have made some adjustment and are concerned with what to do with the rest of their lives may do better with long-term group work.

Most divorce groups described in the literature were structured and combining education and counseling. B. Halpern (personal communication, October 1994) used a structured activity, called an "obstacle checklist," which enumerates common problems. The list, which includes issues such as letting go of the former spouse, making new friends, forgiving the former spouse, sleeplessness, mood swings, and concerns over sexual involvement, helps the group focus on specific discussion topics and serves as a progress report for each person. Members use the list to record insights or ideas on how to handle each problem. Some of the checklist items apply to widowed persons, as well as to divorced persons, but the groups are seldom mixed. Widowed persons, who are working on not deifying their late spouses, may find it much too difficult to listen to people who are vilifying their "exes."

Groups for Widowed Persons

In a chapter on groups for people experiencing major losses, Vernon (1992) stated that although the bereavement process involves common feelings and stages, group members may benefit from a group that addresses their specific kind of loss. Being widowed, for instance, arouses innumerable feelings, some of which are difficult to discuss with family and friends. For example, a widow who is left with limited resources and seemingly unlimited responsibilities may be angry with her spouse for dying and guilty or depressed about her anger. It may be easier for her to discuss these feelings with other people in the same situation rather than with her children who are grieving themselves.

The opportunity to express such feelings and the hope of gaining some catharsis are important aspects of groups for the bereaved. On a more tangible level, members can also exchange ideas on ways to handle various aspects of their lives, from finances to sexuality.

Vernon (1992) described the flow and sequence of one structured group. During the first three sessions, members focus on the past. They tell their stories of losing their partners, discuss loneliness and aloneness, and consider the areas in their lives in which they feel most deprived. The counselor can stimulate such discussions by asking members to bring in photographs or by asking questions about what people miss most and least about their mates. By the fourth session, counselors can encourage members to discuss the new things they are learning to do and areas in which they may now be experiencing growth.

About halfway through the workshop, group members begin to address pragmatic changes. As the group moves to a discussion of the future, the counselor can encourage members to talk about how their lives might be in 6 months or a year. Counselors can ask members about where they might be living, how and with whom they might be spending their time, and what kind of feelings they might be experiencing. As the group terminates, members need an opportunity to express appreciation and regrets and to say their good byes. They also need a chance to discuss strategies they can use to continue to get the support provided by the group.

As mentioned, AARP is a major resource for those interested in establishing groups for widowed persons. Based on the work of Silverman (1980, 2004) and her associates at Harvard University, AARP established the Widowed Persons Service. A trained group leader, herself a widow, reaches out on a one-to-one basis to new widows before they attend their first group session.

AARP launched a special program for widowed Chinese individuals in Phoenix, AZ, staffed by bilingual volunteers. As reported in the Newsletter for AARP Volunteers (1991), "Normally, the grieving process is very private to the Chinese. . . . But Maggie Eng, director of the Chinese Senior Center, saw needs in the members who had left their native country and no longer could rely on large extended families for support at the time of their loss" (p. 1). Volunteers, who translated into four dialects, provided instrumental help with Social Security and housing arrangements and also encouraged widowed persons to begin socializing again.

Groups for Caregivers

As people live longer, more older adults need caregiving from spouses, adult children, friends, and/or paid caregivers. The mix of love and frustration that often accompanies having major responsibilities for a parent or other older adult is well documented. Fortunately, the need for help is becoming more widely recognized, and groups for caregivers are springing up at hospitals, nursing homes, senior centers, family service agencies, religious organizations, libraries, and community centers.

Counselors who work with caregivers need to be familiar with a variety of community resources, which can serve as formal supports. Counselors also need to understand the feelings of caregivers, who may be emotionally drained and physically exhausted—sometimes by family conflicts as well as by their caregiving responsibilities—and yet are often reluctant to use external resources. In dealing with people suffering from severely disabling illnesses, particularly dementia, caregivers may find that "the mourning process may be even more debilitating when the lost loved one is still alive" (Dobson & Dobson, 1991, p. 188).

Johnson (1990) developed a useful concept that helps caregivers understand the difference between giving up and letting go. It is a graphic presentation of the Serenity Prayer used in many 12-step programs: God grant me the serenity to accept the things I cannot change, the courage to change the things I can, and the wisdom to know the difference.

Using the graphic form (Figure 8.1), group members are asked to distinguish between situations that can be controlled and those that cannot be. In all situations they need to decide whether or not to take action. If the decision is one that can be controlled, and they take action, then they are achieving mastery; if they do not they are giving up. For example, if an older person wishes to stay in his or her home, and assessment indicates that this

	(1) Can Be Controlled	(2) Cannot Be Controlled
(A) TAKE ACTION	MASTERY	CEASELESS STRIVING
(B) DO NOT TAKE ACTION	GIVING- UP	LETTING- GO

Figure 8.1 Achieving mastery: the action/decision model. (*Source:* Richard P. Johnson, Ph.D., "Back to the Basics." *Co-op Networker: Caregivers of Older Persons,* 6(1), © 1990, Mercy Family Practice Center, St. John's Mercy Medical Center, St. Louis, MO. Used with permission.)

is possible with appropriate support, then the caregiver is achieving mastery if she or he arranges for adult day care and appropriate home care.

On the other hand, there are situations that cannot be controlled. For example, if a parent, whom the adult child thinks is depressed, absolutely refuses to consider counseling, then the daughter who continues to bring up the issue is engaged in ceaseless striving, or "banging her head against the wall." With assistance from the counselor, group members can often help each other make appropriate decisions and "let go" without guilt.

GROUPS FOR PEOPLE FACING CAREER-RELATED DECISIONS

Counselors hear about many different work-related transitions—looking for jobs, changing jobs, being promoted or laid off, not securing a desired job, or retiring. In most such situations, clients may have to let go of dreams or expectations or establish new goals. As they do this, the line between career transitions and other parts of an individual's life often blurs.

Transitions That May Bring Clients to a Career-Related Group

As we have seen, transitions are sometimes internally triggered, stemming from a person's desire to initiate a change. At other times, a transition may be thrust upon the individual. The context in which transitions arise affects the type of group experience that is most helpful. For example, counselors working with people who are angry about being laid off or forced to take an early retirement must attend to the anger before they can expect group members to begin career planning or a job search in earnest.

Client reactions to a career program may change over time. At the conclusion of a 2-day workshop, adult women clients reported that the affective aspects of the group experience, particularly measures of Yalom's (1985) therapeutic factors of universality, catharsis, and cohesiveness, were most important. In a follow-up study 2 months later, participants still valued the affective aspects of the workshop but reported that cognitive factors, such as information on resources and occupations, and on self-understanding, were the most tangible benefits of the group (Mawson & Kahn, 1993).

Career counselors can enhance the impact of group processes "by sequencing activities, choosing exercises, and structuring client participation to ensure the appropriate balance of attention to task (cognitive factors) and members' feelings (affective factors)" (Mawson & Kahn, 1993, p. 245). Readers are encouraged to keep that balance in mind as they consider situations that might bring their adult clients to career groups.

Career-related changes, whether made by choice or necessity, are apt to raise concerns about mastery, competency, balance, and identity. These recurring themes can be addressed through groups that combine providing career-related information with opportunities for group support. Peer counselors can also serve as supportive "veterans," an important element recommended by Weiss (1976). Several union–management-sponsored groups use this approach. Former union workers, who have already made a transition to retirement or other employment, facilitate small groups.

At times of career transition, the need for support can become enormous. Adults making career transitions frequently need an opportunity to talk to others who are "in the same boat" or further along in the process. As many people struggling with career decisions or trying to find a new job are reluctant to ask friends and coworkers for assistance, their usual sources of support may be cut off. Therefore, the support of members of a career-counseling group may be particularly important and may serve as a model encouraging people to seek support from others.

Many of the coping strategies necessary for success in career decision-making, job search, job retention, and retirement planning can be taught and practiced in groups. For example, members can learn to set goals and develop action plans for achieving them. Groups can be particularly valuable in encouraging compliance with the action plan. Members who might procrastinate on commitments made to themselves will be less likely to do so when they have made a promise to other group members.

Being able to identify and talk about one's values, interests, and accomplishments constitutes an important strategy in planning a career and searching for a job. The modeling and role-playing opportunities in a group make group counseling a valuable modality for honing these strategies. Similarly, networking is a key strategy needed by job seekers. The process can begin in a group, in which members frequently suggest contacts to each other.

Shared experiences make it easier to laugh at otherwise difficult situations, and humor can be a valuable strategy to make looking for, retaining, or leaving a job easier. For example, in both job search and post-retirement planning workshops, people who need time to pursue their paid or unpaid job search can laugh together over the "honey, do" lists developed by partners who think the unemployed individual now has limitless time to perform chores. Many of these strategies are taught in the sample programs described below.

Illustrative Career-Related Programs and Techniques

Career-counseling groups for adults in transition are offered through schools and universities, at the workplace, and in community settings. Examples of programs in various settings are discussed below.

Career Planning Programs

Zunker (2001) suggested a model for developing career counseling programs for adults in transition that includes strategies such as identification of experience, interests, and skills; clarification of values and needs; planning for education, training, or occupations; and movement toward a plan for life learning. He then suggested techniques and specific tasks for each strategy. For example, he recommended using interviews and autobiographies to help adults identify their experiences. Working in this way facilitates clients in identifying and evaluating previous work experience, assessing familial relationships, and identifying reasons for job change, along with career satisfaction variables. According to Zunker, such specific tasks are important because adults in transition often overlook skills they have developed in other contexts. His model included techniques for teaching decision-making skills, a central part of many career-counseling programs.

Another group approach uses quilts as a metaphor "to more effectively see and portray events and meanings in women's lives and work . . . quilts and quilting offer a new way of thinking about careers that overcomes the weaknesses of devaluing women's experiences and splintering their lives" (Sagaria, 1989, p. 13). Counselors ask group members to describe their quilts and give each other feedback based on questions such as "How is this quilt like Susan?" or "How does what Susan told us about her quilt fit with what she has told us about her career goals?" The quilts reflect the importance of relationships and serve as a vehicle for helping group members recognize their commonalities.

Another useful technique, storytelling, "serves a powerful function in career counseling, because storytelling enlightens the narrator and the audience" (Jepsen, 1992, p. 3). The stories, complete with what Jepsen called the "trouble" or the drama that keeps our attention on a story, provides an interesting way to discuss career decisions and career problems. "The audience (counselors, peers, group members) helps shape several aspects of the story . . . the special skills of a counselor are critical to a full telling of a career story" (p. 7).

Some career-planning groups are targeted to people facing particular transitions. The Jewish Vocational Service (JVS) of Detroit publicized a program for displaced homemakers with an attractive brochure entitled "When It's Time to Start Over." Inside the brochure, the description explains the value of the group in a simple manner. "First there's support . . . then there's hope . . . then there's work." This program adds job club services and monthly women's network meetings to the usual career-planning topics.

A more specialized JVS service, designed to assist Russian refugees, includes assessment of work-related English and explanations of the American work culture, along with sessions on job search techniques.

Many of the immigrants have difficulty understanding that in this country people compete for jobs and need to see this for themselves. In the former Soviet Union, they were assigned to jobs. According to the director of the program, "The concepts of productivity and efficiency are totally foreign" (R. Moxley, personal communication, 1994). At the same time, women immigrants may find it hard to understand that in this country there is no subsidized day care or standard paid maternity leave.

Counselors face special challenges when leading groups of people with physical disabilities who want to return to work or cope more successfully with their work situation. A combination of information about the disability and support designed to restore damaged feelings of competence and self-esteem seems to be essential. In addition, special skills may be needed for particular disabilities. For example, silence in a group is likely to be very upsetting to blind participants, so the counselor may need to explain what is going on when one member is thinking. Clients with a hearing impairment are likely to become passive, so assertive skills may be an important component of their career planning groups (Livneh & Pullo, 1992). When working with people with physical disabilities or from different cultures, it is important for counselors to listen carefully for the values and assumptions of the individuals.

Job Search Groups

Many adults in transition already know what they want to do or "be" but need help in putting their plans into action. Typically groups for job seekers teach participants how to identify their strengths and abilities, analyze an employer's needs, and attempt to identify a fit. Goodman & Hoppin (1990) developed one widely used, competency-based program that included useful strategies for self-assessment, decision-making, planning a job-search campaign, communicating with employers, interviewing, retaining the job, and preparing for the next one.

USING THE 4 S MODEL WITH GROUPS

When working with groups, as well as with individuals, counselors can integrate the Hackney–Cormier (2005) counseling model with the transition model. This integrated model, shown in Figure 7.1, fits well with the four stages of group development—exploratory, transition, action, and termination—identified by Gazda (1989).

During the exploratory stage, counselors help members get acquainted and begin to assess their problems and needs in view of their life changes. In the transition stage, they set goals and begin to move to action. In the action stage of groups, counselors intervene to help members develop new coping strategies. Whether working with individuals or groups, counselors should view the termination stage as the appropriate time to assist clients in evaluating their progress and making a commitment to follow-up.

In almost any groups designed for people considering, anticipating, or experiencing a transition, the first step is to encourage them to describe their transitions. What happened or may happen? The major job of counselors after that is to encourage group members to assess and improve their resources for coping in each of the four areas of the Transition model.

Although we talk about the 4 S's separately in the following discussion, it is important to remember that the lines among them blur. In some ways, the situation of any individual includes aspects of the other three S's. Each individual's personal environment is unique. Thus, four women in the same job-seeking group may have very different resources in terms of socioeconomic Situation, Support systems—friends, extended family, work colleagues, spiritual resources—and coping Strategies. An effective group can help each member identify and enhance his or her unique available resources.

For example, a woman who has lost her job and is feeling helpless in terms of finding another may get useful feedback from other group members who help her realize how successfully she has weathered other transitions. The group may also help her see her network of supportive friends and her ability to take care of herself as assets in her present situation. A group can help one woman who is financially able to be unemployed for a short time see this as an asset in that it enables her to be more selective about other jobs. At the same time, the group may be able to persuade another woman, whose financial situation is tenuous, that it is appropriate to accept government assistance to tide her over.

Situation

In groups, members can explain how, from their point of view, the context in which they operate affects the impact of the transition. They can also discuss the extent to which the transition alters their lifestyle, what we have earlier called their roles, relationships, routines, and assumptions. As the other group members offer feedback, each of the group members can realize that although they may all be experiencing a similar transition, their individual situations differ.

Self

Under skilled leadership, a group may be particularly valuable in helping members assess Self factors. For example, individuals concerned that they do not have the psychological resources to cope with major losses may be reassured to learn from other members that their degree of turmoil is normal. They may also profit from hearing ideas as to how people experiencing similar transitions gained some measure of control over their lives.

Many transitions, particularly those involving role losses, lead to a drop in self-esteem. People who feel they are no longer needed can benefit just by having group members glad to see them each week. When members share resources, their ability to contribute to someone else may positively affect their view of themselves.

One activity, which is part of a job-seeking workshop developed by Goodman and Hoppin (1990), illustrates the value of group feedback. To demonstrate the concept of transferable skins, the leader asks one member to come to the front of the room and write the title of a recent job on a simulated theater marquee. The marquee has the words "Star of the Cineplex" at the top. The "Star" explains the job and, with the help of other group members, lists as many skills as possible involved in that job. Then the group discusses ways in which the skills and personal characteristics of the group member can be transferred to other jobs and settings. Frequently, "stars" leave with a more positive view of their skills and abilities and a more optimistic outlook about finding another position. This activity also helps members prepare for their job search, with positively identified skills they may have taken for granted.

Group counselors can maximize the effectiveness of feedback by encouraging interaction and humor. For example, to enliven the discussion of transferable skills, the counselor can tell the story of a man who, with no background in the field, got a job in labor relations. He convinced his employer that as a former basketball referee he knew how to make quick decisions and take the heat!

Support

By their very nature, well-functioning groups provide support. In addition, they can encourage members to explore and enhance their individual support systems. Regardless of the type of transition, clients need to consider who or what has been supportive for them in the past and how they have accessed that support.

Pearson (1990) developed a model for using social support-oriented concepts and procedures in counseling practice. The first step is to identity the strengths and deficiencies in an individual's support system. If this assessment indicates that client-based barriers, such as withdrawal, ineptness, and alienation, are the major causes of the problem, then the task of the counselor is to help the client make some changes. Depending on the theoretical orientation of the counselor, client-based interventions might focus on restructuring attitudes or changing behaviors through modeling and communications skill training. Opportunities to practice new skills in a group can be particularly valuable.

If the initial assessment suggests that the barriers lie more with other individuals or the larger social context in which the person operates, then interventions must focus outside the individual. These can range from counselor contacts with the client's network to political advocacy.

Using Pearson's (1990) model, a useful group activity for the assessment stage is to have people evaluate their own support systems. The idea of a support system can be explained to most clients in words like, "people who are there for you" or "in your corner." To facilitate self-evaluation, counselors can use a worksheet listing needs such as acceptance, self-esteem, peers, guidance, and role models. Next to each need is a brief description of the type of support provided. For example, to meet our need for acceptance we need people who like us and to meet our need for peers, we need people who *are* like us. In a blank column on the worksheet, clients fill in the name of the person or group who supplies that type of support to them (Waters & Samson, 1993; see also the surveys in the Appendix of Pearson, 1990).

Another approach is to use a version of the convoy worksheet (see Figure 3.2), based on the work of Kahn and Antonucci (1980). Group members can fill out this sheet, entering the names of their personal supports in the appropriate concentric circle. These kinds of assessments help group members to identity the strengths and "holes" in their system. Once the resources and deficits have been identified, group members can help each other develop strategies for shoring up those deficits stemming from internally created barriers. Strategies may include ideas on how to meet new people, investigate community resources, or learn to ask for help.

Asking for help is difficult for many people. "Knowing how to take care of yourself is a sign of adulthood" we say to ourselves, or "If he loved me he'd know what I need." Explaining the concept of cosmic accounting, mentioned in an earlier chapter, may help group members be a little more willing to ask for help. The term *cosmic accounting,* developed by Sarah Uhle (personal communication, 1988), refers to the tendency of people to keep mental records of what they give and receive. Many of us have in our heads an accounting system that deals with simple exchanges such as who owes whom a dinner invitation or a favor. Cosmic accounting represents a more complicated exchange in that people may "pay back" somebody else, rather than the person who helped them. The following example may bring the concept to life.

Three women, dressed in business suits, were on their way to a conference in a new car when a tire blew. As it was such a new car, not even the owner knew where the jack was. The three were standing forlornly by the

side of the road, trying to figure out what to do, when a passing motor-
cyclist stopped. He not only changed the tire, but also gave the women
instructions on how to change it themselves in the future. When he finished, the owner asked if she could pay. "Oh no," he said, "Just promise
me that the next time you see someone who needs help you'll stop."

The notion of "passing a favor along" is a key element of cosmic
accounting. Stories such as this one often make it easier for group members to understand the concept and may trigger a realization that they
already have a number of "credits" in their cosmic account on which
they can draw.

To return to Pearson's (1990) model, if the problem with the support
system seems to lie outside of the control of the individual, then the counselor can help group members work in a larger context. Sometimes this
involves linking informal supports with formal ones. This linking may be
particularly important with some of the caregiver groups discussed
above. In other situations, working in a larger context may mean that
clients and/or the counselor move to advocacy.

Strategies

Throughout this book we have mentioned three types of strategies for
coping with a transition: those aimed to modify the situation, those
designed to change the meaning of the situation, and those serving to help
individuals manage the stress of change. Groups can help in all three areas.

Coping Effectiveness Training

Folkman et al. (1991) developed a pilot program of Coping Effectiveness
Training for groups of 8 to 10 people infected with the human immun-
odeficiency virus, commonly called HIV. The program was based on
cognitive–behavioral principles with the goal to improve people's skills
in appraising, coping, and obtaining social support when experiencing
stressful situations.

The first step, appraisal training, teaches people to break down global
stressors into specific problems. The global stressor of being infected with
HIV is overwhelming. It may be more manageable to think about specific
details such as not having enough energy to work a full day, having to tell
close friends and relatives that one has HIV, or the demands of a treatment
schedule. Each of these stressful contexts can be narrowed further to specific
stressful situations. For example, "not having enough energy . . . to put in a
full workday might be narrowed to the specific incident of requesting a
transfer to a less taxing job" (p. 252). The task of the counselor is to help

participants be as specific as possible about their stressors so they can establish goals for coping with them.

The next step is training people to expand their repertoire of coping skills. Based on the Lazarus and Folkman (1984) typology, group leaders teach the difference between problem-focused and emotion-focused coping. The former tends to be more useful with situations that are amenable to change, the latter with situations that cannot change. In problem-focused coping, participants are taught how to apply decision-making skills to manage problem situations more effectively. Emotion-focused training is designed to reduce distress through application of cognitive and behavioral strategies. Examples of cognitive strategies would be selective attention, reframing, humor, and the use of spiritual or religious resources. Behavioral strategies include exercise, relaxation, and engaging in activities the person finds pleasurable. Another component, social support training, helps people identify the kinds of support they need and develop strategies to obtain and maintain the support. These skills are taught in three parts, which the program developers call "Choosing it," "Obtaining it," and "Keeping it."

In designing the program, Folkman et al. (1991) included brief didactic lectures, modeling by the group leaders, and opportunities for participants to practice skills. They also developed a workbook that summarized key points of each session and presented homework exercises. "To keep the workbook from being too serious, material . . . tends to be humorous, and cartoons are used throughout. The humor may be more effective if it is tailored to issues that are relevant to the group" (p.251).

Comparisons of treatment and control groups indicated that treatment groups improved in terms of coping skills, particularly a reduction in self-blame. After 6 weeks, the treatment group exhibited less depression and more positive morale than the control group. Although their model was piloted with persons with HIV, the authors expressed a belief that it "holds a promise as a brief intervention to help people in diverse settings manage the stressful demands of daily living" (p. 257).

Other Stress Management Programs

Stress management programs are of particular importance to adults in transition because stress is often associated with change. In groups, clients can share both their sources of stress and their stress relievers. Such sharing can help members better understand why they may be feeling stress, as well as broaden their ideas about what might help relieve it.

Counselors can help group members realize the tremendous variability in terms of what is stress producing and what is stress reducing. This difference often constitutes a source of stress in families and among friends.

If one person's stress reducer, be it big parties, skiing, or political discussions, is a stress producer for his or her partner, negotiations are clearly needed. The group counselor can help members develop their negotiating strategies.

Group counselors can also introduce exercises, such as those suggested by Tubesing and Tubesing (n.d.) to help members develop more stress management techniques. Stress Bingo is one that works well in groups. Bingo-like cards are made up with a variety of possible stress relievers, such as listening to music, taking a hot bath, walking in the woods, reading a novel, or calling an old friend, printed in the boxes on the cards. Group members are instructed to talk with each other and to ask others to put their initials in the boxes that contain relievers they actually use. In addition to getting their cards filled up with signatures, group members are able to get ideas on how various people use the stress relievers. Typically, Stress Bingo leads to much laughter, which is itself a tension reliever, as well as to a productive exchange of ideas.

WORKING WITH SELF-HELP GROUPS

The last half of the 20th century was described as the era of the self-help or mutual-aid group (*Harvard Mental Health Letter*, 1993). In this report it was estimated that in the United States at least 6 million people participate each year and that 12 to 15 million Americans will participate at some time during their lifetime. There are more than 1,100 national, international, model, and online self-help support groups for a variety of specific issues listed in one database alone. These include self-help groups addressing issues such as addictions, bereavement, health, mental health, disabilities, abuse, parenting, caregiver concerns, and other stressful life situations. Mental Health Net (http://www.selfhelpgroups.org/), self-described as the oldest and largest online mental health guide, lists both local and worldwide self-help groups and provides a registration service for both face-to-face and online groups.

A search of http://mentalhelp.net/selfhelp/ found 48 topics in the A's alone, and these were indicated to be just a sample. Another site listing online support groups, Psych Central (http://psychcentral.com/resources/), listed 389 groups for medical diseases alone, 21 for obsessive compulsive disorder, 91 for bipolar disorder, and 157 for depression. This brief sampling demonstrates that although we are too newly into the 21st century to draw conclusions, it seems that the self-help movement is still strong.

Members of these groups are people with a symptom, disorder, situation, or experience in common who unite to fulfill a need, overcome a handicap, or cope with a crisis. The main purposes of self-help groups are mutual solace, education, and personal change. By talking to others with similar problems, members heighten their own understanding. They see how their actions affect others and how others cope with troubles similar to their own.

Most self-help groups are designed for people experiencing or anticipating a variety of transition events or non-events. The groups can be helpful to people who need support as they look at themselves in their changed roles, analyze their situations, and look for new strategies to help them navigate the transition. Indeed, Davies (1996) found that peer support groups can be especially effective because participants give as well as receive support. In other words, they matter.

Using a very broad definition of support groups, Wuthnow (1994) said that "4 out of 10 Americans belong to a small group that meets regularly and provides caring and support for its members" (p. 4). Indeed, even in the mid-19th century, De Toqueville (1839/2001) observed that Americans were joiners, a fact he noted that distinguished them from the Europeans of the time. More recently, Putnam (2000) disputed this allegation in the book *Bowling Alone*, using the title phrase as a metaphor for what he found in his research to be a decrease in Americans' propensity for joining. Putnam found that numbers of people in bowling leagues were declining, whereas the sport of bowling itself was increasing in popularity. According to Putnam, "We sign fewer petitions, belong to fewer organizations that meet, know our neighbors less, meet with friends less frequently, and even socialize with our families less often" (Putnam, R. D., 2005, Introduction, p. ii). Although this may seem to reflect a more isolated existence for our society today, not all trend watchers agree.

The title of Wuthnow's (1994) book, *Sharing the Journey: Support Groups and America's New Quest for Community,* articulates his basic belief that such support groups represent a major trend in American society. He wrote: "For as long as most Americans can remember, our society has been described to us as being composed of individualists. But the standard wisdom now needs to be challenged. Bible studies, prayer fellowships, self-help groups, twelve-step gatherings, therapy sessions, recovery groups—all have been gaining increasing importance in recent years, as both sources of emotional support and settings in which millions of Americans are seeking spirituality" (p. ix). Did America change between 1994 and 2000? Did Putnam look at a different set of data than Wuthnow? We do not know. What we do know is that self-help groups continue to proliferate.

Advantages and Limitations of Self-Help Groups

Humphreys, Macus, Stewart, and Oliva (2004) conducted research on health-related self-help groups among middle- and lower-income people in two California urban areas with minority–majority populations.

They designed English- and Spanish-language radio public service announcements and posters that were disseminated in Oakland and Los Angeles. They found that areas with the active outreach had more telephone calls for service and more involvement in the self-help groups themselves.

This evidence of efficacy is reinforced by Leung and Arthur (2004) who examined the effectiveness of self-help groups in the rehabilitation of people recovering from mental illness. They found that the members felt the experience to be a positive one, as did the professionals and volunteers who were involved. Of interest, all respondents in their study indicated that a spiritual dimension was an important factor in the group's cohesiveness and in their rehabilitation. This certainly is in line with the previously discussed power of spirituality in enhancing coping of persons in transition.

There are a number of reasons why self-help groups are so popular. As stated earlier, they provide an opportunity to help others as well as to receive help. They also provide a way for people to get assistance without feeling that they are being labeled as "crazy," "mentally ill," or another stigmatized label. As we discussed in Chapter 7 on groups for people in transition, these sorts of experiences provide support merely by helping individuals feel less alone. They also frequently help members access other supports, through resource sharing, through referrals to services, or through support provided outside of the group by group members. Some self-help groups, for example, provide new members with a 'buddy' who they can call or who will call them to offer additional support.

In the view of some analysts, however, self-help groups also pose a danger as lay people may be involved in dealing with serious mental health issues. Others fault self-help groups and their members for being too tied up with their own needs or for encouraging people to stay "stuck" in their situations rather than moving on. In her book, *I'm Dysfunctional, You're Dysfunctional,* Kaminer (1992), suggested that self-help groups encourage simplistic thinking. She criticized many of the groups for stressing somewhat rigid techniques and devaluing complex ideas or uncertainties. Wuthnow (1994) underlined the divergent opinions about the value of support groups. He observed that whereas proponents see them as a way of saving American society and redeeming individuals from destructive addictions, critics deem such groups artificial, "contributing more to a narcissistic obsession with self than to a more responsible society" (p. ix). Counselors may want to keep these concerns in mind as they work with self-help groups.

How Counselors Relate to Self-Help Groups

Mental health professionals can play a variety of roles vis-à-vis self-help groups. Wax (1985) suggested that helping professionals are in a good

position to provide logistical support, start-up assistance, help with organizational and group development issues, consultation, reciprocal referrals, and help with political action, advocacy, and public education. All
such cooperative efforts, of course, require sensitive communications and
patience on the part of both counselors and representatives of the group.

In some situations, counselors and other helping professionals may initiate self-help groups as they see a need for their clients to have peer support.
In various parts of the country, for example, professionals have helped
organize groups for grandparents who are raising their crack-addicted children's children (Trupin, 1993; Waters, 1994). Sometimes groups are organized by laypersons who then seek professional assistance. Despite the fact
that the trend toward formation of self-help groups came, in part, as a rebellion against the formal and threatening mental health system, the relationship between counselors and self-help groups has a long history (Riordan
& Beggs, 1987). The authors noted, for example, that during the 19th century,
social workers assisted immigrants in forming mutual aid societies.

Riordan and Beggs (1987) also observed that as the self-help movement grew in this country, the suspicions that lay people and leaders of
self-help groups had toward professionals were by no means one-sided.
"For their part, professionals initially reacted with dismay that ranged
from clinical hostility to ambivalence. The recent literature now reflects
not only a receding ambivalence but a strong trend toward symbiotic
cohabitation . . . the group is encouraged to remain autonomous while
having access to professional help as desired" (pp. 427–428).

Many support groups arise out of one individual's desire to make
meaning out of a personal tragedy or to find company in a particular situation. Single Mothers by Choice (2005), an example of this phenomenon, was founded in 1981 by a psychotherapist who was herself a single
mother by choice. In 2005 the group had several thousand members and
chapters in 24 areas, double the number it had in 2002. The group
attracts not only single mothers, but those women thinking about having
children without a partner.

Groups for families of murdered individuals and families of murder-
ers are poignant examples of the desire to find comfort in shared troubles.
An unusual support group, Aftermath, helps families of criminals cope
while the offenders are in prison (Dawson, 1993). Its founder "spends
most of her time with women whose husbands, brothers, or fathers have
committed murder, rape, or other sexual offenses. Discovering that someone they love has committed a hideous crime devastates most people"
(p. 12). Negative publicity, friends who desert them, and neighborhood
hostility can add to the pain of an already difficult transition. An indication
of the need for such a group is that 5 years after its founding, Aftermath
had branches all over Great Britain.

Many counselors refer their clients to self-help groups as an adjunct to individual counseling or as a source of support when they terminate their relationship with a client. Counselors may also help with "recruiting" for self-help groups if they give public talks about transitions and mention the value of self-help groups to people approaching, moving through, or moving out of a transition.

In addition, some counselors train facilitators and/or group members who lead self-help groups. For example, Schlossberg, Waters, Goodman (1995) worked with P-FLAG (Parents and Friends of Lesbians and Gays). Members of this group come together to support each other as they deal with a variety of transitions, such as realizing their child is gay or facing the possible non-event of missing out on becoming a grandparent. The counselor originally offered a workshop to train group facilitators in basic communications and group management skills. She had them practice active listening, effective questioning, and caring confrontation. Since then she has consulted informally on issues such as how to handle "difficult" group members, particularly those who withdraw from or dominate group discussions. The range of self-help groups currently in existence provides many opportunities for counselor involvement. We describe a few of these below.

Types of Groups for People Experiencing Various Transitions

A glance at the community activities section of any metropolitan newspaper, as well as retrieval of a large number of hits on an Internet search, attests to the variety of self-help groups. People experiencing individual transitions will find groups where they can search for meaning in life, sometimes with an emphasis on spirituality. Here, too, are the host of groups for persons learning to cope with various disabilities from shyness to cancer and the variety of 12-step programs, such as Alcoholics Anonymous or Gamblers Anonymous. A hallmark of 12-step programs is that people are always defined as in transition; they are "recovering," not recovered.

Sometimes groups are gender-specific. Ever since the publication of *The Feminine Mystique* (Friedan, 1963), there have been consciousness-raising groups for women. We described earlier a group for single mothers by choice. More recently, such groups for men arose. Hassan (1992) said that self-help groups offer men, who typically lack opportunities for intimacy, "A sanctuary in which they can share their emotions without fear of being disdained" (p. 18). Other groups specifically targeted to men include those promoting rights for noncustodial fathers, men who often feel they receive short shrift from the courts during divorce proceedings.

Among the most popular groups are those for people who have experienced or are anticipating family or other relationship-related transitions.

Groups for singles include some individuals wishing to change that status and others wishing to find friendships and intimacy while remaining single. There are also self-help groups for divorced and bereaved people, expectant and new parents, parents of teenagers, parents without partners, adult children of alcoholics, and children of aging parents. The Internet, as mentioned earlier, has spawned a profusion of chat groups, list serves, group blogs, and other on-line group relationships. Self-help will never be the same!

Self-help groups for people experiencing work transitions may involve displaced homemakers, people searching for jobs, those considering or coping with retirement, or those being hired into positions that are non-traditional for their gender or ethnic group. Thus, there are groups for male nurses, women in the construction trades, and black business owners. Counselors can be involved in helping to establish such groups or helping them increase their effectiveness once they are under way.

Self-Help Groups: A Summary

Clearly, the self-help movement is a significant force in current American society, involving at least 6 million people per year. There are groups for people experiencing intrapersonal, interpersonal, and work-related transitions. Many of the topics self-help groups focus on are also discussed in counseling groups. The difference is that the former are led by group members who share the "problem," whatever it may be, and the latter are led by professional counselors, who may or may not be in the same situation. Although they do not generally lead self-help groups, professional counselors can be involved with self-help groups in many ways including recruiting and referring members, assisting with organizational and marketing tasks, helping groups set goals and develop strategic plans, and training and supporting group leaders.

SUMMARY

In this chapter, we have discussed the value and limitations of groups for adults in transition, described a number of group counseling workshops and specific techniques, and talked about how to use the transition model in group settings. In groups, clients have opportunities to hear about a variety of sources of support and coping strategies used by others. When we ask adults what has helped them survive, we most often hear about a sense of humor, support from special people, and faith. All our discussions underlined the importance of group support, the idea with which we began this chapter.

CHAPTER 9

Consultation, Program Development, and Advocacy

When we hear the word *counseling,* most of us envision a professionally trained helper working face-to-face with one or more people considered clients. Indeed, individual and group counseling is what we are trained to do and what most of us like to do. But this is not the whole story. Increasingly, counselors are being called upon to act in other ways to assist adults in transition.

Some counselors now work in the corporate world, and others are community organizers; some counselors design programs in colleges and universities, whereas others develop workshops for senior centers; some walk the halls of legislatures as lobbyists, whereas still others talk about preventive mental health on talk shows. For some counselors, these broadened roles represent an exciting challenge; for others, they are an intrusion or a necessary evil.

As part of their training, counselors are taught to be supportive, encouraging, and accepting. In contrast, advocacy and legislative efforts may involve controversy and adversarial relations. In a random sampling, mental health counselors expressed limited interest in learning how to lobby more effectively or provide psychoeducational services to clients (Wilcoxon & Puleo, 1992), probably because such activities take counselors out of their comfort zone. On the other hand, the Legislative Institutes sponsored by the American Counseling Association draw a number of counselors each year who are eager to learn advocacy skills, albeit are sometimes nervous about their capabilities.

No longer can counselors be merely good listeners. As consultants, trainers, advocates, and program developers, counselors have opportunities to make organizations and systems more responsive to the needs of adults. If clients are to look for available supports in the community, those supports must be there. And counselors can play a role in putting them in place. In some cases counselors' efforts can help create structures that favorably tip the ratio of resources to deficits for adults in transition.

It is our opinion that although counselors should not impose their own values on their clients, counselors should act on their values to bring about needed societal changes. In this chapter, we talk about a variety of ways counselors can do this, including consulting, developing programs, and advocacy.

CONSULTING WITH ORGANIZATIONS AND THEIR EMPLOYEES

Consulting gives counselors a chance to have an impact on adults' everyday environment. Consulting can take many forms. In their introduction to two special issues on consultation of the *Journal of Counseling & Development,* editors Kurpius and Fuqua (1993a) noted that there is no universally accepted definition of consulting. However, most agree that "consultation is a process for helping individuals, groups, organizations, and communities function more effectively and efficiently, with greater satisfaction" (p. 596). When counselors are involved as consultants they have an opportunity to assist adults in transition indirectly rather than directly.

A major difference between consulting and counseling is that consulting is triadic. Counselors work directly with clients; consultants work with consultees who, in turn, serve a client system. The consultee may be an individual, a group, or an organization. The form of the consultation can be varied, but, at the broadest level, writers distinguish between expert consultation and process consultation. Consultants function in the expert role when "the consultee needs some knowledge, advice, or service that the consultant can provide" (Dougherty, 2000, p. 34). Although this can be a satisfactory arrangement, Dougherty noted the danger that individuals or organizations may get used to having somebody else perform the service and not develop their own problem-solving abilities.

Process consultation casts consultants in a less directive and more interactive role with the consultee. The consultant helps the consultee examine how problems are being addressed, rather than focusing on what the problems are. "The expert mode includes heavy responsibility for the consultant for the design, implementation, and success of an intervention. The process mode emphasizes shared responsibility between consultant and consultee and provides for the consultee to internalize planned change process as an acquired capability" (Kurpius & Fuqua,

1993b, p. 599). Counselors can function as consultants in either mode if they have the required skills.

Summarizing the skills that are integral parts of every counselor's repertoire, Dougherty (2000) concluded that effective counselors have the interpersonal skills and communication skills that we associate with effective counseling, including the so-called core conditions (Rogers, 1957) of empathy, genuineness, and unconditional positive regard. He also stated that effective consultants need problem-solving, organizational, and group skills, skills in dealing with cultural diversity, and skills to be able to practice ethically and professionally. The 2005 American Counseling Association Code of Ethics specifically addresses counselors' role in consultation in sections B8 and D2.

It is important to remember that multicultural issues arise during consultation, just as they do in counseling. Jackson and Hayes (1993) provided suggestions for the consultant encountering client organizations whose members or some of whose members are different culturally from the consultant. The first suggestion is that the consultant either have a familiarity with the culture of the consultees or learn about it from the clients or from others and second is that the consultant acknowledge the differences and his or her own lack of information as appropriate. They suggested that the consultant pay particular attention to verbal and nonverbal expressions, location of consultation, written versus verbal agreements, and time assumptions. They pointed out that it is important to understand and pay attention to high-context or low-context cultures and the implications of this dynamic. If this is not done, they suggest that the outcome may be "(a) lack of mutual goals . . . (b) frustration, and (c) disappointment" (p. 145). They concluded that "to continue down the existing training and consulting path using monocultural philosophies and strategies, consultants, along with the profession of consultation, will be seen as ineffective, nonresponsive, and potentially identified as nonessential" (p. 147). These are strong words, and we hope that readers will therefore be motivated to enhance their multicultural competencies.

Dougherty (2000) developed a generic model of consultation that included four stages: (a) entry, (b) diagnosis, (c) implementation, and (d) disengagement. At all stages, consultant and consultees work together. During Stage 1, the consultant enters the organization and explores organizational needs. In Stage 2, diagnosis, the focus is on gathering information, defining the problem, setting goals, and generating possible interventions. Stage 3, implementation, is the action stage of a consultation. Consultants and consultees choose an intervention, then formulate, implement, and evaluate that plan. Stage 4, disengagement, requires evaluating the consultation process, and planning for necessary follow-up. These stages relate closely to the stages of counseling identified in the

Hackney and Cormier (2005) model, described in Chapter 7, that is, (a) rapport and relationship building, (b) problem assessment, (c) goal-setting, (d) initiating interventions, and (e) termination and follow-up.

As part of the action or implementation stage of a consultant relationship, counselors can teach administrators and managers about the transition model. Managers who understand the significance of adult transitions will be more understanding of their employees' behavior and better able to provide support. Sargent and Schlossberg (1988) directed the following remarks to managers to demonstrate this aspect of consultation:

> As a manager, you need to know that people in transition are often preoccupied and a little confused, even if the transition is a desired one. For example, a promotion to a first supervisory job can be exciting, yet the new supervisor—whose roles, relationships, assumptions, and routines have been altered—will be disoriented while he or she figures out what is expected in the new role. In addition, the isolation from friends who were colleagues and who are now subordinates can be upsetting. . . .
>
> When adults start new jobs, for example, they find themselves suspended awkwardly between their old role and the new one. During that period, they need special help, such as new employee orientation and the rapid development of support systems. . . . The move from incompetence to competence can be tortuous. Managers can help by acknowledging the rough transition rather than denying it, and by offering support and specific strategies to learn new competencies. (pp. 58–60)

Consultants may also be able to help organizations set up a transition management program. Some of the transitions in private business and industry organizations that lend themselves to the assistance of consultants include: diversity and multicultural evolution, restructuring of a workforce (which often includes down-sizing or outsourcing employment), team building, and mergers or divestitures. Management of nonprofit organizations, governmental agencies, and nongovernmental organizations may wish to use counselors and consultants when they develop strategic missions, change the focus of their services, or change, voluntarily or by necessity, their sources of funding.

Counselors who want to be more involved in the business world get experience outside of their usual environment, read business journals as well as counseling journals, and attend meetings of organizations such as the American Society of Training and Development. They also need to talk with other consultants and trainers and watch them work. Cosier and Dalton (1993) offered a variety of suggestions on how counselors interested in becoming consultants could plan the change, enter the new field, and promote themselves successfully. Included in their recommendations is a list of relevant professional associations.

Consultants Morin and Cabrera (1991) designed interventions to be used with employees who lose their jobs. Thus, they are functioning primarily as expert consultants. They stated that "our business is career continuation (often called outplacement counseling), and we teach ex-employees the skills they need to continue their careers quickly and efficiently" (p. xxi). Companies provide such services, partly out of concern for their employees and partly because they have found that if former employees make a smooth transition from one job to another, it saves money in severance pay and avoids possible legal actions. Workers who remain with the company are also reassured when they see that their former coworkers have been helped.

Noel (1993) stated that many organizations do a much better job with those they are firing than with those who are staying, those who, in our terms, have experienced a non-event transition. He used the term *layoff survivor sickness* to describe an illness characterized by a variety of feelings, including fear, anger, depression, guilt, and betrayal. In his view, "only compelling multilevel interventions can affect the pathology of layoff survivor sickness" (p. 2). Toward that end, he designed a model, including interventions, which clarifies the process, facilitates grieving, breaks some existing patterns, and creates new systems.

Many of those interventions are based on skills that counselors can use either directly or as consultants to company employees. The examples just discussed illustrate the use of expert consultation skills. The following case study shows how a counselor used process consultation skills to help a group deal with the need to lay people off.

A Case Study of the Transition Model in Action

One of the authors (Schlossberg) had an opportunity to consult with a group of six nurse managers and a professor of nursing in a Canadian city. The problem, as they saw it, stemmed from a Canadian health care crisis. Nursing supervisors had been "ordered" to dismiss almost half of their trained nurses. As each spoke, the situation began to sound hopeless: The nurses had to be fired, they would never get other jobs in the field, it was unfair, but the supervisors had to carry out the orders.

The consultant's first step was to listen to what the clients were saying and reflect it back. She heard catastrophe, no hope, and no way out of this dilemma. Therefore, the goal of the consultation became (a) to help the nurse managers put this negative transition in perspective and (b) to provide skills so they would feel competent to help those they fire learn how to negotiate transitions.

Addressing the feelings of the nurse managers was critical to helping them take control of their role as "messengers of bad news." If they felt hopeless, they would communicate this to those they had to fire. After discussing their feelings, they began to see that while the situation was negative, it was not a disaster. Joblessness can be a defeat and leave one hungry and homeless, or it can be an opportunity to think about getting different training and reshaping goals. Once they could begin to redefine it as a challenge, albeit a negative one, they were on their way.

The supervisors expressed fear that they might some day lose their own jobs. The consultant helped them see that if in fact they were fired, they did not have to give up hope of ever being a nurse again. They might have to temporarily work outside the field, or they might see this as an opportunity to explore where the economy needs workers and how their skills could be transferred.

In addition to feeling guilty about having to fire people, the managers were concerned that they did not have the skills to do it. As they were dealing with transitions, and actually creating transitions in other people's lives, they needed to learn how to help people negotiate transitions. So the consultant helped them learn to teach others how to (a) approach change, (b) assess their resources for coping with change, and (c) develop action plans to take control of the change.

She suggested that in discussing ways to approach change, the managers give all those being fired an opportunity to express their views of the transition. For example, Do they see it as positive, negative, or neutral? If the firings were being discussed in a group, group members might be able to suggest alternate ways to view the situation to each other. Perhaps some will see it as an opportunity to do life planning, rethink their careers, or start over.

To help the managers assist the fired nurses in assessing their resources, she taught them how to explain the 4 S's model. Managers were to help nurses identify their resources and deficits with respect to their Situation at the time of their job loss, their Self, their Support at work and at home, and their Strategies. In teaching the managers to help nurses develop an action plan, she suggested the use of group discussions, including brainstorming, to encourage the nurses to identify resources they could strengthen.

In describing this consultation, the counselor noted that three groups needed attention—the supervisors who had to convey the bad news, those being fired, and those not being fired. In this situation, as in many others, "survivors" may be preoccupied with a fear of impending doom. Consultants must remain aware of the needs of all three groups, rather than just the person or group they are with.

Many organizational development consultants come from the ranks of counselors. They may be hired to implement a career development program. In that case they would work with the management to understand the advantages to the company of employees who are satisfied as well as satisfactory, to use the words from work adjustment theory (Dawis & Lofquist, 1984). Often one level of management is interested in the contracted for consultation, but others need to be 'brought along' to see the advantages of investing time and money in the process. Often managers fear that if employees receive career decision-making assistance and skills training, they will take their skills elsewhere. A persuasive argument used by one CEO was to point out that if other companies did not want his employees, why should he?

In other cases, counselors are hired to improve the organization's multicultural competency. Many of these consultants start with the American Counseling Association's (1992) multicultural competencies and also use the companion operationalization guidelines (AMCD Professional Standards and Certification Committee, 1996). In this endeavor consultants are asked to help organizations consciously create a transition to a more multiculturally competent entity. This transition is one that often creates resistance, as exemplified in *Who Moved My Cheese?* (Johnson, 1998). In his best-selling book, Johnson presented an allegory of mice that resist change to the point of starvation and compares them to mice that accept change and move on. The lessons learned by the "resilient" mice are (a) change happens, (b) anticipate change, (c) monitor change, (d) adapt to change quickly, (e) change, (f) enjoy change, and (g) be ready to quickly change again and again. The underlying message is that not only is change constant, but also that one must embrace change and see it as leading to more positive outcomes. It is beyond the scope of this book to describe the transition of an organization to a more multicultural one, but it is certainly fruitful ground for counselor consultants.

Another transition that may be addressed by counselor consultants is when organizations engage in strategic planning. Whether this takes the form of strategic visioning or the more traditional detailed planning, carrying out the vision or plan will lead to both big and small transitions for the people who work in or connect to the organization. Whenever counselors engage in consultation roles, they find that their counseling skills are necessary precursors to developing the relationships that facilitate effective consultations. Counselors can also assist individuals and organizations manage transitions by designing and delivering programs and workshops.

DEVELOPING PROGRAMS AND WORKSHOPS

Another way that counselors can expand their impact on adults in transition is through designing and presenting structured workshops and acting as program developers. We define a *program* as an array of services offered by an organization, and a *workshop* as a short-term educational or growth experience. Thus, the program of any organization may include several workshops as well as other activities.

Obviously, a competent counselor can be extremely helpful to an individual suddenly conscious of being middle-aged, to a divorced person, or to a job seeker. The same counselor, however, can reach many more people by offering a workshop on midlife changes, divorce, or job-seeking skills. And the workshop may add the bonus of group support.

In addition, some adults who are reluctant to seek counseling may find it easier or more socially acceptable to attend a workshop. Participation in the workshop may be enough to help some people through the transitions. Others may find that they are now more comfortable with the idea of counseling.

Counselors involved in designing workshops or programs may find Brookfield's (1986) ideas on adult learning useful. He recommended flexible programs that build in opportunities for serendipitous learning, and he cautioned against over-reliance on predetermined objectives that leave little room for such unanticipated learning. This may be particularly important in programs for adults in transition because the needs of participants may change as they learn more about *themselves* and their *situations* and see a need to develop new sources of *support* and alternative *strategies*.

Designing Programs

Setting up a comprehensive program is a complicated procedure. It requires that program planners look broadly at the environment, and consider the needs of the individuals to be served, as well as those of the organization and the community. Typically, designing a program requires identification of specific tasks and a time line.

The National Occupational Information Coordinating Committee (1989) developed the useful three-stage model for program design shown below (Kobylarz, 2005):

Stage One. Planning (0–6 months)
- Form committees
- Conduct needs assessment
- Establish program standards
- Initiate evaluation planning

Stage Two. Development (7–12 months)
- Direct committees in program development
- Review the current program
- Revise the plan
- Design the evaluation
- Identify staff development needs

Stage Three. Implementation (13–24 months)
- Involve committees in program implementation
- Conduct staff development
- Monitor program implementation
- Evaluate and use results for program improvement

Because formative evaluation is a continuous process, used to improve program design, discussion of evaluation procedures continues throughout the process. Committees are also involved in all stages. When committees are broadly based and include community representatives, they can assist in marketing and recruiting as well as program design.

Reentry students are the target group for a variety of college and university programs. Jacoby (1991) developed a model for serving adult students. The four components of the SPAR model—services, programs, advocacy, and research—can be a useful guide for counselors. According to her definitions, services are performed *for* students and must be scheduled to accommodate their multiple roles. Programs are carried on *with* students, often through adult student organizations. Advocacy on *behalf* of students is designed to see that the policies and practices of educational institutions are responsive to student needs. Research helps counselors and other professionals better understand the needs of adult students and evaluate existing programs.

Orientation courses for adult learners, such as the one at the University of Maryland, College Park's Counseling Center, addresses issues of identity, comfort with academics, and concerns about balancing work, family, and study. In interviews, adult learners frequently mention the sense of community that results from participation in these workshop courses (B. Greenberg & B. Goldberg, personal communication, 1995).

Designing and Presenting Workshops

By virtue of their training and experience, counselors already have many of the communications skills necessary for conducting workshops. Typically, counselors know how to listen to workshop participants, ask clarifying questions to make sure that participants understand the information, "read" the group's nonverbal language, and promote group interaction.

Effective workshop leaders must also know how to present information clearly and use examples that are appropriate for particular individuals and groups. Counselors can learn these skills. A study of training needs of career development facilitators revealed a significant interest in learning how to train both clients and other career development facilitators. The authors recommended that "train-the-trainer sessions emphasize training skills and that only experienced, effective trainers be used to train other personnel" (Hoppin & Splete, 1994, p. 85).

Counselors interested in designing effective workshops may find Loesch's (1985) seven-step procedure helpful. The seven steps—define your goals, profile the participants, profile the setting, design your agenda, prepare your resources, prepare yourself, and practice—can be applied to almost any workshop. If, for example, you have been asked to design a workshop for dislocated workers in your community and you know the workers are concerned about their ability to look for jobs, your goals might be to provide practical information about job-search techniques and labor-force projections, as well as to build worker confidence. In designing the agenda, you might want to consult both local employers and a list of competencies needed by job seekers, such as that contained in Goodman and Hoppin (1991).

In planning workshops it is important to think of who, what, where, and when. Who and what need to be carefully coordinated so that the content and manner of presentation fit the needs of a particular clientele. Thus, a workshop for adults who have recently learned they have attention deficit disorder should not be done in a straight lecture format. A variety of activities, many experiential, should be included. The leader of a workshop for returning learners needs to inform students about resources of the college or university and give them an opportunity to express some of their concerns about their new role.

Workshop planners also need to consider the cultural background of their participants. After investigating the self-esteem of Arab adults studying English as a second language, Klee (1994) urged counselors and teachers to cooperate in tailoring programs for their special needs. She suggested that single-gender workshops might be more appropriate for this population and also recommended that workshop participants have "opportunities for cultural and linguistic interactions with native English speakers outside of the classroom . . . [possibly through] field trips, 'pot lucks,' forums, guest speakers, or language exchange partners" (p. 31).

The time at which a workshop is offered also affects who can come. Workshops for displaced homemakers with young children can be offered during the day if child care is available. If a business wants spouses to attend a retirement planning seminar, it usually needs to be an evening program so spouses do not have to take time off from their own jobs. Workshops for older adults often have to be scheduled when transportation is available. Safety issues are also important. In their publicity, sponsors may want to mention secure, lighted parking if that is apt to be an issue. Having representatives of the targeted population involved in the planning process increases the likelihood that the right questions about who, what, where, and when will be asked.

A Sampling of Workshops

Earlier in this chapter, we identified a number of topics that could be the focus of support groups for people experiencing individual, family, and work-related transitions. Many of those topics lend themselves to a workshop format, if a more educational focus is desired. This section contains ideas for workshops counselors can conduct or promote, and descriptions of a few we considered innovative.

Sometimes the approach of community-based counseling represents a blending of the stated desires of adult clients with the perceptions of counselors as to their needs. In conducting career decision-making groups, counselors typically want their clients to engage in a comprehensive decision-making process. Adult clients, on the other hand, particularly those adults whose career change is not voluntary, want help in finding a job. Goodman (2006) described this circumstance as an "unconscious conspiracy" (p. 69) between the counselor and the client to look for short-term solutions to deeper problems.

A National Career Development Association-commissioned Gallup poll (Miller, 2000) found that one tenth of Americans stated that they needed assistance with career planning in the past year. Furthermore, 69% said that if they were starting over, they would seek more information and more assistance than they had during their first occupational decision. The data also indicated that career assistance was not available to everyone equally. Minority individuals and youth received substantially less help than the population in general (Herr, Cramer, & Niles, 2004). Programs such as the Adult Career Counseling Center at Oakland University (Goodman & Savage, 1999) and the One Stop Career Centers around the nation are designed to address both immediate needs and the need for comprehensive planning.

An innovative career-counseling program, Operation ABLE, provides classroom-based training and self-paced instruction in a variety of computer applications, as well as offering a "Career Resilience Center" for older workers who need assistance with employment and career decisions, resume development, interview preparation and coaching, and job search assistance (Operation ABLE of Michigan, 2000, p. 13). The Resilience Center also offers skills and aptitude testing and professional career counseling. Classes are also offered in basic skills such as reading, math, and grammar.

Job Link targets food stamp recipients who do not have dependents. The program provides job skills training and placement services to help its clients find job placements. Employment Link works with homeless individuals referred by Med-Link and provides job skills training and placement services to help them find job placements. Work Connect helps hard-to-place individuals with histories of incarceration, substance abuse and other obstacles to find jobs. Skills remediation and employment services help them successfully enter the job market.

Women reentering the work world can benefit from workshops that include a counseling component. For example, PROBE (Potential Reentry Opportunities in Business and Education) was designed to help divorced, separated, and widowed women enter professional and other nontraditional careers. Empowerment of women is a major goal of the program, which is "based on feminist principles . . . [and] relies heavily on women already placed in the community as role models and sources of support" (Towns & Gentzler, 1986, p. 160). Program organizers also work with potential employers to develop jobs.

In the Winter 1990 issue of *Generations,* the journal of the American Society on Aging (Capuzzi, Gross, & Friel, 1990), several counselors from different parts of the country mentioned that they make speeches and present community workshops to introduce ideas about adult development and psychological change to older adults and their families. These programs often serve as a recruiting tool, as attendees may then seek counseling for themselves or refer others.

Educational experiences do not always take place in classrooms. In San Francisco, a vacant lot turned into an urban garden is the site of an innovative program for people being released from prison. People experiencing this transition may find that their preprison support system is no longer intact, and their previous strategies for coping with their lives are no longer appropriate. The Garden Project, founded in 1991, is a model project designed to help recently released ex-offenders reenter their communities, learn new skills, and avoid the temptations of the street.

A press release about the program, undated and simply titled, "The Garden Project", noted, "To help achieve personal goals, 'students' in the program also fulfill requirements to participate in alcohol and drug rehabilitation programs, as well as pursue continuing education studies." An article about the project in the *New York Times* characterized the fruit and vegetables of the garden as "metaphors for what went wrong in a prisoner's troubled past. . . . The simple process of weeding is a good place to start re-examining a life gone wrong. The weeds are whatever got in the way: smoking crack or whoring or stealing" (Gross, 1992). In addition to the metaphorical value of planting, cultivating, and weeding, gardeners are paid for their efforts from the revenue earned by the produce. Local businesses support the project by their purchases, and several foundations have supplied additional income.

Another San Francisco garden program, Fresh Start Farms, hires homeless people to work as organic gardeners. According to an article in the *San Francisco Examiner,* "The homeless workers will be bused to the garden daily, paid minimum wage, then given a bonus of $5,000 at the end of the first year to help them make a go of it in the mainstream market. They can also earn $9 an hour to train other homeless gardeners" (Nakao, 1993). Although these projects are not typical workshops for adults in transition, they represent innovative efforts for which counselors can advocate.

WORKING AS ADVOCATES

In *Webster's New Collegiate Dictionary* (1980) *advocate* is defined as "one who defends, vindicates or espouses a cause." Social scientists talk about functioning as change agents, but, in lay terms, we may think of advocacy as standing up for what you believe. Whatever the definition, in this discussion we are talking about counselor efforts to make life more fair to and more supportive of adults in transition. Sometimes those efforts involve working to empower adults so they can act in their own behalf. In other situations, counselors may need to intervene on a broader level, urging organizations and systems to be more responsive to the needs of adults.

Lewis, Arnold, House, and Toporek (2005) (see Figure 9.1) developed a set of advocacy competencies for the American Counseling Association. These competencies address client, community, and public arenas from the perspective of acting with and acting on behalf of clients. They help the counselor–advocate move from the micro to the macro level, using the appropriate advocacy skills for each circumstance. They were developed in response to a perception that many counselors want to advocate for their clients, but do not know how to be effective. The competencies were designed to help counselors to operationalize the necessary skills.

Let us look at some of the competencies. In the category of client empowerment, the authors recommend identifying potential allies—a support system in the terminology of this book. When they approach advocating at the community level, they discuss finding groups already involved in the same or similar efforts and suggest that counselors join those efforts. In those and other advocacy efforts, they suggest that counselors contribute their particular expertise in communications, training, and research. Similarly, the competency suggestions encourage counselors to use their existing skills in listening, identifying strengths, and knowledge of human development.

Another approach to helping counselors become more effective advocates was undertaken by Lewis and Bradley (2000). They commissioned a series of articles, first published in the American Counseling Association (ACA) newsletter, *Counseling Today,* over a period of months, then

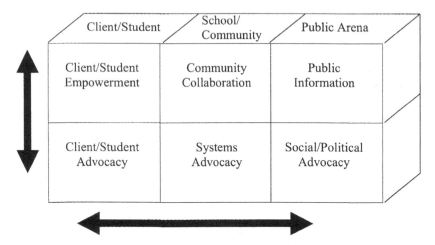

Figure 9.1 Advocacy competency domains. (*Source:* The American Counseling Association Web site, http://www.counseling.org/Resources/. Reprinted with permission. No further reproduction authorized without written permission from the American Counseling Association.)

presented at the ACA national conference, and finally published as chapters in the above referenced book. The chapters provide theory and ideas for approaching advocacy for specific groups, for example, youth, multiracial families, and women in the criminal justice and addictions treatment systems. Each chapter includes suggestions for action and resources; that is, these are not authors who just describe the problems, they are authors who want to help readers have the tools to work toward solutions. In other words, they are advocates. Toporek (2000), in her contribution to the book, provides the rationale for this focus, "Historically, the focus of counseling has been to facilitate clients towards *adapting to the environment* [emphasis added]. However, advocacy in counseling asserts that the environment must change and that both the counselor and the client may be instrumental in this change" (p. 5).

Toporek makes the further point that although it may be important for clients to learn advocacy skills and be empowered by advocating for themselves, this position represents a particular, culturally determined, worldview. She argues that there are many circumstances in which advocating for clients is appropriate and indeed necessary. This position is supported by the ACA ethical standards (2005) as they state, "When appropriate, counselors advocate at individual, group, institutional and societal levels to examine potential barriers and obstacles that inhibit access and/or the growth and development of clients" (p. 5). This affirmative ethical responsibility requires that counselors, to best help their clients, be aware of institutional or societal barriers and take steps to change those barriers. Two case examples follow.

The Case of the Reluctant Gadfly

John McMahon was a counselor at a large urban university. One of his clients, Susan Cooper, was depressed and anxious about her academic performance. She was a 35-year-old freshman who had not been involved in anything remotely academic since finishing high school 17 years earlier. She was taking an extra heavy course load, 16 credits, as she was only going to receive 3 years of alimony before she had to support herself and have the major responsibility of support for her three children, and she hoped to graduate in 3 years. She was doing adequate work in three of her classes, those in the social sciences in which she felt comfortable, but she was drowning in her required English class. She had handed her first paper in late; one of her children broke her wrist and she had to take time to handle that emergency—time she had planned for writing. Her grade was reduced because of that. Further, she had panicked on the midterm exam and performed very poorly. She assured Mr. McMahon that she knew the material, but that her anxiety had been debilitating. Susan was considering dropping out of school and was petrified that she would not meet her financial responsibilities. Mr. McMahon was most comfortable working with individuals, not engaging in advocacy, but he knew he would have to go further to help Susan manage the impending crisis.

The counselor looked at the situation from both the perspective of how he could help Susan and what system interventions might be necessary. Following the ACA advocacy model, he first worked with Susan to see her options. He encouraged her to not only speak with the professor in the class she was failing, but also to let her other professors know that she had extreme test anxiety. On her behalf, he contacted the disabilities office to see if they provided accommodations for test anxiety. When he found out that they did not, he advocated within the system to educate them about test anxiety and persuaded them to add this disability to their list of required accommodations. To do so, he researched other universities' policies, found a model that fit, and provided that to the disabilities office. He gently prodded the office until they added test anxiety to their list, encouraged Susan to register with the office, and asked them to notify her professors that she needed this assistance. Furthermore, he discussed Susan's situation (anonymously) with his colleagues at the next staff meeting, so the entire staff would be aware of this potential service for all of the students they saw. Thus, he advocated at the individual and system levels.

The Case of the Furious Job Counselor

Maria Villanova worked in a one-stop career center as a vocational counselor. Her job was to help clients who were unsuccessful in their quest for employment—those who had been looking for work for more than 3 months. Many of her clients had multiple barriers to employment: their age, inadequate education, or demanding family responsibilities. Sam Wright was that type of client. Sam had lost his manufacturing job at age 55 when his company moved overseas. He had received 1 year of benefits, but these were now expired, and he was getting desperate for work. Sam had been successful at the unskilled job he had held since dropping out of school, but had only a 6th grade education. This unwanted transition had left him with a very poor self-image, and his life was complicated by the fact that his wife had recently been diagnosed with cancer. His children were grown, but none lived close enough to take her to her numerous medical appointments.

Dr. Villanova believed that Sam Wright was being discriminated against because of his age and his educational record. She believed that his work record should be considered as more important than his schooling and that his performance and attendance at his last job were more telling indicators of his abilities than his age. She believed that he could do well at a job that required maturity, steadiness, and judgment and hoped he could find one with some flexibility so he could take his wife to her appointments. She also believed that there should be some support to help him with that latter responsibility.

Her first step was to talk to Sam about his Situation, Self, Support, and Strategies. She believed that he needed to bolster his support system by learning to ask for help; for example, he had a neighbor who had offered to drive his wife to her treatments some of the time, but he had not taken her up on the offer. Second, Dr. Villanova believed that her client needed more job-seeking strategies, so she referred him to her organization's job club. But, Dr. Villanova also believed that Sam was being discriminated against. She educated herself on her county's and her state's laws about age discrimination; she contacted the local equal opportunity office to see what assistance they could offer; she contacted the local office of services to the aging to see what assistance they could offer; and she contacted her state legislators to see if they were able to help in any way. She found that although there were adequate laws on the books, they were not being enforced, and indeed that those responsible for enforcement were understaffed and overwhelmed. She joined with a coalition of organizations that was lobbying for increased funding for this function, lending her counseling expertise and network to this cause. Her hope was that even though Sam might not be helped by these efforts, future clients would be.

Advocacy as Empowerment

In our quest to be supportive of various groups of adults, we must be careful not to take over for them. McKnight (1990) contended that "more and more conditions of human beings are being converted into problems in order to provide jobs for people who are forced to derive their income by purporting to deliver a service" (p. 5). Applying this idea to the needs of an older population, he suggested that scholars conducting research on "old as a deficiency . . . [should be asked instead] to define the competence, the skills, and the capacities of old" (p. 9). McKnight's message can serve as a reminder to counselors to direct their advocacy efforts toward empowerment not the creation of dependency.

In many situations, counselors need to operate on more than one level. In terms of the transition model, counselors can help clients develop more effective *strategies,* and counselors and clients can work together to improve available institutional *support.* For example, counselors in college and university settings may be able to empower returning students through workshops that build self-esteem and teach assertive skills and effective study techniques. At the same time, these counselors can encourage their educational institutions to have evening advising hours, offer financial aid for part-time students, and generally be more supportive of the needs of returning learners.

As an example, the University of Maryland, College Park, has a returning student fund that offers grants to adult learners experiencing financial emergencies. These grants, ranging from $100 to $500, have enabled a number of students to stay in school and continue to provide for their families. Several of the recipients spoke of the grants as a tremendous source of motivation, in part because they made the students feel they really mattered to someone.

To assess the degree to which adult learners feel they matter to their institutions, Schlossberg, Lasalle, and Golec (1991) developed "The Mattering Scales for Adult Students in Higher Education." These easily administered scales give students an opportunity to record their perceptions about their educational environment in five different areas: administration, advising, peers, multiple roles, and faculty. Questions deal with issues such as the degree to which students feel appreciated or missed when they are not in class, and the degree to which they find the policies of the institution cognizant of the competing demands in their lives. Data from the scales provide information for change. Administrators and student development educators can pinpoint the areas in which adult learners feel they do not matter and then take appropriate action to create a more hospitable environment.

Counselors in the workplace can also urge the employing organization to create a more supportive environment by establishing flex-time schedules and/or making dependent care available. Intergenerational day care that serves both preschool children and older adults at the workplace may be one approach counselors can recommend (Waters, 1991).

Counselor–advocates can also work to make nonprofit agencies more "user friendly" for their adult clients. At one employment office, an official of the U.S. Department of Labor heard many unemployment counselors talking among themselves about how "their hearts ached for the people who had to stand in line to collect their checks and wait to talk with them." After looking over the office, the official suggested several changes to make the environment more supportive. He recommended that people take numbers and be able to sit down while retaining their place "in line." He also recommended changing the physical environment so that clients could sit in chairs rather than lean over a counter when talking with counselors (Robinson, 1994).

Minkler (1983) reported another example of working with and on behalf of adults. The Tenderloin Senior Outreach Project was designed for older adults living in single-room occupancy hotels in inner-city San Francisco. Graduate students used weekly blood pressure screening in the hotel lobby as an opportunity to talk with residents and facilitate interaction. As the initial discussion group became popular, residents of other hotels expressed interest. When group discussions indicated that crime was the worst problem, students encouraged residents to develop an interhotel coalition to fight crime. The report is full of poignant stories of the support residents provided each other. In Minkler's view, the project led to gradual empowerment of the elderly residents as individuals and as a community. To see how one counselor engaged in advocacy activities in the service of empowerment, we turn to another profile.

Acting at the Local, State, and National Level

When one is working with an individual client, advocacy often takes the form of "running interference," often as part of the referral process. Operationally that means you do not just give your clients the name of an agency that might provide the services they need, but you call the agency yourself, verify the services they offer and the hours they provide them, and perhaps alert them to your clients' special needs. Also, adults who are apprehensive about negotiating a transition, whether it be returning to school, attending the first meeting of a widowed persons' group, or looking into Alcoholics Anonymous, may need the name of a particular person to look for, or perhaps a "buddy" to accompany them. You can be of help there.

Clients may also need help in coping with bureaucracies. The thought of going for the first time to an employment (or unemployment) office, admissions office, social security building, or senior center can appear daunting to many adults in transition. Counselors can help by walking clients through the process, literally or with an in-office rehearsal. To make appropriate referrals, counselors need to be knowledgeable about local resources. The process of helping adults with such practical concerns may also build trust and open the door for dealing with their emotional problems as well.

Dealing with bureaucracies can pose additional problems for people in certain ethnic or minority groups. Non-English-speaking adults may have particular problems if the agency staff speak only English and if the forms they must fill out are only in English. Counselors can advocate by encouraging the agency to provide translators or bilingual staff members.

A major transition for adults may come when they need to deal with the criminal justice system for the first time. Whether they are the victim of a crime or the family member of a perpetrator, the thought of going to the police can seem overwhelming. This may be particularly true for adults who come from groups that historically have experienced adversarial relationships with the police. Counselors can intervene both to help clients reframe their views of police as potential helpers and to work with police to help them become more receptive to clients from diverse ethnic backgrounds.

Sometimes, in their advocacy role, counselors see a need for a particular service and find a way to provide it. For example, the Adult Day Care Center in Ada, OK, exists because of the efforts of a counselor–educator there (B. Shelton, personal communication, 1990). The retired executive director of the Chamber of Commerce called her to seek help for a former Chamber member who had Alzheimer's disease. They discussed the value of adult day care and set up a community meeting involving potential users of the service, as well as leaders of the business community and legislators to discuss it.

In Ada, the human services people and the business people worked well together. The first group knew what a day care center could do; the business people knew how to incorporate and access funding. This coalition worked well in part because the members were powerful people. A major challenge for counselors is to assist less powerful people to explain their needs and find ways to meet them.

McCrone (1991), writing to urge efforts on behalf of those with disabilities, suggested that lobbying, testifying at hearings, supporting helpful legislators, organizing witnesses, and drafting bills will enable grassroots rehabilitation professionals to participate in the evolution of disability-related Federal law. Such laws can play a crucial role in the lives of adults who become disabled.

Smith (1994) gave a broader rationale for counselor involvement in public policy. In his view counselors are fulfilling only part of their professional obligation if they work with individual clients but fail to see the larger impact they can have by being involved with public policy. He stated that we "must be involved with legislation . . . regarding aid to education or career development, or the issues of accessibility for the physically disadvantaged . . . with discriminatory practices in the work place and the legislation or lack of legislation that works to eliminate that discrimination" (p. 15).

Smith mentioned but a few of the many issues for which lobbying may produce helpful legislation. There are a host of issues involving health care, funding for schools at all levels, security and portability of pensions, and community-based programs to provide assistance to adults experiencing temporary crises or long-term difficulties.

As discussed earlier in this chapter, counselors can advocate in many different ways. For example, they can represent the interests of adults to community organizations and educational institutions. This may mean recommending that colleges and universities schedule supportive services at convenient hours for adults, testifying at a local hearing of a planning agency about the need for additional transportation services for persons with disabilities, or urging libraries to establish in-home services.

Some advocacy efforts are best done by counselors acting individually, whether in their professional roles or as private citizens (Politicians do pay attention to letters and phone calls from constituents.) Other times counselors can maximize their effectiveness by working with an advocacy group representing their point of view. For example, Citizens for Better Care (CBC) is an advocacy organization monitoring conditions in nursing homes. When counselors are aware of CBC's findings, they can help families locate dependable facilities with a well-trained staff and avoid those where CBC has found instances of mistreatment. When counselors have this information, they can make appropriate referrals and perhaps ease the transition of placing a family member in a nursing home. Increasingly, professional associations of counselors are becoming involved in advocacy efforts.

Two noted organizations whose members see their primary role as advocacy are Counselors for Social Justice and Psychologists for Social Responsibility. The stated purpose of the organization Psychologists for Social Responsibility (2005), is to use "psychological knowledge and skills to promote peace with social justice at the community, national and international levels" (Our Mission, 1). Their goals are stated as the following:

Through our Action Committees and Steering Committee we work to

- Apply the growing body of knowledge about conflict resolution and violence prevention.
- Facilitate positive changes for victims and survivors of personal, community, and civil violence.

- Advocate for basic human needs—including actions that decrease poverty, ensure ethnic and gender equality, increase work opportunity, promote healthy and sustainable environments, and achieve a wiser balance between human needs and military budgets.
- Ensure that relevant information from psychology is used in local, national, and international public policy (Our Mission, 2).

Counselors for Social Justice (CJS, 2005), a division of the American Counseling Association, is described as:

a community of counselors, counselor educators, graduate students, and school and community leaders who seek equity and an end to oppression and injustice affecting clients, students, counselors, families, communities, schools, workplaces, governments, and other social and institutional systems. CSJ is committed to

- Challenging oppressive systems of power and privilege.
- Implementing social action strategies including the Social Justice Advocacy Competencies through collaborative alliances with other ACA entities, counselor education programs, and N–16 schools and community organizations.
- Disseminating social justice scholarship about sociopolitical and economic inequities facing counselors and clients/students in schools and communities.
- Maintaining an active support network online and in person for engaging in social justice activities in schools and communities.
- Providing lively professional development to enhance counselor, counselor educator, and graduate student competency in social justice advocacy via ACA annual conference programs (Day of Action/Day of Learning), branches, regions, counselor education programs, N–16 schools, and community agencies.
- Maintaining social justice advocacy resources online (Mission, 1).

The ACA's Government Relations Committee, composed of association members, as well as professional staff, advocates for the interests of both clients and counselors. The Committee's mission is to identify and initiate proactive and reactive positions on public policy issues confronting professional counselors, human development professionals, and those whom they serve.

The committee urges its members to contact their legislators on a wide range of human service needs, to provide the lawmakers with information, and to express appreciation when their actions are in line with the interests of clients and counselors. Counselors can support advocacy efforts by joining these and similar organizations, as well as by their personal advocacy efforts.

Another major benefit of counselor advocacy has been the move toward counselor credentialing. At the national level, in 2005 almost 40,000 counselors have opted for voluntary certification through the National Board for Certified Counselors (2005). As of 2005, 48 states and the District of Columbia had a counselor licensure law. Certification and licensure serve as a way for counselors to indicate their commitment to professionalism. Certification also makes it easier for adults in transition to identify qualified counselors.

Many advocacy activities can have considerable impact on the opportunity structure for adults. In our view, that is a major reason for counselors to be involved beyond their office doors.

SUMMARY

Because adults live, work, and play in environments that encompass a broad range of possibilities, multiple interventions are typically necessary. Let us consider two different clients we might encounter and briefly discuss some of the interventions we might use to enhance their coping resources.

A 40-year-old displaced worker who decided to return to school might benefit from individual and/or group counseling. We, as supportive counselors, can help him explore his Situation. For example, we might find it important to evaluate his financial resources by asking him questions about whether his previous employer will cover any educational expenses, whether he has a working partner, and whether the family has health insurance. Our counseling would also provide an opportunity for him to express his feelings about two major role changes: (a) being laid off and (b) returning to school.

Before helping him set realistic goals, we, as counselors, could also help him explore the Self resources he brings to the transition. What is his attitude toward change and his general outlook on life? Answers to questions about both Situation and Self might be important in determining whether to refer him for financial aid and in helping him decide how many courses to take the first semester.

If we were serving as consultants to the school, we might encourage the administration to engage in a self-study and work with faculty and staff to help them become more sensitive to and supportive of the needs of returning students. We might help them establish a returning student center, help them design programs to meet the special needs of nontraditional students, and/or consult with existing campus offices to add or modify services to serve this population. As advocates, we could testify before the state legislature to urge additional funding to support the establishment of special programs for students as well as retraining for faculty and staff. As advocates we might also work with university administrators to understand the need for evening hours for campus services such as the bookstore, career advising, and even child care. We might even advocate with campus life staff or student activities officers to encourage them to reach out to nontraditional students.

If, on the other hand, our client is a 54-year-old grandmother suddenly faced with the task of raising grandchildren, she might need counseling to help her deal with her changing roles, relationships, responsibilities, and assumptions about herself. Her life plan has probably changed dramatically. We might work with a local hospital to offer parenting classes designed for grandparents, or, in what might be considered a role reversal, work with local adult education programs to design workshops for teenagers being raised by grandparents.

In our role as consultants to school districts, we might encourage teachers and counselors at the schools attended by the grandchildren to participate in in-service training to familiarize them with appropriate ways of handling this special group of youngsters and their grandmothers. As advocates at the state or federal level, we could argue for policy changes that would provide better financial benefits for grandmothers raising their grandchildren. As advocates at the local level, we might suggest that schools change standard notes home from "Dear parent" to more inclusive terminology. We might encourage those in charge of "parent–teacher associations" to broaden their reach.

We hope these two examples underline what we have been saying throughout the chapter and the book. Counseling adults in transition is an exciting and challenging job that gives us an opportunity to function at many different levels.

Afterword

This book has been predicated on a number of assumptions that we hope have been clear as well as comprehensive. In an effort to tie it all together, we will briefly review our assumptions.

ASSUMPTION 1: PRACTICE MUST BE TIED TO THEORY

The scientist-practitioner model, so prevalent in counseling, is based on the notion that practice stems from research and theory. In this book we present a theory of individuals in transition—a theory that lays the groundwork for the many practices, programs, and strategies suggested.

Transition theory posits a structure for viewing *any* change, whether it is anticipated or unanticipated, positive or negative, a success or a failure, or an event or a non-event. The persons and issues vary; the structure remains the same.

Transition theory states that individuals manage transitions differently. The variability stems largely from differences in people's resources and deficits as they approach transitions. The theory categorizes potential resources such as the individual's *Situation, Self, Support,* and *Strategies*—the 4 S system. The practice details what can be done to assess these resources and compensate for deficits that may exist.

An example of the interface between theory and practice relates to coping. It was found that people cope by either changing a situation, changing the meaning of a situation, or managing their own reactions to it. Knowledge and understanding of these categories can guide counselors as they work with clients in an individual or group setting.

Leonard Pearlin and his colleagues also emphasized that no magic coping strategy exists. Effective coping involves utilizing numerous coping strategies as appropriate. Sometimes one may use humor, other times one may need to engage in confrontation, at times mediation may be necessary, and occasionally one may choose to do nothing.

To illustrate, we will share a travel story of Nancy's with you. Several years ago, she went to Denver to make a speech. When she arrived at the hotel she was perplexed. The hotel had no record of the meeting. Nancy called the conference coordinator to discover that the meeting was scheduled for November, not October. She had arrived a month early. As Nancy said:

> I cannot describe my feeling of shock and utter dismay. I immediately called my husband and started to cry. Steve was initially empathetic, but then confronted me with, "Nancy, you've got to cope. Your book, *Overwhelmed: Coping with Life's Ups and Downs,* will be out in 1 month and you can't fall apart in Denver." That did it. I thought, if my book has anything to offer, then I should be able to pull out some strategies to help me get through this experience. I did several things. First, I went to an elegant restaurant, and as the maitre d' was trying to seat me, I refused to sit down. I knew I needed a support system, and he was it. As I started telling him my sad saga, he ordered me a drink, sat down, and let me talk. Then (to myself) I reviewed the coping strategies discussed in the book. Could I change the situation? No, it was October, not November, in Denver. Could I change the way I saw the situation? Yes. Instead of labeling it a failure, a disaster, I decided to reframe it. I could redefine myself as someone who is able to go to Denver for lunch or perhaps San Francisco for dinner. On a more serious side, I decided that as a mental health professional, I could utilize this episode to help others. People could compare their calendar mixups to mine and realize theirs were not as bad. And finally, I knew I had a great opening for the speech in Denver the next month: "You have never had a speaker more eager to talk. I even came a month early."

Although this is a minor example, it illustrates what one can do in a stressful situation or at a time when spontaneous coping is necessary. One can refer to the scientific findings about coping and then decide on an appropriate strategy.

ASSUMPTION 2: WE CAN TAKE THE MYSTERY—IF NOT THE MISERY—OUT OF CHANGE

Change is not as mysterious as it seems. By looking at the degree to which a transition changes one's roles, relationships, routines, and assumptions, counselors can help clients gauge how traumatic a transition will be. Then counselors can help clients examine their potential resources for coping and identify deficits, and can then jointly plan ways of compensating for those deficits by deciding whether to change them, change their meaning, or manage the resultant stress. One can also better understand a client's stress by looking at where the client is in the transition process.

ASSUMPTION 3: COUNSELORS CAN FOLLOW THE THEORY-TO-PRACTICE MODEL BY ORGANIZING THEIR THINKING AROUND THREE QUESTIONS

The three questions are

1. What do counselors need to know?
2. What are counselors likely to hear?
3. What can counselors do with what they know and hear?

The final section focuses on specific strategies and interventions that incorporate the knowledge counselors have about transitions with their counseling skills. These may be used in either individual or group counseling. Counselors will also utilize this knowledge when they work as consultants or advocates to best meet their clients' needs.

We hope that this theory-to-practice book is useful as you help clients become better able to work, love, and play.

APPENDIX

Helping Clients Deal with Non-Event Transitions

Nancy K. Schlossberg

Counselors hear stories about what might have been, about what should have been, and about what did not happen. Yet, much research and counseling advice has been focused only on marker events such as marriage, childbirth, changing jobs, divorce, or being fired. Most of these events are observable; many have rituals and celebrations attached to them. Counselors have enormous power to help clients exchange heartbreaks for heartmends. There are many ways in which they can work with clients—individually, in groups, in workshops, and at brown-bag lunch discussions. Whatever mode they use to help people deal with lost dreams in their lives, they need to be aware of special characteristics associated with these heartbreaks.

The study of non-events—what they are, how they change lives, and ways they can be transformed—is new and needed. To that end, a team of researchers at the University of Maryland, College Park conducted two studies. In the first study they examined non-events using multidimensional scaling. This method uncovered the dimensions that differentiate one non-event from another. Just as we can all tell the difference between cars, such as Fords, Mustangs, and Cadillacs, they felt it would be important to identify the dimensions that differentiated between the disappointed mother and the disappointed doctor. To do that, Nancy Schlossberg, Jan Altman, Leah Steinberg, and Robert Lissitz collected accounts of non-events from graduate students, training directors from business and industry, and returning students. From these, they developed eight prototypical non-events for use in the multidimensional scaling study.

Armed with the findings of this early research, they began searching for additional answers. They arranged interviews with a random sample of 45 men and women 55 and older who served as retired volunteers in the Office of Experiential Learning at the University of Maryland. Other interviews of adults aged 20 to 55 were added to broaden the perspective. These interviews allowed them to hear first hand what the non-events of these adults were, how they changed their lives, and what they did to cope.

Combining qualitative and quantitative data allowed the research team to learn about the drama of the unseen, the unlabeled, and the heartbreaks that occur in all our lives. This research resulted in a book written for the general public by Nancy K. Schlossberg with Susan P. Robinson, entitled_Going to Plan B (1996). But more is needed. Counselors need to help clients deal with non-events. Thus, this Appendix focuses on specific suggestions and strategies for counselors to use with their clients.

I suggest a three-step program for counselors to use as they help clients work through their non-events. The three steps are counselors need to use are

> Step 1: Understand the concept of non-events as a way to listen with a third ear.
> Step 2: Develop specific strategies for clients to use as they cope with non-events.
> Step 3: Teach lessons for life literacy.

STEP 1: UNDERSTAND NON-EVENTS

The following discussion of non-events will illuminate their role in the lives of adults and help counselors listen with a new sensitivity to what did not happen in the lives of their clients. Here are some examples of this phenomenon from the lives of people who were interviewed:

- I gave up my career to stay home and raise my children, but they did not turn out as expected. I had a picture of them with sweaters tied around their shoulders and going to Eastern colleges. Instead, one, who had to go to a special school, now works in a grocery store. Another dropped out of school and hasn't made a comeback. The third is a janitor. There is nothing wrong with them or what they are doing. I just spend my life expecting something different. I am so jealous when I read about other families in which the children moved up and made something of themselves. Why do I walk around feeling depressed?

- I always expected to be a parent. I love children and feel I have a lot to give. My wife and I discovered we can never have children, and my wife refuses to adopt. Am I going to spend the rest of my life being angry at my wife and feeling cheated about not having children? I am really struggling with what to do now.
- My father never realized his dream of becoming a physician. Instead he sells pharmaceutical supplies and is a chronically unhappy individual. The problem is that his lost dream has affected our whole family—my mother, my sister, myself. You wouldn't think someone else's lost dream would affect so many lives. We walk around him as if on egg shells. Is there a healthier way for our family to function?

People often ask, "Am I alone in wondering what might have been?" The answer is "No." In fact, these stories, in a sense, are everyone's stories. Each of these people has experienced that sense of what-might-have-been, the earnest expectations that were not met, the dreams that somehow got lost along the way. It is true that some non-events might seem more significant than others perhaps, but who is to say? Does a thwarted beauty queen feel less pain than a childless man? And how might these adults deal with their pain and give new shape to the future?

Where Do Unmet Dreams Reside?

The researchers found that their respondents' non-events fell into the following domains: relationships that did not materialize; family problems such as internality or not becoming a grandparent; career issues such as not getting a job, not being promoted, or missing an educational opportunity; and issues related to self such as not shedding those extra pounds. In other words, their subjects and people in general dream about love, family, success, legacy, and self-image.

We recognize that life is not tidy—what starts out as a dream about career can impact dreams about self and family. The woman who discussed her father's career disappointment—not becoming a doctor—noted how it has influenced the family. His depression affected his wife. His disappointment in himself projected onto his adult children. He expected them to perform, perform, and perform some more.

What Triggers Non-Events?

The triggers can be external such as a colleague getting promoted, while you are still in the same job; others are internal, such as some highly personal reminders that an expectation may never be realized. Whether internal or external, the underlying issue relates to feeling "off time." Non-events are triggered when people feel that the events they expected should have occurred and they are woefully behind. Despite what we know about variability in timing of transitions in adulthood, people still hold onto a picture of age-appropriate expectations.

Maria cried the night before her 27th birthday: "I don't give a damn about a career. I want a baby and family. It has not happened, and I am beginning to believe it is never going to happen. I don't want to celebrate my birthday." For several reasons, Maria has decided that her timetable has not been met. She is Hispanic with a family-oriented cultural heritage, and her sense of timing has triggered a feeling of great loss.

At the same time, another single woman Maria's age might be delighted that no family responsibilities interfere with a desire to advance her career. Clearly, what is a non-event and off time for one person, might be a desired state of affairs for someone else.

What Types of Non-Events Exist?

Generally, four types of non-events can be identified: personal, ripple, resultant, and delayed.

1. Personal non-events refer to individual aspirations and might include not having a baby, not being promoted, or never marrying. For example, a person who has been in the same job for 20 years might present an example of nothing happening externally, yet everything changes internally; that is, the person's assumptions about competency and identity are gradually shaken. The expected job change never occurred, altering that person's assumptions.

2. Ripple non-events refer to the unfulfilled expectations of someone close to us, which in turn can alter our own roles, relationships, and assumptions. The parents of two young adults who were interviewed described their children to friends as "just fine." Yet they are upset because neither child has married. The parents are in their late 60s and are not the grandparents or in-laws they expected to be. What is not happening to the adult children means that certain expected events are not happening to the parents. As we examine such disappointments more closely, we see that a non-event for one person may ripple significantly into another's life.

3. Resultant non-events start with an event that leads to a non-event. Take the example of the mother who gives birth to a child with multiple disabilities. From this traumatic event may come the resultant non-event of never being able to have another child.

Or consider a rejection from medical school: The resultant non-event is failing to become a physician. The events themselves have a beginning and an end. Not being a physician can last a lifetime.

4. Delayed events are paradoxical. In their interviews, the research team found that adults keenly felt the loss of their dreams, the fear of never realizing a cherished expectation. Yet, they can be convinced that possibly their losses are merely delayed events. During the middle years, whenever they come, people begin to face the possibility that they are experiencing non-events, not delayed events. They begin to give up hope and lose confidence that they can make the dream come true. The question of when an unrealized dream becomes a non-event rather than a delayed event is not clear-cut.

Are All Non-Events the Same?

Schlossberg, Altman, Steinberg, and Lissitz found that non-events differ in three critical ways: They can be *hopeful or hopeless, sudden or gradual,* or *in or out of one's control.* The most crucial way in which these non-events differ is in terms of the degree of hope surrounding them. One man, a political exile, gave up all hope of ever returning to his country because of his political standing. And though his sadness remains, he has refused all offers of help. For him the situation is without remedy, and he is stuck in his private despair. Infertility, not having grandchildren, and rejection from a professional school are also viewed as hopeless. Absence of marriage, surprisingly, was not seen as hopeless. As long as there is breath, our respondents felt, there is a chance to meet the mate of one's dreams. Non-events perceived as hopeless will have the greatest impact on the adults who contend with them.

Some disappointments seem to broadside us suddenly. Ralph returned to college at age 50, a hopeful turn after a sudden resultant non-event. He wrote on his non-event questionnaire: "I was groomed from childhood to some day run the family company. That was cut short when my father suddenly sold the business. After some agonizing, infuriating months, I have gone back to graduate school to study gerontology." Ralph faced a number of events: his father's sale of the business and his subsequent return to school. But what is often overlooked is the lost dream. Ralph wrote: "The non-event for me was that I had been groomed since childhood for a certain career. All my adult life, the company and its demands had been given first priority. This determined my relationship to friends, suppliers, employees, friends, wife, and family. My father's precipitously selling the business—a definite event—caused me to no longer have the role for which I had been prepared."

In a follow-up interview a year later, Ralph said, "When your pencil is broken you find out very rapidly who your real friends are. At home it was confusing to my children. I suddenly went from being the provider to a period of uncertainty and then, for want of anything better, I became a student. It was hard to suddenly have no office, no base. It also changed the way I saw myself. For years I had been the customer, not the vendor. I had no idea how difficult it is to sell oneself. But mostly I had expected to peak in my business career by age 50. Instead, I am embarking on a new career. I am glad you are doing this study. Failure of a long expected event to materialize can create more change in lifestyle, attitudes, social support than the occurrence of the event." Some non-events are out of our control, such as infertility or not having grandchildren. But even career and personal non-events can be beyond our power no matter how hard we strive to avoid them. One woman told us: "In 1977, when I entered the Jesuit School of Theology at Berkeley, California, I thought I would be one of the first women to be ordained as a Roman Catholic priest. The papacy became more conservative; the U.S. bishops weakened, and repression of forward-thinking church people was rising. It was out of my control. It was part of the structure and system of the church. It's strange. I look the same to all my friends; I am doing the same thing I have always done, yet I feel so different. I am a perfect example of nothing happening but everything inside changing." Asked how this thwarting of her vocation changed her life, she used words such as *betrayed, angry,* and *powerless* to describe her initial feelings. Over time, she mobilized her anger and founded an organization helping women who feel oppressed. She also entered a doctor of philosophy program, preparing to become a therapist.

Exercise 1: Listen with a Third Ear

1. Listen for the heartbreak. Example: John talks about the physical aspects connected with multiple sclerosis.
2. Counselor listens for what John does not discuss: his dreams for his life that never materialized. John had started law school but did not have the physical stamina to continue. He is experiencing both events—multiple sclerosis and non-events—the life he cannot live.
3. Counselor identifies the impact this has on others: John moved back to his parents' home. He discussed his feelings on dependency, anger, and gratefulness. Counselor is aware of how John's life is impacting his parents.
4. Counselor listens for the future. Is there hope? What is in John's control? John's condition was gradual but now is very debilitating. At first, he had hope that his condition would not interfere with

his career plans. Because of the severity of his condition, he had to withdraw from school and move home. He feels out of control of much of his life, but in control of his attitude about what has happened to him.

STEP 2: DEVELOP SPECIFIC STRATEGIES FOR CLIENTS TO USE AS THEY COPE WITH NON-EVENTS

Just as there is no magic coping strategy, there is no magic counseling strategy. It is impossible to present a formula for working with all clients. It is important, however, for counselors to continually examine current research as a basis for helping themselves listen and act with new sensitivity. Theory and practice must continually inform each other.

In an analyzing how people cope with non-events, Lisa Heiser and Nancy Schlossberg in one study and Susan P. Robinson and Nancy Schlossberg in later conceptualizations of the work identified four major ways people cope with non-events: discovering, grieving, re-focusing, and reshaping.

Coping with non-events may demand special strategies, because most non-events are hidden, most are losses, and there is usually no rehearsal for them. Although many go through a process that includes discovering, grieving, re-focusing, and reshaping, each person's story is unique. Each person goes through a process, not necessarily in the same order and not necessarily covering every part of the process. This is a process that takes time. People often ask, "How long will it take?" It would be great to provide a definitive answer, but the amount of time depends on the person, the particular non-event, and the supports the person has.

Discovering

Usually the first step is to discover the non-event and give it a name. This has the double effect of diluting the power a non-event can have and of helping an individual to take control of the situation. Strategies that give non-events clarity include acknowledging it, making meaning, labeling it, telling a story about it, and using metaphors to describe it.

When first interviewed Betty said she thought the study was interesting, but it did not apply to her—she was in the midst of too many events, not non-events. She had just started a business, had two young children, and a husband. Betty called back the next day asking for another interview. The realization had hit her: No, she had not experienced any non-events overnight, but she realized that her father's lost dream, his non-event, had significantly influenced her life. She felt he was pressuring her to be a superb wife and mother, while achieving great success in her business. Living with a depressed father and a disappointed mother had not been easy. Their non-events had rippled unhappily into her life. She said that just hearing the term *non-event* had helped her greatly to become aware of what had been going on in their family. The awareness of the concept enabled her to articulate what her parents' problems were and how they influenced her.

Louis, who experienced a career non-event—he was passed over for promotion for 7 years—did not know how to deal with this blow. Alternately, he felt anger, humiliation, and even guilt that he should have performed better at work. His reactions were confusing and unsettling. Fortunately, he talked with his company's human resource person who helped him take a reality check. He realized he was in a dead-end situation. He began talking about his career non-event and his emotional reactions to it. This enabled him to stop blaming himself and focus his energies on career planning. He also developed a story to tell his friends. His new mantra became "It's time for a change."

The biggest difference between events and non-events relates to the fact that non-events are undercover. Therefore, it is particularly important for clients to listen for what did not happen. Was the lost dream one that rippled from someone else, one that resulted from an event, or one that was solely the individual's? Is it a delayed event rather than a non-event? Encourage clients to tell a story about the non-event; the story will then demystify the experience. The question of how to acknowledge your non-events to others is very important. People do not usually go around saying: "Let me tell you about my career non-event, or the job offer that never came." Unless you let others know you are experiencing a painful non-event, they will not know how to comfort you or even that you need comforting. So telling a story, making your pain explicit, can also help mobilize others to mobilize you.

Exercise 2: Tell Your Story

1. Have the client tell the story of the non-event as if the client were to blame for it. (I'm no good, that's why I was not promoted.)
2. Have the client retell the story attributing a different cause. (Times are bad in my field. What happened is inevitable.)
3. Ask the client to now tell the story that could be told to friends. (Things were at a dead end at work so I am rethinking my career. Any ideas?)

Grieving

Many respondents reported the need to grieve for the loss of a dream. For example, it is easy to recognize the grief that accompanies the death of a significant person in one's life. But most people do not recognize the grief that persists over never finding a companion or significant other. To ease this loss, respondents sought support, wrote in journals, talked about their faith, and, of course, invoked humor.

People are expected to grieve over events such as a death or rejoice over events such as a promotion. But how do we help others to deal with their grief over what did not happen—a baby that was never conceived, a book that was never published, or a relationship that never materialized? Grieving for non-events is difficult because the reason for the grief is unrecognized by others. Once the non-event or loss is acknowledged and named, then coming to terms with it can occur.

This is where the counselor can play a critical role. The counselor is someone to whom a person can moan about non-events, the counselor can arrange support groups of others with the same issues so that they can share their losses, and the counselor can encourage the person to keep a journal, chronicling the reactions over time to the non-event.

Kenneth J. Doka described a disenfranchised grief—a special kind of grief that is not recognized by society. This type of grief is particularly applicable to non-events, because they are not public. Grieving, for them, is disenfranchised. There are no wakes, no chicken soup. The sadness is intensified: There is the loss of a loved one or dream and the loss of recognition from others. Labeling the grief and sharing it with others who have similar issues can be very helpful.

Counselors can start non-event support groups. For example, a support group for those sharing the loss of a dream can provide an opportunity for each person to state the particular lost dream and comfort others regarding their loss. It is easier to share with others experiencing similar pain, even if the lost dream is different, than to bury the emotions and try to go on. We need "good grief" before we can move on.

Exercise 3: Sharing the Loss of a Dream with a Group

1. Each person tells the story of the lost dream. (I never had the baby I wanted; my child is a disappointment to me, etc.)
2. Group members identify ways to help each other grieve.
3. Group members suggest ways to initiate help from friends and family outside the group.

Refocusing

The next part of the process can be difficult because it requires letting go of old expectations and reframing the non-event. People often have difficulty changing their perceptions of themselves and the world and moving to a new vision. However, shifting focus is necessary as we shape new goals by reframing our future selves and forcefully identifying a new dream, a new vision, or a new self.

A major way to assist this transformation is through the use of rituals. The late anthropologist Barbara Myerhoff discussed the role of rituals, ceremonies, or rites of passage as a way to help people separate from the past and move into a new place. Rituals help people make sense out of the contradiction and paradox of many transitions—the paradox being that there is no single truth, there are many truths and that individuals are part of the past, but also of the future. Myerhoff described the three stages of any ritual: First, the individual is segregated as in a graduation ceremony; second, the ritual acknowledges the somewhat bewildering phase in which the individual is between the old and the new; and third, the ritual helps the individual move into a new identity.

Unfortunately, non-events are too often bereft of rituals, and non-events need rituals even more than events. Yet how to develop them is a bit more difficult. However, through an article in *Ms.* magazine we begin to see the endless possibilities for developing non-event rituals. The following announcement says it all:

Alice and Carl Hesse

are pleased to announce their daughter

Susan A. Hesse

is settling into

joyous old maidhood

after which she shall cease

looking for Mr. Right

and begin giving

scintillating dinner parties and soirees.

To help celebrate this wonderful occasion,

gift-place-settings

are available at

Macy's Department Store

Counselors can help clients develop non-event rituals by using the form in the following exercise as guidance.

Exercise 4: Developing a Non-Event Ritual

1. Name your non-event. Example: A 17-year-old adolescent announced to her parents that she was not going to college, was moving out of their home and into an apartment with a roommate, and going to work as a waitress. The parents' non-event was their disappointment with their daughter's plans. Their expectations, based on their own experience, was that their daughter would be like all their friends' children and move from high school to college as expected.
2. Identify your emotional reaction to the non-event. Example: They were embarrassed, disappointed, and even angry.
3. Design a ritual to help clients grieve for the past that might never have been and move them closer to the future, keeping in mind that the ritual needs to be a shared activity with an opportunity for acknowledging and naming the past and a rehearsal for the future. Example: To ease their pain, they invited another family (the daughters' godparents) over for a special dinner—a shared activity. They then made a speech to their daughter, giving her the money to install a phone but then saying she would have to pay the monthly bills. They also acknowledged her need to follow her own muse, stating that they would support any kind of future education or training when she was ready. *Note:* Their daughter eventually went to college, but the use of the ritual enabled the family to avoid the usual screaming fights that can attend such a decision. The ritual also helped the family define this transition as a positive, not a negative, transition.

Reshaping

Shifting focus is necessary as we shape new goals by reframing our future selves and forcefully identifying a new dream, a new vision, and a new self. This shift includes taking stock, regaining control, and transforming the dream by imagining another, more possible, self.

Margy's 30th birthday was approaching. She refused to let her parents plan any celebration; in fact, she dreaded her birthday. She felt her life was nowhere. She had always expected to marry, have children, live on a farm, and produce her art. Instead, she lived in a condo in a suburban area and had no prospects of marriage. She did have a job she liked, but the celebration of a birthday was not where she was, rather she wanted to grieve for unmet dreams. Instead, Margy went to the beach with a friend. When she returned, she announced to her parents that she realized she was focusing on the total dream. She was willing to have a piece of the dream and control the part she could. She put her condo up for sale; it took 9 months to sell. She searched and finally bought a farmette with an historic house on it. The house was in terrible shape, but Margy realized she would spend the next 10 years fixing it up. Actually, she is still teaching and is now raising angora goats, free-range chickens, and produce. She still has no husband or child and sometimes grieves deeply about that. Although she has not given up hope, she moved on to live a life that incorporated some of what she wanted.

Counselors can help clients examine their lost dreams and make proactive decisions about what to do. Counselors can help clients make decisions about whether the non-event is in the client's control, when to give up hope and move on, and when to hold onto the dream and keep trying to make it. Hope and control are critical dimensions differentiating one non-event from another. For example, the immigrant man who gave up hope of ever returning to his homeland or seeing his family again differed from the woman who wanted a baby, was not married, but had not given up hope. If the author of the best seller, *Ladies of the Club*, had given up it would have gone unpublished. She kept on working and hoping. It was published when she was in a nursing home. The dilemma is when to hold on to hope using new strategies or when to reshape the dream all together.

The following exercise may help clients figure out how to move ahead despite their sadness.

Exercise 5: Your Dream Reshaping

1. Your lost dream. Example: Daniel expected to write musical comedies. He enrolled in a music school on the G.I. Bill. However, his wife became pregnant. He then dropped out of music school and followed in his father's footsteps by going to law school, and became a labor arbitrator.
2. Is there any hope? Example: Daniel gave up hope. He now regrets giving up a music career and thinks he should have stuck with it longer.
3. If so, what can you still do to make the dream come true? Example: Daniel plays the piano and writes musical comedies for his church. His nonwork life is devoted to music.
4. If not, the choice is yours. Do you want to modify the dream or put the dream to bed and develop a new dream? Example: Daniel gave up the dream for his vocation but held onto the dream as an avocation.

STEP 3: LESSONS FOR LIFE LITERACY

Lessons for life literacy can be learned through individual or group settings and with professionally trained counselors, support groups, or just plain living. Whatever the format, the lessons are the same. They are lessons that can help clients as they face the ups and downs of living.

Lesson 1: Always Have a Plan B.

Because life does not follow a preordained script, it is important to have backup plans. In a recent program on *Sixty Minutes,* Mike Wallace interviewed Oprah Winfrey. During the interview he showed a videotape of their first interview just as Oprah was beginning her show. Wallace asked her what she would do if the show were not a success. Her answer was she did not know, but she was more than her show and would develop something else. Quite different was the response of one of the women in the movie, *Waiting to Exhale,* when asked what she was going to do now that her husband had left her for another woman. She said, "I don't know. I never had a Plan B."

All of us will have scripts for our lives that are interrupted and do not go according to plan. All of us have surprises—some positive and others negative. We cannot count on life just following a neat, arranged, linear script. Part of life is having alternative plans—from A through Z.

Lesson 2: Challenge Assumptions About "Age-Appropriate Behavior."

Many individuals catastrophize about what it will be like to get old—having less fun, less sex, and less power—but rarely take into account the fact that each age has new possibilities. We often identify each decade with less than the last. Yet we can probably all think of people in their 70s and 80s who fall in love, start new relationships, and pursue new volunteer or business possibilities. It is true that there are losses, but one must remember the gains also. Newer research on the emergence of wisdom confronts negative attitudes about aging.

The MacArthur Foundation sponsored a series of studies on midlife. The conclusion was that midlife is a benign period with endless possibilities. The *midlife crisis* is an artifact of the media.

Lesson 3: Explore Options Even if You Think There Are None.

Jim, a stockbroker, lived a double life: life in his head of the outdoors, roughing it and the life he lived in business suits and fancy offices. He had seen no way to reconcile these two lifestyles. Finally, he broke out of his it-can't-be-done mode. He convinced his company to let him open an office in Bozeman, Montana. He goes to work in boots, lives an outdoor life, and keeps in touch with clients by e-mail, fax, and phone. He could have spent his whole life not living out the dream. Instead he created options.

Of course, that is easier for some than others. The person working for McDonald's does not have the same options as a stockbroker. And the goal is not to dream the impossible. But we find that there are often opportunities to think in new ways about our lives. Sometimes, there are seemingly more barriers than one can overcome. Who would have ever thought that Christopher Reeve could still produce and act in movies? Another example is the film, *My Left Foot,* in which a person with physical handicaps, who came from an impoverished family, created new options for himself.

Lesson 4: It Is Never Too Late to Put Meaning Back in Your Life.

Larry McMurtry, in the book, *Duane's Depressed,* described the sudden shift in one man's life. Responding to the death of a neighbor, Duane wondered about his life and felt deep regret for all the things he never accomplished. The book chronicles Duane's struggle to put meaning back in his life. And that is something we can help our clients do—put meanings back in their lives. To quote Gayle King, assistant pastor of St. Boniface church in Sarasota, FL, "you can have it all but maybe not at the same time." And remember the Latin phrase, *carpe diem*—Seize the day.

Exercise 6: Practice Lessons for Life Literacy

1. Have client identify a cherished goal. Then ask the client to think of a Plan B if the goal is not realized. Example: "I had always planned to have lots of children. I am not married, I am 40 and will either adopt a hard-to-place child or become a foster parent."
2. Challenge assumptions about what you cannot do. Example: "I can't start a doctoral program. I am 53 years old." Think of those who started such programs. Aina enrolled in a doctoral program at 55. Now at 65, she has completed her work and has embraced a new career as a licensed therapist.
3. Have clients who say it cannot be done begin to brainstorm options. Example: Marcy, a manicurist, began lying and saying she was an interior designer. When confronted by her counselor about this discrepancy and challenged to begin training as an interior designer, Marcy explained all the reasons that was impossible. Over time, Marcy did find an evening program and is beginning her training.

AND IN CONCLUSION

Be aware that what looms as a lost dream for one person might not be an issue for someone else. Clients' expectations and feelings guide both the professional counselor and the client in seeking solutions for these silent forms of heartache. In the long run, we are all looking for hope to outlast the broken dreams and for a promise to ease the sorrow of defeat. By giving non-events their place in adult development, professional counselors can offer that brighter reality—and even redirect our own lives as well.

References

Adler, A. (1954). *Understanding human nature.* New York: Fawcett Premier. (Original work published 1927)

Ager, S. (1994, February 3). At 40, at midday, a time for change. *Detroit Free Press,* p. F1.

American Association of Retired Persons. (1989). *Reminiscence: Finding meaning in memories. A training kit.* Washington, DC: Author.

American Association of Retired Persons. (1991 September–October). Widows overcome barriers to grieving. *Highlights, 9*(5), 1–10.

American Association of Retired Persons. (1993). *Grandparents raising their grandchildren, what to consider and where to find help.* Washington, DC: Author.

American Counseling Association (1992). *Cross-Cultural Competencies and Objectives.* Retrieved October 20, 2005, from http://www.counseling.org/Content/NavigationMenu/RESOURCES/MULTICULTURALANDDIVERSITYISSUES/Competencies/Competencies.htm.

American Counseling Association (2005). *ACA code of ethics.* Retrieved October 20, 2005, from http://www.counseling.org/Resources/CodeOfEthics/TP/Home/CT2.aspx?.

AMCD Professional Standards and Certification Committee. (1996). *Operationalization of the multicultural counseling competencies.* Retrieved October 20, 2005, from http://www.counseling.org/Content/NavigationMenu/RESOURCES/MULTICULTURALANDDIVERSITYISSUES/MCC96.pdf.

Amundson, N. E. (1996). Supporting clients through a change in perspective. *Journal of Employment Counseling, 33*(4), 155–162.

Anderson. M. (2005). *Spirituality and coping with work transitions.* Unpublished doctoral dissertation, Oakland University, Rochester, MI.

Ashmos, D., & Duchon, D. (2000). Spirituality at work: A conceptualization and measure. *Journal of Management Inquiry, 9,* 134–145.

Aslanian, G. B., & Brickell, H. M. (1980). *Americans in transition: Life changes as reasons for adult learning.* New York: College Entrance Examination Board.

Association for Specialists in Group Work (ASGW). (1998). ASGW best practice guidelines (Prepared by L. Rapin & L. Keel). *Journal for Specialists in Group Work, 23,* 237–244.

Astin, H. S. (1984). The meaning of work in women's lives: A socio-psychological model of career choice and work behavior. *Counseling Psychologist, 12,* 117–128.

Azrin, N. H., & Besalel, V. A. (1980). *Job club counselor's manual: A behavioral approach to vocational counseling.* Baltimore: University Park Press.

Baldwin, A. L. (1948). Socialization and the parent-child relationship. *Child Development, 19,* 127–136.

Bandler, R., & Grinder, J. (1975). *The structure of magic I.* Palo Alto, CA: Behavior Books.

Bandura, A. (1982). Self-efficacy: Mechanism in human agency. *American Psychologist, 37*(2), 122–147.

Bandura, A. (1997). *Self-efficacy: The exercise of control.* New York: Freeman.

Barnett, R. C., & Hyde, J. S. (2001). Women, men, work, and family. *American Psychologist, 56,* 781–796.

Barrett, F. (2004). Coaching for resiliency. *Organization Development Journal, 22,* 93–96.

Bateson, M. C. (1989). *Composing a life.* New York: Grove Press.

Belavich, T. G. (1995). *The role of religion in coping with daily hassles.* Paper presented at the 103rd Annual Convention of the American Psychological Association, New York, NY. (ERIC Document Reproduction Service No. ED393042).

Belenky, M. J., Clinchy, B. M., Goldberger, N. R., & Tarule, J. M. (1986). *Women's ways of knowing.* New York: Basic Books.

Bennett, K. M. (2005). Psychological wellbeing in later life: the longitudinal effects of marriage, widowhood and marital status change. *International Journal of Geriatric Psychiatry, 20,* 280–284.

Bergin, A. E., Masters, K. S., Stinchfield, R. D., Gaskin, T. A., Sullivan, C. E., Reynolds, E. M., et al. (1994). Religious styles and mental health. In L. B. Brown (Ed.), *Religion, personality, and mental health* (pp. 69–93). New York: Springer-Verlag.

Bergman, G. (n.d.). Fresh currents in the stream of life. *Gray Panther Network.* Philadelphia: The Gray Panthers Newsletter.

Bergquist, W. H., Greenberg, E. M., & Klaum, G. A. (1993). *In our fifties: Voices of men and women reinventing their lives.* San Francisco: Jossey Bass.

Berkman, L. F., & Syme, S. L. (1979). Social networks, host resistance and mortality: A nine-year follow-up study of Alameda County residents. *American Journal of Epidemiology, 109,* 186–204.

Berne, E. (1964). *Games people play.* New York: Grove.

Bertaux D. (1982). The life course approach as a challenge to the social sciences. In T. K. Hareven & K. J. Adams (Eds.), *Aging and life course transitions: An interdisciplinary perspective* (pp. 127–150). New York: Guilford Press.

Betz, N. E. (1989). Implications of the null environment hypothesis for women's career development and for counseling psychology. *Counseling Psychologist, 17,* 136–144.

Black, C. (1987). *It will never happen to me.* New York: Ballantine Books.

Bloch, D. (2004). Religion, spirituality, and health: A topic not so new. *American Psychologist, 59,* 52.

Bloch, D., & Richmond, L. (1998). *Soul work: Finding the work you love, loving the work you have.* Palo Alto, CA: Davies-Black.

Bly, R. (1990). *Iron John: A book about men.* Reading, MA: Addison-Wesley.

Bolles, R. (2000). *How to find your mission in life*. Berkeley, CA: Ten Speed Press.

Bolles, R. N. (2006). *What color is your parachute?* Berkeley, CA: Ten Speed Press.

Bonanno, G. A., Wortman, C. B., & Randolph, M. N. (2004). Prospective patterns of resilience and maladjustment during widowhood. *Psychology and Aging, 19,* 260–271.

Bosworth, K., & Walz, G. R. (2005) *Promoting student resiliency.* Alexandria, VA: American Counseling Association Foundation.

Brammer, L. (1991). *How to cope with life transitions: The challenge of personal change.* New York: Hemisphere.

Brewer, E. W. (2001). Vocation souljourn paradigm: A model of adult development to express spiritual wellness as meaning, being and doing in work and life. *Counseling and Values, 45,* 83–93.

Bridges, W. (1980). *Transitions: Making sense of life's changes.* New York: Addison-Wesley.

Bridges, W. (1988). *Surviving corporate transition.* Mill Valley, CA: William Bridges & Associates.

Bridges, W. (2004). *Transitions: Making sense of life's changes.* Cambridge, MA: Da Capo Press.

Bright, J. E. H., & Pryor, G. L. (2005). The chaos theory of careers: A user's guide. *Career Development Quarterly, 53,* 291–305.

Brim, O. G., Jr., & Kagan, J. (Eds.). (1980). *Constancy and change in human development.* Cambridge, MA: Harvard University Press.

Brim, O. G., Jr., & Ryff, C. D. (1980). On the properties of life events. In P. B. Baltes & O. G. Brim, Jr. (Eds.), *Life-span development and behavior* (Vol. 3). New York: Academic Press.

Britnell, E. S., Madill, H., Montgomerie, I. C., & Stewin, L. L. (1992). Work and family issues after injury: Do female and male client perspectives differ? *Career Development Quarterly, 41,* 145–160.

Broderick, P., & Blewitt, P. (2003). *The life span: Human development for helping professionals.* Upper Saddle River, NJ: Merrill Prentice Hall.

Brody, E.M. (1985). Parent care as a normative family crisis. *The Gerontologist, 25* (1), 19–29.

Brody, E. M. (2004). *Women in the middle: Their parent-care years* (2nd ed). New York: Springer Publishing Company.

Brookfield, S. D. (1986). *Understanding and facilitating adult learning: A comprehensive analysis of principles and effective practices.* San Francisco: Jossey-Bass.

Brott, P. E. (2001). The storied approach: A postmodern perspective for career counseling. *Career Development Quarterly, 49,* 304–313.

Brown, D. (1996). Status of career development theories. In D. Brown, L. Brooks, & Associates (Eds.), *Career choice and development* (3rd ed., pp. 1–13). San Francisco: Jossey-Bass.

Brown, R. (1988). Unpublished materials distributed at a workshop at Oakland University, Rochester, MI.

Brown, S., & Lent, R. (2000). *Handbook of counseling psychology.* New York: Wiley.

Buhler, P. (2000). The 10 most significant changes of the 90's and how they impact the workplace of the 21st century. *Supervision, 61,* 16–19.

Bureau of Labor Statistics. (1998). *News: United States Department of Labor* (USDL Publication No. 98-253). Washington, DC: U.S. Government Printing Office.

Burke, M. T., Hackney, H., Hudson, P., Miranti, J., Watts, G., & Epp, L. (1999). Spirituality, religion, and the CACREP curriculum standards, *Journal of Counseling & Development, 77,* 251–257.

Burke, M. T., & Miranti, J. G. (1995). *Counseling: The spiritual dimension.* Alexandria, VA: American Counseling Association.

Burn, S. M. (2004). *Groups.* Belmont, CA: Wadsworth.

Burnside, I. M. (Ed.). (1984). *Working with the elderly: Group process and techniques* (2nd ed.). Monterey, CA.: Wadsworth.

Busse, W. M. O., & Birk, J. M. (1993). The effects of self-disclosure and competitiveness on friendship for male graduate students over 35. *Journal of College Student Development, 34,* 169–174.

Butler, R. (1963). The life review: an interpretation of reminiscence in the aged. *Psychiatry, 26,* 65–76.

Byars, A. M. (2001). Rights-of-way: Affirmative career counseling with African American women. In W. B. Walsh, R. P. Bingham, M. T. Brown, & C. M. Ward (Eds.), *Career counseling for African Americans* (pp. 113–138). Mahwah: NJ: Erlbaum.

Caine, L. (1974). *Widow.* New York: William Morrow.

Campbell, J. (1988). *The power of myth.* New York: Doubleday.

Caplan, G. (1976). The family as support system. In G. Caplan & M. Killilea (Eds.), *Support systems and mutual help: Multidisciplinary exploration* (pp. 19–36). New York: Greene & Stratton.

Capuzzi, D., & Gross, D. R. (1992). *Introduction to group counseling.* Denver, CO: Love.

Capuzzi, D., Gross, D., & Friel, S. E. (1990). Recent trends in group work with elders. *Generations, 14,* 43–48.

Carlsen, M. (2000). The sustaining power of meaning. *Generations, 23,* 27–30.

Charner, L., & Schlossberg, N. K. (1986). Variations by theme: The life transitions of clerical workers. *Vocational Guidance Quarterly, 34,* 212–224.

Cheng, C. (2003). Cognitive and motivational processes underlying coping flexibility: A dual-process model. *Journal of Personality and Social Psychology, 80,* 814–833.

Cheng, C., & Cheung, M. (2005). Cognitive processes underlying coping flexibility: Differentiation and integration. *Journal of Personality, 73,* 859–886.

Cherlin, C., & Furstenberg, F. F. (1992). *The new American grandparent: A place in the family, a life apart.* New York: Basic Books.

Chin, J. W. (1993, June). Letter: Multicultural education does not always include all cultures. *Guidepost, Newsletter of the American Counseling Association,* p. 2.

Chiu et al. (2004). An integrative review of the concept of spirituality in the health sciences. *Western Journal of Nursing Research, 26*(4), 405–428.

Chodoff, P. (1976). The German concentration camp as a psychological stress. In R. H. Moos (Ed.), *Human adaptation: Coping with life crises*. Lexington, MA: Heath.

Christensen, K. A., Stephens, M. A., & Townsend, A. L. (1998). Mastery in women's multiple roles and well-being: Adult daughters providing health care to impaired parents. *Health Psychology, 17,* 163–171.

Cochran, L. (1997). *Career counseling: A narrative approach*. Thousand Oaks: Sage.

Cohen, F. (1980). Coping with surgery: Information, psychological preparation, and recovery. In L. Poon (Ed.), *Aging in the 1980s, Psychological issues*. Washington, DC: American Psychological Association.

Colgrove, M., Bloomfield, H. H., & McWilliams, P. (1991). *How to survive the loss of a love*. Los Angeles: Prelude Press.

Constantine, M. G., & Parker, V. F. (2001). Addressing the career transition issues of African American women: Vocational and personal considerations. In W. B. Walsh, R. P. Bingham, M. T. Brown, & C. M. Ward (Eds.), *Career counseling for African Americans* (pp. 99–112). Mahwah: NJ: Erlbaum.

Continuum Center, Oakland University (1978). *Paraprofessional preventive mental health programs: Final report to the National Institute of Mental Health*. Rochester, MI: Author.

Conyne, R., Wilson, F. R., & Tang, M. (2000). Evolving lessons from group work involvement in China. *Journal for Specialists in Group Work, 25,* 252–267.

Cooke, D. (1994, October). *A multicultural look at the transition model*. Speech at the conference on Transition: Thriving on Change, University of Maryland, College Park.

Corey, G. (1995). *Theory and practice of group counseling* (4th ed.). Pacific Grove, CA: Brooks/Cole.

Corey, G. (2005). *Theory and practice of counseling and psychotherapy* (7th ed.). Pacific Grove, CA: Brooks/Cole.

Corey, G., & Corey, M. S. (1982). *Groups: process and practice*. Monterey, CA: Brooks/Cole.

Corey, G., & Corey, M. S. (2003). *Groups: process and practice* (2nd ed.). Monterey, CA: Brooks/Cole.

Corlett, E., & Millner, N. (1993). *Navigating midlife*. Palo Alto, CA: Davies-Black.

Corrie, S. (2002). Working therapeutically with adult stepchildren: Identifying the needs of a neglected client group. *Journal of Divorce and Remarriage, 16,* 135.

Cosier, R. A., & Dalton, D. R. (1993). Management consulting: planning, entry, performance. *Journal of Counseling & Development, 72,* 191–198.

Costa, P. T., & McCrae, R. R. (1980). Still stable after all these years: Personality as a key to some issues in adulthood and old age. In P. B. Baltes & O. G. Brim, Jr. (Eds.), *Life-span development and behavior* (pp. 66–102). New York: Academic Press.

Covington, S. (1994, June 21). Treatment of women in and out of the criminal justice system. Presentation at the University of Utah School of Alcoholism and Other Drug Dependencies. Salt Lake City, UT.

Counselors for Social Justice (2005). *Mission.* Retrieved October 22, 2005, from http://www.counselorsforsocialjustice.org/mission.html.

Coyle, J. (2001). Spirituality and health: Towards a framework for exploring the relationship between spirituality and health. *Journal of Advanced Nursing, 37,* 589–597.

Croteau, J. M., Lark, J. S., Lidderdale, M. A., & Chung, Y. B. (2005). *Deconstructing heterosexism in the counseling professions: A narrative approach.* Thousand Oaks, CA: Sage.

Cudney, M. R. (1980a). *Instructors guide for the book for eliminating self defeating behaviors.* Kalamazoo, MI: Life Giving Enterprises.

Cudney, M. R. (1980b). *Workbook for eliminating self defeating behaviors.* Kalamazoo, MI: Life Giving Enterprises.

Cutler, L. (1985). Counseling caregivers. *Generations, 10,* 53–57.

Dailey, R. J. (n.d.) The stress resistant personality. Unpublished workshop handout. Rochester, MI: Continuum Center, Oakland University.

Davies, G. (1996). The employment support network—An intervention to assist displaced workers. *Journal of Employment Counseling, 33,* 146–154.

Dawis, R. V., & Lofquist, L. H. (1984). *A psychological theory of work adjustment: An individual differences model and its applications.* Minneapolis, MN: University of Minnesota Press.

Dawson, T. (1993). Relatively guilty. *New Statesman & Society, 6*(278), 12–13.

De Jong Gierveld, J., & Peeters, A. (2003). The interweaving of repartnered older adults' lives with their children and siblings. *Aging and Society, 23,* 187–205.

De Toqueville, A. (2001). *Democracy in America.* New York: Signet. (Original work published 1839.)

Deaux, K. (1993). Reconstructing social identity. *Personality and Social Psychology Bulletin, 19,* 4–12.

DeLucia-Waack, J., & Donigian, J. (2004). *The practice of multicultural group work.* Belmont, CA: Brooks/Cole.

Depner, C., & Ingersoll-Dayton, B. (1988). Supportive relationships in later life. *Psychology and Aging, 3,* 348–357.

Dewey, J. (1933). *How we think: A restatement of the relation of reflective thinking to the educative process.* Boston: Houghton Mifflin.

Didion, J. (2005). *The year of magical thinking.* Toronto, Ontario, Canada: Random House.

Dobson, J. E., & Dobson, R. L. (1991). Changing roles: an aging parents support group. *Journal for Specialists in Group Work, 16,* 178–184.

Doerr, D. C. (1993, October). *Existential therapy, men, and careers.* Paper presented at a meeting of the Minnesota Career Development Association, Minneapolis, MN.

Dohrenwend, B. S., Krasnoff, L., Askanasy, A. R., & Dohrenwend, B. P. (1978). Exemplification of a method for scaling life events: The Peri life events scale. *Journal of Health and Social Behavior, 19,* 205–229.

Dougherty, A. M. (2000). *Psychological consultation and collaboration in school and community settings* (3rd ed.). Belmont, CA: Wadsworth.

Douglas, J. D. (1990). Patterns of change following parent death in midlife adults. *Omega, 22,* 123–137.

Downing, N. E., & Rousch, K. L. (1985). From passive acceptance to active commitment: A model of feminist identity development for women. *The Counseling Psychologist, 13,* 695–709.

Dubin, K. (1994). *Change of life.* Unpublished play.

Ebaugh, H. R. F. (1988). *Becoming an ex: The process of role exit.* Chicago: University of Chicago Press.

Egan, G. (1994). *The skilled helper: A problem management approach to helping* (5th ed.). Pacific Grove, CA: Brooks/Cole.

Ellis, A. (1984). *Rational-emotive therapy and cognitive behavior therapy.* New York: Springer Publishing Company.

Ellison, C. W. (1983). Spiritual well-being: Conceptualization and measurement. *Journal of Psychology and Theology, 11,* 330–340.

Ellison, C. W., & Smith, J. (1991). Toward an integrative measure of health and well-being. *Journal of Psychology and Theology, 19,* 35–48.

Elmer, V. (1994, July 11). Loyalties die as companies change, shrink. *Detroit Free Press,* p. 5A.

Erikson, E., Erikson, J., & Kivnick, H. Q. (1994). *Vital involvement in old age.* New York: Norton.

Erikson, E. H. (1950). *Childhood and society.* New York: Norton.

Evans, K. M., Rotter, J. C., & Gold, J. M. (2002). *Synthesizing family, career, and culture.* Alexandria, VA: American Counseling Association.

Fassinger, R. E. (1991). The hidden minority: Issues and challenges in working with lesbian women and gay men. *The Counseling Psychologist, 19,* 157–176.

Feldman, R.S. (2006). *Development across the lifespan.* Upper Saddle River, NJ: Prentice Hall.

Fiske, M. (1980). Changing hierarchies of commitment in adulthood. In N. J. Smelser & E. H. Erikson (Eds.), *Themes of work and love in adulthood* (pp. 238–264). Cambridge, MA: Harvard University Press.

Fiske, M., & Chiriboga, D. A. (1990). *Change and continuity in adult life.* San Francisco: Jossey-Bass.

Fitzgerald, L. F., & Harmon, L. W. (2001). Women's career development: A postmodern update. In F. T. L. Leong & A. Barak (Eds.), *Contemporary models in vocational psychology* (pp. 207–230). Mahwah, NJ: Erlbaum.

Fitzgerald, L. F., & Weitzman, L. M. (1992). Women's career development: Theory and practice from a feminist perspective. In H. D. Lee & Z. D. Leibowitz (Eds.), *Adult career development: Concepts issues and practices* (2nd ed., pp. 124–160). Alexandria, VA: National Career Development Association.

Folkman, S., Chesney, M., McKusick, L., Ironson, G., Johnson, D. S., & Coates, T. J. (1991). Translating coping theory into an intervention. In J. Eckenrode (Ed.), *The social context of coping* (pp. 239–260). New York: Plenum.

Folkman, S., and Moskowitz, J. (2004). Coping: Pitfalls and promise. *Annual Review of Psychology, 55,* 745–774.

Fowler, J. W. (1991). Stages in faith consciousness. *New Directions in Child Development, 52,* 27–45.

Fox, C., & Halbrook, B. (1994). Terminating relationships at midlife: a qualitative investigation of low income women's experiences. *Journal of Mental Health Counseling, 16,* 143–154.

Fraenkel, P. (2003). *Contemporary two-parent families: Navigating work and family challenges.* In Walsh, F. (Ed), Normal family processes: Growing diversity and complexity (pp. 61–95). New York: Guilford Press.

Frankl, V. (1963). *Man's search for meaning.* Boston: Beacon Press.

Freud, S. (1961). *Complete psychological works* (Vol. 21). New York: Norton.

Frey, D. (1993, March–April). Play therapy can be a tool in working with adults. *The National Psychologist, 21.*

Friedan, B. (1963). *The feminine mystique.* New York: Norton.

Garrett, M. T., & Carroll, J. J. (2000). Mending the broken circle. *Journal of Counseling & Development, 78,* 379–388.

Gazda, G. M. (1989). *Group counseling: A developmental approach* (4th ed.), Boston: Allyn & Bacon.

Gelatt, H. B. (1991). *Creative decision making: Using positive uncertainty.* Los Altos, CA: Crisp.

Gelatt, H. B. (1993, November). *Career development in organizations.* Paper presented at the California Career Conference, San Diego.

Gendlin, E. T. (1981). *Focusing.* New York: Bantam.

Gentry, M., & Shulman, A. (1988). Remarriage as a coping response for widowhood. *Psychology and Aging, 3,* 191–196.

George, L. K., & Siegler, I. C. (1981). *Coping with stress and coping in later life: Older people speak far themselves.* Durham, NC: Center for the Study of Aging and Human Development and Department of Psychiatry, Duke University Medical Center.

Gergen, K. J. (2000). An invitation to social construction. London: Sage.

Gerzon, M. (1996). *Listening to midlife.* Boston: Shambhala.

Gilligan, C. (1982). *In a different voice.* Cambridge, MA: Harvard University Press.

Gilligan, C. (1988). Remapping the moral domain: New images of self in relationship. In C. Gilligan, J. V. Ward, & J. M. Taylor (Eds.), *Mapping the moral domain* (pp. 3–19). Cambridge, MA: Harvard University Press.

Gilligan, C. (1993). *In a different voice.* Cambridge, MA: Harvard University Press.

Gladding, S.T. (1999). *Group work: A counseling specialty.* Upper Saddle River, NJ: Prentice Hall.

Gladding, S.T. (2003). *Group work: A counseling specialty* (4th ed.). New York: Merrill.

Gomez, M. J., Fassinger, R. E., Prosser, J., Cooke, K., Mejia, B., & Luna, J. (2001). Voces abriendo caminos (Voices forging paths): A qualitative study of the career development of notable Latinas. *Journal of Counseling Psychology, 48,* 286–300.

Gooden, W. E. (1989). Development of Black men in early adulthood. In R. L. Jones (Ed.), *Black adult development and aging* (pp. 63–90). Berkeley, CA: Cobb & Henry.

Goodman, J. (1992). The dental model for counseling. *American Counselor 1,* 27–29.

Goodman, J. (2006). Toward a holistic view. In D. Capuzzi & M. D. Gross (Eds.), *Career counseling: Foundations, perspectives, and applications.* Boston: Pearson.

Goodman, J., & Hoppin, J. M. (1990). *Opening doors: A practical guide to job hunting* (2nd ed.). Rochester, MI: Continuum Center, Oakland University.

Goodman, J., & Hoppin, J. M. (1991). *Leader guide for opening doors: A practical guide for job hunting* (2nd ed.). Rochester, MI: Continuum Center, Oakland University.

Goodman, J., & Savage, N. (1999). Responding to a community need: Oakland University's adult career counseling center. *The Career Development Quarterly, 48,* 19–30.

Goodman, J., & Waters, E. B. (1985). Conflict or support: Work and family in middle and old age. *Journal of Career Development, 12,* 92–98.

Gordon, A. (1990). *Safe at home.* Toronto, Ontario, Canada: McClelland & Stewart.

Gore-Felton, C. (1999). Enhancing women's lives: The role of support groups among breast cancer patients. *The Journal of Specialists in Group Work, 24,* 274–287.

Graham, S., Furr, S., Flowers, C., and Burke, M. T. (2001). Religion and spirituality in coping with stress. *Counseling and Values, 46,* 2–13.

Gross, J. (1992, September 3). A jail garden's harvest: Hope and redemption. *The New York Times.*

Gutek, B. A., & Larwood, L. (1989). *Women's career development.* Newbury Park, CA: Sage.

Gutmann, D. (1987). *Reclaimed powers: Toward a new psychology of men and women in later life.* New York: Basic Books.

Gwyther, L. (1986). Family therapy with older adults. *Generations, 10*(3), 42–45.

Hackney, H., & Cormier, S. (2005). *The professional counselor: A process guide to helping* (5th ed.). Boston: Pearson.

Hagestad, G. O. (1986). Dimensions of time and the family. *American Behavioral Scientist, 29,* 679–694.

Hagestad, G. O., & Burton, L. M. (1986). Grandparenthood, life context, and family development. *American Behavioral Scientist, 29,* 471–484.

Hagestad, G. O., & Neugarten, B. L. (1985). Age and the life course. In E. Shanar & R. Binstock (Eds.), *Handbook of aging and the social sciences* (2nd ed.). Mimeograph.

Haley, J. (1982). *Problem solving therapy* (2nd ed.). San Francisco: Jossey-Bass.

Halstead, R. W. (1991). Career counseling and culture: The case of Ebo. *Career Development Quarterly, 40,* 24–35.

Hansen, S. (1997). *Integrative life planning: Critical tasks for career development and changing life patterns.* San Francisco: Jossey-Bass.

Hansen, S. (2001). Integrating work, family, and community through holistic life planning. *The Career Development Quarterly, 49,* 261–274.

Hansson, R. O., Jones, W. H., Carpenter, B. N., & Remondet, J. H. (1986). Loneliness and adjustment to old age. *International Journal of Aging and Human Development, 24,* 41–53.

Hareven, T. K (1992). Family and generational relations in the later years: A historical perspective. *Generations, 16*(3), 7–12.

Harris, J. (2005). Black women's identity from a black feminist perspective: The interaction of race and gender. (Doctoral dissertation, 2005). *Dissertation Abstracts International, 65,* 9B, Southern Illinois University of Carbondale; pages: 00272.

Harvard Mental Health Letter (1993, March). Self-help groups—Part 1. *9*, 1–3. Boston: Harvard Medical School.

Hassan, G. (1992). No holds barred. *New Statesman & Society, 5*(215), 15–27.

Hattie, J., Myers, J., and Sweeney, T. (2004). A factor structure of wellness: Theory, assessment, analysis, and practice. *Journal of Counseling & Development, 82*, 354–364.

Hawley, L. D., Goodman, J., & Shaieb, M. (2002). Research in context. In K. M. Evans, J. C. Rotter, & J. M. Gold (Eds.), *Synthesizing family, career, and culture* (pp. 123–128). Alexandria, VA: American Counseling Association.

Hedberg, A. (1989, October). Caring for your aging parents. *Money*, 136–145.

Heith, S. (2004). Transforming friendship: Are housemates the new family? *Sociology Review, 14*, 8–13.

Helms, J. E. (1990). *Black and white racial identity: Theory, research and practice.* New York: Greenwood.

Helms, J. E. (1995). An update of Helm's White and People of Color racial identity models. In J. G. Ponterotto, J. M. Casas, L. A. Suzuki, & C. M. Alexander (Eds.), *Handbook of multicultural counseling* (pp. 181–198). Thousand Oaks, CA: Sage.

Helson, R., & Srivastava, S. (2001). Three paths of adult development: Conservers, seekers, and achievers. *Journal of Personality and Social Psychology, 80*, 995–1010.

Hennig, M., & Jardim, A. (1977). *The managerial woman.* New York: Doubleday.

Herr, E. L., Cramer, S. H., & Niles, S. G. (2004). *Career guidance and counseling through the lifespan* (6th ed.). Boston: Pearson.

Hill, R. (1965). Generic features of families under stress. In H. J. Parad (Ed.), *Crisis intervention: Selected readings.* New York: Family Service Association of America.

Hiner, N. R. (1985). Adults in historical perspective. In N. K. Schlossberg, et al. (Eds.), *The adult years: Continuity and change* (pp. 47–53). Columbia, MD: International University Consortium and Ohio University.

Hobfoll, S. E. (2001). Social and psychological resources and adaptation. *Review of General Psychology, 6*, 307–324.

Hodge, D. (2001). Spiritual assessment: A review of major qualitative methods and a new framework for assessing spirituality. *Social Work, 46*, 203–214.

Hof, L. (1993). The elusive elixir of hope. *The Family Journal: Counseling and Therapy for Couples and Families, 1*, 220–227.

Hoffman, E. (1990). *Lost in translation: Life in a new language.* New York: Penguin Books.

Holmes, T. H., & Rahe, R. H. (1967). The Social Adjustment Rating Scale. *Journal of Psychosomatic Research, 2*, 213–218.

Hoppin, J., & Splete, H. (1994). *Training needs of career development facilitators.* Rochester, MI: Career Development Training Institute at Oakland University.

Hopson, B. (1981). Response to the papers by Schlossberg, Brammer, & Abrego. *The Counseling Psychologist, 9*, 36–39.

House, R. M., & Tyler, V. (1992). Group counseling with gays and lesbians. In D. Capuzzi & D. R. Gross (Eds.), *Introduction to group counseling* (pp. 183–204). Denver, CO: Love.

Howard, J. (1978). *Families*. New York: Simon & Schuster.

Howell, L. (2001). Spirituality and women's midlife development. *Adultspan, 3*, 51–60.

Hudson, F. M. (1991). *The adult years: Mastering the art of self renewal*. San Francisco: Jossey Bass.

Hudson, F. M. (1999). *The adult years: Mastering the art of self renewal* (Rev. ed.) San Francisco: Jossey Bass.

Hughes, A., & Graham, S. (1990). Adult life roles. *Journal of Continuing Higher Education, 38*, 2–8.

Humphreys, K., Macus, S., Stewart, E., & Oliva, E. (2004). Expanding self help group participation in culturally diverse urban areas: Media approaches to leveraging referent power. *Journal of Community Psychology, 34*, 413–424. Abstract retrieved October 13, 2005, from PsycINFO database.

Isenhart, M. W. (1983, November). *Passages: Rafting the Green River as an analogy to the mid-life transition*. Paper presented at the annual meeting of the Speech Communication Association, Washington, DC.

Ivey, A. E., & Ivey, M. B. (2003). *Intentional interviewing and counseling: Facilitating client development in a multicultural society* (5th ed.). Pacific Grove, CA: Brooks/Cole.

Jackson, D. N., & Hayes, D. H. (1993). Multicultural issues in consultation. *Journal of Counseling & Development, 72*, 144–147.

Jacoby, B. (1991). Today's students: Diverse needs require comprehensive responses. In T. K. Miller & R. B. Winston, Jr. (Eds.), *Administration and leadership in student affairs* (pp. 281–307). Muncie, IN: Accelerated Development.

Jepsen, D. (1992, March). *Career as narrative*. Paper presented at the annual meeting of the American Counseling Association, Baltimore, MD.

Jewish Vocational Service. (2000). *JVS 2000 Annual Report*. Southfield, MI, Author.

Johnson, R. P. (1990). The Serenity prayer. *Group Networker* (Newsletter from the Family Practice Center, St. John's Mercy Medical Center, St. Louis County, MO), 6(1), 2.

Johnson, S. (1998). *Who moved my cheese?* New York: Putnam's.

Johnston, L. (1994, February 17). *For better or worse. Detroit Free Press*, p. 6F.

Jones, S. L. (1996). A constructive relationship for religion with the science and profession of psychology: Perhaps the boldest model yet. In E. P. Shafranske (Ed.), *Religion and the clinical practice of psychology* (pp. 113–147). Washington, DC: American Psychological Association.

Joseph, J. (1987). Warning. In S. Martz (Ed.), *When I am an old woman I shall wear purple* (2nd ed.). Watsonville, CA: Papier-Mache.

Josselson, R. (1987). *Finding herself: Pathways to identity development in women*. San Francisco: Jossey-Bass.

Jung, C. J. (1933). *Modern man in search of a soul*. New York: Harcourt Brace.

Kobasa, S. C. (1980, September). *Alienation and illness*. Paper presented at the 88th Annual Meeting of the American Psychological Association, Montreal, Quebec, Canada.

Kobasa, S. C., Maddi, S. R., & Kahn, S. (1982). Hardiness and health: A prospective study. *Journal of Personality and Social Psychology, 42*, 168–177.

Kagan, J. (1980). Perspectives on continuity. In O. G. Brim, Jr. & J. Kagan (Eds.), *Constancy and change in human development*. Cambridge, MA: Harvard University Press.

Kagan, J. (1998). Biology and the child. In W. Damon (Series Ed.) & N. Eisenberg (Vol. Ed.), *Handbook of child psychology: Vol. 3. Social, emotional, and personality development* (5th ed., pp. 177–236). New York: Wiley.

Kahn, R. L. (1975, June 2). *Memorandum to SSRC Committee on Work and Personality in the Middle Years*. Ann Arbor, MI.

Kahn, R. L., & Antonucci, T. E. (1980). Convoys over the life course: Attachment, roles, and social support. In P. B. Baltes & O. G. Brim, Jr. (Eds.), *Life-span development and behavior* (pp. 383–405). New York: Academic Press.

Kalish, R. A. (1985). *Death, grief and caring relationships* (2nd ed.). Monterey, CA: Brooks/Cole.

Kaminer, W. (1992). *I'm dysfunctional, you're dysfunctional*. Reading, MA: Addison-Wesley.

Kamya, H. (2000). Hardiness and spiritual well-being among social work students: implications for social work education. *Journal of Social Work Education, 36*, 231–240.

Kanter, R. M. (1977). *Men and women of the corporation*. New York: Basic Books.

Kanter, R. M. (1993). *Men and women of the corporation*. New York: Basic Books.

Kapes, J. T., & Whitfield, E. (2002). *A counselor's guide to career assessment instruments* (4th ed.). Alexandria, VA: The National Career Development Association.

Kaplan, D. (Ed.). (2003). *Family counseling for all counselors*. Greensboro, NC: CAPS.

Kay, S., & Schlossberg, N. K. (2006). *The transition guide*. Alexandria, VA: Transition Works (http://www.transitionguide.com).

Kessler, R. C., Foster, C., Webster, P. S., & House, J. S. (1992). The relationship between age and depression in two national surveys. *Psychology and Aging, 7*, 119–126.

Kidder, T. (1993, October–November). Inside Linda Manor. *Modern Maturity, 55–56*.

Kimmel, D. C. (1990). *Adulthood and aging: An interdisciplinary developmental view* (3rd ed.). New York: Wiley.

Kincade, S. (1987). *A delegation workshop*. Toledo, OH: Unpublished manuscript.

Klee, K. B. (1994). Self-esteem among Arab adults: Studying English as a second language. *Michigan Journal of Counseling and Development 22(2)*, 27–32.

Kobasa, S. C., Maddi, S. R., & Kahn, S. (1982). Hardiness and health: A prospective study. *Journal of Personality and Social Psychology, 42*, 168–177.

Kobylarz, L. (2005, June). *National career development guidelines overview*. Unpublished document delivered at the conference of the National Career Development Association, Orlando, FL.

Kohlberg, L. (1984) *Essays on moral development* (Vol. 2). New York: Harper & Row.

Kohn, M. L. (1980). Job complexity and adult personality. In N. J. Smelser & E. H. Erikson (Eds.), *Themes of work and love in adulthood* (pp. 193–210). Cambridge, MA: Harvard University Press.

Krohne, H. W., & Slangen, K. E. (2005). Influence of social support on adaptation to surgery. *Health Psychology, 87,* 354–362.

Krumboltz, J. D. (1991). *Career beliefs inventory.* Palo Alto, CA: Consulting Psychologists Press.

Krumboltz, J. D., & Hamel, D. A. (1977). *Guide to career decision-making skills.* New York: Educational Testing Service.

Kübler-Ross, E. (1969). *On death and dying.* New York: Macmillan.

Kurpius, D. J., & Fuqua, D. R. (1993a). Introduction to the special issue. *Journal of Counseling & Development, 71,* 596–597.

Kurpius, D. J., & Fuqua, D. R. (1993b). Fundamental issues in defining consultation. *Journal of Counseling & Development, 71,* 598–600.

Labouvie-Vief, G., & Diehl, M. (2000). Cognitive complexity and cognitive-affective integration: Related or separate domains of adult development. *Psychology and Aging, 15,* 490–504.

Lambert, J. D. (1998). Marital status continuity and change among young and midlife adults: longitudinal effects on psychological well-being. *Journal of Family Issues, 19,* 652–637.

Land, G., & Jarman, B. (1992). *Breakpoint and beyond: Mastering the future today.* New York: Harper Collins.

Larson, D., & Larson, S. (2003). Spirituality's potential relevance to physical and emotional health: A brief overview of quantitative research. *Journal of Psychology and Theology, 31,* 37–51.

Layton, P. L. (1984). *Self efficacy, locus of control, career salience, and women's career choice.* Unpublished doctoral dissertation, Minneapolis: University of Minnesota.

Lazarus, R. S. (1980) The stress and coping paradigm. In L. A. Bond & J. C. Rosen (Eds.), *Competence and coping during adulthood.* Hanover, NH: University Press of New England.

Lazarus, R. S., & Folkman, S. (1984). *Stress, appraisal, and coping.* New York: Springer Publishing Company.

Lehrer, T. (Speaker). (1990). An evening wasted with Tom Lehrer. Reprise/Wea.

Leibowitz, Z., Schlossberg, N. K., & Shore, J. E. (1991, February). Stopping the revolving door. *Training and Development Journal,* pp. 43–49.

LeMasters, E. E. (1957). Parenthood as crisis. *Marriage and Family, 19,* 352–355.

Lent, R. L., & Hackett, G. (1987). Career self-efficacy: Empirical status and future directions. *Journal of Vocational Behavior, 30,* 347–382.

Leung, J., & Arthur, D. G. (2004). Clients and facilitators' experience in a Hong Kong self help group for people recovering from mental illness. *International Journal of Mental Health Nursing, 13,* 232–241.

Levine, S. V. (1976). Draft dodgers: Coping with stress, adapting to exile. In R. H. Moos (Ed.), *Human adaptations: Coping with life crises.* Lexington, MA: Heath.

Levinson, D. J. (1978). *The seasons of a man's life.* New York: Ballantine.

Levinson, D. J. (1986). A conception of adult development. *American Psychologist, 41,* 3–13.

Levinson, D. J. (1989, May). Speech presented at the national conference on new options for adult counselors, University of Maryland, College Park.

Levinson, D. J. (1996). *The seasons of a woman's life.* New York: Knopf.

Lewin, K. (1943). In D. Cartwright (Ed.), *Field theory in social science* (pp. 43–59). New York: Harper.

Lewin, T. (1993, November 8). Conflict for working couples: When he retires, must she? *The New York Times,* pp. A1, B9.

Lewis, J., & Bradley, L. (Eds.) (2000). *Advocacy in counseling: Counselors, clients, & community.* Greensboro, NC: CAPS.

Lewis, J., Arnold, M., House, R., & Toporek, R. (2005). *Advocacy Competencies.* Retrieved February 28, 2005, from http://www.counseling.org/counselors.

Lieberman, M. A. (1975). Adaptive processes in late life. In N. Datan & L. H. Ginsberg (Eds.), *Life-span developmental psychology* (pp. 135–159). New York: Academic Press.

Lightsey, O. R. (1996). What leads to wellness? The role of psychological resources in well-being. *Counseling Psychologist, 24,* 589–735.

Lindeman, B. (1987, July). Nana, I can't visit you. *50 Plus,* p. 4.

Lindemann, E. (1965). Symptomology and management of acute grief. In J. J. Parad, (Ed.), *Crisis intervention: Selected readings* (pp. 7–21). New York: Family Service Association of America.

Lipman, A. (1986). Homosexual relationships. *Generations, 10*(4), 51–55.

Lipman-Blumen, J. (1976). A crisis perspective on divorce and role change. In J. R. Chapam, & M. Gates (Eds.), *Women into wives: The legal and economic impact of marriage: Vol. 2. Safe yearbook in women's policy studies.* Beverly Hills, CA: Safe Publisher. Lipman-Blumen, J., & Leavitt, H. J. (1976). Vicarious and direct achievement patterns in adulthood. *Counseling Psychologist, 6,* 26–32.

Lips-Wiersma, M. S. (2000). The influence of 'spiritual meaning making' on career choice, transition and experience. DAI 61, no 14A. University of Auckland; pages: 00299.

Livneh, H., & Pullo, R. E. (1992). Group counseling for people with physical disabilities. In D. Capuzzi & D. R. Gross (Eds.), *Introduction to group counseling* (pp. 141–164). Denver, CO: Love.

Livneh, H., & Sherwood-Hawes, A. (1993). Group counseling approaches with persons who have sustained myocardial infarction. *Journal of Counseling and Development, 72,* 57–61.

Locke, D. C., & Parker, L. D. (1994). Improving the multicultural competence of educators. In P. Pederson & J. Carey (Eds.), *Multicultural counseling in schools: A practical handbook* (pp. 39–58). Needham Heights, MA: Allyn & Bacon.

Loesch, L. C. (1985). Guidelines for conducting workshops. Unpublished manuscript prepared for Continuing Education in Aging for Professional Counselors, a project of the American Association of Counseling and Development.

Loevinger, J. (1976). *Ego development: Conceptions and theories.* San Francisco: Jossey-Bass.

Loevinger, J. (1993). Ego development: Questions of method and theory. *Psychological Inquiry, 4,* 56–63.

Looby, E., & Sandhu, D. (2002). Spirituality in the workplace: An overview. In D. Sandhu (2002). *Counseling employees: A multifaceted approach.* Alexandria, VA: American Counseling Association.

Lopata, H.Z. (1987). Widows and their families. In C. S. Chilman, E. W. Nunnally, & F. M. Cox (Eds.), *Variant family forms* (pp. 133–149). Newbury Park, CA: Sage.

Lovén, A. (2003). The paradigm shift: Rhetoric or reality? *International Journal for Educational and Vocational Guidance, 3,* 123–135.

Lowenthal, M. J., & Weiss, L. (1976). Intimacy and crises in adulthood. *The Counseling Psychologist, 6,* 10–15.

Lustbader, W. (1994, March). Presentation on Caregiving at the Annual Convention of the American Society on Aging. San Francisco.

Lustbader, W., & Hooyman, N. R. (1994). *Taking care of aging family members: A practical guide.* New York: Free Press.

MacKinlay, E. (2001). Aging and isolation: Is the issue social isolation or is it lack of meaning in life? *Journal of Religious Gerontology, 12*(3–4), 88–99.

Maddi, S. (2002), The story of hardiness: Twenty years of theorizing, research, and practice. *Consulting Psychology Journal: Practice and Research, 53,* 175–185.

Markides, K. S., & Mindel, C. H. (1987). *Aging and ethnicity.* Newbury Park, CA: Sage.

Marks, N. F., & Lambert, J. D. (1998). Marital status continuity and change among young and midlife adults. *Journal of Family Issues, 19,* 652–686.

Martin, W. E., Jr. (1991). Career development and American Indians living on reservations: Cross-cultural factors to consider. *Career Development Quarterly, 39,* 273–283.

Maslow, A. (1954). *Motivations and personality.* New York: Harper & Row.

Mawson, D. L., & Kahn, S. E. (1993). Group process in a women's career intervention. *Career Development Quarterly, 41,* 238–245.

May, R. (1982). *Will and spirit: A contemplative psychology.* San Francisco: Harper & Row.

Mayer, K. U., & Schoepflin, U. (1989). The state and the life course. *Annual Review of Sociology, 15,* 187–209.

McCarn, S. R., & Fassinger, R. E. (1991, September). *Embracing our diversity: An inclusive model of lesbian development.* Paper presented at the annual convention of the Association for Women in Psychology, Hartford, CT.

McCrone, W.P. (1991). The federal legislative process for rehabilitation counselors. *Journal of Applied Rehabilitation Counseling, 22,* 1620.

McEwen, M., Komives, S., & Schlossberg, N. K (1990). *A pilot study of college presidents leaving the presidency.* Unpublished manuscript.

McKnight, J. L. (1990, July). *The need for oldness.* Paper presented at a meeting of the elderly cluster of W. K. Kellogg Foundation grantees, Minneapolis.

Meichenbaum, D. H. (1977). *Cognitive-behavior modification: An integrative approach.* New York: Plenum.

Merton, R. K. (1957). *Social theory and social structure.* Glencoe: Free Press of Glencoe. OK.

Mihovilovic, M. A. (1968). The status of former sportsmen. *International Review of Sport Sociology, 3,* 73–96.

Miller, J. V. (2000, Summer). Career trends: The fourth NCDA/Gallup national survey of working America. *Career Developments.*

Minkler, M. (1983, November). *Building supportive networks in a "gray ghetto": The Tenderloin Senior Outreach Project.* Paper presented at the annual meeting of the Gerontological Society of America, San Francisco.

Minuchin, S., & Fishman, H. C. (1981). *Family therapy techniques.* Cambridge, MA: Harvard University Press.

Mitroff, I. I., & Denton, E. A. (1999). *A spiritual audit of corporate America: A hard look at spirituality, religion and values in the workplace.* San Francisco: Jossey-Bass.

Moen, P., & Fields, V. (2002). Midcourse in the United States: Does unpaid community participation replace paid work? *Aging International, 27,* 21–48.

Molinaro, V. (1997). Holism at work: Exploring the experiences of individuals creating a new holistic story of work. (Doctoral dissertation, 1997). *Dissertation Abstracts International, 59,* no. 06A, University of Toronto; pages: 00227.

Montenegro, X. P. (2004, May). Divorce experience: A study of divorce at midlife and beyond conducted for *AARP The Magazine. AARP,* May 2004.

Moody, H. R. (1988). Twenty-five years of the life review: Where did we come from? Where are we going? In R. Disch (Ed.), *Twenty-five years of the life review: Theoretical and practical considerations* (pp. 7–21). New York: Haworth.

Moody, R. A. (1978). *Laugh after laugh: The healing power of humor.* Jacksonville, FL: Headwater.

Moore, C. J. (2004). *In other words: A language lover's guide to the most intriguing words around the world.* New York: Walker.

Moos, R. H., & Tsu, V. (1976). Human competence and coping: An overview. In Moose, R. H. (Ed.), *Human adaptation: Coping with life crises.* Lexington, MA: Heath.

Moradi, B. (2005). Advancing womanist identity development: Where we are and where we need to go. *The Counseling Psychologist, 33,* 225–253.

Morin, W. J., & Cabrera, J. C. (1991). *Parting company: How to survive the loss of a job and find another successfully.* San Diego: Harcourt Brace Jovanovich.

Mosak, H. H. (1987). *Ha ha and aha: The role of humor in psychotherapy.* Muncie, IN: Accelerated Development.

Myerhoff, B. (1984). Rites and signs of ripening and intertwining of ritual, time and growing older. In D. Kertzer & J. Keitch (Eds.), *Age and anthropological theory* (pp. 305–330). Ithaca, NY: Cornell University Press.

Myerhoff, B. (1985) (Producer). *Rites of Renewal* [Motion picture]. Owings Mills, MD: International University Consortium and Ohio University.

Myers, J. E., & Perrin, N. (1993). Grandparents affected by parental divorce: A population at risk. *Journal of Counseling and Development, 71* (1), 62–66.

Myers, J. E., Sweeney, T. J., & Wittmen. M. (2000). The wheel of wellness, counseling for wellness: A holistic model for treatment planning. *Journal of Counseling and Development, 78,* 251–266.

Myers, J., & Williard, K. (2003). Integrating spirituality into counselor preparation: A developmental, wellness approach. *Counseling and Values, 47,* 142–153.

Myers, I. B. & Briggs, K. C. (1977). *Myers-Briggs Type Indicator.* Palto Alto, CA: Consulting Psychologists Press.

Nakamura, J., & Csikszentmihalyi, M. (2002). The concept of flow. In C. R. Snyder & S. J. Lopez (Eds.), *Handbook of positive psychology* (pp. 89–105). New York: Oxford University Press.

Nakao, A. (1993, November 2). New roots from tender shoots. *San Francisco Examiner,* pp. B1, B7.

National Board for Certified Counselors (2005). Retrieved October 12, 2005, from http://www.nbcc.org/stats.

National Occupational Information Coordinating Committee. (1989). *The national career development guidelines (Trainer's manual).* Washington, DC. Author.

Neugarten, B. L. (1968). The awareness of middle age. In B. L. Neugarten (Ed.), *Middle age and aging* (pp. 93–98). Chicago: University of Chicago Press.

Neugarten, B. L. (1979). Discontinuities in the study of aging. In T. K. Hareven & K. J. Adams (Eds.), *Aging and life course transitions: An interdisciplinary perspective* (pp. 55–74). New York: Guilford Press.

Neugarten, B. L (1982, August). *Successful aging.* Paper presented at the 90th Annual Meeting of the American Psychological Association, Washington, DC.

Neugarten, B. L., & Neugarten, D. A. (1987). The changing meanings of age. *Psychology Today, 21,* 29–33.

Nevill, D. D., & Schlecker, D. L. (1988). The relation of self-efficacy and assertiveness to willingness to engage in traditional/non-traditional career activities. *Psychology of Women Quarterly, 12,* 91–98.

Newman, B. M., & Newman, P. R. (2003). *Development through life: A psychosocial approach.* Pacific Grove, CA: Brooks/Cole.

Newlon, B. J., & Arciniega, M. (1992). Group counseling: Cross-cultural considerations. In D. Capuzzi and D. R. Gross (Eds.). *Introduction to group counseling* (pp. 285–306). Denver, CO: Love.

The New York Times (1993, November 8), p. A12.

The New York Times (2005, August 14), pp 1, 15–17.

Niemela, P. (1987). The significance of the 50th birthday for the woman's individuation. *HotFlash, 6,* 2–3.

Noel, D. M. (1993). Leadership in an age of layoffs. *Issues & Observations, 13,* 1–5.

Occupational Outlook Handbook (2004–2005). Washington, DC: U.S. Department of Labor. Retrieved November 2, 2005, from http://www.bls.gov/oco/home.htm.

Operation ABLE of Michigan (2000). *Annual report.* Southfield, MI: Author.

Orr, T. E. (2000). *The social construction of difference and inequality: Race, class, gender, and sexuality.* Mountain View, CA: Mayfield Publishing.

Osborn, D. S., & Zunker, V. G. (2006). *Using Assessment Results for Career Development* (7th ed.). Pacific Grove, CA: Brooks/Cole.

Pahl, R. (2000). *On friendship.* Cambridge, England: Polity Press.

Paloutzian, R., & Ellison, C. W. (1991). *Manual for the Spiritual Well-Being Scale.* New York: Authors.

Pargament, K. (1997). *The psychology of religion and coping: Theory, research and practice.* New York: Guilford Press.

Parkes, C. M. (1971). Psycho-social transitions: A field for study. *Social Science and Medicine, 5,* 105–115.

Parkes, C. M. (1982). Attachment and the prevention of mental disorders. In Parkes, C. M., & Stevenson-Hinde, J. (Eds.). *The place of attachment in human behavior* (pp. 295–309). New York: Basic Books.

Pearlin, L. I. (1980). Life-strains and psychological distress among adults. In N. J. Smelser & E. H. Erickson (Eds.), *Themes of work and love in adulthood* (pp. 174–192). Cambridge, MA: Harvard University Press.

Pearlin, L. I. (1982). Discontinuities in the study of aging. In T. K. Hareven & K. J. Adams (Eds.), *Aging and life course transitions: An interdisciplinary perspective* (pp. 55–79). New York: Guilford Press.

Pearlin, L. I., & Lieberman, M. A. (1979). Social sources of emotional distress. In R. Simmons (Ed.), *Research in community and mental health* (Vol. 1, pp. 217–248). Greenwich, CT: JAI Press.

Pearlin, L. I., & Schooler, C. (1978). The structure of coping. *Journal of Health and Social Behavior, 19,* 2–21.

Pearson, R.E. (1990). *Counseling and social support: Perspectives and practice.* Newbury Park, CA: Sage.

Pearson, R. E. (1992). Group counseling: Self-enhancement. In D. Capuzzi & D. R. Gross (Eds.), *Introduction to group counseling.* Denver, CO: Love.

Pearson, R. E., & Petitpas, A. J. (1990). Transitions of athletes: Developmental and preventive perspectives. *Journal of Counseling & Development, 69,* 7–10.

Pearson, S. M., & Bieschke, K. J. (2001). Succeeding against the odds: An examination of familial influences on the career development of professional African American women. *Journal of Counseling Psychology, 48,* 301–309.

Peavy, V. (1998). A new look at interpersonal relations in counseling. *Educational and Vocational Guidance Bulletin, 62,* 45–50.

Peck, T. A. (1986). Women's self-definition in adulthood: From a different model? *Psychology of Women Quarterly, 10,* 274–284.

Peluso, E., & Peluso, L. S. (1988). *Women and drugs: Getting hooked, getting clean.* Minneapolis: CompCare.

Perosa, S. L., & Perosa, L. M. (1985). The mid-career crisis in relation to Super's career and Erikson's adult development theory. *International Journal of Aging and Human Development, 20,* 53–68.

Peter, L. J. (1978). *Peter's quotations: Ideas for our time.* New York: Bantam Books.

Peterson, G., Sampson, J., & Reardon, C. (1991). *Career development and services: A cognitive approach.* Pacific Grove, CA: Brooks/Cole.

Peterson, L. (1995). *Starting out, starting over.* Palo Alto, CA: Davies-Black.

Phillips-Miller, D., Campbell, N., & Morrison, C. (2000). Work and family: Satisfaction, stress, and spousal support. *Journal of Employment Counseling, 37,* 16–30.

Phinney, J. S. (1990). Ethnic identity in adolescents and adults: Review of research. *Psychological Bulletin, 108,* 499–514.

Phinney, J. S. (2000). Identity formation across cultures: The interaction of personal, societal, and historical change. *Human Development, 43,* 27–31.

Piaget, J. (1952). *The origins of intelligence in children.* New York: International Universities Press.

Plath, D.W. (1980). Contours of consociation: Lessons from a Japanese narrative. *Life-span Development and Behavior, 3,* 287–305.

Polanski, P. (2002). Exploring spiritual beliefs in relation to Adlerian theory. *Counseling and Values, 46,* 127–136.

Prince, M. J., Harwood, R. H., Blizard, R. A., Thomas, A., & Mann, A. H. (1997). Social support deficits, loneliness and life events as risk factors for depression in old age. The gospel oak project VI. *Psychological Medicine, 27,* 323–332.

Psychologists for Social Responsibility. (2005). *Mission.* Retrieved October 22, 2005, from http://www.psysr.org/about%20us.htm

Putnam, R. D. (2000) *Bowling alone: The collapse and revival of American community.* New York: Simon & Schuster.

Putnam, R. D. (2005). Retrieved October 12, 2005, from http://bowlingalone.com.

Random House Dictionary of the English Language. (2000). New York: Random House.

Raphael, L. (1994, February). Journey through menopause. *Hers, 1*(6), 10.

Raskin, P. M. (2002). Identity in adulthood: Reflections on recent theories and research. *Identity, 2,* 101–108.

Remondet, J. H., Hansson, R. O., Rule, B., & Winfrey, G. (1987). Rehearsal for widowhood. *Journal of Social and Clinical Psychology, 5,* 285–297.

Reynolds, A. L., & Pope, R. L. (1991). The complexities of diversity: Exploring multiple oppressions. *Journal of Counseling & Development, 70,* 174–180.

Riordan, R. J., & Beggs, M. S. (1987). Counselors and self-help groups. *Journal of Counseling & Development, 65,* 427–429.

Ritter, K. Y (1985). The cognitive therapies: An overview for counselors. *Journal of Counseling & Development, 64,* 42–45.

Roberts, B., Helson, R., & Klohnen, E. (2002). Personality development and growth in women across 30 ycars: Three perspectives. *Journal of Personality, 70,* 79–102.

Roberts, P., & Newton, P. M. (1987). Levinsonian studies of women's adult development. *Psychology and Aging, 2,* 154–163.

Robinson, J. (1994, August). *Making informed labor market choices: The right tools, the right times.* Presentation at the national conference of State Occupational Information Coordinating Committees, Danvers, MA.

Rockquemore, D. A. (2004). Negotiating racial identity: Biracial women and interactional validation. In A. R. Billem and C. A. Thompson (Eds.), *Biracial women in therapy: Between the rock of gender and the hard place of race* (pp. 85–102). New York: Haworth Press.

Rodin, J. (1990). Control by any other name: Definitions, concepts and processes. In J. Rodin, C. Schooler, & K. W. Schaie (Eds.), *Self directedness: Cause and effects throughout the life course.* Hillsdale, NJ: Erlbaum.

Rogers, C. R. (1957). The necessary and sufficient conditions of therapeutic personality change. *Journal of Counseling Psychology, 21,* 95–103.

Rokach, A. (2002, June). *Loneliness in old age: the effects of culture on coping with it.* Paper presented at the 4th Biennial Convention of the Society for the Psychological Study of Social Issues. Toronto, Ontario, Canada.

Rosen, J. L., & Bibring, G. L. (1968). Psychological reactions of hospitalized male patients to a heart attack: Age and social class differences. In B. L. Neugarten (Ed.), *Middle Age and Aging* (pp. 201–211). Chicago: University of Chicago Press.

Rosenbaum, J. E. (1979). Tournament mobility: Career patterns in a corporation. *Administrative Science Quarterly, 24,* 220–241.

Rosenberg, M., & McCullough, B. C. (1981). Mattering: Inferred significance to parents and mental health among adolescents. In R. Simmons (Ed). *Research in community and mental health* (Vol. 2). Greenwich, CT: JAI Press.

Ross, D. B. (1984). A cross-cultural comparison of adult development. *Personnel and Guidance Journal, 62,* 418–421.

Rubin, L. (1981). *Women of a certain age: The midlife search for self.* New York: Harper & Row.

Rubin, L. (1986). On men and friendship. *The Psychoanalytic Review, 73,* 165–181.

Ruffin, J. E. (1989). Stages of adult development in Black professional women. In R. L. Jones (Ed.), *Black adult development and aging* (pp. 31–62). Berkeley, CA: Cobb & Henry.

Sagaria, M. A. (1989). Toward a woman-centered perspective of careers: The quilt metaphor. *Journal of Employment Counseling, 26,* 11–15.

Sand-Pringle, G., West, J. D., & Bubenzer, D. L. (1991). Family counseling rituals: A case study. *Journal of Mental Health Counseling, 13,* 500–505.

Sargent, A. G., & Schlossberg, N. K. (1988). Managing adult transitions. *Training and Development Journal, 41,* 58–60.

Satir, V. (1972). *Peoplemaking.* Palo Alto, CA: Science & Behavior Books.

Savickas, M. (1997). The spirit in career counseling: Fostering self-completion through work. In D. P. Bloch & L. J. Richmond (Eds.), *Connections between spirit and work in career development: New approaches and practical perspectives* (pp. 3–25). Palo Alto, CA: Davies-Black, pp. 3–25.

Savickas, M. L. (2001). Toward a comprehensive theory of career development: Dispositions, concerns, and narratives. In F. T. L. Leong & A. Barak (Eds.), *Contemporary models in vocational psychology: A volume in honor of Samuel H. Osipow* (pp. 295–320). Mahwah, NJ: Erlbaum.

Savickas, M. L. (2003, September) *The career theme interview.* Paper presented to the International Association of Educational and Vocational Guidance, Berne, Switzerland.

Savickas, M. L., Passen, A. J., & Jujoura, D. G. (1988). Career concern and coping as indicators of adult vocational development. *Journal of Vocational Behavior, 33,* 82–98.

Scheier, M. E., Matthews, K. A., Owens, J. F., Magovern, G. J., Lefebvre, R. G., Abbott, R. A., & Carver, C. S. (1989). Dispositional optimism and recovery from coronary artery bypass surgery: The beneficial effects on physical and psychological well-being. *Journal of Personality and Social Psychology, 57,* 1024–1040.

Schlossberg, N. K. (1981). A model for analyzing human adaptation to transition. *The Counseling Psychologist, 9,* 2–18.

Schlossberg, N. K. (1984). *Counseling adults in transition.* New York: Springer Publishing Company.

Schlossberg, N. K. (1991). *Overwhelmed: Coping with life's ups and downs.* Lexington, MA: Lexington Books.

Schlossberg, N. K. (2004). *Retire smart, retire happy: Finding your true path in life.* Washington, DC: American Psychological Association.

Schlossberg, N. K., Lassalle, A., & Golec, R. (1991). *The mattering scales for adult students in higher education.* College Park, MD: University of Maryland.

Schlossberg, N. K., & Leibowitz, Z. B. (1980). Organizational support systems as buffers to job loss. *Journal of Vocational Behavior, 18,* 204–217.

Schlossberg, N. K., Lissitz, R., Altman, J., & Steinberg, L. (1992). *Non-events: Describing a new construct.* Unpublished manuscript.

Schlossberg, N. K., Lynch A. Q., & Chickering, A. W. (1989). *Improving higher education environments for adults.* San Francisco: Jossey-Bass.

Schlossberg, N. K., & Robinson, S. P. (1993). Non-events: Another name for heartbreak. *American Counselor, 2,* 21–25.

Schlossberg, N. K., & Robinson, S. P. (1996). *Going to plan B.* New York: Simon & Schuster.

Schlossberg, N. K., Waters, E.B., and Goodman, J. (1995). Counseling adults in transition (2nd ed.). New York: Springer Publishing Company.

Schmidt, S., Nachtigall, C., Wuethrich-Martone, O., & Strauss, B. (2002). Attachment and coping with chronic disease. *Journal of Psychosomatic Research, 53,* 763–773.

Schneider, M., & Corey, J. (2005). *Groups: process and practice* (7th ed.). Belmont, CA: Wadsworth.

Scofield, M. (1993, June 6). About men: Off the ladder. *The New York Times Magazine,* p. 22.

Seligman, M. (2002). *Learned optimism.* New York: Knopf.

Sharify, N. (1988, June). Views of an educator. In S. Karkhanis (Ed.), *How to avoid dead end in your career: An Asian/American perspective, and library services for the Asian/Pacific American Librarians Association: Papers of the 1987 Program of the Asian/Pacific American Librarians Association,* San Francisco.

Sheehy, G. (1995). *New Passages.* New York: Random House.

Sherman, E. (1987). Reminiscence groups for community elderly. *The Gerontologist, 27,* 569–572.

Sholk, J. C. (1983) Untitled poem. *Journal of Counseling and Development, 78,* 121.

Shoptaugh, C., Phelps, J., & Visio, M. (2004). Employee eldercare responsibilities: Should organizations care? *Journal of Business and Psychology, 19,* 179–196.

Siegel, B. S. (1986). *Love, medicine, and miracles: Lessons learned about self healing from a surgeon's experience with exceptional patients.* New York: Harper & Row.

Silverman, P. R. (1980). *Mutual help groups: organization & development.* Beverly Hills, CA: Sage.

Silverman, P. R. (2004). *Widow to widow.* New York: Springer Publishing Company.

Silverstone, B. (1994, March). *You and your aging parent revisited: A 20-year retrospective on family caregiving.* Lecture presented at the 40th Annual Meeting of the American Society on Aging, San Francisco.

Sinacore, A. L., & Akcali, F. (2000). Men in families: Job satisfaction and self esteem. *Journal of Career Development, 27*, 1–13.

Singer, V. I., Tracz, S. M., & Dworkin, S. H. (1991). Reminiscence group therapy: A treatment modality. *Journal for Specialists in Group Work, 16*, 167–171.

Single Mothers by Choice (2005). Retrieved October 13, 2005, from http://mattes.home.pipeline.com/.

Slife, B., & Richards, P. (2001). How separable are spirituality and theology in psychotherapy? *Counseling and Values, 45*, 190–206.

Smelser, N. K., & Erikson, E. H. (1980). *Themes of work and love in adulthood.* Cambridge, MA: Harvard University Press.

Smith, G. C., Kohn, S. J., Savage-Stevens, S. E., Finch, J. J., Ingate, R., & Lim, Y. (2000). The effects of interpersonal and personal agency on perceived control and psychological well-being in adulthood. *Gerontologist, 40*, 458–468.

Smith, H. (1994). Rationale for counselor involvement in public policy. *Quest, 27*, 15.

Spencer, S. A., & Adams, J. D. (1990). *Life changes.* San Luis Obispo, CA: Impact.

Spierer, H. (1977). *Major transition in the human life cycle.* New York: Academic Press for Educational Development.

Stachow, D. M. (1993, November). *Beyond awareness: The key to designing a non-biased model for counseling individuals over sixty.* Presentation made at conference of the Association for Adult Development and Aging, New Orleans, LA.

Staudinger, U. M., Fleeson, W., & Baltes, P. B. (1999). Predictors of subjective physical health and global well-being: Similarities and differences between the United States and Germany. *Journal of Personality and Social Psychology, 76*, 305–319.

Stephan, N. (1989). *Finding your life mission.* Walpole, NH: Stillpoint.

Stewart, A. J., & Vandewater, E. A. (1999). "If I had it to do over again . . .": Midlife review, midcourse corrections, and women's well-being in midlife. *Journal of Personality and Social Psychology, 76*, 270–283.

Stroebe, M., Stroebe, W., & Schut, H. (2001). Gender differences in adjustment to bereavement: an empirical and theoretical review. *Review of General Psychology, 5*, 62–83.

Sue, D. W., & Sue, D (2002). *Counseling the culturally different: Theory and practice* (4th ed.). New York: Wiley.

Super, D. E. (1980). A life-span, life-space approach to career development. *Journal of Vocational Behavior, 16*, 282–298.

Super, D. E., & Knasel, K. G. (1979). *Development of a model, specifications, and sample items for measuring career adaptability (vocational maturity) in young blue collar workers.* Cambridge, England: National Institute for Careers Education and Counselling, and Ottawa, Ontario, Canada, Canada Employment and Immigration.

Super, D. E., & Knasel, E. G. (1981). Career development in adulthood: Some theoretical problems and a possible solution. *British Journal of Guidance and Counselling, 9*, 195–201.

Super, D. E., & Nevill, D. D. (1984). Work role salience as a determinant of career maturity in high school students. *Journal of Vocational Behavior, 25,* 30–44.

Super, D. E., & Nevill, D. D. (1985). *The salience inventory.* Palo Alto, CA: Consulting Psychologists Press.

Sussman, M. B. (1972). An analytic model for the sociological study of retirement (pp. 28–73). In F. M. Carp (Ed.), *Retirement.* New York: Human Sciences Press.

Sweeney, T. J. (1998). *Adlerian counseling: A practitioner's approach.* Philadelphia: Accelerated Development.

Szapocznik, J., & Kurtines, W. N. (1993). Family psychology and cultural diversity: Opportunities for theory, research, and application. *American Psychologist, 48,* 400–407.

Tannen, D. (1990). *You just don't understand: Women and men in conversation.* New York: William Morrow.

Taylor, S. E. (1989). *Positive illusions: Creative self-deception and the healthy mind.* New York: Basic Books.

Taylor, S. E. (2005). *Health psychology* (5th ed.). New York: McGraw-Hill.

Taylor, S. E., Sherman, D. K., Kim, H. S., Jarcho, J. J., Takagi, K., & Dunagan, M. S. (2004). Culture and social support: Who seeks it and why? *Journal of Personality and Social Psychology, 87,* 354–362.

Ternes, R. (1984). *Living with an empty chair.* New York: Irvington.

Thomas, J. L., Sperry, L., & Yarbrough, M. (2000). Grandparents as parents: Research findings and policy recommendations. *Child Psychiatry and Human Development, 31,* 3–22.

Toossi, M. (2002). The century of change: The U.S. labor force, 1950–2050. *Monthly Labor Review, 125,* 15–28.

Toporek, R. L. (2000). Developing a common language and framework for understanding advocacy in counseling. In J. Lewis and L. Bradley (Eds.), *Advocacy in counseling: Counselors, clients, & community* (pp. 5–14). Greensboro, NC: CAPS.

Towns, K., & Gentzler, R. (1986). Empowering reentry women: An organizational case study: The story of PROBE. *Women and Therapy, 5,* 159–66.

Trupin, S. (1993). Moral support for "grandparents who care": A nursing success story. *American Journal of Nursing, 93,* 52–57.

Tubesing, N. L., & Tubesing, D. A. (n.d.) Structured exercises in stress management (Vols. 1–4). Duluth, MN: Whole Person Associates.

U.S. Department of Commerce, Bureau of the Census (2004). *Statistical abstract of the United States* (113th ed.). Washington, DC: Author.

Vaillant, G. E. (1977). *Adaptation to life.* Boston: Little, Brown.

Vaillant, G. E. (1982, May). *Maturity over the life cycle.* Paper presented at the meeting of the Helpers of Adults, College Park, MD.

Vaillant, G. E. (2002). *Aging well.* Boston: Little, Brown.

Valach, L., & Young, R. A. (2004). Some cornerstones in the development of a contextual action theory of career and counseling. *International Journal for Educational and Vocational Guidance, 3,* 61–81.

Van Gennep, A. (1960). *The Rites of Passage.* Chicago, IL: The University of Chicago Press.

Ventis, W. L. (1995). The relationship between religion and mental health. *Journal of Social Issues, 51*(2), 33–48.

Vernon, A. (1992). Group counseling: Loss. In D. Capuzzi & D. R. Gross (Eds.) *Introduction to group counseling* (pp. 263–281). Denver, CO: Love.

Viorst, J. (1976). *How did I get to be forty . . . and other atrocities.* New York: Simon & Schuster.

Wa, J. (1985). Self-help groups. *Journal of Psychosocial Oncology, 3,* 1–3.

Walsh, F. (1998). *Strengthening family resilience.* New York: Guilford Press.

Walter, J., & Peller, J. (1992). *Becoming solution-focused in brief therapy.* New York: Brunner /Mazel.

Wapner, S. (1981). Transactions of persons-in-environments: Some critical transitions. *Journal of Enviromnental Psychology, 1,* 223–239.

Waters, E. B. (1990). The life review: Strategies for working with individuals and groups. *Journal of Mental Health Counseling, 12,* 270–278.

Waters, E. B., & Goodman, J. (1990). *Empowering older adults: Practical strategies for counselors.* San Francisco: Jossey Bass.

Waters, E. B., & Samson, J. (1993). *Strengthening your team: A training program for volunteers and staff who work with older adults.* Rochester, MI: Continuum Center, Oakland University.

Waters, R. (1991, October). Intergenerational day care! Young and old alike. *Parenting,* pp. 74–79.

Waters, R. (1994, October 12). Women who make a difference: Help for grandparents. *Family Circle, 106,* 17–18.

Watts, A. (2004, June). *Career guidance policy: A Report on the OECD, EU and World Bank Review.* Address delivered to an International Symposium on "International Perspectives on Career Development," the International Association for Educational and Vocational Guidance and the National Career Development Association. San Francisco.

Wax, J. (1985). Self-help groups. *Journal of Psychosocial Oncology, 106,* (14), 1–3.

Webster's new collegiate dictionary (1980). Springfield, MA: G & C Merriam.

Weenolsen, P. (1986, August). *Life and self meaning: The process of their creation.* Paper presented at the 94th Annual Convention of the American Psychological Association, Washington, DC.

Wegscheider-Cruse, S. (1989) *Another Chance: Hope & Health for the Alcoholic Family* (2nd ed.). Palo Alto, CA: Science and Behavior Books.

Weiss, R. S. (1976). Transition states and other stressful situations; their nature and programs for their management. In G. Caplan & M. Killilea (Eds.), *Support systems and mutual help: Multidisciplinary explorations* (pp. 17–26). New York: Grune &: Stratton.

Wheatley, M. (2002). Spirituality in turbulent times. *School Administrator, 59,* 42–46.

Whiston, S. C., & Brecheisen, B. K. (2002). Practice and research in career counseling and development—2001. *The Career Development Quarterly, 51,* 98–154.

Whitbourne, S. K. (1996). *The aging individual: Physical and psychological perspectives.* New York: Springer Publishing Company.

White, B. (1992) "Me—the Helpee." *Feedback* (Newsletter of the Continuum Center, Oakland University), *20*, 7–8.

White, J. E. (2002). *Racial identity development among college students: An examination of five students' perspectives.* (Doctoral dissertation, 2002). *Dissertation Abstracts International, 62,* no. 08-A, Oregon State University; pages 00158.

White, M. F. (1996). *Constructive therapies.* New York: Guilford Press.

Wilcoxon, S. A., & Puleo, S. G. (1992). Professional development needs of mental health counselors: Results of a national survey. *Journal of Mental Health Counseling, 14,* 187–195.

Wittmer, J. M., & Sweeney, T. J. (1992). A holistic model for wellness and prevention over the life span. *Journal of Counseling & Development, 71,* 140–148.

Worden, J. W. (1991). *Grief counseling and grief therapy* (2nd ed.). New York: Springer Publishing Company.

Wuthnow, R. (1994). *Sharing the journey: support groups and America's new quest for community.* New York: Free Press.

Yalom, L. D. (1985). *The theory and practice of group psychotherapy* (3rd ed.). New York: Basic Books.

Yang, J. (1991). Career counseling of Chinese American Women: Are they in limbo? *Career Development Quarterly, 39,* 350–358.

Young, C. L (1983). *Inscape: A search for meaning.* Rochester, MI: Continuum Center, Oakland University.

Young, J., Cashwell, C., & Shcherbakova, J. (2000). The moderating relationship of spirituality on negative life events and psychological adjustment. *Counseling and Values, 45,* 49–57.

Young, P. R. (1988, June). Experiences of an Asian/American librarian. In S. Karkhanis (Ed.), *How to avoid dead end in your career: An Asian American perspective, and library services far the Asian/Pacific American Librarians Association: Papers of the 1987 Program of the Asian/Pacific American Librarians Association,* San Francisco.

Zaleznik, A., & Jardim, A. (1967). Management. In P. F. Lararsfeld, W. H. Sewell, & H. L. Wilensky (Eds.), *The uses of sociology* (pp. 193–234). New York: Basic Books.

Zimpfer, D. G. (1990). Groups for divorce/separation: A review. *Journal for Specialists in Group Work, 15,* 51–60.

Zunker, V. G. (2001). *Career counseling: Applied concepts of life planning* (4th ed.). Pacific Grove, CA: Brooks/Cole.

Index